Contested Meanings

Contested Meanings

THE CONSTRUCTION OF
ALCOHOL PROBLEMS

Joseph R. Gusfield

THE UNIVERSITY OF WISCONSIN PRESS

The University of Wisconsin Press
114 North Murray Street
Madison, Wisconsin 53715

3 Henrietta Street
London WC2E 8LU, England

Printed in the United States of America

Library of Congress Cataloging-in-Publication Data
Gusfield, Joseph R., 1923–
Contested meanings : the construction of alcohol problems/
Joseph R. Gusfield
384 p.   cm.
Includes bibliographical references (p. 337) and index.
ISBN 0-299-14930-7 (cloth: alk. paper).
ISBN 0-299-14934-X (pbk.: alk. paper)
1. Alcoholism—Social aspects—United States.   2. Drinking of alcoholic beverages
—Social aspects—United States.   I. Title.
HV5292.G77   1996
391.1'3'0973—dc20   95-43786

To the Memory of Fred Davis,
Admired Colleague and Friend

Contents

Acknowledgments

We all stand on the shoulders of our colleagues. It is a rare scholar who can recite the pedigree of every idea or turn of phrase in his or her armamentarium. I can only indicate those who have been especially helpful in a direct sense and within my faulty memory. Two names especially come to mind—Harry G. Levine and Robin Room. Both in their own writings and in friendships across the past twenty years their enthusiasm for ideas and their own work in alcohol studies have been sources of provocative insights. My informal association with the Alcohol Research Group has always been extraordinarily beneficial to me. They have listened to my colloquies without obvious boredom and have provided library facilities and, through Andrea Mitchell, librarian extraordinaire, helped me find just the right materials. In addition to the three staff members just cited, I am particularly indebted to Patricia Morgan, Ron Roizen, Richard Speiglman, Susanna Barrows, Walter Clark, Connie Weisner, and Denise Herd, both for conversations and for their own work.

During the 1980s, I was much affected by members of the theory section of the Society for the Study of Social Problems. Those to whom I owe a debt of gratitude include Joel Best, John Kitsuse, Joseph Schneider, Craig Reinarman, Ron Troyer, and James Orcutt. My colleagues and graduate students in the Department of Sociology at the University of California, San Diego are the intellectual context essential to scholarship. Without the competent and concerned office staff little could be accomplished. As always, my thanks to Irma Geller Gusfield are too profound to enumerate.

I dedicate this book to the memory of Fred Davis, onetime fellow student, longtime friend and colleague. He is painfully missed.

La Jolla, California
November 1994

Contested Meanings

Chapter One

Introduction
The Social Problems Context
of Alcohol Studies

In 1807, Sir John Sinclair, as part of his four-volume *Code on Health and Longevity*, compiled a list of writings on the topic of personal hygiene. The list contained 1,878 books (Blake 1974, 31). I doubt that a list of books on alcohol at the time could have been longer, but a list of books on the social aspects of alcohol today would be considerably longer than Sir John's modest one. Certainly the historians, sociologists, and other social scientists who have contributed to that vast jungle of scholarship constitute a large number of scholars. Despite the mountains of papers and books devoted to describing and analyzing the subject, the scholarly study of alcohol by historians and social scientists has only in the past fifty years emerged from the battlefields of partisanship into the quieter fields of a more detached and sober mien. The work of the Committee of Fifty in the late 1890s was an exception to the partisan immersion of alcohol studies in the struggle over legislative policies (Levine 1983). The establishment of the Yale School of Alcohol Studies (now at Rutgers) in the early 1940s marked the beginnings of a more detached perspective in the study of drinking in America. With some noble exceptions, such as John A. Krout's *Origins of Prohibition* (1925) and Peter Odegaard's *Pressure Politics* (1928), the historical study of alcohol in America has had to wait until the generation engulfed by the struggle between wets and drys disappeared from the legislative and electoral conflicts of American politics. Since then, scholars have conducted many survey and interview studies of drinking and its detrimental consequences, the pathology of drinking (Clark and Hilton 1991, ch. 1). A nonpartisan approach to the political issues of alcohol has been made manifest in historical studies of the antialcohol movements and legislation of the nineteenth and early twentieth centuries (Blocker 1989).

These studies have led to a reconceptualization of much that constituted popular and conventional wisdom. The surveys and other sociological studies have forced a revision in the perception of alcoholism, substituting a more flexible and variegated view of the "problem drinker" for the rigid and one-dimensional concept of an alcoholic career (Cahalan, Cisin, and Crossley 1969; Cahalan and Room 1974). James Timberlake (1963), Brian Harrison (1971), and I (Gusfield 1963) began to treat the temperance and Prohibition movements in the United States and in England as a part of the general movement toward social reform and not as a chance event, an aberrant expression of the unique Puritanism of American culture.

The corpus of social research on drinking, as I describe it in this volume, has been dominated by the view of alcohol use as a "social problem." In the past twenty or so years, the study of social problems has been deeply affected and, in my biased judgment, enriched by intellectual and scholarly perspectives which have had a transforming influence on research and on the conception of social problems. Alcohol studies has shared in this transformation but only to a limited degree. This book is, I hope, one step toward a more flexible, self-conscious, and politically sensitive understanding of social problems. The ideas and interpretations offered here are set in the context of a social constructionist perspective toward social problems.

Characteristically both the public discussion of social problems and issues and the studies and conclusions of sociologists are viewed as pronouncements about a real situation independent of the speakers and researchers. They are predicated on a view of a factual world independent of the observers. We need not, and ultimately cannot, dispense with that assumption of a reality that is, in Woolgar and Latour's phrase "out there" (Latour and Woolgar 1979). But in understanding the character of social problems in contemporary society, it is valuable to conceive social realities as products of the interaction between observers or actors on the one hand and an objective world on the other. Social problems are definitions of phenomena and responses to those definitions and interpretations of a particular kind. To describe that kind is a primary goal of this book. Social reality seldom comes to us clearly marked and with overwhelming authenticity. It is shaped and defined by human beings with beliefs, interests, and commitments, whose implicit and explicit frameworks produce an interpreted reality. As such, it is possible to see social problems as the outcome of a process and the products of sociological research as stages in the process of problem definition. Examined reflexively, the judgments and pronouncements of laypeople and sociologists may be viewed as part of that process. This is distinguished from seeing the study of social problems as substantive, as the determination of what is "out there." That substantive approach is not without merit, but is not the stance of this volume, although it certainly can be appropriate as well (Merton 1976, ch. 1).

One implication of the constructionist approach to social problems is that such problems are subject to change in public attention and definition without a clear relation to their existence as conditions of life. Thus, social problems, both as a concept and as a set of policy concerns, are historical matters and need to be studied in their cultural as well as institutional contexts. The application of this perspective toward alcohol problems is basic to this volume.

While I have made some minor revisions and added material to my previously published articles that serve as some of the chapters of this book, I have not sought to revise these chapters so as to bring them up to date. In my career as a general sociologist, part of whose work has been in alcohol studies, I have written for diverse audiences, primarily in academic sociology and in the policy area of alcohol controls. My warrant for publishing papers already published elsewhere is that what was readily accessible to one audience may not have been to the other.

Written at different times and for different occasions, these chapters necessarily contain some information that is no longer accurate and that may be inconsistent with that in other chapters written at other times, as well as a certain measure of intended and unintended self-plagiarism. Many of the chapters published in the past are most valuable for their analytic method. These should not be taken as accurate descriptions of current activities. They represent a general perspective toward the analysis of social or public problems.

In recent years, issues of alcohol policy have been placed on the agenda of public attention to a much greater degree than at any time since Repeal in 1933. However, I am less concerned in this volume with setting policy or with the analysis of policies per se than with understanding the frameworks with which social problems and policies develop in the United States.

The study of drinking and the public control of drinking behavior has been, for me, an area in which to explore aspects of American life and processes of political and legal change, which are concerns of sociologists, whatever their specialized "fields" might entail. At the same time, I have tried to bring to the specialized area of "alcohol studies" the broader insights and perspectives which come from the general sociologist and historian.

Two themes are sounded throughout this volume. The first I refer to as the social construction of social problems. The second is the difference between the public discourse about social problems and the less formal, less public modes of behavior and ideas that constitute an indigenous culture. Both of these themes are implicated in recent ways of thinking about alcohol studies and in approaching research on the topic. Each involves more than methodological or theoretical viewpoints within sociology and history. Each has a political connotation which cannot be ignored. The political impacts of scholarly and intellectual changes can affect how problems are understood and given meanings. This consideration is the major thrust of my perspective.

THE SOCIAL CONSTRUCTION OF SOCIAL PROBLEMS

In my 1981 book on drinking-driving, *The Culture of Public Problems,* I drew on the recent theory of the social construction of social problems. Holders of this theory emphasize the interaction between the objective conditions of a "real" world and the subjective sense of the active individual (Berger and Luckmann 1966), and such is the perspective I hold in this book. While I am not uncritical of that approach (Gusfield 1984a), it has led to many useful understandings of the context in which public issues emerge. It also leads me to a particular perspective toward the efforts to control alcohol use, as ways in which cultural authority is manifested and sought in American life. In sociology, the theory has shifted attention from analyzing and describing conditions to studying how and why conditions become understood as public or social problems and how and why they are defined in particular fashions (Spector and Kitsuse 1977).

What the social constructivist orientation has made possible is an uncovering of the implicit assumptions and the framework of limits in the emergence and definition of social problems. Robert Scott's early work in this perspective showed how the definition of blindness in use by governmental agencies widened the public definitions of blindness to include a large contingent of people whose blindness is, to many people, debatable, a social creation of its definers. Scott uncovered a political conflict about coverage which might otherwise be accepted as consensus (Scott 1969). This is only one illustration of the focus on the processes of thought and social movements involved in the development of social problems. To use Spector and Kitsuse's terms, social problems can be seen as "claims-making activities."

In the area of alcohol studies a focus on the frameworks of research makes it possible to examine the implications of the pathological emphasis in alcohol studies. It leads me to analyze the self-imposed limits on alcohol research and the consequent meanings of drinking in America which they affect.

PUBLIC PROBLEMS AND INDIGENOUS CULTURES

A second theme in the volume is the focus on the less directly political arena of behavior, not the social movements that sought to develop public policy but the behavior of groups occurring in the less formal arenas of social life.

The historians of the 1960s, including myself, accepted in the main the general framework of alcohol study contained in the political conflicts of the temperance and Prohibition movements. We made such movements for the social control of drinking the center of much research, especially in history. It is not that our work was pro-wet or pro-dry but that it revealed what Michel Foucault would have called our "gaze" (1974, ch. 7). That would not have made our work as directly ideological and unscholarly as were the diatribes of officials of movements and their enemies. What was chosen for significance was the issue of drinking as it appeared in the arena of public concern.

The first stage in the scholarship of alcohol history has been framed by attention to the political conflict and has ignored the ways in which drinking has been a part of the social organization and culture of segments of the American population. It is not that we who produced that first rush of scholarship ignored the clashes of groups and cultures. What is central to my argument is that we confined our studies to the reformist impulse and, in so doing, took as our subject matter the organized movements rather than the way in which drinking was related to the social organization and the culture which people used in their daily life. What we produced was political history and political sociology. In this sense it was elite history, narrative history, a history of events.

Social history breaks away from the heavy hand of Prohibition and pathological drinking. It focuses on the ordinariness of drinking in ordinary lives. In this stage of alcohol studies it is represented by the work of social historians studying drinking behavior rather than the temperance

or Prohibition movements. Works by W. J. Rorabaugh (1979), R. Rosenzweig (1983), and P. Duis (1983) illuminated the drinking behavior of Americans and analyzed tavern life and everyday drinking behavior.

The move toward social and cultural history is not, despite the codes
of objective scholarship, without its political agenda, its ideological meaning. Turning away from the political questions of legal and political controls as subject matter also means seriously examining drinking as a significant part of the lives of those whom controls have sought to regulate
on the assumption that their drinking was pathological, damaging to
them, and nonbeneficial. The shift in frameworks is consequential because it denies the assumption that drinking is an excrescence, an en-
cumbrance, and a failing.

The social historians have broken the pattern of concentration on the
pathological character of drinking and asserted that drinking is an aspect
of culture and behavior which is either ignored or denigrated in the public policy arenas and the research of alcohol studies. Students of the sociology of law have been placing an emphasis on indigenous legal processes, the ways in which disputes are settled outside of legal institutions.
I hope in this volume to place attention on the study of the indigenous
cultures in which drinking is a part of the processes of leisure in American life, to be studied as behavior apart from a pathological frame of reference. The dominance of the pathological frame, implicit in the historical study of temperance movements and the sociological focus on social
problems, serves to deny a cultural position for drinking. The emphasis
on the political arena often hides the significant aspects of movements
that occur in everyday life and personal interactions (Gusfield 1981a;
forthcoming; Gusfield, Kotarba, and Rasmussen 1979).

Some years ago I interviewed a Prohibitionist party official. Attempting to draw him out, I criticized his emphasis on alcohol as the cause of
alcoholism. After all, I said, alcoholism was only a symptom of some underlying difficulty in the alcoholic. "Curing" alcoholism would only treat
the symptom; the deeper problem would emerge in another symptom.
His reply has stayed with me for almost thirty years: "Some symptoms are
better than other symptoms."

CULTURAL AUTHORITY AND CONTESTED MEANINGS

Cultural authority and contested meanings constitute both the general
orientation of the first section and a major thrust of the entire volume.
Recognition of the interpretive character of human action leads to the

problem of meaning as central to sociological study and to alcohol problems in particular. Chapter 2 sounds the general theme of contested meanings and cultural authority. Which interpretations are dominant and are sources of public response is not given by the nature of things but is part of a process which may involve a working consensus or intense conflict.

Whose standards shall prevail becomes a political question in a society like the United States where division, conflict, and contention are so characteristic. Thorstein Veblen, probably the most eminent sociologist in the field of consumer behavior, referred to "canons of decency" in describing aspects of status symbolism (1934). Who, if anyone, sets the standards of decency, propriety, and tolerance in American society? From this angle, the study of the conflicts over the use, or misuse, of alcohol is grist for the sociologist's mill as a study of cultural authority, how it is sought, achieved, or lost.

Within this process, the interpretations given to conditions that label them as social problems are themselves ways of construing meaning to events and situations, as well as ways of intervening in what is acceptable fact. Consensus is not a given status but is sought after and itself either posited or created by the very acts of assuming it. In this sense, "social problems," as a concept, is itself part of the process of generating the authority to compel belief.

The contested or uncontested meanings may be acknowledged or ignored. In chapter 3 I present a detailed analysis of major alcohol research studies with an eye toward achieving an awareness of how these studies present an uncontested meaning that ignores the otherwise contested character of alcohol in American life.

From what perspective and for what social groups is the study of drinking and drunkenness conducted? Does the operative definition of pathological behavior reflect societal consensus or does it reflect a situation of conflicting standards of propriety and impropriety? In examining studies of drinking in America I am analyzing the image of the drinking experience projected by the choice of questions and the theoretical frames of research, the cognitive structure that precedes the work of research and provides its very definition of relevant data. That structure of the research process limits the imagery of its subject matter and the consequent interpretation of its data. How it does so and with what implications for the meanings of drinking is the focus of chapter 3.

Both of these chapters introduce the issue of cultural authority. In projecting one or another image and meaning of objects and events, social research affects the culture of belief and experience. It grants a degree of acceptance or rejection of belief. In modern societies some beliefs possess a high degree of consensus—the spherical character of the earth or the deleterious consequences for children of sexual advances by adults, for example. Some beliefs are hotly contested in contemporary America—the moral status of abortions or homosexuality, for example. In each of these, the actions themselves possess little meaning that can govern responses to them. They are perceived and conceptualized from one perspective or another. They are given meaning by interpretation.

Cultural authority is the ability to influence interpretation, to grant some meanings a legitimate status as true. The cultural authority is one source of legitimating or delegitimating a meaning and a belief. Social research may do so by findings or by the framework of its studies. It may create a sense of consensus or of conflict within the society. It is in this sense that research enters the world of the political. Meanings may be described, implicitly or explicitly, as contested or uncontested. In this fashion the corpus of alcohol studies, by its general structure of research, becomes a player in the game of political and moral conflict.

DRINKING AND THE CLASH OF CULTURES

In my study of the American temperance movement I dwelt on the clash of cultural groups expressed in the political arena where temperance issues were fought over. During the nineteenth century, Catholic, immigrant, and urban Americans were on one side and Protestant, native-born, rural Americans were on the other on the issue of temperance (Gusfield 1963). The clash of cultures became a source of electoral and legislative conflicts, as other historians have described it for other issues as well (Jensen 1971; Kleppner 1970). In today's public parlance, we speak of "culture wars."

But the political arena is not the same as the indigenous, everyday behavior, although it does bear some relationship (Reinarman 1987). In parts 2 and 3, I focus on the informal behavior and drinking actions of contemporary Americans, but with an eye on differences.

The two chapters in part 2 are analyzed in light of divergent orientations in American society toward drinking. They are concerned, in one way or another, with the meanings of alcohol in divergent groups in American history. Chapter 4 is an analysis of how drinking plays a role in specific contexts in the shift of orientations within the modern agenda of life—from work to play, from hours to after-hours, from day to night and week to weekend.

Chapter 5 is more historical, charting both policy and institutions, such as the police, which form the contexts of dominant and alternative cultures in American life. These are seen in the context of American leisure and its changing historical conditions.

My aim in these chapters has been to put the phenomenon of American drinking in the arena of everyday life rather than placing almost exclusive emphasis on the political institutions. Drinking, and nondrinking as well, takes place in a complex context of institutions, personal interaction, social ritual, physical environment, and cultural meanings and beliefs that prescribe and proscribe how, where, what, and with whom it occurs.

INDIGENOUS SOCIAL CONTROL

The analysis of drinking in the context of group and culture provides a different path of analysis than the description and examination of public policies and legal actions. In chapter 5 I point out how the concept of social control has now come to mean public policy. An older usage emphasized the informal, interactive processes by which people influenced and controlled each other. Studies of drinking-driving are concentrated on the impact of legislative and judicial action on the events. In chapters 6 and 7 of part 3, originally a single report, I present field observations of bars with an emphasis on how the specific aspects of situations operate to affect drinking-driving behavior.

These field observations were made by me and my assistants in 1979 and should not be taken as descriptions of current actions. Their value lies in the analysis of behavior. As such they are efforts to observe and analyze behavior in bars and to place drinking-driving in the context of one kind of everyday, ongoing life, that of taverns, bars, and public places of drinking. They are, therefore, distinguished from much of the analysis of drinking-driving which concentrates on the attributes of the drinking-driver or specifies context only in general terms, such as "bars" or "home."

My focus in these chapters is on the ways in which the specific contexts of persons, institutions, and the self exercise, or fail to exercise, social control over bar patrons. I found it necessary to analyze a number of different elements which provide an understanding of the social control mechanisms at work. The four bars we observed are varied: one for regulars, one for transients and regulars, an upscale restaurant-related bar, and the large singles "meat market" type. Studying different types of bars made it possible to analyze how different contexts bear on actions.

These observations serve to remind the reader that drinking is an event as well as an attribute of the person. "Social control" and "policy" are by no means only public, political acts. There is an indigenous culture which is highly significant and exists both in relation to public policy and outside of it. In this respect my attention to the natural world of drinking is similar to the work of M. Galanter (1981), which points out that courts and legal institutions are only one aspect of how law is used in American life. It also reflects the recent interest in the study of how a variety of social movements impact the interactions of daily life, in contrast to their more political impacts (Gusfield 1982).

THE EVOLUTION AND DEVOLUTION
OF SOCIAL PROBLEMS

Divorce was once considered a leading social problem in America. Today it is accepted; even the family and social problems texts see it only as one anticipated outcome of marriages. Social problems of yesterday may disappear off the communal agenda as new ones take their place. Social problems are historical occurrences that emerge or disappear without any necessary relationship to the conditions of their existence. It is doubtful, for instance, that a greater occurrence of "child abuse" accounted for its recognition and emergence as a public concern in the early 1970s (Pfohl 1977; Nelson 1984).

In part 4 I return to the focus of historical change, examining alcohol "abuse" and the drunkard as historically produced statuses. Chapter 8 is a frequently reprinted article first published two decades ago. I include it here because it gives a general analysis of the process of definition and redefinition of deviants and deviant behavior in American society.

The very production of deviance and stigma is not only historical but may result from deliberate efforts to create identities which are stigmatizing (Goffman 1963b). In chapter 10, I report field observations of drinking-driving offender classes and probationary interviews, both of which I interpret as processes designed to bring the offenders to see themselves as deviant drinkers, as potential or established alcoholics and in need of treatment. Medical definitions and legal definitions of behavior are not necessarily congruent and have different implications for the image of self-identity. The change in alcohol identity from legal offenders to sick people is not necessarily construed as favorable by all drinking driver offenders, as I find in the observations presented in chapter 10.

We have been accustomed to thinking of stigma and deviance as isolating and depriving statuses. We have also been accustomed to assuming that such statuses occur, are recognized, and remain statuses to be removed. In contemporary United States this view ignores the consequences of institutional developments oriented to help the stigmatized. In chapter 9 I analyze how welfare, medical, and legal concerns have created professionals who champion the entitlements of some deviant and stigmatized people for financial and other aid. This is particularly, but not uniquely, the case in the groups who have the status of "alcoholics." The idea that people may have rights and entitlements that stem from stigmatized statuses is important to our understanding of how these statuses are derived and how their public positions may evolve. Here the impact of professions to control "troubled persons" are seen to be important agents in a changed meaning of "deviance" in American life.

INTERPRETIVE PERSPECTIVES AND PUBLIC POLICY

In part 5, the final section of the book, I return to the theme of interpretation and alcohol problems in public policy arenas. In chapter 11 I attempt to sketch an alternative way of "seeing" public problems of alcohol, a way now also pressed by some analysts in the field of illicit drugs under the concept of "harm reduction." The objective here is to see a social problem from an alternative standpoint, to locate it in a different conceptual space. The result is to broaden the means of coping with a problem by seeing it in a variety of differing modes.

In chapter 12 I examine the historical changes in the public concept of alcohol problems, shifting from a focus on deviant drinkers to a conception of the general population as a focus of policy. This chapter applies the viewpoint of constructivism and historical location to the alcohol policy area in an analysis of how meanings change.

Finally, chapter 13 takes up the issue of contested meanings again but with a focus on the divergent meanings which may underlie agreements on policies. What a public policy means to one set of participants may be quite different from what it means to another, although these meanings are often latent and inexplicit. Again, as indicated in part 2, the symbolic meanings of drinking events and public policies is central to my analysis. The policies that are similar in drinking-driving countermeasures are nevertheless set in very different conceptions of the problem. How traffic professionals, alcohol experts, and citizen anti-drinking-driving movements conceive the problem of auto crashes and alcohol impairment differs considerably both in their commitment to specific countermeasures and in the emotional content of their support. Here again divergent meanings are at work even when there is superficial consensus.

The general drift and sometimes march of alcohol studies, and American historical scholarship in general, toward a disengagement from the political conflicts over drinking has been hailed as intellectual progress by scholars, especially in the period from 1940 to 1970. Today's scholar is often excoriated for a failure to recognize the unavoidability of moral judgment and even the importance of writing engagé. Both these viewpoints seem to me too stark. A more useful formulation may be to recognize that history and sociology, like human thought in general, operate within frameworks of perception and conception which bound and define their subject matter. Volumes on theory and methodology are filled with debate over visions and revisions: quantitative and qualitative; political and social history; Marxist and Centrist; nationalist and cosmopolitan; events versus *longue duree;* narrative versus analysis. Such academic battles do not involve ideological prefigurations in the sense of scholarship dedicated to moral judgments about their topics. Yet every shift in meaning and method is a new way of seeing, and consequently a new constellation of concerns and interests.

Over and above the dusty issues of scholarship is the struggle for cultural dominance for which history and sociology can serve as legitimator and defender or as dissenter and critic. We might wish to be aloof from the moral and political conflicts we write about. We may hope that our "pure" research would be unpolluted by the objective rigor of methodology. That is an illusion devoutly to be wished but often to be rejected.

Part 1

Contested and Uncontested Meanings:
Social Problems, Alcohol Studies,
and Cultural Authority

Chapter Two

Contested Meanings and the Cultural Authority of Social Problems

What is involved in calling a condition or situation a "social problem"? Naming a condition a "social problem" frames the phenomena as pathological, troublesome behavior. It minimizes the activity as "natural" and normal and defines it as a condition opposed to a public interest, a condition which should be eradicated or alleviated by public action. "Social problems" are a contrast to a frame of social and political conflict. They assume a standard or frame from which the condition can be labeled as problematic and thus in need of remedy. As such, the act of naming a condition as a "problem" is part of a process in the attempt to create a consensus about that standard or frame. It is in this sense that cultural authority is involved.

As a rhetorical device, the concept of "social problem" is a claim that some condition, set of events, or group of persons constitutes a troublesome situation that needs to be changed or ameliorated. Those who define the problem do so from a standard which involves them in the role of legitimate spokespersons for the society or public interest. Having defined the condition as a "social problem" there is then a legitimate basis for bringing public resources to bear on it in the manner defined. That such claims are often rejected as well as supported in the process does not reduce their rhetorical character or their bid to engage public resources. To speak of "child abuse" involves a definition of the condition and a set of principles, whether explicit or implied, from which "abuse" can be identified. To be a "social" or public problem those definitions and the standards from which they are judged needs also to be identified as shared throughout the society, as part of its culture. The process of con-

17

structing the idea of "social problem" and giving it a distinctive meaning is also a part of the process of creating or discovering the standard. Facts take on significance through the processes by which they are selected for attention, named, classified and given a relationship to each other. "Social problem" is a term that, like others, has its historical location and terminological functions as a linguistic instrument for ordering our understanding and suggesting action. As such it is itself a part of the process which it describes. "Child abuse," "child maturation," and "child rights": to call one a "social problem," another a "biological process," and another a "legal issue" is not a neutral action. Each has implications and consequences.

THE SOCIAL PROBLEMS CULTURE
AND THE WELFARE STATE

Sociologists and their students are not the only ones who live in the shadow and sunlight of "social problems." As an object of attention, social problems are a part of modern societies. It is not that contemporary societies generate conditions which are problem-laden and cry for reform and alleviation, while primitive and preindustrial ones do not. It is that modern societies, including the United States, display a culture of public problems. It is a part of how we interpret the world around us that we perceive many conditions as not only deplorable but as capable of being relieved by and as requiring public action, most often by the state. A "social problem" is a category of thought, a way of seeing certain conditions that provide the source for a claim to change through public actions. The concept is a part of modern language; the idea is a part of modern culture.

All human problems do not by that reason alone become public ones. Unrequited love, disappointed friendships, frustrated ambitions, parent-child disputes, and biological aging are among the most searing experiences of life, but they have not yet been construed as matters requiring public policy or even capable of being affected by public actions. Much that in primitive and nonindustrial societies has been either resignedly accepted or coped with in the confines of the family, including drinking, is now construed as the responsibility of public institutions. In his excellent book *Total Justice* (1985), the legal historian Lawrence Friedman has described the many new legal rights which have emerged in American justice in the past fifty years. These have created legal entitlements to answer grievances for which, in the past, the only response was "lump it" (Friedman 1985). A small but instructive example makes the point: the special ramps and parking spaces to which physically handicapped people are now entitled in the United States. Add to these civil rights, women's rights, prisoners' rights, children's rights, gay rights, and other examples that would take too much space to unpack. There is an inflationary trend in modern societies that expands the areas described as "social problems."

The cultural concept of "social problems" is not something abstract and separate from social institutions. The late Ian Weinberg used the term "referral agencies" to describe the institutions and professions to which people turn for the tasks of coping with "public problems," a term I prefer to "social problems" (Weinberg 1974). To give a name to a problem is to recognize or suggest a structure developed to deal with it. Child abuse, juvenile delinquency, mental illness, alcoholism all have developed occupations and facilities which specialize in treatment, prevention, and reform. Shelters for runaway adolescents and battered women, alcohol and drug counselors and recovery centers, community services for the aged, legal aid for the indigent, and community mental health counseling are all provided by most communities. New professions and new rights are continuously emerging. We may even be on the way to making sexual satisfaction a public responsibility. As sexual therapy becomes a recognized field requiring training and as medical insurance is extended to it, that is no longer a far-fetched possibility.

Both as a feature of contemporary culture and as a matter of social structure, the conceptualization of situations as "social problems" is embedded in the development of the welfare state. When I speak of "the welfare state" I have in mind the long-run drift in modern societies toward a greater commitment to use public facilities to directly enhance the welfare of citizens as a matter of right rather than as charity (Ehrenreich 1985; Wilensky 1975). This disposition to turn many private and familial problems into public ones is a characteristic of most modern societies. It reflects both a higher gross national product and a democratized politics that insures a floor to the grosser inequities of life and the free market (Briggs 1961; Heilbroner 1989). Underlying both of these is the optimism of a sense of progress, the views that most of life's difficulties are inherently remediable. The welfare state culture accepts and demands a degree of welfare functions from public agencies. It also has a social structure in which a significant portion of the labor force is employed in resolving and minimizing social problems.

The development of the welfare state has been marked by two attitudes or processes of action. First, it has meant a benevolent orientation toward people defined as pathological, abnormal, or deviant. The disposition to act for the benefit of problem people is found even in criminal cases, where the rehabilitation of the criminal and the special consideration of juveniles is one element in punishment and incarceration (Platt 1969). Second, the welfare state marks an inroad on the principle of the free market. As Briggs suggested, it puts a floor under that market. It establishes a minimum below which the market is no longer the principle governing the activity or inactivity of the state or other public agencies (Briggs 1961).

The development of professions dedicated to benevolence, the so-called "helping" professions, depend upon and accentuate the definition of problem populations as "sick," as objects of medical and quasi-medical attention. The "troubled persons" industries consist of the professions which bestow benevolence on people defined as in need. Such occupations include counselors, social workers, clinical psychologists, foundation administrators, operators of asylumlike centers, alcohol rehabilitation specialists, and those whose task it is to bring people viewed as trouble to themselves or to others into the stream of "adjusted" citizens.

To be sure not everything that smacks of public benevolence had its origins in the welfare state. Certainly the poor, the orphan, the insane, and other handicapped or flawed persons have been a public concern for long before the rise of contemporary welfare policies. But the extent of public commitment of resources and interests and the numbers of areas drawn into public concern has greatly increased since the days of the Poor Laws. Further, those problems approached as matters of law enforcement, crime especially, have not involved a concern for "troubled persons" but rather a concern for "troublesome persons" acted on as a matter of law enforcement. Here too, as the above discussion of rehabilitation suggests, a problem may be acted upon in a welfare mode as well as, for instance, a law enforcement mode.

The key term is "treatment" ("rehabilitation" is analogous) and can be contrasted with two alternative forms of understanding: that of sin and that of institutional organization. The former places the onus for the problem on the choice of the "troubled person." The latter seeks responsibility for the problem in the institutional arrangements under which the person lives. A concept of sin or choice leads to an emphasis on law and criminalization as policies. The latter leads to a search for changes in institutional structure, an effort to change or reform existing arrangements within which the individual has been acting. Policies that aim to increase job opportunities as a means to diminish crime are one example.

Treatment presents a view of the problem as largely a medical one and the policy needed is that of cure of individuals. The example I use here is the disease concept of alcoholism. To "see" alcohol problems as primarily those of persons suffering from a condition akin to other diseases operated to do two things. First, it weakened the onus of the chronic drunk as responsible for his or her condition. In that sense it marshaled attitudes of commiseration and benevolence. The alcoholic was someone to be helped and not condemned. Second, it made it reasonable to develop a body of knowledge and a corps of people who could be trained in the skills and knowledge needed to help alcoholics. (To a significant degree, it also provided employment for recovering alcoholics who now had capital in their past troubles. They could serve as counselors and practitioners to other alcoholics.) The same logic exists in the development of juvenile delinquency and the rehabiltative orientation toward criminals.

For deviants and troubled people to be "returned" to society requires a special group of workers trained to accomplish the task and to administer the institutions which accomplish it. If, however, the difficulties are understood to be those of moral diversity, of contested meanings, than the problem is, in whole or part, a political issue, and no system of training can eradicate the moral and political conflict involved. If the condition is perceived as that of individual illness or deficiency, then there can be a social technology, a form of knowledge and skill that can be effectively learned, whether it requires medical or institutional skills. That knowledge is the mandate for a profession's license to "own" their social problem. Insofar as it is accepted, it constitutes the source of ownership of a problem.

To "own" a problem, as I have written elsewhere (Gusfield 1981a) is to be afforded the recognition and obligation to have the claims to the existence of a problem and to information and ideas about it be given a high degree of attention and credibility. To "own" a social problem is to possess the authority to pronounce that a condition constitutes a "problem" and to suggest what might be done about it. It is the power to influence the marshaling of public facilities—laws, enforcement abilities, opinion, goods, and services—to aid the resolution of the problem. To disown a problem is to claim that one is not responsible. In the nineteenth and early twentieth centuries the Protestant churches were the dominant "owners" of the alcohol problem, a status which has since been lost to or shared with medical, governmental, and academic institutions. The beer, wine, and liquor industries have generally sought to "disown" the problem, as in the slogan: "The fault is in the man and not in the bottle."

CONSENSUS AND CONFLICT:
THE PUBLIC STATUS OF SOCIAL PROBLEMS

An interpretation of a social problem as one of individual deficiencies and the emergence of professions based on such assumptions limit the perception of institutional features at work. Patricia Morgan has suggested that the definition of social problems as those of "troubled persons" is a form of depoliticizing problems (Morgan 1980). There is much merit in this view. The psychologizing or medicalizing of phenomena, as a way of seeing, draws attention away from the institutional or structural aspects. As Morgan maintains, from 1955 to 1975 the California liquor, beer, and wine industries actively promoted the redefinition of alcohol problems described in the term "the alcoholism movement." Ron Roizen has asserted that one consequence of that movement was to "de-villify" alcohol (Roizen 1991), to focus attention on the drinker rather than the nature and availability of the drink. A defect of the drinker replaced availability of alcohol as focus of the problem.

What Morgan and others maintained is that the alcohol industries sought to prevent an alternate view, summed up in the phrase contrasting to "substance abuse": "abusive substance." Such a view would make the insititutions that support the sale and distribution of alcohol targets of public policy. The "alcoholism movement" depoliticized the alcohol problem in that it deflected an alternative: recognition of fundamental conflicts about the acceptance or rejection of alcohol as a commodity.

In the process of owning or attempting to own a problem, those in the public arena claim to represent a societal consensus, to speak for society. The definition of the condition as a problem, as calling for public action, is presented as beyond need of argument. The language and rhetoric of "social problems" is a language which assumes and points toward a basic consensus about the problematic character of the condition deplored. In the same fashion a physician can assume that his or her patient wants to be cured. Child abuse, alcoholism, mental illness, prostitution, gender and racial discrimination, crime, and drug addiction are just a few among many social problems which are imbued with an aura of consensus about their status as problems. To challenge their status as social conditions requiring eradication or at least minimization is unthinkable in the contemporary public arenas. The point is illustrated in one of my favorite comic strips, "Miss Peach." The first-grade teacher has told her class that next week they will have a speaker on the topic of juvenile delinquency. "Oh, goody," says one of her young pupils. "Will he be for it or against it?"

Miss Peach's student made a profound utterance about most of the situations sociologists customarily study under the rubric of "social problem." They involve an assumed public consensus from which the behavior targeted for change or reform is perceived as outside the norm, as opposed to societally shared values. It is not publically acceptable for anyone to be "for" mental illness, alcoholism, gender or racial discrimination, poverty, drinking-driving, air pollution, homelessness, or almost all the titles of chapters in the various texts in the field. To see a situation as a social problem is to set in motion a particular form of discourse and to channel policies in a particular direction. To speak of "child abuse" is to focus on the active abusive role of parents and guardians vis-á-vis the child. To speak of "child neglect" is to focus on institutions as well as instead of specific acts of family, on poverty and indifference. The image of the first is of a parent beating or sexually molesting a child. The image of the second is of homeless children, living on the streets.

From time to time conditions may pass into or out of the realm of "social problems." The gay rights movement has succeeded in turning the deviant status of the homosexual from a "social problem" to a matter of social and political conflict (Greenberg 1988). Child abuse became a social problem in the 1970s as it was discovered through the efforts of radiologists and pediatricians, although the actions had existed well before the discovery (Nelson 1984; Pfohl 1977).

Claims to use public resources for reform posit a "society" which is homogeneous, against which the problem situation can be contrasted. In this the nature of "social problems" has not changed much since 1943 when C. Wright Mills published his justly classic paper, "The Professional Ideology of Social Pathologists" (1943). In his critical examination of the field, Mills described the method of defining social problems by sociologists as "in terms of *deviation from norms*. The 'norms' so used are usually held to be the standards of the society" (531–32). A pluralism of values or political power is denied.

A point made by Murray Edelman in his analyses of the language of social problems is instructive (Edelman 1977). Aid to farmers, he pointed out, is called "parity," aid to business in the form of tax cuts is simply called aid to the general economy, aid to people at the poverty level is called "welfare" or "help." Differing language frames mean differing assessments and evaluations. Currently this is recognized at a public level in the term "corporate welfare."

Edelman's discussion is pertinent. We use terms such as "welfare" and "helping" and "social problem" to emphasize the temporary and un-committed nature of benevolence or control rather than the language of rights, which creates a different meaning. To use the language of "social problem" is to portray its subjects as "sick" or as "troublesome." We do not use a language of personal deficiencies to talk about economic con-cerns, describing recession as the problem of sick businessmen and in-vestment counselors as "market therapists." The income of the client af-fects the language of the profession. Subsidies to the auto industry are not "aid to dependent factories."

Nor is that consensus, illustrated by Miss Peach, something inherent in the objects attended to. Agreement is a social construction in which an assumed accord is not contested. It can be contrasted with issues such as abortion or gun control or vivisection where the existence of diversity, of conflict, is so evident that the claim to represent a public or even elite consensus falls on its face. In these areas a claim to represent the "soci-ety" appears patently unacceptable. We recognize that in undertaking so-cial policies somebody loses and somebody wins, unless some compro-mise occurs. The fact of conflict is recognized, as is the case with gay rights. Where consensus is assumed that is not the case. Even the word *issue* is less utilized in the language of social problems. The deviant, the pathological, cannot argue that his or her vice is really virtue. To do so seriously is to change the definition of the condition.

In 1989 the California State Supreme Court affirmed a lower court decision that prohibits staff members of mental hospitals from forcibly administering antipsychotic drugs to patients committed for three- to fourteen-day periods. An attorney for one of the hospitals, in comment-ing on the case, objected to the decision saying: "This decision may sat-isfy someone's notion of an abstract principle but the patients who sup-posedly would benefit are going to be denied effective treatment" (*Los Angeles Times* 1989). The speaker asserts a claim to be recognized among those who "own" a part of the problems of mental disorder. The speaker does more than state a personal opinion, he makes a claim to represent more than himself, to speak for the interests of the public and the inter-ests of those the hospital personnel are acting toward. The speaker as-serts that the condition of the patients is to be considered a problem even though others—the patients—may not see it as such. He represents him-self as speaking for a consensus—a "society," a "true public interest."

The situation, as he presents it, is not that of a divergence of standards but that of a consensual society and a deviant minority, a presumed normality and an abnormal condition. It is not a political issue between differing points of view and interests. It is a social problem, and a united societal consensus affirms it. There is no room for a diversity of views; no contest of meanings. In the sense used in literary criticism, the "voice" of the writer is that of the abstract authoritative "society" (Gusfield 1976a).

In her study of child abuse and the making of a public agenda, the political scientist Barbara Nelson distinguished between "valence issues" and "position issues." She writes: "A valence issue such as child abuse elicits a single, strong, fairly uniform emotional response and does not have an adversarial quality. 'Position issues,' on the other hand, do not elicit a single response but instead engender alternative and sometimes highly conflictful responses" (1984, 27). This is similar to the distinction now being made in social movements literature between conflict movements and consensual movements (Lofland 1989; McCarthy 1988) or among political scientists between consensus issues and conflict issues (Hayes 1981; Crenson 1971). Abortion is a conflict issue; pro-life and pro-choice are conflict movements and countermovements. It was the absence of controversy, of adversaries, that made the child abuse legislation develop so rapidly, Nelson maintains.

This discussion of the concept "social problems" points up how the use of public resources to alleviate a "social problem" is carried on as an attempt to present policy expressing a societal consensus and to deny or gloss over a pluralism of norms or values. Some in the society claim to carry out actions which will benefit others or will change the behavior of those that are troublesome to the claimants and the "society." The troublesomeness is abnormal or clearly morally indefensible.

Such assertions have to be seen as part of the process by which that nebulous "generalized other" we call "society" is created. The status of consensus is not a characteristic of the condition or issue. It is a result of human actions and processes which succeed or fail in their efforts. How a condition is defined and how that definition comes to dominate or fails to dominate public arenas is not preset. For many years the performance of abortions was a "social problem" and a criminal act. With the rise of the medical and feminist movement to legalize abortions, that consensus became less dominant. In the continuing public conflict over the abortion question, the decisions of the Supreme Court have been so important, in part, because the Court claims to "speak for society."

CONTESTED AND UNCONTESTED MEANINGS
AND THEIR TRANSFORMATIONS

Whether particular public policies occur in a context of consensus or conflict is not a matter of the policy or issue. The definitions of conditions is itself open to conflict and change. The gay rights movement is a good example of how the meaning of conditions as "social problem" can be transformed. That movement is perhaps the most salient example of how the ability to mobilize has enabled a subject group to transform its status. During this century, homosexuals have been thought of as sinful or as sick—objects of condemnation or of medical benevolence. What the gay rights movement did was to resist the public designation of deviance, of abnormality, by attacking the presumed norms, to deny that homosexuality constituted a social problem. In doing this the phenomena of homosexuality lost its status as a "social problem" and became a matter of political and cultural conflict about the recognition of alternative sexual styles. What had been an uncontested meaning has been transformed into a political contest over the meaning of homosexuality. The gay rights movement has succeeded in removing social problem from the definition of homosexuality. Symbolically, the American Psychiatric Association removed homosexuality from its list of psychiatric disorders, thus demedicalizing it (Bayer 1981). The meaning of a condition as a "social problem" is itself either a source of political and social conflict or the result of such processes.

The case of child abuse illustrates how a social problem has been transformed from one kind into another. Nelson's analysis of child abuse as a valence issue presumes that its character results from its content. That needs to be demonstrated rather than assumed. Pfohl's description of the earlier child abuse movement, of the late nineteenth century, indicates the possibility that children might well be experienced as the subjects of a more politicized framework. The similar conception of "child neglect" emphasized the homelessness and malnutrition of children of poverty and threw the onus on the social structure and public institutions which associated poverty with child neglect. This is a much more adversarial, political definition of the "child abuse" problem. It touches on the institutional arrangements of social and political organization. It cannot be "handled" through reforming persons or law enforcement. Although there have been some efforts to counter the current emphasis on the problems of parental abuse of children with alternative conceptions or to emphasize the rights of parents against state intervention, these have not been mobilized to a point of converting the dominant definition of child abuse from an apolitical to a political one. It now is experienced through the concrete image of good people and bad people, villains and victims. A similar process has occurred in the status of smoking in the United States. Once, in the early twentieth century, it was decidedly a moral-oriented movement. In the 1960s it reemerged within a discourse of health, which in several ways masked the moral elements still at work (Gusfield 1993).

The change to "social problem" from "political issue" is significant in the construction of phenomena in the public sphere. In his 1977 presidential address for the Society for the Study of Social Problems, entitled "The Politics of Speaking in the Name of Society," Bernard Beck pointed out that, under the guise of being a social problem, many interests can be served (Beck 1978). "Working politicians have discovered the usefulness of conducting politics under the guise of treating social problems" (357). Beck used the example of the deinstitutionalization of custodial organizations such as mental asylums. There, as in the case of the decriminalization of public drunkenness, action taken with an eye toward state budgets is justified as benevolence toward people with troubles. Politicians, asserted Beck, shun the conflicts that embitter and divide their electorates. They are happy when they can "turn over" issues to technicians or to legal decisions. It depoliticizes the issue by defining it as one expressive of societal consensus.

The effort to define situations as "social problems" is far from always successful. Some groups are capable of mobilizing to bring about change or to resist the controlling definitions. The gay rights movement transformed an uncontested meaning into a political contest. The attempt of an organization of prostitutes, ex-prostitutes, and interested persons to remove the charge of vice has failed to affect that status (Jenness 1993).

KNOWLEDGE, POLICY, AND CULTURAL AUTHORITY

The political scientist E. E. Schattschneider expressed one aspect of my thought in this chapter when he wrote: "All forms of political organization have a bias in favor of the exploitation of some kinds of conflicts and the suppression of others because *organization is the mobilization of bias*. Some issues are organized into politics while others are organized out" (1960, 71).

Knowledge in the field of social problems often serves to take issues out of politics by defining the meanings of the arena, condition, or events as uncontested. (In the following chapter I will show how this occurred in the field of alcohol studies.) The problem of analysis is not one of denying a societal consensus but of examining what is contained in the meanings given to the problem as social research has used it.

Max Weber's discussion of science and politics as vocations is a good place at which to begin to discuss differing forms of knowledge and their relation to social problems as a sociological field and cultural authority as an object of analysis (Weber 1946; 1949, 77–159; Schluchter 1979.) Most pertinent are the distinctions between fact and value and between an ethic of absolute ends and an ethic of responsibility.

The distinction between fact and value has been a cornerstone of much discussion of the social sciences. Values influence the processes of research by modes of selection and procedures of study. Yet values are perceived as an impediment to good research, a flaw rather than a model. The distinction between fact and value has both merit and limits. Certainly, scientists, unlike religious leaders, do not present themselves as prophets declaring ultimate meanings in life. They do present themselves as declaring conditions which are "out there" and which need to be considered by those who undertake action.

For Weber, as for others, science was not simply a means to achieve ends and values supplied by other institutions or elites. It was also a value in itself, a process of searching for knowledge which gives meaning to existence. As such, it has no easily given set of constraints on what to search for or where to conduct its searches.

For Weber, politics was not only the art of the possible. Unlike Science, Politics was the realm of values, of goals, of visions of the Good. The politician must take stands; must make judgments of values. He or she cannot act "objectively." In Harry Truman's famous aphorism: "The buck stops here."

But this distinction between knowledge and action is also too simple. Weber's discussion of an ethics of conviction and an ethics of responsibility is central both for our analysis and for his comments on politics as a vocation. An ethics of conviction is also called an ethics of absolute ends *(Wertrationalitat)* and contrasted with an ethics of multiple ends *(Zweckrationalitat)*. For the politician bound to absolutist ethics there is no need to recognize the costs and benefits, the consequences of choosing one end or value and ignoring others. There is no need to choose, to arbitrate, to compromise, or to measure and predict consequences. For one bound to an ethics of responsibility, the necessity of weighing one value against another, of recognizing the costs of attainment and benefits to be gained, is central. Ethical and political action are not clearly given. For Weber, rational action in a pluralistic society requires an ethics of responsibility, of pluralistic values and hence of a politics of rational understanding of the totality of possibilities.

For an ethics of absolute ends, science becomes administrative; that is, it provides the means to achieve the singular value to which the politician is committed. For a politics of ethical responsibility, as Wolfgang Schluchter suggests, science becomes value-relevant. It makes available to policymakers and publics those elements of value diversities which make up the political landscape. Such knowledge is irrelevant to those for whom action is dictated by monistic values. As Schluchter puts it: "In a society in which there is no objective knowledge about causal and value relations it is impossible, strictly speaking, to act 'responsibly.' Value-free but value-relational knowledge creates the very facts which can then be evaluated. In this way modern science has not only a necessary but a critical relationship to responsible action" (Schluchter 1979, 91). I would underline the word *critical,* giving it a less ambiguous meaning, that of comment and explication of the values with which an ethics of responsibility must cope.

This discussion leads to a further distinction between three forms of knowledge: scientific, administrative, and political. Political knowledge is the wisdom and judgment that is involved in making choices among goals and values. Administrative, technical knowledge is the "art of the possible," the knowledge of how to achieve the political goals. It is the bureaucratic side of political action, illustrated in the many discussions of civilian-military relations. Much of Weber's fear of democratic politics was that of leaderless administration, administration devoid of the directions and standards that come from political decision and bias. Scientific knowledge remains outside the political process, is indeed a critic and an assessor of the political. It must include the processes of value-formation and value-existence in its study. It is this view of social science that underlies my perspective in this volume.

Insofar as a social problems approach blunts the question of consensus and dissensus, it hides the conflicts that exist in the society. Such covering impedes the essential clarification needed both for understanding and for rational action. It is bad scholarship, and it makes for bad politics.

In analyzing what are commonly called "social problems" we need to keep in mind the transformational possibilities. Beneath the serene facade of consensus we may discover the maelstrom of groups in conflict. The capacity of an ownership group to make its version of reality the only acceptable one is a mark of cultural authority. Where conflict rages, it is also a bid for that authority, to assert a cultural hegemony over the field. When meanings become contested it indicates that, at least in that area, there is no group that can articulate and define situations in a way that can make them acceptable throughout human society. Political choice cannot be avoided.

In a way, this chapter is a sermon. The moral is not contained in any summative sentence, but it is a plea to move the study of social problems closer to the study of how social movements and institutions affect and are affected by the interpretations, the language, and the symbols that constitute seeing a situation as a social problem. It is a plea to see "social problems" as a process of designation and not only a recognition of a given situation. At the same time, we need to take care not to separate the study of meanings from the study of their historical and institutional settings.

As interpreters of social problems, we sociologists earn our living by other people's troubles. One person's poison is another's mead. (Not George Herbert or Margaret.) What we can best contribute to assuage our guilt is to cast an ironical eye on the passing scene so as to make us all more aware of the possibilities and opportunities that the veils of cultural meanings and institutional arrangements hide from us. It is out of this humanistic and reflexive self-awareness that societies may yet achieve some control over their own destinies.

Chapter Three

"No More Cakes and Ale"
The Rhetoric and Politics
of Drinking Research

I begin with a specific question: Why are there so few studies of drinking in America? To those of you exposed to the thousands and thousands of studies in the bibliographies of alcohol research this will seem like the inane maunderings of an uninformed or facetious writer, attempting to misinform or mislead his naive readers. Evidently I am playing on ambiguities and diversities in the meanings and understandings of the word *drinking.* What I wish to convey is that among the multitudinous papers, occasional books, and mountains of reports of and about drinking by social scientists there are few that describe, interpret, or analyze the drinking events in which Americans drink, drinking perceived as having no or few troublesome consequences for the drinker or for others. Most studies of American drinking, I submit, are either about what is defined as pathological drinking or are dominated by the framework of pathology, of drinking as a social problem. This chapter, as well as others in this volume, is about the domination of the pathological framework and its consequences for understanding drinking in America and for public policy toward it.

In the sequence of festivities in many European countries, Carnival (or Mardi Gras), with its licensed release from many prohibitions on drinking, eating, sexuality, aggression, and social hierarchy, occurs before and in contrast with the ascetic period of Lent. The two holidays also appear as metaphors and figures for alternating and opposed attitudes toward life. In his detailed study of popular culture in early modern Europe, Peter Burke points to a Bruegel painting in which a fat man sitting on a barrel combats a thin old woman on a chair. The historian remarks that this is a literal enactment of a common battle in Shrovetide rituals. He interprets the fat man, "who belongs to the tavern side of the picture," as symbolic of the Carnival spirit of traditional popular culture and the thin old woman as the embodiment of Lent, associated with the "high culture" of the clergy who were then (1559) attempting to reform, if not suppress, many popular festivities (Burke 1978, 207).

Alcohol research generally emerges on the side of Lent and as an opponent of Carnival. Despite repeated avowals of support for "moderate drinking," the substance of studies of drinking in the United States adds up to a condemnation of drunkenness and thus a condemnation of a significant facet of American leisure and popular culture. Operating with an assumption of a societal consensus about drunkenness, the field of alcohol studies possesses a rhetoric which ignores the moral conflicts about alcohol use which pervade the reality of its uses. In doing so, the current state of research on drinking in America creates an apolitical image of drinking behavior and reinforces a view of consensus about drinking that glosses over moral and political conflicts in American life. In its character as apolitical analysis of a social pathology, alcohol research functions politically to the detriment of understanding drinking and thus ignoring the sources of political and moral conflict.

Social research is frequently social criticism, whether the authors are so aware or not. This basic tenet of the sociology of knowledge extends well beyond the popular conception of bias, the idea that the values of the researcher are reflected in what he or she finds and reports. In one formulation, social research, whatever the dispositions of its authors, has consequences for public policies and private aspirations. In the preface to the English translation of Karl Mannheim's seminal work, *Ideology and Utopia*, Louis Wirth summed up this view: "The distinctive character of social science discourse is to be sought in the fact that every assertion, no matter how objective it may be, has ramifications extending beyond the limits of science itself" (Mannheim 1949, xvii).

But there is an even more revealing understanding of how knowledge both is affected by and in turn affects culture. This understanding has emerged from the analysis of the very ways in which inquiry is conducted and reported upon to audiences. Here the emphasis is on the framework or paradigms which lead the researcher to ask some questions but not others, to study some objects and situations and not others, to interpret his or her data in one way and not in another, to write or report his or her study with one choice of words and phrases rather than another.

One aspect of this critical approach to social research has taken the form of analyzing the documents of research as themselves modes of persuading an audience to accept the conclusions or assertions of the social scientist. While the word *rhetoric* has had a discredited connotation as a form of deception it has come to be recognized that most communication, including science, is a form of persuasion, whatever the rules of the communication game. The art of scientific and social research involves persuasion in written or oral form. It therefore possesses a rhetoric, a mode of persuading an audience (Latour and Woolgar 1979; Gusfield 1976a, 1981a). The analysis of social science research as rhetorical acts does not exhaust the modes of analysis nor does it necessarily conflict with the truth or falsity of the author's assertions or impugn the scientific integrity of the creators. What it can do, however, is uncover the dominating frameworks within which research is conducted and which influence the implications of the research for public policy. Factual representation involves selection, interpretation, and communication so "events in the same set are capable of functioning in order to figure forth different meanings—moral, cognitive or aesthetic" (White 1978, 127).

Sociological writing, like most of social science, is rhetorical in that it presents an argument; it is an effort to persuade (Perelman and Olbrechts-Tytecka 1969; Toulmin 1950). How persuasion is accomplished is a legitimate inquiry. Style, structure, language, metaphors, and visual material are germane to the analysis of scientific reports as they have been to literary materials. The very style and organization of a discipline is itself an essential aspect of its conventional rhetoric (Gusfield 1981a, chs. 2–4; Bazerman 1989).

THE SOCIAL CONSTRUCTION OF REALITY

We are persuaded by argument but we are also persuaded by what is attended to and what is ignored in research. In many ways this is a more powerful form of persuasion because it is less readily noticed. The character of the object studied is often more implicit than explicit. It constitutes the reality of the work and its context. As such it often is taken for granted and contrasting or conflicting aspects of study are unnoticed. In this sense, reality is itself a social construction, in part if not in whole.

An interpretive approach to the study of human action begins with the realization, or perspective, that in much of human action the real, everyday world in which we act is not the objective, unmediated world of a pristine, self-contained reality. It is infused with meanings and posesses an interactive character. "Reality" is thus a construction of meanings which interpret raw sense data. The reality of fact which is assumed to be independent of the observer is a product of an interaction between the facticity of the world and the frames, categories, interests, and concepts of the observer (Berger and Luckmann 1966). I need not go so far as to deny a real world, what Charles Taylor calls "brute data" (1979). It is not a metaphysical position, about the nature of reality, but an epistemological one, about how we know or believe we know.

It is the socially shared element of facticity, the meaning given to phenomena, "raw data," as social problem that is the focus of my attention in this chapter. Facticity constitutes the underlying approach in the individual studies that make up the bulk of this book. I am intent on understanding how situations are and are not defined as "social problems" and how they are imbued with specific characteristics. In this I follow the seminal work of Spector and Kitsuse's *Constructing Social Problems* (1977) and expand on the analysis contained in my study *The Culture of Public Problems* (1981a). As Spector and Kitsuse put it: "If a sociologist of occupations studying prostitution would look for people earning their livings, a sociologist of social problems would look for people engaged in defining (or promoting) the prostitution problem" (75).

The example of prostitution suggests another mode of framing events and conditions, of particular importance to drinking as a social problem. The "same" data (prostitution) is seen from different interests. What is centrally attended to by one kind of interest—the sociology of occupations, for example—is only marginally attended to by the other, the sociologist of social problems. In one frame, that of occupations, prostitution has many similarities to other occupations such as accounting, law, and construction. In another frame, that of social problems, it has many similarities to other "vices" such as drug abuse, alcoholism, and homelessness. The income of the prostitute would be of great importance for the sociologist of occupations but only marginal for the social problems sociologist. As Erving Goffman wrote, "There is a sense in which what is play for the golfer is work for the caddy" (1974, 8).

In understanding the rhetorics of social research it becomes imperative to observe what is not studied as well as what is studied. We need to be sensitive to the multiple possibilities that might have been explored as well as those that were. The sociologist Pitirim Sorokin once remarked that probably the last thing a fish realizes is that it is swimming in water. Only when it is out of it, gasping for breath on dry land does it realize where it has been. We need to listen for the silences as well as the noises. Only then can we "hear" the frame.

FRAME AND IMAGERY IN ALCOHOL
CONTROL POLICIES

Attempts by officials and established institutions to limit, control, and re-press drinking and drinking patterns run through the history of many countries like rivers winding through the landscape, now swollen by spring rains, now dried and thin by the heat of summer. Social scientists are interested in explaining and understanding the flow of drinking controls. They find themselves equipped with a set of conflicting and contrasting perspectives with which to study social hydrodynamics.

The joys of drinking and drunkenness have been celebrated in story, in song, in poetry, and in folklore, humor, and legend. So too have the woes of drinking and drunkenness. In American society drinking and drunkenness have been a source of division between groups and between styles of leisure. Attitudes and behavior associated with drinking have been a marker by which propriety and respectability have been assessed and evaluated. While many people have been enlisted as partisans or supporters of efforts to restrict or abolish the use of beverage alcohol, others have either ignored or actively rejected the advice or coercion of laws and public standards about drinking.

The analysis of drinking involves understanding the frame in which the study of and policy toward drinking has occurred in the United States and the consequences of different frames applied to it. The dominant frame is that of drinking as a social problem. The concept of "social problem," as an aspect of our language, in turn implies a general framework. Both the frame and the concept have consequences important both to general understanding of what happens when phenomena are labeled "social problems" and to the specific understanding of drinking and public policy in America.

Social problems do not emerge spontaneously nor are their characteristics given unilaterally by the force of facts on observers. What is noticed, what is emphasized, what is selected for effective policy is a product of the interaction of ideas and events. The interpretive frame of the alcohol problem has shifted and changed through its history. Such frames, or what Robin Room (1974) calls "governing images," limit as well as direct public perception and the policies associated with them. They are the paridigmatic schema within which a social problem is defined and experienced as "real." In the last sixty years in the United States several such frames have existed as dominant images of the alcohol problem.

With Repeal of the Eighteenth Amendment in 1933, alcohol continued to be perceived in the public policy arena in America as a dangerous commodity. All states passed legislation setting a minimum age below which sales were prohibited. Most localities set hours as limits to sale both on- and off-premises. States developed Alcohol Beverage Control Boards to grant or refuse licenses to sell. Public drunkenness was everywhere made illegal. Alcohol was once again subject to specific taxes. Prohibition remained in several states and many localities voted themselves dry. Spirits, beer, and wines were not, by virtue of Repeal, now accorded the same legal status as other foods or liquids.

Such strictures became part of the taken-for-granted framework within which drinking and drunkenness were objects of public concern. However, the problem of alcohol use, of drinking and drunkenness, underwent a major change. During the decades from 1933 to 1970 the problem of alcohol became defined as the problem of alcoholism, and the policies associated with alcohol largely were those of finding and treating alcoholics (Roizen 1991). (See chapter 12 of this volume.)

With the emergence of Alcoholics Anonymous, the growth of treatment facilities and associations of recovering alcoholics and of a profession of people who treated alcoholics, the perception of problems associated with alcohol became restricted to a population of deviant drinkers—people who were unable to control their disposition to drink. It was those deviant people, unable to limit their drinking and addicted to alcohol, who became the object of attention. The normal drinker, the occasional drunk, was not seen as generator of a public problem, for himself or for others. Even where problems other than the individual addiction were stressed, they were seen as consequences of a chronic alcoholism, either fully existent or incipient (Waller 1967). The social problem of alcohol was perceived as that of chronic alcoholism. In Roizen's apt phrase, drinking was "de-villified" (1991).

The "alcoholism movement" was supported by another belief that gained currency in the 1940s: that alcoholism was a form of disease (Jellinek 1960). There were two facets to this belief. First, that the problem of alcohol was confined to a deviant group of people whose condition created problems for themselves and, to some extent, others. Second, that policies to resolve the problem of alcohol were medical. The subject of policy—of the alcohol problem—was the addicted person, the alcoholic.

The Public Health Movement in Alcohol

By the early 1970s the alcoholism movement began to lose its dominance in public and policy areas. What emerged and is active today is a perspective or frame frequently labeled the "public health perspective" (Bruun et al. 1975; Beauchamp 1988; Room 1985). The development of the public health perspective is an instance of what Robin Room has called "problem inflation" (1984). From this perspective, alcohol problems include more than just alcoholism. The policies recommended affect the total population of drinkers, not just alcoholics. In their influential World Health Organization report, eleven authors from more than a half-dozen countries stated: "our main argument is well-substantiated: *changes in the overall consumption of alcoholic beverages have a bearing on the health of the people in any society. Alcohol measures can be used to limit consumption: thus, control of alcohol availability becomes a public health issue"* (Bruun et al. 1975, 12–13).

From the perspective embodied in the WHO report, the focus is on two objects of concern. First, the range of behaviors to be avoided are found in nonalcoholics as well as alcoholics. Work absenteeism, drinking-driving, rowdiness, public drunkenness, and crime are not exclusive to alcoholics or always the result of addiction to alcohol. Second, such undesirable behaviors do not necessarily call for clinical treatment of individuals. They are best dealt with by preventive measures which constrain availability or which control the detrimental consequences of drunkenness on the drinker and on others. Like measures of public sanitation or mass innoculations, they involve the total population of normal, common drinkers.

Here the object of concern has again changed. *The* alcohol problem has a different reality and consequently calls for different policies. The idea of the problematic drinker and of problematic drinking is a different object. The concept of the deviant, or social drinker, has been deconstructed and in the process changed.

In practice, the prevention movement has been largely associated with attempts to diminish the total consumption of alcohol through measures such as increased taxation and laws which mandate signs or education about such issues as the fetal alcohol syndrome and the dangers of drinking and driving. It has also been associated with another policy orientation which, unlike the prevention movement, is marked by a very different interpretation of the alcohol problem or problems.

The Criminalization Movement

The prevention movement perceives drunken behavior as dangerous both to the drinker and to others. Adherents emphasize the event in its environmental and institutional context. The aim of policy is thus to design the environment and institutions so as to lessen the danger. The drinker is viewed as a patient, to be helped. Still another perspective is possible: to "see" the drinker as an enemy of the people whose action is criminal. From this perspective, the aim of prevention is best carried out by criminalization through laws.

In the early 1980s, impelled by anti-drinking-driving movement associations, such as Mothers Against Drunk Drivers (later "Drivers" was changed to "Driving"), and with federal support, all states that had not yet done so passed legislation dropping the minimum age for legal sale of alcoholic beverages to eighteen. States have also increased punishment for drinking-drivers and lowered the minimum blood alcohol level needed for the misdemeanor. The aim of such legislation is to deter the drinker through criminalization of behavior. In this, and in other ways, the act of drunken behavior is given a different interpretation as deviant (Ross 1992; Mäkelä and Room 1985). The drunkard is not sick but immoral and antisocial.

The criminalization of drunkenness operates, as does much of current law, in commitment to deterrence theory (Zimring and Hawkins 1973; Ross 1992; Lawrence, Snortum, and Zimring 1988). The drinker is assumed to be a rational person for whom increased punishment and risk of apprehension leads to compliant behavior.

The ease with which drinking ages were lowered, the increased punishment for drinking drivers, and the general disposition to consider constraints on drinking suggest a growing criminalistic construction of drinking in America. It is represented in a more coercive and harsh orientation toward the drunkard (Mäkelä and Room 1985). The drinker and the drunkard are objects of moral disapproval and less worthy of social consideration than are others. The criminalization movement is a return to an open moralism.

THE PATHOLOGICAL FRAME

All three of the perspectives—treatment, prevention, and criminalization—share a significant element in common: they all are attentive to drinking as pathological behavior, as behavior which leads to unwanted consequences. In framing the perception of drunkenness as pathological, they minimize and obliterate a vision of drunkenness which recognizes virtues and benefits that impel many drinkers to something more than "moderate drinking." They do not endorse any policies for making drinking easier or acceptable. With some exceptions, the policies aim at reducing consumption by inducing abstinence among alcoholics, by reducing availability, or by deterring the drinker from drinking through fear of punishment. To a significant degree they concentrate on limiting or eliminating the use of intoxicating drink. They ignore or place little attention on designing contexts or facilitating contexts which accept drinking patterns and seek to make drinking safer.

The interest of those who study or create policy regarding drinking is in "drunkenness" and its dangers. Research is oriented toward pathologies and "excessive" drinking. There are few studies of drinking and drunkenness as behavior in a context, few studies of "normal" drunkenness, in which there have been few or no damages. Yet, as a few studies indicate, even the pathologies are more often the result of less than heavy drinking or are the actions of people who cannot be construed as alcoholic or having other alcohol-related problems. To be sure, heavy drinkers are disproportionately associated with pathological behavior, but there are so many more "normal" drinkers than alcoholics so that their contribution may outweigh that of the chronic inebriate. A study of Air Force personnel found that while chronic alcoholics accounted for approximately 6 percent of the drinkers and 25 percent of the participants in drunkenness events, the remaining 75 percent of the participants in drunkenness events were accounted for by personnel who were not afflicted with chronic problems (Polich and Orvis 1979; also see Knupfer 1984; Kreitman 1986; Bacon 1979).

Both the public health and the criminalization perspectives are then policies which, like the antismoking campaigns, seek to change drinking and drunkenness. Like that campaign, their objective is diminishing consumption.

There is one exception to this. The public health perspective does speak of measures to provide a safer environment in which the dangers associated with drunkenness can be lessened. This is what some have labeled the "make the world safe for drunks" approach or what I refer to as the difference between *drinking* problems and drinking *problems*. (See chapter 11 of this volume.) Ralph Nader once remarked that Detroit ought to produce an automobile on the assumption that fools and drunkards would drive it. Building a safer auto, making roads user safe, making a car difficult to start if the driver is drunk, providing cheaper and more reliable forms of public transportation, and providing incentives for designated driver programs are some measures that could lessen the dangers of drunkenness. While such modes have been discussed or written about occasionally, they are glaringly absent from much of the corpus of social science research on alcohol.

Being drunk, or some variant such as "high" or "tight," is a part of the leisure time acts of many Americans. It remains outside the frame of social research except as pathology. Within the frame of pathology, getting drunk is something to be prevented. From this perspective, the partying, bar attendance, and frequent drinking of many, many more Americans than those who get into trouble with drinking must be construed as deviance or unsocial behavior.

"Seeing" drinking behavior as a social problem represents a concentration on the risks and dangers of drunkenness, but it also has produced a blindness to virtues and benefits to drinking as a possible "good" among consumer goods. The attempted social control of alcohol plays a role in the conflict over styles of life and the definition of propriety in American life. The secure and accepted life of sobriety is set out as the definition of what is right and proper, and drunkenness is condemned as being deviant and improper.

The frame of drinking as a social problem takes on significance in examining the corpus of research on alcohol. The area of alcohol studies has been a major foundation for much of alcohol policy in the post-Repeal years.

ALCOHOL AND THE ASSUMPTION OF MALEVOLENCE

Selden Bacon, undoubtedly the leading sociological researcher of drinking in the past generation, frequently and emphatically pleaded for the study of "normal" drinking and intoxication to be a major focus of alcohol research (Bacon 1969; 1976; 1979). In a trenchant article on priorities in alcohol research he carried this a step further. He saw the ubiquity of the pathological frame as both a distortion of American drinking patterns and a form of limited scholarship.[1] Bacon wrote: "It is not a dark secret, nor is it difficult to perceive, that the established intellectual research disciplines . . . when they turned their attention to alcohol, man and society, focused upon the painful aspects. They studied "drunks," not drinkers; intoxication rather than drinking; the awful sequels of alcohol ingestion, not the usual. Studies of the causes of alcoholism, for example, are legion, but studies of the causes of drinking are rare" (1979, 9).

In a review and assessment of the impact of alcohol on wife beating and child abuse, Claire Hamilton and James Collins, Jr., coined a useful phrase to describe a significant element in much current alcohol research. It is worth quoting the passage in detail:

> On the other hand, the family violence literature, especially that which deals with intervention strategies to address the problem, often assumes that alcohol is a cause of violence between family members. This literature is not theoretically satisfying. It is not explicit about how alcohol fits the causal scheme. The characteristics and details of violent events in the family that involve alcohol are not distinguished from those where alcohol is not present. A *"malevolence assumption"* appears to operate [emphasis added]. An offender with a drinking problem or the presence of alcohol in an incident of family violence is assumed to demonstrate that alcohol has explanatory power.
>
> The moral and political debates about alcohol and its effects have not been confined to the moral and political arenas. These perspectives also have influenced scientific analyses and interpretation. This influence has often been expressed in the following logic: alcohol is destructive and evil, and therefore one is likely to find destruction and evil where alcohol is found. We refer to this as the "malevolence assumption" and it is an implicit attitude in much of what is written on family violence. (1981, 261)

The "Malevolence Assumption" in Drinking-Driving Studies

Elsewhere I have examined the social construction of the problem of drinking-driving (Gusfield 1981a, pt. 1) Here I want to point to several ways in which the research on drinking-driving, through the assumption of malevolence, limits or hides the place of drinking-driving and drunkenness in the everyday lives of many drinkers. One is found in a clear use of the assumption that wherever alcohol use is found, it is the causal factor responsible for the accident. After twenty-four years of reading hundreds and hundreds of studies of drinking-driving, only in 1994 did I find more than one which attempted to examine and assess the fault of the alcohol factor, or even the drinking motorist, in the accident.[2] Bacon has presented evidence of researchers overlooking several studies which appear to cast doubt on the assumed relation between drinking and pathological outcomes (1979, 11–13).

The language is often less definitive. Conclusions are often couched in such phrases as "Alcohol was involved in x percent of the cases." From this, however, policy considerations are drawn just as if a causal conclusion had been drawn. Journalists and public officials are less cautious, moving easily from "involvement" to cause (Gusfield 1981a). Even in the professional research, "involvement" is not investigated further to determine in what fashion alcohol was involved.

In two other ways the possible role of drinking and drinking-driving in the leisure and culture of groups is hidden. It is evidenced less by what is studied than by what is not. In the first case, drinking-driving is studied apart from a situation; as a specific activity it is seldom studied in relation to purposes, interactions, or contexts of the life of the drinker. For example, in the hundreds and hundreds of drinking-driving studies there is none that seeks to understand how drinkers do manage to drive safely. There is a distinct repulsion toward studies which might entertain any suggestion that drinking might be less than dangerous or might be made to be less dangerous (Husak 1994). The deviant character of drinking and drunkenness is not examined for differences and diversities. It is not treated as a "natural" activity but as pathological behavior. The bar studies in chapters 6 and 7 of this volume suggest that the conventionality of drinking-driving is at least a tenable hypothesis that bears study.

The second way that alcohol studies of drinking-driving limit the perception of group conflicts is in the dominance of the concept of limiting drinking as the major countermeasure in drinking-driving literature. Possibilities of alternative transportation and of safer autos or technological devices, such as ignition interlocks, occupy a marginal place in the panoply of ways to curtail accidents and deaths attributed to drinking. The emphasis on limiting drinking, as opposed to other safety measures such as making more one-way roads, increasing use of safety belts, and designing vehicles with more safety features, accentuates the dangerous and deviant character of drinking.

Looked at as a corpus of advice, legislation, and public understandings, alcohol studies and policies add up to the condemnation of drunkenness of all degrees and in all circumstances and contexts. If the policies toward alcohol are discussed in terms of costs and benefits, the costs are the focus and the benefits are rendered invisible. A focus on benefits would involve study of with whom, where, and how drunkenness exists, and could redefine the issue as one of preserving benefits as much as is possible within policies for preventing or limiting costs.

The implicit assumption of much alcohol research is that "rational, socially moral persons never allow themselves to be under the influence of alcohol." The acceptance of drunkenness is then a concession to human frailties and political realities. Those who drink to a point of some level of drunkenness are implicitly presumed to be fools, knaves, or insane. The moral deviance of alcohol use is thus underlined and assumed. In this fashion a consensus about alcohol use is further assumed, not argued or even considered a matter of legitimate conflict.[3]

The ubiquitousness of drinking to points of drunkenness suggests its important role in human leisure. What constitute the benefits and attractions which it may bring? This central question of research is glaringly absent in scholarship. Studies abound of how drunkenness results in dangerous behavior or in detrimental results, such as injury, death, or addiction. Studies of drunkenness that does not have such results are absent from the literature. Drunkenness is not studied as "normal" or "natural" behavior.

It is possible to approach the study of drinking with other frames. My emphasis here is on drinking and drunkenness as an aspect of leisure events in American life—of social gatherings, bar activities, personal interaction. This is not the only frame, the only prism, through which to view drinking, but through this approach I can seek to understand drinking first as behavior, both pathological and nonpathological.

The Frame of Alcohol Research

Drinking and drunkenness are a part of American life and have been a part of the leisure life of many people in many societies. As a part of social life, of taverns and parties, of solitude and isolation, drinking and drunkenness by no means always, or even usually, create risks to the drinker or others. Even when they do, as with other forms of risk, a "rational" view would not automatically dismiss all risks unless the activity is counted as without use. "Use" is itself a matter of value, and the norms of what is morally allowable, a question of cultural standards. What is deeply embedded in alcohol studies is its assumption and perspective of the pathological character or valuelessness of drinking and drunkenness. How does the frame of the pathological operate in alcohol research? Here I move to consider the specificity of research projects.

STUDIES OF ALCOHOL USE

Ralph Berry and James Boland's 1977 book *The Economic Cost of Alcohol Abuse* has played a significant role in arguments establishing the basis for policies restrictive of alcohol use. A reading of it illustrates how a social problems perspective is constructed through treating the condition as one about which consensus exists. The perspective is embedded in the frame of the study. On the first page the authors announce: "This book is intended to look at the phenomenon of alcohol abuse from an economic perspective." But in defining the research problem as a pathological condition, they eschew assessing the benefits, to the individual and to "society," of drinking and drunkenness which is nonpathological.

Nowhere in their book do the authors attempt to weigh costs against benefits. Is a "hangover" worth the fun and revelry of an evening's drinking? Would an analysis of toxic wastes, of auto usage, of coffee use avoid examining its benefits either to "society" or the individual consumer?

Others have also noted that Berry and Boland's study assesses only the negative and none of the positive effects of alcohol (Weiner 1977). How many marriages are held together as well as destroyed by the use of alcohol? How many criminal acts are inefficently carried out and caught through the use of drink? How much is nonpathological or socially useful drinking worth, as a consumer good? Here again, the malevolence assumption has guided research. It is, however, the operational omission of alcohol's possible benevolence, its importance for the styles of enjoyment and leisure of some, that makes the control of alcohol inherently part of the continuous efforts to control and shape popular culture.

The Benevolence Assumption

There is an opposite assumption seldom found in the social science literature of alcohol as a social problem. It is illustrated in the famous sentence from *The Rubáiyát of Omar Khayyám:* "I wonder often what the Vintners buy, / One half so precious as the stuff they sell" (Fitzgerald 1928, 683).

Both mass entertainment culture and popular legend and folklore accept the uses of alcohol as a positive blessing as well as a potential danger. For many, the attempts to limit and control drinking appear as undue infringements on the liberties of the people's enjoyment. The controllers are cloaked in the apparel of the Puritan, the spoiler of fun and frolic. Alcohol becomes the symbol of release from restraint, the harbinger of a life that contrasts with the work-directed and constrained existence that minimizes the carnival spirit of play and leisure.

In this examination of the benefits of drinking, I am interested not in drinking that is limited to decorous and marginal aspects of sociability but in a level sufficient to affect the character of interaction, perception, and emotional tone, some form of intoxication. "Drunkenness" is a commonsensical standard, and the effects of drinking can be conceptualized in folk terms such as "tight," "high," "pickled," and "stewed," terms indicating levels of drinking that engage attention and create mood. It is the mood-setting and mood-changing implications of drinking that constitute both its benefits and its costs.

The benevolence assumption is the belief that drinking is all benevolence and no malevolence. At least for American culture, I do not mean to deny any danger in drinking. The very releasing character of drinking is dangerous for some and risky for others. But how much risk is allowable and acceptable? How much is "normal"? Under what conditions? How to maximize benefits and minimize costs is a question most cultures and societies both pose and solve. As a society we have certainly decided that automobile traffic is worth the risk of injury and death that accompanies it. Public policy is oriented toward both the expansion of auto use and the alleviation of the problems engendered by it. Few analysts of traffic accidents have seriously suggested, as Ivan Illich has, that a severe reduction in the use of the auto should be adopted as a means to achieve auto safety (Illich 1974).

THE PATHOLOGICAL FRAME IN STUDIES OF DRINKING

The dominance of the pathological frame is evidenced as well, and more subtly, in efforts to study drinking practices. Here the questions studied, the modes of study and the interpretations reveal the centrality of problem-drinking as the focus of drinking research. The paradigm of social problems is more cultural than a matter of bias in the conventional sense of the word. It inheres in the assumptions about what is to be studied and what is to be focus or backdrop. Such elements are less matters of awareness than they are matters of what is taken for granted. In this sense, what I am studying is the culture of alcohol research.

The matter was put exceptionally well by George Maddox and Bevode McCall:

> A primary reason why research attention has typically been
> directed to the pathological aspects of alcohol use is that all drinking
> has frequently been conceived as abnormal, as maladaptive, or as only
> a prelude to alcoholism. . . . This focus . . . has put a stamp on
> orientations to the study of drinking, to the formulations of research
> questions, and on the types of explanations of drinking behavior
> which have been proposed. The personal and social dysfunctions of

drinking have been emphasized almost to the exclusion of any broader considerations of drinking as an acceptable form of social behavior. (Maddox and McCall 1964, 10–11)

I shall examine this assertion through analysis of three major studies of drinking. Two of these have been of major influence in the field and the third has been published most recently but will probably be widely read and accepted by alcohol researchers. The first, *Drinking in College* by Robert Straus and Selden Bacon, was published in 1953 and marked the first major sociological study of drinking in America. For many years it was a model of social research in the field. The second, *American Drinking Practices,* part of a series of such studies involving D. Cahalan as joint author, was published in 1969 and is still a widely cited model. The books in this series were extremely influential in directing attention away from alcoholism as the only problem of alcohol studies. The third work is a series of special studies edited by Walter Clark and Michael Hilton titled *Alcohol in America* published in 1991.

I have chosen these works, spanning thirty-eight years, for their impact and anticipated impact on the field, both in content and as research models, and for the excellence of their authors as methodologists. My aim is not to criticize the studies but to analyze the preconceptions and purposes which affected their design and execution. I am not concerned with the validity or reliability of the conclusions or the status of the methods except where they impinge on the questions of content. The questions that did and did not guide the research constitute my focus. My aim is to demonstrate the way in which the pathological framework directed the study of drinking in these areas where problematic drinking was not the asserted or sole end of the study. That each of these works uses the method of the social survey is of significance, but it is not vital to my argument.

Drinking in College

Straus and Bacon's *Drinking in College* is, of the three studies, the one most oriented toward the study of "normal" drinking. It was the first of the tradition of social surveys in alcohol research. It was financed by grants from the Yale Laboratory of Applied Physiology and from a private individual. Straus was then a young scholar, and Bacon, was then, as well as for most of his career as a sociologist, the "dean" of sociologists in the field of alcohol research. In several papers, in appearances at conferences, and in the introduction to *American Drinking Practices,* Bacon was critical of the focus of alcohol studies on pathological drinking. As indicated earlier, he was a constant advocate for studies of "normal" drinking; however, he usually advocated it as an essential prelude to studies of alcoholism and pathological drinking, as a needed benchmark against which to study pathology. While Bacon and Straus are much more concerned with typical and normal drinking than are the authors of the other two volumes, their survey of drinking among college students is nevertheless dominated by the pathological framework and its confines.

The first two chapters of their book are largely introductory ones in which the authors sound the theme of placing the study of drinking on a basis of scientific objectivity. In this goal, they contrast themselves with the temperance movement's domination of American public attitudes toward drinking. These, they assert, were formulated in a period when alcohol use was seen as antithetical to the progress of civilization and family morality. In that perspective drinking possessed no virtues at all (26–27, 30–31). It is that social response to the American customs of drinking which has made the perception of college student drinking so flamboyantly distressing to the American public.

The major conclusions of the study hearken back to the problems of image versus reality. Having presented the findings of their survey, Straus and Bacon engage in what Robin Room would call "problem deflation" (Room 1984). They find that college students drink very much in keeping with their gender, religion, income, and other social identities. There is no specific pattern of college drinking, nor are college students any more "deviant" in their drinking than is the general population of the country.

What can *Drinking in College* tell us about "normal" drinking other than the correlational accounts of group attributes? While the study divides respondents into drinkers and nondrinkers and classifies them by a quantity-frequency index, it also questions students about experiences of being "high," "tight," or "drunk." Being at least "high" is an experience that most of the male drinkers (73 percent) and female drinkers (58 percent) report having had at least 10 percent of the times they have used alcohol (131). There was, of course, considerable range among the students in the frequency of any of these degrees of intoxication. Nevertheless, there was a pattern of customary levels of intoxication displayed in the data.

Patterns of intoxication, their consequences, and student responses to them are examined in three chapters of that work, one on the potential problem drinker, one on student attitudes toward drinking, and one on beliefs about drinking and sexual behavior. These chapters concentrate on the pathological consequences of drinking. The chapter "The Potential Problem Drinker" probed the social complications of drinking, such as loss of job, missed appointments, missed classes, and so forth, but not the benefits, although these are mentioned. The overcoming of shyness or increased sociability are not developed. In the chapter "What Students Think of Drinking," the focus is on what students think about the drinking of others. Questioned about attitudes toward drunkenness, students registered much disapproval, but the definition used emphasizes loss of control and inability to respond. Attitudes toward being "high" or "tight," though included in experiences of students, are not probed with follow-up questions (180). A chapter on drinking and sexual behavior focuses on disinhibition as a source of danger. Despite finding (chapter 12) that about one-third of the men and one-quarter of the women feel that a party is a "flop" without alcohol, the use of alcohol in creating social atmospheres was not a basis for questioning. Nor are the peer pressures to drink or not to drink systematically studied.

The authors succeed in their effort to rid the colleges of the onus of being places of increased drinking. Yet they leave untouched the question of the uses to which alcohol is put by students. Interestingly, in their conclusion Bacon and Straus make an assertion that cuts to the crux of the framework of pathology that underlies so much of alcohol research. They state: "It should hardly be necessary to add that the education we are referring to does not involve 'teaching students to drink.' *Alcohol does not appear to do anything for youth which cannot be achieved more effectively and with greater social acceptance in other ways* [emphasis added]. However the majority of adults in our society do use alcoholic beverages, and ignorance or misinformation about the subject on the part of the user or nonuser has nothing to commend it" (212). This pious conclusion is nowhere examined. Just what alcohol does for youth and adults is not clarified by this study, nor do the authors anywhere discuss what might be alternatives. Without a clear view of how alcohol functions in other than pathological ways, the task of classification would be quite difficult. Here, as in the other two studies, the frame of pathology governs the procedures and contents of the study. The study tells us as much by what it leaves to silence as by what it talks about.

American Drinking Practices

Cahalan, Cisin, and Crossley's study was part of a monograph series published by the Rutgers Center of Alcohol Studies, then the most prestigeful site for social research on alcohol in the United States. The book, subtitled *A National Study of Drinking Behavior and Attitudes,* reports the results of a national survey conducted by the Social Research Group at George Washington University under a grant from the National Institute of Mental Health.

The study is based on a lengthy questionnaire completed by approximately 2,700 persons of a national sample. The basic format of the study is the familiar one of dependent and independent variables. The dependent variable, to be explained and characterized, is that of consumption amounts. Based on responses, the sample is classified into abstainers, light drinkers, moderate drinkers, and heavy drinkers. These types are then correlated with such items as subgroup membership (sex, age, occupation, and so on), opinions about drinking, circumstances of drinking, drinking effects and problems, personality attributes, and changes in consumption. Special attention is given to the "escape drinker." None of the chapter titles mention problems connected with alcohol use.

The study is dominated by attention to consumption types measured by usual quantities and frequencies of drinking. This is the central question by which respondents are described. Who drinks how much, what, and why are the major questions under consideration. "Analysis of behavior and attitudes related to drinking should help to facilitate understanding of the reason why some people drink moderately, some drink heavily and some do not drink at all" (71). What is meant by drinking practices is largely the amount and frequency of alcohol use. Inquiries about the occasions of drinking or the effects, described below, are subsidiary. As we shall see, the search for the heavy drinker and his or her correlates is a major orientation of the study.

Three elements of the study represent its focus, both in the presentation of data and in the conclusions. The first element is the demographic and sociological correlates of consumption. This is the standard sociological examination of such attributes as age, gender, class, and so forth, and is a major focus of the study. Much space is given to discussion of methods of measuring consumption, and the main category used to describe the sample is that of amounts of alcohol consumed.

The second emphasis of the study is on the heavy drinker and his or her motivation for drinking, even though people in that category made up only 15 percent of those studied. As Selden Bacon points out in his introduction, the "escape" drinker is the only category used to describe the quality of the drinking practice in the book. The material on the drinking practices of other categories is subsumed under general rubrics.

Thus, who people drink with or where they drink is confined to such categories as "restaurant or bar" or "friends." The occurrences of drinking at parties, on dates, in automobiles, or following personal crises are ignored. There is no data on the consequences of drinking either per se or in relation to events. Such levels as drunkenness or folk terms such as "high" and "tight" are absent. Questions on effects are asked in open-ended, write-in form. Two-thirds of the drinkers in the sample used the form, and two-thirds of those reported "no effects." As the authors point out, probing might well have uncovered many more positive and negative effects (125).

"Escape drinking" emerged as significant in the analysis (164–283). Four of nine possible reasons for drinking ascribed by respondents as "escape," the others "social." The category of "social" was neither analyzed further nor discussed. While "escape" drinking was a more frequent response among heavy drinkers, light and moderate "escape drinkers" made up a much larger percentage of the total sample than did heavy drinkers (169). This is because there were many more light and moderate than heavy drinkers in the sample.

A third main element of the study involves a theory of heavy drinking. The work is relatively limited in development of theoretical presentations to explain its findings. However, the authors do present a theory to account for heavy drinking. Here they utilize the material on "escape drinking" as well as personality characteristics displayed on psychological tests (201–10). "This and other studies have clearly indicated that there are basic differences in individual mechanisms for coping with stress" (206). The modes of coping with stress through alcohol are not discussed as a facet of nonheavy drinking, and there is a strong implication, stated even explicitly, that "self-reliant people" do not need such resources as alcohol to deal with stress (206–7).

To sum up this analysis, *American Drinking Practices* focuses attention on only one segment of drinkers and drinking in America, that of heavy drinkers and especially those who drink to "escape" stress. The framework of pathology ignores the study of recreational drinking, of occasional drunkenness, of ritual and ceremonial drinking, and of the role of drinking occasions and sites such as parties, bars, and weddings.

Alcohol in America

Even in its full title, *Alcohol in America: Drinking Practices and Problems* is a sequel to *American Drinking Practices*. While differing from that earlier study in several significant ways, it is set in the same framework of concerns that guided the 1964 national survey. Published in 1991, it uses the data of that earlier study as a base for comparison with a 1979 national survey and one done in 1984. The 1964 and 1984 surveys were both conducted by the same research center, the Alcohol Research Group (called the Social Research Group in 1964). This study was part of a grant from the National Institute on Alcoholism and Alcohol Abuse (NIAAA) to the Alcohol Research Group (ARG) as part of its status as a National Alcohol Research Center. The editors of this volume, Walter Clark and Michael Hilton, were both members of the ARG at the time of the 1984 studies. They have written, singly or together, most of the chapters in that volume. (Three were written by Robin Room and one by Thomas Harford and two associates.)

Alcohol in America is an in-depth presentation and analysis of survey data, with an emphasis on the changes and trends across the two decades from 1964 to 1984. The presentations are largely of empirical data with little effort at construction of general theories, such as that of "escape drinking" in the earlier study. There is a greater concern for data on intoxication and drinking contexts than in the earlier volume. Nevertheless, the emphasis is still that of pathological drinking. This dominance is quite clear to the editors. As Clark writes early in the introductory chapter: "one central reason for doing such surveys is to determine the relationship of various drinking patterns to the occurrence of various kinds of alcohol-related problems" (Clark and Hilton 1991, 3).

The authors are sensitive to issues involved in intoxication and in the contexts of drinking, but the basic methods of data collection and analysis are still the relation between three kinds of variables: the independent variables of demogarphic characteristics (age, sex, region, "ethnicity," and so forth), amounts consumed, and the dependent variables of behavior. The consequences of drinking were all presented to respondents as negative. The terms "drinking problems" and "alcohol-related consequences" are used interchangeably (Clark and Hilton 1991, 54–55, 142, 198–201, 218–21). Pleasurable or other possibly positive consequences are ruled out by their absence. The reader is again led to conclude that only fools, knaves, or insane people drink, especially to a point of mood alteration.

Many anomalies in the study lead the authors to raise some questions and present some data that does bear on drunkenness rather than consumption and on the drinking of other than heavy drinkers. Thomas Harford and two associates, in keeping with Harford's past research on

social drinking, present a chapter on frequency of intoxication and its relation to average daily consumption and to alcohol-related problems
(Harford, Grant, and Hasin 1991, 213–37, in Clark and Hilton 1991). As
they point out: "It is intoxicated behavior that evokes a societal response
and not merely the amount of alcohol consumed" (237). While heavy
drinkers were found to be intoxiated more frequently than lighter drinkers and to have more problem consequences, "most drinkers do not report experiencing problems related to their drinking" (16). Intoxication
is by no means confined to heavy drinkers, nor do most heavy drinkers experience problems. Those reporting intoxication two or fewer times a year
account for as high a percentage of all those experiencing problems as do
those intoxicated once or twice a week (223). As in the Air Force study described earlier, the absolute number is significant in ways that the rates do
not catch. These aspects of "normal" drinking and drunkenness are
touched on but not given much attention in *Alcohol in America*, as in the
two studies described earlier.

Studies of "Normal" Drinking

Greater clarity for my argument can be attained by examining two others studies. In these, the focus is on the ways in which alcohol is used in
"normal" activities rather than on pathology. In *Liquor License* (1966),
sociologist Sherri Cavan studied bar behavior in a variety of different
types of bars in San Francisco, including convenience bars, singles bars,
nightspots, and bars patronized by specific social groups. What interested
her was the moral order of the bar, what behavior is permissible in bar
settings but not in other public places. Her central conclusion is summed
up in the phrase "time-out." In much of the daily activities of life, behavior is consequential and serious, governed by constraints and anxi-
eties. But there are places and occasions which are "unserious." Among
these are such public events and places as the public drinking place, holidays, carnivals, social parties, vacations, conventions, and picnics. In
these situations, we are freed from the relation between "the here and
now and the there and later" (11). Bars permit an escape from the work
of "normal" behavior to the play of "time-out" in Cavan's view: "The
characteristic feature of these unserious times and places is that they
grant the right to be indifferent about matters that would otherwise
obligate concern by absolving them of the consequences they would otherwise be expected to have. They establish, as it were, a time-out period
when the constraint and respect the social world ordinarily requires is no

longer demanded and, hence, they permit even for the ordinarily prudent what would otherwise be considered social licentiousness" (1966, 235). Cavan emphasizes that the bar is not an unregulated place where anything goes but that it has a moral order, rules of its own which govern the ways in which patrons can act toward each other and which govern the ways in which the governance of "serious" life can be suspended.

In their analysis of ethnographic literature on a wide variety of human societies, Craig MacAndrew and Robert Edgerton emphasize the importance of settings and cultures in understanding the consequences of drinking and drunkenness as well as the "time-out" characteristic in the uses of alcohol. In *Drunken Comportment* (1969), they present the thesis that the consequences of drinking and drunkenness are regulated by cultural norms and are not the result of the chemical effects of alcohol. Nevertheless, in the societies they studied, drunkenness is recognized as a distinct condition and contrasted with other conditions of the person. Drunkenness is a state of "socially sanctioned freedom from the otherwise enforceable demands that persons comply with the conventional proprieties" (89).[4]

The truth or falsity of these two studies is irrelevant to my argument. Both of them study the mood-inducing aspects of drinking, emphasizing the settings within which drinking takes place. In this sense, they are far closer to the "folk" view of alcohol as "disinhibiting" and, in that characteristic, providing a basis for enjoyment and escape or "time-out." Both studies ask different kinds of questions about drinking than do the surveys described earlier.

It is this lack of attention to the popular view of "normal" drinking that the pathological framework induces. It is worth noting that the 1969 study by Cahalan and associates makes no mention of Cavan's book, published in 1966, nor does the 1991 study mention *Liquor License* or *Drunken Comportment.* Reading through the many studies of drinking that now fill the journals and the shelves, I am led to wonder why competent, "serious" people ever would engage in the drinking behavior summed up in such "folk" terms as getting "high," "tight," or "drunk." If the only behavior studied with depth are the troubles connected with drinking, this question is appropriate.

THE POLITICAL RHETORIC OF ALCOHOL STUDIES

This extended comment on alcohol studies is not just an "academic" project, significant for the history of ideas and movements. I assert that different frames within the study of drinking have consequences for the political realm. In placing the research problem in differing frames they support or undermine varying sides in public issues.

For these reasons, the study of a social arena is not devoid of political meaning. How we as researchers perceive and understand the "others" when we study them is filled with consequences because our predispositions are acted out in a relationship that is filled with domination or appreciation. Ethnographers have in recent years been exceptionally sensitive to this as those who were colonized have begun to talk back to the colonizers (Said 1978; Clifford and Marcus 1986).

The political consequences of such rhetoric is that only a pathological conception of drinking is presented. The opposition to alcohol control policy is not understood, and policy is not informed by that opposition. A "false" consensus is developed. (See chapter 2 of this volume.)

That struggle to define what Thorstein Veblen termed the "canons of decency," the standards of propriety, is implicated in efforts to control public morality. It is the recognition of this struggle that makes the study of alcohol controls pertinent to the study of how cultural authority is shaped and sustained. Alcohol research, akin to many other forms of study, is involved in the process of creating and reinforcing a representation of legitimated cultural standards. It is not just discovering or uncovering, it is also recovering and covering over. It becomes a denial of alternatives and, in this fashion, whether explicit or implicit, assumes a position in social conflict.

In confining the study of drinking to the study of pathological drinking, alcohol studies hides the moral and political conflict that would be more recognizable were drinking to be studied from a variety of frameworks, as behavior both troublesome and rewarding. It is in this sense that I have used the well-known quotation from Shakespeare's *Twelfth Night* as the title to this chapter. In the play Malvolio upbraids Sir Toby Belch for his vices, of which drunkenness is specifically mentioned. "Is there no respect of place, persons, nor time in you?" Malvolio pleads with Sir Toby to "separate yourself and your misdemeanours." The reply is classic: "Dost thou think because thou art virtuous, there shall be no more cakes and ale?" (1938, 2.3.98–99, 104–5, 123–25).

Part 2

Drinking and Leisure

Chapter Four

Passage to Play
Rituals of Drinking Time
in American Society

A number of years ago I led an undergraduate class discussion of Aldous Huxley's novel *Brave New World*. Huxley's work was an anti-Utopian vision of a future world in which human hedonism ran rampant at the expense of human qualities of spirit, independence, and creativity. All material needs and desires and all sensual gratifications were satisfied. I began the discussion by asking a student if he would like to live in Huxley's future society. "No," he replied, "but I'd sure like to visit on weekends."

That answer has seemed to me to encapsulate a characteristic of the modern, organizational society: its division of time into periods of different quality as well as function. To use the weekend as a contrast to the week implies a routinized scheduling of time in which a period of work and a period of play exist as contrasts. In the response of that undergraduate, the weekend becomes a release from the rules and the tasks of daily routine.

The clock is as much a symbol of modern civilization as shoes, print, and the steam engine. Contemporary industrialized societies are time-bounded. The hour, the day, and the week are definite and fixed units. Punctuality and attention to time, subdivided into minutes and even seconds, is a fundamental part of social organization (Zerubavel 1981). Earlier, preindustrial, societies reckoned their time divisions by more natural rhythms prescribed by sunrise and sunset, religious calendars of festival, Sabbaths, and feast days; by the ebb and flow of the bodily energy (Dumazedier 1968, 248–54; Le Goff 1980, 43–52). As life moved into cities and work into factories and organizations, predictability and constancy came to be prized (Reid 1976; Thompson 1967). Time was cut up into smaller units and the flow of time secularized and made into routine, fixed elements.

It is in this context that I want to consider the symbolic uses of drinking in the time frames of American life. While many societies have distinguished periods of play from periods of other activity, the conception of leisure as a definite and bounded part of time is a feature of the industrial and post-industrial world of work.[1] This very distinction between work and leisure must be viewed as a development of industrialized society and its normal definition and division of time (Dumazedier 1968; Marrus 1974, 1–10). Leisure is a historically emergent category, dependent on the separation of work from home and thus from one period of the day to another. In the routinized, secularized, and disciplined activity of the factory, modern life has found its metaphor, a metaphor dramatized and characterized in Chaplin's classic film *Modern Times.*

With industrial labor there came a new conception of time. Instead of working in spurts and splutters, with long bursts and short rests, the daily round was transformed into a regular and repeated process, with beginnings and endings clearly stated and enforced, with a specified length of work defined in units of time ("the hourly wage" or "the monthly salary") and with a definite work-week (Thompson 1967; Gutman 1977, 3–79). Historians of nineteenth-century Europe have written about "Saint Monday" as a form of resistance to the appearance of fixed schedules of work. The high degrees of absenteeism by workers at the beginning of the week seems analogous to the many saint days by which work was punctuated in an earlier, less secular, and less rationalized work-time (Kaplow 1981; Reid 1976). With the rigid time schedules of industrial organization, everyday life becomes as a set of impermeable membranes and the flow of time experienced as a passage from one period to another; from organization to home; from work to play.

As a characteristic of modern life, leisure must be seen in its contrast to the demands of work. The different contexts of time are also different contexts of comportment; areas of life in which contrasting attitudes exist toward the activities and objects of attention. Leisure is not-work; work is not-leisure. The terms separate areas of self-control required at work from those expressed at play: supervision; standardization and utilitarian forms of thought and criteria of action from areas of release, of spontaneity; of action for its own satisfactions. Boundaries must be maintained, but within the confines of leisure there is a wider range of choices and behaviors. The culture of time in modern life is symbolized in the slogan of some American labor unions in their struggle for the eight-hour day in the 1890s: "Eight Hours of Work; Eight Hours for Sleep; Eight Hours for What We Will" (Rosenzweig 1983).

Day and night; week and weekend; work and vacation—these comprise much of the rhythm of our lives (Melbin 1978). Work and play; workplace and home; organization and community—these comprise much of the shifts we pass through in the course of daily existence. Spontaneity, disorder, relaxation, freedom, equality—these are some of the terms of description for the time and area of play and leisure. Leisure has its meaning in modern life in the contrast to work—to the controlled, disciplined, orderly, hierarchical nature of organizational tasks. The world of work requires and demands from us behavior that stands often in opposition to the license and leeway of playful motivations and attitudes. Routine involves us in fixed boundaries of time, in a limitation of choice of activity and in a definite sequence of behavior (Zerubavel 1981, 44–49).

The great threat to organization is disorganization: the failure to conduct ourselves in accordance with rules. Leisure provides, in the British phrase, a "free time." To mix the two domains becomes a danger to the serious side and an opposition to the playful. If play and leisure constitute countercultures of release from the discipline and ruled nature of "serious" work they are not completely unruled. Social organization governs both the dominant culture and the release from its claims (Rieff 1966, 1–28). What the rationalistic, modern impulse has demanded is that the hedonistic, the playful, the irresponsible, the nonserious not be permitted to enter the domain of the "serious" areas of making a living and earning a livelihood.

In the agenda of everyday life we pass from one arena to another. We go through the time periods in spatial passage. We travel from organization to home; from work to play. Alcohol, in the particular historical context of the United States, has developed symbolic properties which serve to facilitate this passage in a generally, though not always, orderly manner. Alcohol has symbolic meaning in the temporal organization of daily and weekly life for a large segment of the American population.

THE SYMBOLISM OF FOOD AND DRINK

Culture as Language

It has been conventional in anthropology to think of drinking as a ritual act, used as an adjunct to religious rituals or a focal point of Dionysian rites (Heath 1975; Jellinek 1977). From this and other perspectives alcohol has been analyzed for its tension-reducing properties or its unifying effects in rituals of solidarity. Such approaches have studied drunkenness rather than drinking. The occurrence of limited, recurrent occasions of drinking rather than drunkenness is closer to the subject of this chapter. It is drinking as a cultural object that occupies my attention.

My use of culture and its embodiment in food and drink is a perspective of the understanding of meanings. From this viewpoint, culture can be seen as symbol systems with which life is organized into an understandable set of actions and events (Gusfield 1981a). Clifford Geertz has stated this is an excellent fashion: "both so-called cognitive and so-called expressive symbols or symbol-systems have, then, at least one thing in common: they are extrinsic sources of information in terms of which human life can be patterned—extrapersonal mechanisms for the perception, understanding, judgment and manipulation of the world. Culture patterns . . . are—'programs'; they provde a template or blueprint for the organization of social and psychological processes (1973, 216). That food and drink are used as symbols of social position and status is an old theme in sociology. Thorstein Veblen's classic study of conspicuous consumption and status symbols created a mode of analysis which has been the staple of sociological studies of consumer behavior since its original publication in 1899 (Veblen 1934). More recently the study of food and drink has been as attentive to the text, the content of consumption, as to its context, the setting and the participants (Douglas 1984, 1–39). Mary Douglas makes the distinction between the interest in food as material and as symbolic by referring to eating as a "field of action. It is a medium in which other levels of categorization becomes manifest" (30). In her own analyses of British meals and of the Judaic rules of *kashruth* she has demonstrated how what is eaten and how it is eaten constitute a mode of communication and can be read as a cultural object, embodying the attributes of social organization or general culture (Douglas 1966).

Others have made use of somewhat similar orientations to the study of food. Marshall Sahlin's distinction between animals that are improper to eat and those proper to eat in Western societies laid emphasis on the "human-like" qualities attributed to "pets," such as dogs, horses, and cats, as compared to those perceived as less than human, such as pigs, sheep, and cows (Sahlins 1976). Barthes' analysis of steak as a male food or sugar as symbolic of a "sweet time" again show the use of food as a system of signs and symbols capable of being read for their meaning; what they say as well as what they denote as material sustenance (Barthes 1973, 1979; also see Farb and Armelagos 1980, ch. 5). Claude Lévi-Strauss's

The Raw and the Cooked is, perhaps, the seminal work in this approach to the study of food as a symbol and as a medium of communication (Lévi-Strauss 1969).

In his recent analysis of taste and social structure, Pierre Bourdieu presents both an empirical study of consumer habits and an interpretive theory which, applied to food and drink, sees in the content of meals and foods the communication and representation of more general orientations to lifestyles. In his surveys of the French population, Bourdieu found sharp differences in both the foods eaten and the nature of meals among various classes and occupational groups. Among the working classes, the emphasis in eating is on the material and the familial. Guests not closely related to the household are seldom invited. The sequence of courses is unimportant. The changing of plates is minimal. The food itself is heavy and filling; a focus on plenty. There is a sharp division between male food and female food and a lack of concern for food as creating health or beauty of body. Among petite-bourgeoisie and the bourgeoisie, the opposite is the case. The meal is an occasion for social interaction; it is regulated in manners and sequences; it is preoccupied with considerations of health and aesthetic consequences (Bourdieu 1984, 177–200).

Bourdieu reads these empirical differences as the existence of distinctive tastes; part of fundamental and deep-seated styles of life. In emphasizing the meal as an occasion of social relationships, the bourgoisie deny the primary, material function of eating and maintain the integration of familial with the more disciplined areas of life. Order, restraint and propriety may not be abandoned. In this they express a dimension of the bourgeois' orientation to society as a matter of refinement and regulation, of a "stylization of life" which "tends to shift the emphasis from substance and function to form and manner, and so to deny the crudely material reality of eating and of the things consumed or . . . the basely material vulgarity of those who indulge in the immediate satisfactions of food and drink" (Bourdieu 1984, 196).

In the light of these analyses of food, the relation between alcohol and the passage from one realm to another is to be studied as text, that is, as a statement or language through which a message is being communicated. This does not preclude its status as expressive of a way of experiencing life and expressing culture. At the same time, to understand that message, it needs to be understood in a context. That context is both interactive (where it is occurring and on what kinds of occasions) and historical (the meanings that the past and the particular society have given it). The styles of one group cannot be understood in isolation from their contrasts. Neither can the uses and meanings of alcohol in the passage from work to play be understood apart from its connotations in American history.

THE MEANINGS OF ALCOHOL IN AMERICAN CULTURE

Alcohol in American Culture

Political conflicts over the use and availability of alcoholic beverages have been a persistent part of American history. The efforts of the temperance and Prohibition movements to limit and eradicate the use and the availability of alcohol through persuasion and through law are a salient piece of American politics (Gusfield 1963; 1986, ch. 8). Even after repeal of the Prohibition amendment alcohol has remained a "dangerous commodity," limited in its legitimate use to adults to specific hours and provided by licensed sellers.

Before the 1830s, while drunkenness was observed and condemned, it had an accepted place in American life in both work and play. With the emergence of industrial organization, the separation of work as an area of sobriety and play as an area of permissible insobriety became more common (Tyrell 1979; Rorabaugh 1979). The development of leisure as a contrast to work did much to reinforce the disapproval of drinking as daytime activity. The prohibition against drinking on the job was much like that which occurred in Britain with industrial development: "The frequency of early nineteenth-century protest against working-class drunkenness is as much an indication that the ancient inseparability of work and recreation has become inconvenient as that drunkenness had itself become more prevalent" (Harrison 1971, 40).

In the United States, the association of alcohol with leisure is part of a unique pattern of drinking. Societies differ in the periodicity and manner of drinking as they do in many other forms of behavior. The French drink wine at any time of day. The Finns consume alcohol on the weekend and in large quantities, to get drunk (Beauchamp 1980). Americans also confine alcohol to certain periods of the day, to certain days of the week, to certain areas of the locality. When these norms are breached, the resulting behavior is cause for disapproval, ridicule, and more punishing sanctions.

Whether the use of alcohol is rejected or not, the concept of a proper time for drinking contains a recognition of time frames. There are appropriate settings in time, space, and activity for drinking and inappropriate ones where drinking is to be avoided. The phrase, "It's time for a drink" is used to mark the conclusion of work activities. As studies of behavior in bars has shown, that part of the folk conception of "competent drinkers" lies in not crossing the boundaries that separate acceptable places of drinking and drunkenness from unacceptable ones (LeMasters 1975; Gusfield, Kotarba, and Rasmussen 1981). To appear on time for work and perform adequately, to carry out one's obligations as husband or father, is crucial to the notion of social competence.

There is a time for work and a time for play, a time for drunkenness and a time for sobriety. Day and night, weekday and weekend, work time and leisure time, these mark the boundaries of ordinary separation of abstinence time from drinking time in a wide range of American groups and subcultures.

The Meanings of Alcohol in American Culture

Why alcohol? What is the content of the message conveyed by drinking that makes it a fit object to symbolize and ritualize the transition from work to play?

On one level it exists as a sign. Already segregated and separated from work, it is an index to the appearance of a nighttime attitude. The sight of containers of wine, beer, or whiskey testifies to the time period itself, just as the increased flow of traffic serves to announce the end of the workday to observers of the highway.

But there are deeper meanings to the use of alcohol in American life that stem from its character as a source of conflict and ambivalence in American life. In their comparative study of drunkenness in a large sample of societies, Craig MacAndrew and Robert Edgerton coined the term "time out" to describe the way in which drinking in American culture symbolizes and introduces a degree of cultural remission (MacAndrew and Edgerton 1969; Cavan 1966). By "cultural remission" I refer to the conventionalized relaxation of social controls over behavior. The very derogation of drinking among large segments of American society creates its meaning as quasi-subterranean behavior when practiced within those segments.

As an object, as a form of food, alcohol is believed to be a disinhibitor (Levine 1978a). Some anthropologists, like MacAndrew and Edgerton, attribute the disinhibiting qualities of alcohol to the social definitions of drink and drunkenness rather than to its physiochemical properties. Whatever the correctness of those views, alcohol appears in American society deeply connected with mood-setting. It is a mood which contrasts with the serious and the workaday world.

Several attributes associated with alcohol help to enhance the belief in its mood-setting properties and enhance its ability to symbolize the passage from work to play. One is the "cover" which alcohol provides to the exposure of the self to public judgments. By shifting the burden of explaining embarrassing moments from a reflection of the self to the effects of alcohol, drinking provides an excuse for lapses of responsibility, for unmannerly behavior, for gaucheries, for immoral and improper actions. "I was not myself" is the plea the morning after. In this fashion, the use of alcohol places a frame around action which mitigates effects in other spheres of life.

Second, there is the festive character of alcohol use. Work, especially in the modern formal organization, demands an attitude of serious attention to task. To again refer to an American idiom, "It's no party" is a way of contrasting the festive, fun-oriented attitude with the nature of the regulated, goal-oriented life of organized work. The spontaneity of leisure is not the measured tones of daily labor.

Third, alcohol is an accompaniment of social solidarity. Precisely because it possesses a meaning of contrast to organized work, it is a dissolver of hierarchy. In Victor Turner's term, *communitas,* it is a contrast to structure, a commitment to values of human similarity and antistructure (Turner 1969, 1977). This again highlights its fitness as a marker of time and space for the transformation of the person from a socially bound and limited player of roles into someone of self-expression.

ALCOHOL IN THE RITUAL TRANSFORMATION
OF SPACE AND TIME

The calendrical movement is also a movement of social space and social time, as distinguished from chronological space and chronological time. What is contrasted are styles of behavior which constitute the meanings of a space and a time change. Another way of seeing such changes is as a transformation of frame in which alcohol performs the function of keying events into a new frame.

Framing and Keying

Frameworks of thought and perception enable participants in social action to define the behavior allowable and expected within an area—a space—and within a swath of time. With the carpets rolled up and the chairs and tables placed against the wall, the dining room becomes a dance floor. To "mistake" a dance floor for a dining room is to make a grievous social error. The frame provides the interpretations that enable the actor and the observer to know what set of rules apply because he can now define the meaning of the situation. A clear example of frames is exemplified in the behavior of art models. Posing in the nude during a "sitting," they generally robe themselves during rest periods. To be "working" rather than "playing" is to place action in a different frame and generate a different set of meanings to a situation.

In our everyday lives we shift frames continuously: the shift from work to play being one of the major transformations of daily life. Such shifts are facilitated by stylized, ritualized ways of making the change. Erving Goffman has referred to such social devices through an analogy with music as "keying": "I refer here to the set of conventions by which a given activity, one already meaningful in terms of some primary framework, is transformed into something patterned on this activity but seen by the participants to be something quite else" (1974, 43–44).

Such keys, continues Goffman, operate as cues to establish the beginnings and endings which bound the transformation in time. I will use the concepts of frame and key to describe the uses of alcohol in establishing time frames of play. In nonmechanical work, wine is sometimes used, especially late in the workday, in conjunction with work, such as meetings. It turns a work activity into a more social occasion.

I am also using the concept of keying to include devices and conventions by which new settings and new frames are created within new activities. A related concept, used by an observer of the beer party in an African society, refers to the significance of beer as a "context marker" (Karp 1980, 90). Reference to beer drinking in announcements of mortuary ceremonies indicates a commensal aspect of the occasion.

Alcohol as a Keying Device

The sharp segregation of areas of life from one another in modern societies makes the journey from work to home a liminal period—a transition that is ambiguously framed. From Arnold van Gennep to Victor Turner the concept of rites de passage has been an object of special attention among anthropologists. It has been used to describe the characteristic rituals which mark movement from one status to another, from one stage in the life cycle to another (Van Gennep 1960; Turner 1969;

1977). To see liminality in the journey from work is to analogize the tension and danger associated with liminality in primitive societies to the modern round of the daily and weekly shifts in modern life.

Within the American context, drinking en route to home, to begin the evening or on the threshold of entry into the home is a frequent event among groups where drinking is accepted. I am describing not bouts of drunkenness but the contained and circumscribed "social drinking" which may occur in bars or at home. What is significant is the meaning of drinking as an aftermath to the work period and a prelude to the leisure period. The "cocktail hour" embodies the symbolism of a time period between work and leisure. The term itself connotes a means of ending a period of time and thus a transformation into another. Within the workplace, the expression "It's time for a drink" is used among fellow-workers to signal the end of the workday and the beginning of another style of behavior. It is a way of announcing that one frame—of work—is now ended and another—of play—is about to begin.

The festive character of the occasion is a matter of its frame. Commercial bars have created a new term in recent years to describe the period of drinking of the "cocktail." They use the expression "Happy Hours" to connote the period of time at the end of workday, usually 4–6 P.M., and its attendant shifts in style. Here too the special nature of the time is further symbolized in the lowering of prices during "Happy Hours." In recent years the expression "TGIF" has emerged in American English. An acronym for "Thank God It's Friday," it clearly bestows the meaning of cultural remission on the weekend. It too is celebrated by drinking.

The ritual in which work colleagues celebrate the end of the day or the end of the week is again illustrative of the meaning of drink as solidifying personal relationships. It serves as a cue to permit nonhierarchical relations, unregulated by the structures of organization. At another level it signals the exposure of the self to others within an atmosphere which is also protective. One of the norms of action within the drinking group is a lesser attention to calculations of economic fairness and justice. The buying of rounds is one way in which an exact measure of quid pro quo is replaced by a moral economy in which money must not be "the measure of all things" (Thompson 1978; Rosenzweig 1983). In "rounds" each person takes responsibility for payment of the drink of all members of the group, no matter what his own consumption will be or has been (Gusfield, Kotarba, and Rasmussen 1981).

In another passage of mood, the drink is consumed on first entering the home or shortly after. Here again the demand for transforming the person from a work-oriented to a family-oriented person presents the problem of how this is achieved. Change of dress is another way of changing the person and is another, perhaps substitute, ritual through which the transformation is marked.

Note that the form of drinking described here is not that of drunkenness or unlicensed behavior. Such celebrations are not marked by the drunken behavior and licensed deviation from norms that has often been associated with Saturnalia ceremonies, such as the Christmas office party or the New Year's Eve party (Gusfield 1963). Alcohol may not be consumed in large amounts at all. It is its use as cue to a changed agenda of behavior that is the function under study here.

Alcohol and the Meal: Priorities and Sequences

The gulf that separates work from play, abstinence from drink and alcohol from industry, appears as well in the hierarchy of drinks. Beer and wine, low alcohol content drinks, have a wider use, in more settings, than does whiskey or gin. Hard liquor is segregated even more than "softer" drinks containing less alcohol.

This hierarchy must be understood in analyzing the symbolism of alcoholic beverages in the meal. One rule of taste is that the alcohol served before the meal may be of higher "proof" than that served during the meal. Whiskey or gin may be offered and accepted as a prelude to the meal but not as an accompaniment to the meal. Beer or wine may be offered as well and may also be used as part of the meal. The higher the alcohol content, the less it is viewed as a nutrient. Eating as a physical activity is to be separated, to some degree, from eating as a social occasion.

The prelude to the meal, more characteristic of middle-class homes on occasions of receiving guests, serves a mood-setting function as well as marking the transition from one home to another and, sometimes, the passage from work to play. Food offered in the form of hors d'oeuvres (literally, "outside the main work") is part of the setting of a mood of friendly interaction to which the alcohol contributes both as cue and as disinhibitor.

It is important to note the change which eating appears to have undergone in American life during the past hundred years. Riesman's study of American cookbooks shows a shift from instructions in utilitarian cooking to those teaching the use of exotic foods that display the taste and wide knowledge of the hosts (Riesman et al. 1950, 148–52). This seems close to Bourdieu's differentiation of working-class and bourgeois uses of eating, although the class lines are probably not as clearly defined as in Bourdieu's description (see pp. 76–77, 85). In this shift from utilitarian use of foods to an aesthetic attitude, the continuity between work and leisure is diminished and the experience of eating transformed into an occasion of play. In the American context, the use of alcohol, especially of spirits, defines the nonsubstantiality of the meal as a fun time rather than a refueling stop.

Alcohol as Activity

The cultural definition of alcohol as a liquid which develops and sustains personal and solidary human relationships is significant in cuing occasions. The drinking occasion is a contrast to the rational and hierarchical attitudes of persons as dramatic actors and actresses, as players of roles. In the drinking arena first names are required and organizational placements tabooed. Here again Victor Turner's distinction between structure and communitas is useful. Structure is rule-bound and role-oriented. Relationships between persons are mediated and regulated by their position in the structure: employee and supervisor, doctor and patient, clerk and customer. These are the identities by which we frame relationships. In play such attributions have less claim on our attention and on our behavior.

The ability to shift moods and frames is daily demanded of us in modern life. We are moved to adjust to changes of scene and frame. Sometimes this requires us to act differently toward the same people, as with colleagues outside the workplace. Sometimes it requires us to act differently toward different people, as in going from workplace to home. The drinking situation enables us to provide liminal time; a way of passing from the ordered regulation of one form of social organization to the less ordered, deregulated form of another.

Here the presence of alcohol takes on another meaning: its unpredictability. Insofar as alcohol is believed to relax inhibitions, the outcomes of that disinhibition are never clearly contained even by rules of appropriate drinking behavior. One of the contingencies of drinking arenas is that the social organization may come unglued. While drinking can promote fellow-feeling it can also be a catalyst to angry words, denunciations, and the exposure of those secrets by which social organization is held in place. *In vino veritas* but social order cannot stand too much *veritas*. In enhancing disorder and unpredictability there is also risk and danger. That in itself suggests the meaning of alcohol in developing the frame of antistructure; of passage from serious to the playful; from predictable order to risky role-release.

Coffee: The Passage to Work

In the folklore of drinking there is the belief that coffee is an agent of sobriety. It is what the drinker should drink if he wishes to achieve sobriety quickly. Common talk pictures coffee as the antithesis to alcohol. It is the liquid with which one wakes up in the morning. It is what the workers and the professionals drink on "breaks" or sip alongside their work. Although physiologists disclaim the ability of coffee to eradicate the effects of alcohol, it persists as the symbol of contrast—the food with which we return from the world of leisure to the world of work.

It is the appearance of coffee that symbolically ends the party as it does the meal. As breakfast food, coffee is the "eye-opener," the food that recalls the coffee drinker to the serious mien of the workplace. Coffee stimulates; alcohol relaxes. Its symbolic properties produce its ritualistic usage.

ABSTINENCE AND DRINKING: THE SYMBIOSIS OF CONTRASTS

In America the segregation of the use of alcohol to the period of leisure is largely a product of the nineteenth century. Colonial America did not generally perceive alcohol as inherently evil. Its consumption was not limited to special times and places (Landers and Martin 1982). Its impropriety as an adjunct to "serious" utilitarian pursuits arises with industrial and organizational development. The shift from alcohol as the "goodly creature of God" to "Demon rum" was, however, not simply a response to economic development. The ambivalent and remissive meanings of alcohol owe much to the work of the American temperance and Prohibition movements in creating the public awareness of alcohol as a "dangerous commodity" (Gusfield 1963, 1984).

Alcohol is a point of tension, ambivalence, and conflict in American life, unlike its status in most industrial societies. Only in Finland, Norway, and Sweden have antialcohol movements been as politically salient as in the United States. The many political battles over the regulation of sales; the special restrictions on time of sale, especially to adolescents; the numerous legal measures enacted to limit its availability and use all attest to public ambivalence. The Prohibition amendment was a major restriction on American consumption habits. Even after repeal, alcohol continued to be a restricted commodity and its sale regulated by legal constraints. For large segments of the American population the use of alcohol is minimal and the descriptions of the passage through daily life above are maps to a nonexistent island. It is a Brave New World which many wish neither to live in nor to visit.

Neither is the idea of leisure as play or as cultural remission a uniform feature of American life. Until this point I have used the concepts of leisure and play almost synonymously. That usage is misleading in a way that hides the contrastive character of alcohol in American life. Leisure is a chronological concept—the absence of work and the time period of choice, of "what we will." Play is, as I am using the concept, leisure characterized by spontaneity, by unscheduled action, by a blurring of social boundaries and by activity which is chiefly unproductive from an economic viewpoint.[2] It is "fun time" and opposite in quality and style to the serious activities of life.

It is possible for leisure to be conducted in ways indifferent to or even antagonistic to play and certainly to cultural remission. The distinction made by Zerubavel between profane time and sacred time, following Durkheim, recognizes that leisure may be a time of considerable self-commitment, discipline and contemplation, hardly meriting the description of playfulness. Such sacralizing of leisure is apparent in the Sabbath of major religions (Zerubavel 1985, ch. 4; 1984, passim).

The advent of leisure and the possibilities of play raise problems as well as opportunities. There are diverse possibilities in the continuity or discontinuity between realms of the spirit as there are between periods of the day. For the deeply religious, the secular world of work may push one to wear a mask which abjures the sacred world of spiritual or mystical attainments. Leisure permits the expression of a self for whom the very term "play" is an abomination. To be absent from work is to be able to enter a different world; to be released to God. The cultural remission is not from order but from the profane world to the sacred.

Both the transition from work to play and from the secular to the sacred are transformations of discontinuity. They involve shifts in the styles of thought and behavior that constitute contrasts with the personality and character of the work arena. For many others, work and leisure may be more closely associated. A sermon by a nineteenth-century American minister illustrates the attitude of continuity. In "Christian Recreation and Unchristian Amusements" Reverend Theodore Cuyler cautioned against the attitude that "wants stimulation and excitement." Condemned enjoyments, such as the theater, do not strengthen us for the work of the following day and lack spiritual value (Gusfield 1963, 30–31).

Reverend Cuyler's sermon represents only one form of continuity between leisure and work; one in which leisure is judged on its implications for work. Equally significant is the characteristic lifestyle in which routine, discipline, and scheduling remain central to the daily agenda of life. That playful orientation toward activity in which carelessness and disorder are prized is anathema for this philosophy. The meaning of play as release from the dominance of the "serious" side of life is unattractive and even immoral from the perspective of continuity.

This sense of opposition between drinker and nondrinker as a contrast of cultural themes may also have its analogies elsewhere than the American situation. Pierre Bourdieu, utilizing a survey of the French population, finds a similar set of distinctions: "in abstaining from having a good time and having it with others, the would-be *petit bourgeois* betrays his ambition of escaping from the common present, when, that is, he does not construct his whole self-image around the opposition between home and the cafe, abstinence and intemperance, in other words between individual salvation and collective solidarities" (Bourdieu 1984, 183). Bourdieu's description of the French petite bourgeoisie differs from the American in at least two respects. First, the contrast is situated in a context of class differentiation. In the American case the opposition, once religious and ethnic, has become more characterological and generational (Gusfield 1963). It cuts across the categories of class and ethnicity. Second, in the French case the contrast is a more general one between an emphasis on the here and now, on the utilitarian values of food and drink in the working class and the emphasis on refinement, on escape from the mundane and the useful among the petite bourgeoisie. In the American case, abstinence from alcohol is associated with a utilitarian and religious perspective toward leisure. As Bourdieu also points out, in the French case, among the bourgeoisie foods are also sources of pleasure but with less emphasis on the physical character of food than on its commensal and taste-symbolizing aspects. The individualism is a deeper one in the American context. The person is the dependable source of social control and the group, the crowd, the peer is the mechanism of temptation and disorder. What the antipathy to cultural remission displays in the American context is a fealty to and dependence on the importance of self-control and a distrust of the ability of social and institutional restraints to regulate and constrain human behavior. It is the prized image of the person

who resists temptations and limits worldly desires for spiritual rewards
that the abstinence ethic means in the American setting (Levine 1978a;
Nissenbaum 1980).

AMERICAN CULTURE AND THE SYMBOLISM
OF DRINKING

One of the streams of thought in Temperance literature of the nineteenth
century was the "all or none" character of drinking (Gusfield 1963;
Levine 1978a). The argument for abstinence was for total abstinence on
the grounds that a little would become more and would grow beyond
control. The habitual drunkard, the chronic alcoholic, are the tangible re-
minders of what constitutes the deviant person and the grim prophecy of
what that deviance is and does. The belief extends to limited drinking in
the assertion that release from social controls cannot be a moderated,
regulated, and controlled affair. Once Pandora opens the box, the spirits
that flow out from it cannot again be captured and encaged.

The identification of modern life with rational and systematic thought
and action has been a major theme of contemporary sociological theory.
The rationalization of the institutional framework in the form of organizational structures has been the structural side to the cultural *geist* of rationality and regulation. At the same time that industrialization and capitalism emerged from the cocoon of history the dialectical opposition to
both of them emerged as well. A romantic resistance to rationality has
been a recurrent theme in modern life (Spitzer 1983; Lears 1981; Bell
1976; Gouldner 1980).

Such orientations toward modern life are represented as well in the divergent conceptions of the value of alcohol and those who hold them.
One fears exactly what the other seeks. A Romantic approach prizes the
end of the day and the discontinuity which it makes possible. Those who
accept it look with favor on the "time-out" as a bounded and limited
space and time in which a more authentic self can achieve expression.
The use of alcohol symbolizes a temporal lifestyle and accentuates the
transformation out of the posture of social controls and self-imprisonment.

But the meaning of alcohol as symbolizing and signaling a remission
of social controls is both underlined and shaped by the contrasting condemnation of its use and of the relaxation of control that it presages. The
existence of a once-dominant and still vital culture of continuity between
leisure and work gives the behavior of drinking an even clearer sense of a

"break" in the styles of life that mark the daily routines of work and organizational tasks.

Despite these wide divergences in lifestyles and conceptions of leisure represented in the presence or absence of alcohol in transforming social activities, there is an underlying uniformity of meaning. Both groups—abstainers and users—and those overlapping have a similar understanding of what the presence of alcohol symbolizes. The cognitive understandings are the same even though the evaluational stances are in conflict. The conflict is not possible without the common "agreement" on the definition of the situation. Both see in the use of alcohol the same transformation of the frame from work to play.

This symbiosis within conflict is apparent in two other frameworks for the relation of work to play in which alcohol plays a symbolic role. One is found in certain occupations in which preindustrial forms of organization and culture still exist. In construction industries, for example, there often persists a definition of work as male activity (LeMasters 1975, esp. ch. 2). Drinking is more likely to occur within the work period. Beer and whiskey, but not wine, may be used during worktime in any quantity and not always be seen as antithetical to the day's activities. Such occupational worlds have only partially "surrendered" to the routinized and controlled arenas of bureaucratic organization and factory discipline. Here the idea of a regulated order of space and time has not fully been institutionalized. Work and play are not yet impermeable.

The opposite is also both possible and, perhaps, increasingly found in modern organization and among upper echelons of control. This form is the intrusion of play into work (Riesman 1950). Here work forms take on something of the character of informal sociability. The serving of wine at committee meetings is one such mode in which the meeting is placed, though ambiguously, in the frame of a social occasion. The use of alcohol at business luncheons serves both to remove something of the intrusion of work into "private time" and also to provide a framework of conviviality and social equality where it may be useful to the work of achieving a consensus among possibly conflicting members.

In both of these examples—the construction industries and organizational management—the meaning of alcohol is homogeneous to the others discussed above. What differs is the content of the rituals in the drinking acts. The meanings follow the same code; speak in the same language.

In the perpetual struggle of the individual toward self-expressiveness and social integration, the conflict between work and play, day and night, gains intensity. Release is both a boon and a danger. The alcoholic is the obverse of the workaholic. (Note how the word has been adapted to both poles.) The alcoholic becomes one of the symbols of a fear of falling; of a threat in the personal drama of success and failure that is the key story of American careers. The workaholic is the opposite. Here the danger lies in the inability to let go; to enjoy release from role. That one is pathology and the other only troubling is the difference between cultural subordination and dominance.

Drinking in America remains a point of political, legal, and social conflict. While it retains meanings of cultural remission, the society is able to institute social controls that generally bound and limit the "time-out" character of play. While the use of alcohol continues to be seen as possessing unpredictable danger, its use is generally institutionalized into conventional areas and activities. It is further testimony to the ability of drinkers to regulate and restrict the periods and arenas of cultural remission, "to visit on weekends." That others find "playing" with social controls threatening to their own self-control and to the social organization is testimony to the fear that the "wild man" in us is uncontainable. Once let loose he may not show up for church on Sunday or for work on Monday.

Chapter Five

Benevolent Repression
Popular Culture, Social Structure, and the Control of Drinking

In the sequence of festivities in many European countries, Carnival, with its licensed release from many prohibitions on eating, sexuality, aggression, and social hierarchy, occurs before and contrasts with the ascetic period of Lent. The two holidays also appear as metaphors and figures for alternating and opposed attitudes toward life. In his detailed study of popular culture in early modern Europe Peter Burke points to a Bruegel painting in which a fat man sitting on a barrel combats a thin old woman on a chair. The historian remarks that it is a literal enactment of a common battle in Shrovetide rituals. He interprets Carnival, "who belongs to the tavern side of the picture," as symbolic of the traditional popular culture; Lent, however, he associates with the "high culture" of the church clergy, who were then (1559) attempting to reform, if not suppress, many popular festivities (Burke 1978, 207).

This association between modes of drinking and modes of sobriety, on the one hand, and divisions in the social structure, on the other, is both the inciting point as well as the subject matter of this chapter. Attempts by officials and established institutions to limit, control, and repress drinking and drinking patterns run through the history of many countries like rivers winding through the landscape, now swollen by spring rains, now dried and thin by the heat of summer. Social scientists are interested in explaining and understanding the flow of drinking controls. They find themselves equipped with a set of conflicting and contrasting perspectives with which to study social hydrodynamics. This paper is about structural explanations and opposing frameworks for understanding alcohol controls.

SOCIAL CONTROL AND MORAL REFORM

On my study wall there is a framed slogan, "Work is the curse of the drinking classes." It is an appropriate text with which to begin. Within those few words are several ways in which issues of regulating drinking are frequently treated. First, there is the importance of social structure. Descriptions of drinking involve classes in conflict rather than a societal consensus that is shared throughout society and from which a special category of persons deviates. Second, in transmuting and transvaluing the parent phrase, "Drink is the curse of the working classes," it reverses the usual view of the problem of alcohol use by locating it among the sober and the orderly. It is the view of those inside the drinking culture, not outside of it. Third, the slogan asserts an opposition between work and drink, an irreconcilability often fundamental to temperance adherents. What makes it funny is its agreement with the parent phrase in viewing drinking problems as differentiated by class and its reversal of values. It is the view of Carnival, not of Lent.

Implicitly the two slogans are not mirror images. The more conventional view is that of the altruist for whom the regulation and control of drinking is a matter of helping sufferers, people in trouble. For the humorous sloganeer, the control of drinking is something other people impose on him; the alcohol abuse is something that affects the controllers, not the controlled. The crux of the problem, both as a matter of policy and as an analytical issue, is evidenced in the attempted regulation of dance hall and liquor sale hours in Milwaukee in 1912 (Harring 1983, ch. 8). Frequently the dance halls were part of, or next to, saloon premises. Opponents of restrictive local ordinances, especially the unions, charged that they constituted class legislation since the dance halls were a major form of recreation for working-class youth. A social worker declared: "This is not a fight against the Germans or the Poles. It is not a fight against the pleasures of the working class. All we want to do is lift the moral standards of the city. Give our working girls the liberty of a pure city, pure enjoyment, rather than this personal liberty the opposition speaks of" (Harring 1983, 185).

Analyses by historians and sociologists of what is called moral reform, or sometimes humanitarian reform, often demonstrate one or the other of these polar perspectives. One school, perhaps most frequent among historians, views reforms as actions in which the reformers are inspired by visions of a new and better world for those to be reformed. The relevant questions concern ideas of reformers about what it is that makes some people suffer and what can be done about their suffering. In the opposite perspective attempts to reform others, including drinkers, are inspired by the trouble that they (those being reformed) create for the controllers. These are to be seen as efforts at social control of troublesome behavior. As William Muraskin has put it in characterizing the social control approach, "the first question to ask is: 'Who are the reformers and of what are they specifically afraid?'" (Muraskin 1976, 56).

Such considerations raise the question, For whom is alcohol a source of trouble? In this chapter I examine a group of materials, largely by historians, bearing on the ways, times, and places in which drinking has been troubling. I hope to shed some light on the structural contexts in which policies of alcohol control emerge. This chapter calls attention to the settings in which drinking occurs. The act of drinking, and even drunkenness, has not been the major target of efforts to control alcohol. Such efforts are fruitfully seen as directed against particular forms of usage embodied in particular times and places and involving particular groups. This paper focuses on the context of drinking as part of popular culture, as distinguished from "official" and "high" culture, and its relation to divisions within the social structure.

My attention is drawn to discussions among sociologists and social historians working in other, though allied, fields—the history of crime, deviance, law enforcement, urbanization, popular culture, and what is now termed social control. Those discussions are fertile sources for alcohol studies, both in the theoretical questions they raise and in the sometimes explicit, often implicit material bearing on the social history of drinking.

SOCIAL STRUCTURE AND SOCIAL CONTROL

Like most concepts, social control is one with a long history, though its users often have a short memory. Early sociologists used it as a contrast to governmental, legal, and coercive controls. They emphasized the normative and interactive sources of human coordination as opposed to legal and institutional sources of compliance (Janowitz 1978, ch. 2). In recent years the term appears in two different forms, each a sharp contrast with its earlier uses (Rothman 1983).

Social control has become a buzzword of the alcohol field. Several major reports have stressed the reconsideration of controls as the outstanding development of the 1980s in Europe and America (Bruun et al. 1975; Mäkelä et al. 1981; Moore and Gerstein 1981). Here the reference is to the use of law and institutional regulations in establishing a continuing framework for the availability and use of alcohol. In another arena, among sociologists and social historians, the term has come to mean almost the equivalent of suppression or repression. To show social control is to diminish its claim to do something else—to reform or to help, for example.

Such meanings are observable in the recent stream of sociological materials about health and medicalization. The message has been clear: aspects of medicine such as treatment of mental illness, alcoholism, homosexuality, and drug addiction are construable as means of controlling behavior rather than curing illness (Szasz 1970; Conrad and Schneider 1980). The matter is summed up in a now-classic essay by Irving Zola, "Medicine as an Institution of Social Control" (Zola 1972). The imputation that a particular professional practice is a means of social control serves to impeach its claim to social neutrality. What professes to be a way of helping sick people is then interpreted as a way in which one part of society is trying to enforce its interests, its standards, and its values over the opposite values, standards, or interests of another. What is presented from a posture of benevolent consensus between doctor and patient, reformer and reformed, is unmasked (demystified) as conflict repressed.

My preference for the term *public controls* to refer to this newer usage and *communal controls* to describe the older form is more than a compulsion for clarity and neatness. It calls attention to a feature of human social life that I will explore later, perhaps ad nauseam. Here it is used to distinguish the official, deliberate acts of institutional policy from the normative and structured patterns of social interaction that constitute facets of situated, particular action. The latter—the social controls of specific settings, of popular and often unofficial culture—must be contrasted with the official, public controls of governments and laws as well as church officials and others in public positions. At least since William Graham Sumner's *Folkways* the relation between these two levels of collective life has been a major problem of modern sociology.

I have been recounting a typical intellectual history. Concepts and counterconcepts go together like husband and wife, locked in loving conflict. In the narrow field of alcohol studies today we use controls to contrast preventive measures with treatment approaches. What then is their usage among the social historians and sociologists in allied domains?

Consider the study of mental illness/madness/insanity (the choice of descriptive term is significant, of course). David Rothman's research into the development of asylums in the United States is a study of reformers in the first half of the nineteenth century and why they believed as they did in the then-new idea of asylum: "The asylum was to fulfill a dual purpose for its innovators. It would rehabilitate inmates and then, by virtue of its success, set an example of right action for the larger society" (Rothman 1970, xix). Even though he casts much doubt on its progressive character, Rothman's view of his subject matter is nonetheless that of his subjects; his is a study of reform, of aid to people with troubles. Andrew Scull, in his analysis of the treatment of insanity in nineteenth-century England, shares common ground with Rothman but approaches the subject matter from another perspective. He draws attention to the differentiation that occurred between being employed or unemployable, especially in respect to the indigent poor and the insane. He sees the problem posed by the conditions of economic life: "The establishment of a market economy and, more particularly the emergence of a market in labor, provided the initial incentive to distinguish far more carefully than hitherto between different categories of deviance. . . . [To distinguish] the able-bodied from the non-able-bodied poor, . . . to provide aid to the able-bodied poor threatened to undermine . . . the whole notion of a labor market" (Scull 1979, 37).

These diverse formulations supply differing perspectives and raise different kinds of questions. What one sees as asylum another sees as incarceration. Rothman's subjects see the deviant as a troubled person; Scull sees persons whose existence creates trouble for others. Rothman's emphasis is on cultural meaning, on how mental illness was defined and understood. Scull's is on structure, on the problem posed for others by the ways in which mental illness and poverty were handled in England.

Thus, recent public control perspectives redefine the reform of deviance. Where the rhetoric of reform talks of helping others, the redefinition raises doubts and queries, finding interests and functions at work that contrast with the consensus that the concept of deviance itself implies. As the material on medicalization indicates, the control perspective uncovers social conflicts where consensus was thought to lie.

How, then, shall we go about studying drinking from these different perspectives? In much of the remainder of this essay I will examine some of the efforts to study drinking in the context of how it creates troubles for other people and of how sociologists and social historians have been utilizing ideas of social conflict in the analysis of drinking and deviance. Implicit, and sometimes explicit, in this analysis is a perspective that asserts that the problems of public control of alcohol are seldom those of drinking per se but rather of the contexts and groups within which drinking and drinking behavior occur. It is these contexts that give meanings to, and create troubles for, specific parts of social structures within particular historical circumstances.

THE RATIONALIZATION OF LEISURE

Deep in the conscious experience of modern people is the division of time into distinct periods—minutes, hours, and days. Equally as significant is the overarching difference between times of work and times of play—day and night, week and weekend. As Lewis Mumford and, later, David Landes have pointed out, the clock and the watch are the symbols of modern, organized, systematized life (Mumford 1938; Landes 1983). The contrast between Carnival and Lent has its analogue in the separation of daily work from daily leisure (Melbin 1978; Rodgers 1978, 18–19; Zerabuvel 1981; Zerabuvel 1985).

Leisure is more than play. It is a discrete period set aside for play, a systematized way in which time is divided. It is the counterpart to work. As such, it emerges into the consciousness and daily routine as a consequence of the transition from the home-centered workplace to the workplace—the factory, the office—outside the family and the household (Marrus 1974). It represents a paradox of modern existence—routinization of the time for play. It is here that the major issues of popular culture and drinking are found.

This is not to say that drinking and drunkenness have been issues only in industrialized, modern societies. The attempts to limit the "excesses" of festival and carnival behavior beginning in the sixteenth century in Europe are instructive in two respects. First, they demonstrate a perceived sacrilegious and immoral behavior. A focus on drinking as the source of the gluttony, lechery, and violence of Carnival is part of the efforts of the Protestant and Counter-Reformation Catholic churches to limit the occurrence and activities of Carnival. The ethics and religious sensibilities of the reformers were in conflict with the ethics and sensibilities of popular tradition, "which involved more stress on the values of generosity and spontaneity and a greater tolerance of disorder" (Burke 1978, 213). The persistence of this competition for the control of popular recreation is a major theme of this chapter (Harrison 1982, ch. 3).

The second lesson in the early attempts to control drinking and drunkenness is the division between popular culture and high culture. The rowdiness with which Carnival is associated had become less and less a shared sacred quality of holidays, festivals, and holy days. Sobriety had been more successful at the higher levels of society (Burke 1978, chs. 8 and 9). It gave to drunkenness and festival behavior an added feature of social protest that made the emergence of rowdy behavior even more fearful to those who sought to control it. The content of holiday parades, rituals, and other behavior expressed itself in symbolized protests and sometimes in crowd violence. A similar point about the symbolic content of peasant culture has been made by E. P. Thompson in his distinction between polite culture and plebeian culture (1978).

To what extent are the troubles created by drinking related to its context, to the settings in which drunkenness occurs? For whom are drunken acts troubles? Are they understandable as encounters between cultures— between classes, ethnic groups, and religions—in which what is presented as reform, as aid to troubled persons, can be interpreted as troublesome to controllers?

The conditions of agrarian life and the diffuse character of peasant-patrician relations nevertheless made for a social framework that operated to contain and limit the collision between the forces of Carnival and Lent. One form of the argument about drinking and public controls has been that the rise of industrial work led employers to change the traditional acceptance of alcohol as a feature of the workplace. The resistance of the preindustrial community to the rational conduct of life in an industrial society has often been epitomized in the Saint Monday phenomenon, absenteeism or drunkenness of workers after the weekend. Unaccustomed to a time sequencing that required planning and pacing of the total daily agenda, workers continued to declare holidays and sought to work when they saw fit rather than follow the systematic organization of daily and weekly time that the industrial process made dominant (Gutman 1977, 68–74; Harrison 1971, 40; Thompson 1967; Kaplow 1980; Roberts 1982).

Another way of seeing these processes is to recognize that what was threatening to the development of industrial production was the timing and location of drinking. The new industrial work force had to learn the disciplines of routine, punctuality, and perseverance while overcoming the traditional habits of spontaneity, indefiniteness, and the mix of work and play (Bendix 1954, ch. 2; Boyer 1978, ch. 3; Gutman 1977; Dawley and Faler 1976). Drinking at work became anathema not because it had increased in frequency but because it conflicted with the demands of new forms of coordinating labor into a more routinized life (Lemert 1967, ch. 2). What had to be learned was a new industrial morality that prescribed a more routinized and disciplined use of time (Dawley and Faler 1976; Thompson 1967). As Harrison remarks, the nineteenth-century temperance debate in England was really an argument about how leisure was to be spent. My previous study of the American case is very similar (Harrison 1971, ch. 1; Gusfield 1963, ch. 7).

These perspectives toward emergent controls over alcohol use are two somewhat different forms of class interest theory. The first finds impediments to good workers largely in the physiological effects of alcohol on work. It is the employer who finds in control of drinking means for improving the productivity of an industrial labor force. His conflict is epitomized in the move to end both drinking on the job and payment of wages in whiskey (Tyrell 1979; Rorabaugh 1979; Lender and Martin 1982). In the United States this exclusion of drinking from the workplace, so contrary to earlier practice, was well under way by the 1830s and had become an accomplished fact of American life by the late nineteenth century (Rosenzweig 1983, ch. 2).

A second form of the theory of class interest in the rationalization of leisure focuses attention on the culture of the working classes as it exists in congruence or in conflict with the demands of organized productivity under an industrial capitalism. Here rationalized industry and agriculture are predicated on the existence of a particular kind of person as worker and as citizen—one whose values and habits form the self-discipline, ambition, individualism, and ethical probity that ensure both loyal and competent laborers and neighbors. The interest of the industrial and employing class is in the total way of life of employees, in ensuring that the culture of the working class is consistent with the need of employers for a consistent and productive work force (Gutman 1977; Dawley and Faler 1976). The control of drinking is one means for inculcating a new culture in the working class, a means that benefits the employers by providing the recreation that ensures a more stable and self-motivated workforce.

A crude form of this class struggle analysis is found in Sydney Harring's historical study of police in several American cities in the nineteenth century. Harring describes police as primarily engaged in an effort to control working-class life and leisure for the benefit of employers and elites: "Increasing the degree of exploitation of labor means that the police institution provides a measure of discipline and control over the working class that permits a wider measure of exploitation through the labor process—that is, more work with less resistance" (1983, 13). From this standpoint the functions of "the suppression of working class recreational activity" can be seen, in part, as making the total society more rational with respect to the interests of employers or, as some might interpret it, with respect to the productivity of the total economy (Harring

1983, 151). Others have presented a more sophisticated form of the argument in relation to crime control in general. Surveying the development of a professional, bureaucratized, and public police force, they have concluded that the move to an efficient and organized police was motivated by a demand for both a more orderly form of protection and a more recurrent and predictable social order, one that was not vulnerable to unpredictable work stoppages and political demonstrations (Spitzer and Scull 1977; Spitzer 1983).

This account of the rationalization process extended to alcohol use assesses social controls as aspects of a wider domination of elites. It defines the troublesome character of alcohol as the troubles that one class creates for another. Elites institute drinking controls that benefit themselves and do so in the name of helping others. From another standpoint leisure is itself affected by the same rationalistic impulses that characterize capitalism and Western culture. Here the attempt to curtail drinking and drunkenness in its leisure-time uses is part of the moral demands of a civilization that prizes self-control and organization. Harry Levine's analysis of the pre-Civil War temperance movement is based on a description of the efforts of middle-class people to instill a new psychology of self-control in the middle class, to place the burden of social controls on the individualistic self rather than on the domination of external authority (Levine 1978a). From a similar viewpoint Paul Boyer suggests that participation in, and support of, moral-reform societies was also "less the wish to control others than an impulse toward self-definition, a need to avow publicly one's own class aspirations" (Boyer 1978, 161).

There are many difficulties with explaining drinking controls as serving the interests of employers in employee productivity. For one thing, preindustrial groups do not necessarily resist industrial work. Studies of contemporary industrializing societies do not find the same problems reported for England and the United States. India, for example, appears to experience little intractability in industrial labor (Lambert 1963; Morris 1960). The capacities of people to seal off new from old habits is greatly underestimated (Gusfield 1967b).

What alternatives are available and how effective are they for solving problems or troubles posed by drinking? Samuel Cohn's study of British railway workers, for example, shows that employers made small use of "cultural monitors" (clergymen) to discipline worker drunkenness, although it was an element in the labor problems they encountered. They did, however, utilize the existence of competition from Irish migrant labor to establish systems of wage payment that made the worker avoid absenteeism. In other cases, as in Pullman, Illinois, in the late nineteenth century, the attempt to create a moral atmosphere in the worker community, for whatever motives, led to a fringe suburb of evangelical churches, whorehouses, saloons, and union halls, all outlawed or discouraged in the clean air of the pure residential and paternalistic factory town (Hughes, n.d.; Hutchison 1991).

More significant are Alan Dawley and Paul Faler's studies of working-class culture and labor protest in Lynn, Massachusetts, in the nineteenth century. Similar to Gutman's study of work habits, their work distinguishes between a preindustrial morality associated with traditional culture and an industrial morality associated with modernity and industrial life (Dawley and Faler 1976; Johnson 1978, chs. 1, 2). The traditional preindustrial work ethic in America welcomed spontaneity and a lifestyle in which drinking played an important part. The Temperance movement found strong support among modern workers imbued with an industrial morality they shared with their industrial employers. However, although they shared that morality, it was a matter of neither employer dominance nor support for employer interests.

Paradoxically, the new industrial morality emerged as much from the rural, property-oriented segment of the population as from the working classes. It developed independently of employers. Daniel Rodgers, in his history of the work ethic in America, argues that the ethic of work arose in the agricultural communities of America before industrialization (1978). Moreover, the same qualities that characterized good factory workers also characterized workers who were less obedient and possessed other qualities that made it easier for them to organize. It was among the group most receptive to temperance habits that Dawley and Faler found sources of labor unrest. The more traditional workers were more ready to take orders and more subservient to paternal patterns of labor relations.

There is a vagueness to general concepts like class, capitalism, or industrialism that bedevils much of sociological history in alcohol studies. We need a microhistorical approach that specifies time, place, and group. In the same period that employers of factory labor might be seen as having had an interest in minimizing drinking among workers, commercial farmers had an interest in transporting grain in the form of alcohol (Rorabaugh 1979, ch. 3). The interests of the liquor industry, the glassblowers union, and the steel manufacturers are by no means either all alike or necessarily in conflict. To assume a homogeneity of diverse or similar interests on alcohol questions because of position in the social relations of production is an illusion.

THE PROBLEM OF PUBLIC ORDER

In 1826 the Federalist preacher Lyman Beecher voiced his fears of the new electorate: "The laws are now beginning to operate extensively upon necks unaccustomed to their yoke. . . . Drunkards reel through the streets day after day . . . with entire impunity. Profane swearing is heard." (Gusfield 1963, 42). In this sermon, one of his famous "Six Sermons on Intemperance," Beecher saw drunkenness as a political problem, a symbol of the power of a voting public that rejected the authority of the church and the cultural elite. Yet his fears of the "lower orders" are strikingly contemporary. For much of the nineteenth and twentieth centuries writers, political officials, and public figures found the sources of crime and public disorder among the lower social levels. The poor, the immigrant, and the outcast race or religion have appeared to those in higher positions as threats to personal safety, public order, and established government. In 1872 Charles Loring Brace wrote a widely read book called "The Dangerous Classes of New York City," borrowing a term long in use in England as well (Monkkonen 1975, ch. 2). The term not only has a tone of class antipathy but also conveys a sense of societal crisis. As Alan Silver remarks, "It was much more than a question of annoyance, indignation or personal insecurity. The social order itself was threatened" (Silver 1967, 3). The theme persisted throughout the nineteenth century as cities grew in number and size (Boyer 1978, 161).

In most of the accounts of the "dangerous classes," "the lower orders," or, in contemporary language, "the underclass," drunkenness appears as a necessary, if insufficient, part of the descriptions. How to contain the threat of riot, crime, or just rowdiness is a major problem in the growth of American cities (Gutman 1977; Tilly 1981; Wade 1978; Brown 1970). Both as cause and as content, alcohol and drunkenness are associated aspects of the problem of public order. Some have even related the emergence of a crime problem in European cities to the distillation of gin, its lowered price, and the increased use of liquor among the lower classes (Rubinstein 1973, ch. 1; Braudel 1973, 158).

Although drinking is always a matter of concern, it is seldom treated in isolation from other acts with which it is associated as cause or catalyst. Concern with drinking is entangled with concern for the moral and, as we shall see, the political character of drunken action. A line of continuity runs across centuries and an ocean to the British Act of 1606 controlling the operation of alehouses. It described drunkenness as the cause of "Bloodshed, Stabbings, Murder, Swearing, Fornication, Adultery and such like" (Wrightson 1981, 12).

The image of drunkenness as an adjunct to crime and urban disorder is deeply embedded in the repertoire of middle-class and upper-class perceptions of the social structure, augmented by the growing gap in drinking habits between the classes during the nineteenth century (Kett 1977, pt. 2; Harrison 1971, ch. 2). Susanna Barrows has shown how the French crowd and the mob were perceived in the last half of the nineteenth century as irrational and violent and explained as a consequence of male drunkenness, alcoholism, and the irrational character of women. She quotes the historian Maxime du Camp as describing the Communards as "chevaliers of debauchery; apostles of absinthe" (1983, 45). The poor and the outcast were the drunken enemies of public order.

Public order is, however, a term that means and has meant different things to different people at different times. How much orderliness is demanded, and by whom? The central work of George Rudé, and Eric Hobsbawm on preindustrial crowds has made the important point that the rioting and violence of such crowds was often acceptable and expected. It was neither viewed as a threat to the social order nor as abnormal (Rudé 1964; Hobsbawm 1963). Rudé has also revised the image of the mob as undifferentiated riffraff (Rudé 1959; 1964). In neither England nor France of the seventeenth and eighteenth centuries were crowds irrational, unstable, or drunken. As long as they were not seen as a threat to existing institutions, they could be accepted and rioting seen as a cry of protest falling on often-sympathetic ears. Rudé suggests that the frequent bread riots of eighteenth-century France were a form of price maintenance (Rudé 1959, 200–209). The control of public crime and disorder was often singularly lax by current American standards. Colonial America accepted a much higher level of disorder, including public drunkenness, than did the nineteenth-century United States (Maier 1978).

According to Silver, it was the emergence of a professional and municipal police force that raised the standards of public order (Silver 1967). As regular contact between public authority and the citizenry began to occur, the demands for greater safety, legality, and stability increased. Since the development of regularized police forces the standards of public sobriety appear to have made public drunkenness the major nontraffic violation of law in many Western societies (Gurr 1976, 56; Harring 1983, ch. 7).

Yet a common standard of public order is by no means the case. Public drunkenness, for example, is not accorded the same degree of antipathy everywhere as it has been accorded in the United States. David Bayley's comparison of Japanese and American police reveals a greater acceptance of drunkenness in public areas in Japan than in America. The Japanese take a protective attitude toward fellow citizens drunk in public (Bayley 1976, ch. 3). The sight of drunken men does not create fear in the general public in Japan as it often does in the United States (Plath 1964).

POLICE AND PUBLIC ORDER: ROWDINESS
AND DISSIDENCE

Until recent decades policing has chiefly involved control of lower-class citizens. However, a close analysis of police and the maintenance of public order indicates that the problem of order and the role of alcohol in it is more complex than generalities of class and class struggle indicate. I find it useful to approach this study with some analysis of both sides of the social equation—the institution of policing and the class and ethnic character of leisure.

Studies of police and policing in the United States have been consistent in pointing out two features of law enforcement. First, policing is largely a reactive, rather than a proactive, procedure. The limitations on entry into what is defined as private spaces prevent police from responding to potential or actual crime unless it is reported or observed (Black 1980; Rubinstein 1973; Lundman 1980; Manning 1977; Stinchcombe 1963). The second feature follows from the first and is a key element in understanding the problem of public order and alcohol. Police can best control and supervise events they can observe and to which they can react. The area in question, then, is largely public and observable territory. Streets, sidewalks, parks, alleys, and public plazas are the venue of police (Rubinstein 1973, ch. 4). In the daily activities of police, public order is a matter of keeping the streets and sidewalks safe from crime and minimizing the public's fear of crime or danger.

Where, then, are points of contact between police and citizenry? An understanding of the relation of alcohol to public order would require knowledge about the lifestyles of different groups in specific historical periods. Where do patterns of leisure bring people into public arenas? Are these patterns unique to particular classes or other social groups? Are they socially structured? Much of the work on nineteenth-century policing and regulation of leisure has stressed the role of public drunken-

ness as a major source of arrests and the regulation of drinking areas—
pool halls, dance halls, bars, streets—as a major preoccupation of police
and a source of pressure on them (Harring 1983).

Are the sites of leisure class-patterned? In earlier periods there was apparently more interclass drinking than there is today (Harrison 1982,
ch. 3). If so, are alcohol controls only artifacts of class styles of leisure or
do they maintain the interests of one class against another? The leisure-
time pursuits of Americans bear some relationship both to cultural aspects of immigrant and native populations and to the uses of public areas
and public places. Although the latter relate to cultures, they are also consequences of income. That most of the arrests for public drunkenness in
Milwaukee and Chicago in the late nineteenth century should have been
among the working classes is not surprising (Harring 1983). The amal-
gam of class and ethnic imageries and the problems posed for police by
concerns for public order provided a situation in which drinking became
a point of tension between police and the working class. It should be
pointed out, however, that such regulation was usually itself limited both
by working-class resistance and by police indifference to laws with which
they had little sympathy, being of the working class themselves. Here the
difference between highly professionalized police forces and those with
limited training and professional self-conceptions may be considerable.

The rise of professionalized police forces is by no means adequate to
describe or explain the attempts to control, regulate, and limit drinking in
such periods as the late nineteenth and early twentieth centuries in the
United States. I have elsewhere analyzed the American temperance movement (Gusfield 1963), but here I want to view the public controls from a
slightly different perspective—as aspects of urban history and the control
of popular culture closely related to the form in which drinking occurs.

The theory of police control of alcohol as class struggle has another,
and perhaps more crucial, dimension. The issue here is less that of public
order in the daily sense than in the political sense. Interest in order too
has two dimensions or levels. One is the concern for the prevention of
riots, demonstrations, and dissidence. American life, as we have come to
be aware, has experienced a multitude of violent crowd events (Kett 1977,
ch. 4; Brown 1970). These have lacked the acceptance of lower-class
rioting by elites that existed in Europe and England (Silver 1967; Gurr
1976, 96).

The disposition of authorities and established groups to see political
dissent as irrational, insane actions of impulsive or drunken mobs is one
way of avoiding a confrontation with the issues and conflicts posed by

dissidence (Morgan 1988). As Ted Gurr has put it, "One group's 'political violence' is another group's 'legitimate protest'" (1976, 15). Here too there is great need for careful examination of the role of alcohol in acts of collective behavior and the ways in which the events are interpreted by different observers. What constitutes political disorder and what constitutes crime is also at issue. Is Pearson correct in maintaining that "there is . . . historical continuity between this [traditional] response to the 'mob' and modern accounts of hooliganism and crime as senseless?"! (Pearson 1983, 100). How is the description of the presence of drinking used to strengthen or weaken interpretations?

A second form of political interest, however, is given by a different concern—the political function of the drinking place. Styles of leisure among classes or other politically significant groups are often seen as important to the power aspirations of elites. Here Gareth Stedman Jones seems mistaken when he writes, "Struggles over leisure time do not have . . . inherent antagonism built into them" (Jones 1983, 49). Any point of gathering that is exclusive or mostly so for a specific group becomes a potential and actual source of political mobilization for a class, an ethnic group, or an aggregate. Susanna Barrows, for France, and Patricia Morgan, for Italy, have shown how government opposition to the French working-class cabaret and the Italian laborer's *bettoja* were motivated by the fears of working-class political dissidence (Barrows 1979; Morgan 1988). The drinking place may not be the workingman's club, but it has been a location particularly open to political development. In the attack on the saloon the Progressive movement found a way to challenge the supremacy of the urban political machines. By no means, however, do these considerations explain the prohibition movement and its multiple rural and urban supports. Neither do they, without much more study, explain police attention and inattention to drinking and drinking places.

In this discussion of the problem of public order and drinking I have been stressing the complexity of the act of drinking in relation to social institutions and social structure. Class, as a descriptive term, is itself often too broad for practicable analysis. The distinction made by Britons in the eighteenth century has remained in use, although with different terms: they distinguished between the "rough" and the "respectable" poor (Harrison 1971, ch. 1). Drinking may also be seen as troublesome to those within as well as outside the lower class (Ignatieff 1983). Within segments of the lower classes in the nineteenth century there also existed strong normative systems that enjoined abstinence or decried frequent insobriety. The social controls supported by the middle classes, in turn, were self-oriented, expressing concern about the dangers of drunkenness for their relatives, colleagues, and friends (Gusfield 1986; Levine 1978a).

Since the 1960s America has witnessed the rise of a new "dangerous class" whose relation to the social structure is less determined by the division of labor than by the division of age. The invention of adolescence as a distinct social category in the twentieth century has provided a new image of the criminal class and a new source of threat and fear. Although in the nineteenth century young people were frequently seen as sources of crime and disorder, they were viewed as part of a discrete class. In the past three decades, however, youth has emerged as a distinct part of the social structure. Diversities of occupation and class are submerged in a general category of age (Kett 1977, ch. 4; Gillis 1981).

Crime studies highlight the role of youth and the imagery of crime, delinquency, violence, and disorder. After the repeal of Prohibition, minimum-age laws were one of the few limitations on alcohol availability that were upheld (Mosher 1980). The major recommendation of the 1983 Presidential Commission on Drunk Driving has been the strengthening of such laws. Youth is becoming, if not a substitute for, at least an addition to "the dangerous class."

The contact between youth and police is accentuated both by the use of the automobile and by the leisure patterns of youth and youth communities. Adolescents are today a major user of streets in American society and a major target of police regulation. The control of adolescent leisure has become recognized as a unique area of police activity.

PUBLICIZATION OF DRINKING: CLASS, CULTURE, AND THE SALOON

Studies of antialcohol movements as an arena of political or community conflict have depicted the clash between "dry" and "wet" forces as an outcome of differences between diverse cultures. Various distinctions have been made: the diversity between evangelical and ecclesiastical religions (Jensen 1971); between pietistic and ritualistic religious perspectives (Kleppner 1970); between natives and immigrants, Catholics and Protestants, and urban and rural groups (Gusfield 1963); and between preindustrial and industrial cultures (Gutman 1977). While this emphasis on the continuity of cultural elements is not misplaced, it ignores the specific history of the time and place of conflict. Others are more perceptive in stressing the way in which the experience of both the controllers and the would-be controlled respond to new conditions and experiences in their use of alcohol (Stivers 1976b; Duis 1983; Rosenzweig 1983).

The saloon represents a significant institution in the American history of drinking as well as a lesson in how particular periods of historical existence shape the meanings of alcohol among diverse groups. The saloon (a corruption of the word *salon,* denoting an elegant room in an upper-class home or establishment for dining or for receiving guests) was an invention of the late nineteenth century in America (Rosenzweig 1983, ch. 2). Many conditions of urban and industrial life contributed to its rise to a place of importance in the leisure of Americans, especially the working class. Although continuity with a preindustrial life was apparent, the place and meaning of alcohol consumption was shaped by the experience of life in the cities of industrial America (Boyer 1978; Rosenzweig 1983, chs. 2, 4).

The importance of the saloon in both the imagery and the focus of alcohol controls is a reflection of the public character of the popular culture implicated in those controls. The bar is a quasi-public institution, accessible to strangers and, as a business, adaptable to changes in neighborhoods. Unlike private drinking, drinking in bars is both observable and closely related to public spaces such as streets, squares, and plazas. As Duis remarks, "The disorderly activities inside spilled onto the sidewalk" (Duis 1983, 202). In the long effort of middle-class America to cope with the moral disorder it attributed to urban growth, the saloon was imagined as the home of the dangerous classes and the vivid symbol of a popular culture that spawned immorality.

For the poor and the immigrant, the narrowed confines of housing, a need for social services, and even a concern for the purity of water and milk prevented him from privatizing his life in the same fashion as the native, middle-class American. "English-speaking or native-born predominated at the coffeehouse," reports Duis, "while the immigrants went to their respective saloons (Duis 1983, 202). Within the saloon the worker could also find a multiplicity of functions often not available elsewhere. They ranged from advice on adapting to the city, check cashing, union meetinghalls, and information networks to free lunches, a telephone, conviviality, and more pleasing furnishings than the home could supply. Overall the saloonkeeper, often romanticized by journalists, played an important role in the processes by which what Duis calls a stubborn parochialism supported the autonomy of the ethnic culture and community, apart from the wider metropolitan concerns of the native American middle class (Duis 1983, 142).

Drinking was not limited to the poor and the working class, but saloon patronage largely was. Law and public policy played a role in the development of the saloon as a commercial enterprise. In Worcester, for example, the high cost of licenses effectively spelled the death of the *shebeen,* the Irish institution of selling liquor and drinking in homes, usually a monopoly of widows. Whereas at other levels of urban communities Americans were moving in the direction of family life focused on the nuclear unit with a narrowing of the gender gap, the saloon fostered an isolated male recreational group (Rosenzweig 1983, ch. 2; Sennett 1974). It came to be a space and a time apart both from job and home as well as a refuge from both: "Men left the home as much in search of a place to drink as of something to drink" (Duis 1983, 106).

As Rosenzweig suggests, the saloon can be seen as an embodiment of what Raymond Williams, following Gramsci, calls an alternative culture (Williams 1977). With the increase in discretionary income accompanying the industrial organization of the late nineteenth century, the worker was able to support a social milieu that provided a sharp contrast to the discipline, individualism, and hierarchy represented by the factory model of the rational, market-oriented society. The communal values represented in "treating" were an opposite of the savings ethic that was so much the standard of middle-class advice on achieving mobility (Rosenzweig 1983, 58–59). The values of mutual support, equality, and group solidarity were clearly polar to the individualistic refrain of a market-centered American morality of personal achievement.

One should recognize that what is construed as "public area" is itself not clearly given. For most of their history, colleges in the United States have been places of disorderly conduct and rioting, and college authorities have been ineffective in regulating drinking (Kett 1977; Rudolph 1962). For many reasons, including their origins outside the political structure of municipalities, colleges have had an enclave status; they have been permitted to control their own affairs. With campus officials acting in place of parents, police have refrained from entering college campuses and have frequently left disciplinary problems, including drunkenness, to college authorities. The military have similarly occupied a less public position than most of the citizenry.

Such enclaving was less possible in the density and public-transportation patterns of American cities in the 1880s and 1890s. The saloon itself was an institution that always threatened to move into middle-class neighborhoods. It did find a congenial location on major thoroughfares joining urban sections to one another (Duis 1983, ch. 7). It is not that there was necessarily more or less drinking associated with urbanization but that the character of public drinking made the issues of popular culture and group divisions a center of heightened concern for the preservation of moral standards. The effort to control drinking was isolated neither from the general Progressive movement against political corruption nor from the movements to preserve moral purity, which was felt to be waning among the middle classes. The sense of a traditional moral order under siege pervaded the urban middle classes of the late nineteenth and early twentieth centuries in the United States (Boyer 1978, 13, 14). It is consistent with this view of the context of drinking that the major arm of the Prohibition movement was called the Anti-Saloon League.

PRIVATIZATION OF DRINKING AND THE
INDIVIDUALIZING OF LEISURE

Prohibition may have sounded the demise of the saloon, but it was well on its way out as a central institution of working-class life even before the 1920s. American leisure was undergoing profound changes as new technologies, urban communities, and rising discretionary incomes made new forms of recreation more attractive. A growing egalitarianism between husband and wife added to the emergence of other forms of public leisure, of which the movies were the most striking (Rosenzweig 1983, ch. 8). The development of such urban institutions as amusement parks and spectator sports added to the new commercial leisure that attracted both middle and working classes (Barth 1980). The saloon was not as vital to a working class now more accustomed to city life and new consumption patterns. The outlines of contemporary American society and culture were discernible even as the Eighteenth Amendment was passed.

The America of the past fifty years is sharply at variance with the society of the pre-Prohibition eras. A middle class of small-business and freelance professionals has been replaced by one dependent on jobs in organizational workplaces. The dominance of agricultural ideals has given way to rhythms of life in which consumption is as much a delineator of identity as production. A rise in the general standard of living and a decline in hours of work have meant a standardization of leisure that diminishes the gap between classes in American life.

Such profound changes have sharpened the boundaries between work and leisure in their role both as symbols of character and as times of the day and the week. A description like the following would hardly be expected to gain general assent today as it did in nineteenth-century America: "The responsible young man was the one who knew that his obligations to his employer extended through his off-duty hours as well as through his working-day" (Wyllie 1954, 49). It is not that the ethic of work has disappeared in America, but belief in the moral significance of continuity between spheres of life, of being a person whose work and play are consistent, has become less dominant.

The very notion of rationalizing leisure contains an instructive ambiguity. With the successful eradication of drinking from the workplace the conflicts over the use of alcohol in American life have been about leisure and how it should be used. For some, the world is rationalized by being the arena of a consistent character. Sobriety is enjoined as a sign of the self, of a consistent and continuing person. To rationalize leisure is to make it the locus of the same kind of person, subject to the same set of values and judged by the same criteria. For others, work and play are two different and even contrasting spheres of life. The rational being keeps them separate. Studies of bar behavior and drinking-driving by myself and associates suggest that many drinkers utilize a typology of competence and incompetence in perceiving themselves and other drinkers (Gusfield, Kotarba, and Rasmussen 1979; Gusfield 1981b). Competent drinkers recognize and respect the division between the two worlds and act in accordance with a different normative system in each. Work is work and leisure is leisure, and the twain need never meet.

It may be profitable to speculate on the shift in presentation of moral character implied by these polarities. The relationship between economic activity and moral character was perhaps far more strident in America before the 1930s than it has become today. Daniel Rodgers observes that "to doubt the moral preeminence of work was the act of a conscious heretic (1978). The assumption that a consistent self is essential to either job success or the work life as indicative of other areas of life is by no means routine today.

CULTURAL HEGEMONY: CARNIVAL AND LENT REVISITED

The description of diverse meanings of leisure and play in American life suggests still another way of studying social control, by focusing on the cultural categories and meanings that constitute the tacit sources of aspiration and evaluation. Viewed from the systemic perspectives of Parsonian sociology, these sources point to the elements of a common culture. Viewed from the standpoint of social structure, especially in Marxian orientations, norms of drinking and drunkenness can be seen as ways of achieving, through culture, a social control without force and without the appellation of repression at all. The terms used here have been *dominant ideology, cultural hegemony,* or *legitimization* (Williams 1977). Has some group or class—religious, ethnic, or other—achieved control by having others embrace its beliefs, values, and categories to such an extent that control through repressive means has not been necessary?

Has there been, and is there now, a common set of beliefs and values about beverage alcohol that cuts across major diversities in American life? Do such similarities, if they exist, serve the interests of some groups and work to the disadvantage of others? Elsewhere I have discussed this issue in particular in regard to law as symbolic and to the impact of temperance ideas on the middle classes themselves (Gusfield 1986). Here I will examine temperance ideas and beliefs with reference to the theme of leisure-time uses, especially in relation to the contemporary New Temperance movement.

The focus of this chapter has been on drinking as part of a total context in the emergence of leisure and its uses. By the mid-nineteenth century three aspects of drinking and social control were dominant in American life in the sense that they were shared by most groups, whatever their support of, or hostility toward, the public controls represented by temperance and Prohibitionist policies. One, as Levine has pointed out, was the belief in the disinhibiting effects of alcohol as the cause of drunkenness, accidents, and immorality (1978a). Second was adherence to norms that enjoined the mix of working and drinking. Even among the nonabstinent, drinking had become defined as an after-hours matter. The third aspect was a general attitude of rejection of, disappointment in, and concern for the "habitual drunkard," or, in mid-twentieth-century terms, the "alcoholic." Despite qualifications and marginal groups, these areas of agreement have set outer limits to the conflicts over drinking and public controls in the United States for the past hundred years.

Within these limits, however, there has been active conflict over the systems of public controls. As I have maintained in this essay, such controls have found their battlefield in the efforts to control and constrain playtime. If alcohol is seen as disinhibiting, that fact has caused it to be embraced by some and repulsed by others. It is in the meanings of leisure that struggles over the uses of alcohol have been most productive of political conflict.

In the symbolism with which American culture has invested the use of alcohol, drinking and abstinence have come to be definers of moral character (Gusfield 1963). The respectable leisure habits of some are the disrespectable habits of others. The abstinence and inhibition that mark the temperance ethic is decried as blue-nose intolerance, whereas boisterousness and uninhibited camaraderie are seen by others as irresponsibility and an invitation to the immoral.

The Weberian *geist* of bureaucratization and utilitarian rationality assumes much more system and unity than societies or cultures demonstrate. Whether as a dialectical response to capitalist culture and industrial organization or as historical continuity, the romantic resistance to rationalization has been a recurrent theme of modern thought (Spitzer 1983; Lears 1981; Bell 1976; Gouldner 1980). Drinking has become, especially in the United States, a symbol of the irrational, the impulsive, the "free" side of life. Its association with the uncontrolled and irresponsible, with the unpredictable appearance of trouble, is part of its appeal and danger. There is a constant theme in modern literature that identifies the romantic opposition to a world of calculation, responsibility, and cooperation with the underclass, with youth, and with the dangerous classes. Efforts to rationalize leisure by responsible drinking, for example, are often chasing a contradiction in terms.

The nineteenth-century battlefields have given way to different arenas of contention. Although clear pockets of division still exist (Protestant fundamentalism, for example), the distinctions of American society along cultural lines are no longer as clearly matters of religion, class, region, or even ethnicity as they were in the nineteenth century (Gusfield 1963, ch. 6). The greater standardization of American life has meant that whatever the divisions over alcohol use, they no longer clearly follow nineteenth-century boundaries.

As I argued a number of years ago, the effort to freeze American drinking through the Eighteenth Amendment was an admission of the failure of the temperance ethic to achieve the status of dominance through American society (Gusfield 1963, ch. 6). Neither Prohibition nor its repeal appears to have changed the conflictual status of alcohol in American life. What has changed is the structure of public controls. From 1933 until the late 1970s the repressive character of public controls toward drinking was minimized, although the United States, as compared to other capitalistic and industrialized societies (excepting the Scandinavian) retained a public definition of alcohol as a dangerous commodity. A more permissive and tolerant orientation toward leisure replaced the constraints of the Prohibition era. The "alcohol problem" became the problem of the alcoholic and was thereby sealed off from the playtime activities of most Americans and defined as a medical rather than a political issue.

The recent renaissance of prevention policies means also the return of drinking as a political issue. Measures to restrict the availability or sale of alcohol to the general public or to special groups, such as young adults, restore the effort to define leisure-time drinking and its locations as less than respectable. Yet at no time can we find a dominant or culturally hegemonic ethic. If the achievement ethic or individualism can be construed as dominant in American life, its relation to drinking is by no means clear. As an issue it remains a matter of conflict and opposition.

Part 3

The World of Drinking and Driving:
An Ethnographic Study of Bars

Chapter Six

Competence and Incompetence in Drinking and Driving: Situated Aspects of Control and Autonomy

INTRODUCTION: OBSERVING AND RECORDING

Driving under the influence of alcohol is illegal in all fifty American states. It is also a common experience in American life, as ad hoc observations, mass media reports, and careful research indicate (Borkenstein et al. 1964). Roadside surveys of American motorists in the early 1970s found that for every one motorist arrested for driving under the influence of alcohol there were approximately two thousand others also driving under the influence of alcohol who were undetected, unobserved, or unarrested (U.S. Department of Transportation 1974, 2.) Drinking-driving thus falls into the category of other traffic offenses. It is an action commonly performed and usually without legal sanctions although an offense against specific statute law. This widespread occurrence in everyday American life makes it more like what H. Laurence Ross characterizes most traffic violations—"folk crimes" (Ross 1960).

The problem of drinking-driving has been extensively studied in the United States and Europe for twenty years. A research literature of at least three hundred studies exists and grows larger each year (Cameron and Room 1978). Almost all of the research to date has been marked by a concern for developing solutions to drinking-driving conceived as a public problem. With few if any exceptions such studies have been focused on the drinking-driver's demographic characteristics or characteristics of the accidents in which drinking-driving has been a feature. In almost all of the literature on drinking-driving there is an absence of narrative data drawn directly from drinking-drivers or observations of the drinking-driving phenomenon either prior to accident or unconnected with accident. (For one exception, see Pelz and Schuman 1974.) This chapter is an investigation of the drinking-driving event as a phenomenon—an act experienced by those engaging in it. My aim is neither to solve a public problem nor to study drinking-driving as it is involved in social trouble— arrests, accidents, injuries or death. It is to understand it as a form of human behavior, not as a problem.

In studying drinking-driving as behavior and experience I am not conceiving it as an aspect of illegal behavior or as abnormal, deviant, or unusual behavior. My intent is less clearly concerned with the development of policy. I am interested in the sociology of drinking-driving; the socially shared rules and arrangements governing the nature and occurrence of drinking-driving and the circumstances in which they are applied. As objects of study such rules and arrangements are to be found in the activity of persons who contemplate drinking and driving and not in the legally enunciated rules of courts, legislatures, and officials. These may or may not be congruent with legal arrangements. I want to examine drinking-driving from the standpoint or perspective of those who meet the problem of driving after having consumed alcohol. In situations in which people drink and people drive, what are the social rules governing such behaviors and how do they arise as governing mechanisms?

This is an ethnographic study. The data has been obtained through observation, participant-observation, conversation, and quasi-interviews conducted in four public bars in San Diego County. Two of the bars were neighborhood bars and two were transient in type. (These are fully described in chapter 7.) The data represent more than one hundred hours of observation of interaction in these public facilities. This is a study of the drinking-driving phenomenon as it emerged in the naturalistic setting of barrooms—as a topic of conversation, as behavior, as a response to queries initiated by observers.

ETHNOGRAPHY AND THE STUDY OF CULTURE

Underlying the choice of an ethnographic method are assumptions regarding the nature of social life and the object of this study. While I do seek to uncover the rules of action, such rules are not as clearly discoverable as law is to lawyers—through examination of definitive statements. Most rules of social behavior are tacit and unstated. Frequently they arise in interaction and can only be recognized after the fact rather than a priori.

They are, however, the rules used by participants, not those imposed by others—legal officials, managers, or social observers. An ethnographic analysis is preoccupied with understanding the orderliness in behavior, not with predicting it. In observing behavior, including conversation, my intention is to capture the rules and meanings by which drinking-driving is defined and observed by participants; to understand the cultural categories and meanings through which drinking-driving is assessed, understood, and seen as appropriate or inappropriate and the ways in which such categories are applied in different circumstances. Whatever the system of organization derived from our observations, the result is a set of assertions of how people expect each other to behave within that culture (Tyler 1969, 5–6; Mehan 1980, ch. 5).

Charles Frake has put the same idea in another fashion, likening the ethnographer to the linguist: "it is not, I think, the ethnographer's task to predict behavior *per se,* but rather to state the rules of culturally appropriate behavior. . . . In this respect the ethnographer is again akin to the linguist who does not attempt to predict what people will say but to state the rules for constructing utterances which native speakers will judge as grammatically appropriate. The model of an ethnographic statement is not: 'if a person is confronted with stimulus X, he will do Y', but: 'if a person is in situation X, performance Y will be judged appropriate by native actors'" (1969, 124).

What I am doing in this ethnographic study is attempting to derive from observation of four bars some of the rules and meanings which are available to persons in the particular culture of these settings. To do so I must assume that an order of rules exists by which participants make sense of the interactions and events occurring—that is, that the actors have developed or do develop in interaction those directives which enable them to decide on appropriate action and expression.

COLLECTING DATA

The virtue of ethnography is that social behavior is observed in its natural scene. If, as we assume, social rules are complex and take account of specificity of situations, then efforts to observe them in retrospect are both too general and too much distorted by the character of the communications setting in which they occur (Cicourel 1964). Responses to questionnaires are affected by both of these difficulties: they cannot cover the multifold and highly specific contingencies in which action occurs and they are not responses to the situation to which questionnaires are addressed.

Responses consist of behavior occurring within the situation of question-answer. They are behavior addressed to the question-answer situation rather than to the situation in which the drinking-driving behavior occurs.

More significantly, the attempt to derive the rules and meanings used by participants is limited by the investigators lack of experience or observation of participant's behavior. Put in another way, the sociologist cannot know what questions are sensible, significant, and relevant to the participant's social organization without a prior exposure to it.

Thus the principle of ethnographic data collecting is to derive the data as much as possible from the naturalistic settings in which it occurs. This is not always possible and departures from it were made, but the effort was to keep as close as possible to the setting which was under observation.

More specifically, three units of data were obtained:

1. *Naturally occurring participant observation:* Here the observer either perceived behavior or heard conversation in which he was or was not a participant as a barroom customer. Example: The observed discussion between a bartender and a customer over continuance of service.

2. *Conversation:* and, in a few instances, behavior initiated by the observer on matters of interest to him but introduced as part of the action of him as barroom customer. For example, "steering" a conversation toward topics relevant to drinking-driving.

3. *Quasi-interview:* Here the observer identifies himself as someone "interested in studying drinking behavior" and elicits conversation about previously observed bar behavior or other matters of interest to him. This was only used in the case of bartenders or "bouncers." An example of this is a query to a bouncer about whether he has experienced any troubles from drinking-driving in his work recently.

In this account of different units of data, the role or persona of the observer undergoes change, from observer to participant-observer to interviewer. In all of these postures, the observer assumed a continuous role—that of customer in the bar. In that role is found the reason for selecting bars as the setting of this study.

As several observers of bar behavior have pointed out, bars are areas of unusual accessibility for social interaction. Unlike private homes, bars are public places, formally open to anyone of legal age to enter and to purchase alcohol. But they are also accessible in a way different from private homes and from many other public places such as restaurants, stores, and theaters. In Erving Goffman's phrase, they are "open regions"—places where unacquainted people have the right to engage each other in social interaction (Goffman 1963a, 132; Cavan 1966, ch. 3). Simply by virtue of appearing as a customer, the observer can engage in conversation without seeming to be obtrusive. This characteristic of bars is the feature which makes them especially useful to the ethnographer. The relation between bars and drinking-driving makes them excellent sites for the study of drinking-driving, but so too do parties in private homes. What the bars possess, however, is greater accessibility to observation and to participant-observation.

METHODS OF RECORDING DATA

The very condition of being a customer which enables the observer to gain entrée to the cultural world of the bar also limits his ability to record what he observes. Fieldwork has constantly presented this problem (Schatzman and Strauss 1973, ch. 6). Efforts to record conversation verbatim, through moment-by-moment note-taking or videotape or auditory recording has two drawbacks: it prevents the observer from himself being accessible to others and thus threatens his access to the scene he seeks to enter. It turns the barroom atmosphere into a publicly exposed situation. We assumed any effort to accomplish such a state even if it were allowed by bartenders, would make the observers' later interaction so constrained that the natural interaction would be decisively distorted. Put in another way, it would have put customers "on guard."[1]

The system for recording data used in this study is much like that used in many other bar studies and other field research in contemporary societies (Cavan 1966; Junker 1960, ch. 2). I call it the "stool system," because of the key role of the public toilet in it. The observer functioned as a customer, talking with other customers and/or the bartender. He observed his interaction and other interactions within his perception. He had to rely on his memory to "record" significant conversation and events as they occur. Every possible moment socially acceptable, he left the scene of interaction and went to the men's toilet. Using the toilet stall as a place of privacy, he made quick, mnemonic notes of the previous interaction. On arriving home, or in the car, after the observational period, the short notes were expanded. The expanded version was put on tape and transcribed by secretarial service. It is these expanded versions which constitute the data of the study. The frequency with which the observer was able to make the original, short notes depended upon the interaction taking place and his judgment as to whether it could be missed as well as the risk that too frequent absences would occasion suspicion among fellow customers. Note-writing approximately once an hour was the norm, although we did not keep a record of it. A reputation for weak kidneys is one of the risks of this kind of fieldwork.

ANALYSES: FORMAL AND INFORMAL

Critics of fieldwork of this kind frequently point to its imprecision and selectivity of data. Given the ongoing events in a contained space, the observer attends only to some and not to all that occurs. His record of observations is itself selective because he only places into notes that which is seen as pertinent or "interesting" and even that is limited by the intervening screen of memory (Cicourel 1964). Consequently, field data is not susceptible to the formal analyses of data derived from questionnaires, documents, or videotaped recordings where the totality of data is available for retrieval and can be exhaustively coded by established criteria.

There is no doubt that such criticisms are apt. But social research is seldom able to achieve ideal conditions. Costs must be adjudged against benefits. Perhaps more significantly, however, the goals or results of social research must also be seen as distinctive and different from those of research on natural and nonhuman subjects. Both aspects of this research, its cost-benefit ratio and its particular status as knowledge, need to be examined before the research itself is presented.

The informal analysis conducted here is largely a search for order within the data. I have already indicated the major virtue of field data as compared to more formally collected materials. Participant-observation attempts to see the behavior from the standpoint or meaning of the participants. It is therefore better adapted to discovering hypotheses, theories, and understanding the social organization of a group than are methods which must utilize ad hoc systems of the investigator's for interpreting the meaning of responses and information presented by members (Glaser and Strauss 1967).

It is the "richness" of the data that enables the investigator to produce an understanding of the order of participants that is related to the complexity of social life. By "richness" I mean the variety, depth, and complexity of events occurring in natural conditions. This is illustrated by the crucial way in which I have used seemingly negative data. As a general rule, the people we observed insisted on drinking and driving. In conversation and behavior they uphold this rule of normal drinking behavior, but, in both behavior and conversation, this rule is often broken. Such negative data would suggest that my designation of the rule is false. However, the existence of excuses to explain why the rule is not followed indicates a subsidiary rule defining when exceptions are permissible and supporting the normality of the general rule. As the research leads me to conclude, such "exculpatory defenses" are a crucial part of the social organization of drinking-driving. This form of "analytic induction" takes advantage of the sequential character of field research in that initial interpretations are constantly refined and qualified by further observations (Denzin 1970, 194–97; Becker 1958).

Insofar as I can call my creation of order in the data a form of "method," it is largely a search for how common events or interpretations are contradicted by other events or interpretations in the data and what principles or rules can grant them orderly understanding, that is, reconcile one to the other. Several forms of this process, discussed in detail in the next chapter, illustrate my procedures:

1. *Relation between separate events:* Here a seemingly negative instance supports the general rule because of its differentia. In general, women were given greater license to refrain from driving and there was greater permissibility among others to intervene in preventing them from driving. In one case this was observed not to occur when the observer would otherwise have expected it. In this case, however, the women were viewed by the participants as having acted especially aggressively and "unladylike." Thus the observation of the general rule is strengthened by seeing how the negative event is interpreted.

2. *Relation between statements and events:* One of the virtues of seeing behavior rather than asking about it is that the discrepancy between what is said and what is done is made evident (Deutscher 1973). If we depended only on the conversation in bars to establish the rule that husbands drive and wives are passengers, it would be supported. However, by watching what happens when the couples get into the car, we learned that this is far from the norm. (Incidentally, this also bolstered our general conception of how much barroom talk and action appear as performance before an audience.)

3. *Relation between settings and events:* A major hypothesis of the research was that the application of rules of drinking-driving differed considerably between settings represented by the different kinds of bars. What occurred in the neighborhood bar did not occur in the transient bar. Such observations were essential to the depiction of the different economic elements in each type as a business and the consequences of such differences for the drinking-driving phenomenon. Without comparing events and the absence of events from one setting to another, it would have been difficult to discover the economic factors at work in each.

4. *The absence of data:* Questionnaire and interview methods presuppose the existence of understandings and meaning which enable the investigator to frame questions. Thus they often elicit data which may not emerge in natural surroundings. Being asked for an opinion about an object or event the respondent may frame one but does not do so in the course of natural occurrences. Much may be learned by failures to observe expected data. We were surprised by the infrequent occurrence of talk about drinking-driving apart from specific situations and the consequent absence of talk that would form a set of recipes, hints, or advice on how to drive while under the influence of alcohol, how to prevent arrest, or how to cope with a drinking-driving charge.

My goal in this study was to uncover the social rules, as distinguished from legal rules, which are in use in daily life to govern drinking and driving and to understand how these are used in specific and varying circumstances. I would be less than candid if I maintained that the results are independent of the interpretation and ordering which the author brings to it. Data are no more self-evident than other aspects of life. My general perspective toward social behavior and the problem of drinking-driving has greatly influenced both my work and that of the other two observers. The interpretation of what was observed and selected to be remembered involves a creative act.

While I have attempted to approach drinking-driving as if I knew nothing about it in the beginning, I am not only a member of the American culture but also someone who has faced public issues of drinking and driving. For the past six years I have been studying the problem of drinking-driving, largely as a matter of law, law enforcement, and public policy (Gusfield 1975a; 1976b; 1978; 1981a). This study is itself part of a larger set of studies of how public problems emerge and are defined through institutions of science, law, and medicine.

However, that creative interpretation is not independent of empirical observation. It is governed and controlled at every point by the positive and negative events recorded. They constrain the interpretation and provide the source for emergent ideas. While I have sought to approach drinking-driving de novo as if it were as strange and exotic a behavior to me as the pagan religious rites of the natives on a Polynesian island is to a German anthropologist, such a feat is not possible. But in adopting that stance I come closer to seeing what I may have taken for granted and can now question.

In including protocol statements from the recorded data, I have attempted to support each statement or assertion about the data with either the source or an example of the type of source on which the assertion is based. The reader can then examine his or her agreement with my interpretation.

Finally, the reader must recognize that ethnographic data of this kind, informally collected and analyzed, is not of the same type nor aspires to the same evidentiary status as natural science and propositional knowledge. In general, ethnographic data serves two major purposes:

1. It shows that it is possible to develop a plausible and empirically grounded interpretation of a phenomena which is at variance with some other, often conventionally held, system of interpretation. In this fashion it demonstrates that the other interpretation need not be an exclusively and necessarily "true" account. Such falsifiability is, as Popper suggests, one of the major ways in which knowledge is developed (1976).

2. In a significant manner sociological knowledge is a form of knowledge which is neither Art nor Science but a mix of both. It consists of multiple plausible interpretations of the real world. Each is empirically grounded and self-consistent. The value of such interpretations lies in the understandings and questions which they yield and which are used as a stock of possibilities by which the student or reader can approach new areas and objects. This, I submit, has been the importance of much ethnography of the past decades of social science research. Ethnography creates new images of social life and thereby forces the reader to recognize the rules of behavior which are taken for granted and the alternative possibilities available.

This chapter cannot adequately engage in the fuller methodological analysis for grounding the ethnographic method used here. I have only tried to lay the basis for understanding what I am about in this study. Inherent in the claim of the ethnographer to how understanding is generated from data is a coolness toward summaries, conclusions, and propositions as doing irreparable violence to the complexity of the subject. Discussions of method and theory are then not an adequate substitute for reading the study.

THE BAR: THE CREATION AND MANAGEMENT OF MOODS

Risk and uncertainty are a normal feature of everyday life. The individual recognizes the riskiness of crossing the street, of handling cooking equipment on a hot stove, of leaning out of windows. Drinking alcoholic beverages and driving automobiles are both in a class of actions commonly seen as fraught with considerable risk to personal interaction, to health, and to property. The potentials of violence, accident, embarrassment, and economic loss are always present in the tangible possibility that drinking will lead to drunkenness and driving to accidents. The people we observed are not unique in recognizing these risks. Nor do we believe they are unique in treating them as normal occurrences, risks to be coped with but not, on that account, to be avoided.

My focus in this study is on the nexus of the two risks—of drinking *and* driving. It is part of the common sense, the accepted wisdom about reality that the combination of the two is inherently riskier than driving sober. How that insight affects behavior, however, is not a logical or direct deduction from the abstract character of such generalized understanding. It is, instead, an emerging, situated aspect of behavior; one that arises in a context of other people, alternative possibilities for transportation, and the particular settings which govern interaction with other people and establish alternative possibilities. It is less likely to be faced as a problem through planned and anticipated routines than to be dealt with in situ, as a problem handled only when and how it arises.

In a general sense bars in the United States are public places in which alcoholic and nonalcoholic beverages may be sold by the glass. For the sociologist they are also particular social areas. "They define for the actor what activity can take place as a matter of course and without question, and for what conduct those present will be held accountable" (Cavan 1966, 3.) In the past, observers of bars have attempted to categorize them by the activities other than drinking that go on in them, by their clientele, and by their mood (Cavan 1966; Room 1977; Roebuck and Frese 1976). The mix of clientele and setting creates a specific kind of atmosphere within which the minute-to-minute management of the setting is enhanced or deterred. My focus is on how the atmosphere, mood, or scene affects the management of the setting by the "host" or management—bartenders and servers. What we assert is that the character of the bar is influenced by its setting and the clientele attracted or repelled by that setting. Control of behavior within that setting is in turn influenced by these attributes of the mood. Managerial control is itself an important element in enhancing the mood which the setting has initiated. To understand how self, peer, and managerial controls affect the drinking and driving event requires its being placed conceptually within that social area.

The focus of the description of the four bars observed is on the interaction of physical elements with clientele. Each bar has a particular character which is both attractive to and in turn enhanced by the kind of clientele which is customary to it.

The Club

Geography and Physical Setting

The fastest growing part of San Diego County lies to the north of the city. Along the Pacific coast and eastward lie a series of communities, some newly developed and others older. Both types have become bedroom communities for the county. The Club is situated in one of the older areas along the coast, well within the suburban fringe of the parent metropolis.[2] It is in the midst of a small, local shopping center just off a frontage road that adjoins the coastal highway. The highway is a two-way route that once was the major connection between San Diego and Los Angeles. About two decades ago it was superseded by the interstate expressway, which is about two miles east. Today the coastal route is a major link between San Diego and the suburban communities along the coast. The shopping center is largely a convenience place for local residents. The units of the center, approximately twelve, are clustered in a U across and around a small parking lot, with space for approximately fifty cars.

The Club is flanked on the right by a laundromat and a doughnut shop. The latter is open until 1:00 A.M. and serves coffee as well as fresh doughnuts. To the left of the lounge are a meat market and a liquor store. There are other neighborhood bars in the vicinity but not within easy walking distance. The coastal highway contains several major restaurants and bars, all of which cater to the general county and city population. These, too, are not within easy walking distance, but they are only five or ten minutes from the Club by car.

Appearance

I have chosen "cover names" for our observation sites, to protect their identity and to emphasize the character of the site, although in each case the actual name conveyed much of the character. "The Club" emphasizes the regularized attachment of a core group of regulars who are there most evenings and for whom the bar is a "home away from home," a place where friends meet, help can be obtained, advice is sought, checks are cashed, money is borrowed and lent, and the bartender is "one of the gang." Like the concept implied by the word *club*, it is a predominantly, though not exclusively, male place. The notes of one of us, after his initial entry to the Club, constitutes our dominant image of it: "my attention went immediately to the bar as the center of interaction and the people there, including the bartender. It took me awhile to consciously look around the Club and get my attention away from the four other men sitting at the bar and the bartender himself."

Seen from the outside the Club might be any kind of office or establishment. It has no storefront window. Instead the front is a white brick wall and a glass door. Yellow ornamental lights are hung at the top of the wall. Only the name "The Club" gives any indication of the enterprise going on within. Although the interior is dark in contrast to the adjacent laundromat and doughnut shop, it is well-lit for a bar. Furnishings and patrons can be seen immediately on entry and no time is required for the eyes to adjust to dim light. The room is U-shaped. The bar follows the shape of the room, and there are tables in booths opposite one side of the bar. Most customers used the bar, and the tables served more as a place for overflow than as a primary site. There was a jukebox in one corner with a usual assortment of contemporary country and rock records. Adjacent to the far end of the bar from the entrance is a large, unused room. In general the decor of the Club is neither memorable nor noticeable.

Clientele

The Club is a neighborhood bar, although customers usually drive to it. It has neither entertainment nor recreational equipment to attract clientele. The decor does not convey a specific mood or class which might appeal to one or another age level. It is neither a youth bar nor particularly a couples bar. Its appeal is to a core of regulars for whom it is a "hangout." Its site in a small shopping center precludes many transients from stopping.

The customers are mostly blue-collar and lower white-collar workers—construction workers, shop owners, butchers. Two distinct age groups predominate, one in the late twenties and early thirties and the other close to or at retirement age—late fifties and sixties. The class level of the lounge can be evidenced by its close connection to the Elks organization. A group of regulars, the core continuing clientele, consists of seven or eight customers, all of whom belong to the Elks. Applications for membership are available at the bar.

Two bartenders constitute the staff. (There are no waiters or waitresses.) One is only there a couple of nights a week. The stable center of the lounge is a hired bartender named Frank. He is a short, thin man about fifty years old. He has been at the Club for eight years and is also a member of the Elks. From time to time, one or the other of the regulars helps out as auxiliary bartender, as does the owner.

The regulars sit at the bar and carry on conversation with Frank. They know and are known by many of those who patronize the bar less frequently than the regulars, who are there most every night. On weeknights the bar sometimes closes around midnight, two hours before the legal closing hour. One night at the Club we recorded: "This night was very slow. Some kids came in and Tom left about 10:00 but that was about it. George and I and Frank just sat around and shot the bull, once again talking about sports, gambling, women. Not much was said. There was also a special on TV that we watched and which, according to Frank, accounted for why it was slow."

The focus of our observations was on the regulars—a group of seven or eight customers who come in every night. Central to the group is a man about thirty-five years old named George. He is single, lives in the area but not within walking distance, and works as a butcher at a supermarket in the county. George has been a bartender in the past and served in the military. Like most of the regulars, George is a heavy drinker, beginning early in the evening. Whiskey is the staple drink of the group.

The Club does not vary much from evening to evening or from day to day. On weeknights the customers are fewer and the action slower. The bar may close by 11:00 P.M. or midnight. There is a larger crowd on weekends, but the character of the clientele remains the same. Stability, sameness, and homeyness are the marks of the Club.

Friendly Al's

The Club and Friendly Al's are quite similar, but the differences are significant. As the choice of name attests, this is a bartender's bar, one in which the bartender—often the owner, Al, but also Big Joe, Glenn, and occasionally Dana—closely manages the bar and controls its activities. In the Club the regulars include the bartender as part of their group. In Friendly Al's, he is the fulcrum around which activities emerge.

Geography and Physical Setting

Al's is located on one of the major east-west thoroughfares of San Diego, about three or four miles from the downtown section of the city. It is a street of retail stores, bars, restaurants, and offices. Mesa Avenue is within the route regularly patrolled by the special drinking driver squad of the San Diego Police Department. Friendly Al's is located in a storefront building, one that abuts the front sidewalk. The building is about fifty feet wide and painted black. Large white letters announce the name "Friendly Al's." There is no special place for parking, and patrons must use Mesa Avenue or use the side streets if they park cars nearby. Like the Club, its presentation is not noteworthy and thus announces its local character.

Once inside, it takes a little while for one to become accustomed to the darkness and to see one's surroundings. The entrance door is to the right of a bar, approximately forty feet long, extending the length of the room. Two pinball machines stand in a 7-by-7 foot area near the entrance, and beyond them stands a large pool table. The remainder of the room contains several tables with adjacent chairs. A jukebox is against the wall, across the room from the bar and close to the pool table. Compared to the crowded "feel" of the Club, Friendly Al's seems spacious. The customers' constant crossing of the room from bar or tables to jukebox and the players at the pool table give a sense of activity. The often present country music, the whirr of the pinball machine, and the click of the pool balls form a tonal background to the scene.

Clientele

Al's is a bar with greater differentiation among its clientele than the Club. While it has a core of regulars, it is frequented by loners and, especially on the weekends, couples and groups as well. A protocol excerpt provides a description:

> When I arrived at Friendly Al's at approximately 11:00 P.M. all seats at the bar were taken and four of the tables were occupied as well as the pool table itself . . . the same crowd distribution was present at Al's this evening as . . . is usually present there. By this I mean that to the interior of the bar are the regulars (couples) with whom Al and the other bartenders interact most regularly. At the exterior end of the bar (toward the entrance) were seated the non-group regulars, or what appear to be the more transient of the regular customers at Al's . . . It is at the front of the bar where the loners come in for the most part to sit and drink and occasionally engage in conversation with each other and the bartender. The tables are occupied by young couples, in their twenties, who were either sitting and drinking and/or playing pool at the pool table.

Friendly Al's is almost always kept open until the legal closing time. After midnight the crowd dwindles to mostly the regulars at the bar. During the period of observation there were occasional "events" that made the evening unique, such as Al's birthday, the birthday of one of the regulars, or the return of the bar's pool team from a contest with another tavern. On those occasions food might be available and the bar decorated.

Al's had first come to our attention through a newspaper story on the Breathalyzer machine which he had installed. By depositing twenty-five cents, customers can measure their blood alcohol level and determine whether they are beyond the legal limit. We felt that the presence of the machine might make for ease of introducing the topic of drinking and driving into conversation and would be a focus for natural emergence as well. (As you will see, the machine was largely ignored by customers.) The location of the bar and its character as a bartender-led site convinced us to devote closer attention to it.

The role of the bartender is conveyed in this excerpt from the protocol quoted earlier: "The bar was fairly loud this evening for Al was really carrying on. Al is the kind of bartender whose presence is known in all corners of the bar. He laughs and jokes with all customers at various times of the evening and speaks very loudly. When one is in the bar at Friendly Al's it is hard to be completely anonymous, for Al will regularly come over to all customers, including myself, and at least say a few words."

That Place

The Absence of Management

In both the Club and Friendly Al's the core of regulars and their interaction with the bartender constitute a focus of the activity of the bar and are significant to how both drinking and driving are influenced and controlled. That Place and the Hermitage, although different from each other in important ways, are alike in the limited degree of managerial control. They minimize the public nature of social control and leave the individual to himself and his peers to a greater degree than do the Club or Friendly Al's.

Geography and Physical Setting

That Place is a large, two-story building which, from its exterior, might be a family dwelling. It is located in an area of many bars, restaurants and central shopping, along Arena Drive just North and West of Downtown San Diego, an area which stays awake well after the city has gone to sleep.

Police on the drinking driver squad tell us that Arena Drive is the place to come to when they want to find DUI (driving under the influence of alcohol) offenders. That Place is situated across from the main indoor sports arena in San Diego, the site of major basketball and hockey events and of many rock and roll concerts. Next door to the bar is a large and well-known record store that is open until midnight. Several restaurants are close to the tavern. A parking lot services both the bar and the record shop. Across the street, also opposite the arena, are several very large retail supermarkets with an abundance of parking. Within a few blocks are several "strip" bars and go-go dancing establishments. That Place is about three miles from a major naval training base.

All of this signals a clientele of unmarried, male customers. That is inexact since That Place also has its contingent of single females. It is the youthful clientele of That Place that stands out and its character as a singles bar that provides its atmosphere.

The physical setting is both seemingly disorganized and labyrinthine. There are two floors. There is a large bar downstairs and a small one upstairs, although the smaller one is not always in use. The middle section of the downstairs contains booths along the walls. In the back third of the downstairs area is a dance floor area. On the first week night evening we observed about eight single men in their twenties standing at the downstairs bar, near the entrance. In the dance area eleven single women, seeming in their early twenties, were in small groups of two or three and one group of six. Several young men were also in the area, talking to the women, drinking, or talking to each other by the many pinball machines in the area. Both upstairs and downstairs there are many game machines as well as several machines dispensing free popcorn. There is a steady background of dance music.

The general atmosphere at That Place is set by the unusual decorations massed in all corners and areas of the building. All kinds of memorabilia hang from the walls. An old horse-drawn cart hangs behind the main bar. In the center of the front room is a gasoline pump that serves as an aquarium. Knickknacks hang on the walls.

T-shirts with "That Place" written across the front are on sale. Two tape recorders play music—one for the dance area and one for the other part of the bar.

The result is a sense of areas within areas, of niches and corners. Young men and women stand, sit, dance, talk, play, and make noise. In Friendly Al's the noise is background; here it is foreground. The bar and the bartenders occupy a small corner in this crowd. Waiters and waitresses are around, but the total impression is of groups and persons separated and decentralized. There are bouncers at the front and rear entrances, but they serve mostly to check age limits. Like its name, That Place has an anonymity about it that distinguishes it from the two bars described earlier.

That does not mean that it is without character. Indeed That Place is much like the bars described by Sherri Cavan as "pickup bars" (Cavan 1966, 178ff.). The presence of many single women without male escorts and of single men suggests this, and both conversation with patrons and observation established it. The youth of the clientele and its singles character are the outstanding features.

The management has provided a place in which its customers can play and organize their own activity. It is this absence of direct control over activities which makes That Place so different for our interests in drinking and driving. Unlike at the Club or Al's, the bartender at That Place can neither observe nor supervise his customers.

The Hermitage

Geography and Physical Setting

In many ways The Hermitage and That Place are very different kinds of bars appealing to very different clientele. Yet in both, the customers are the major source of normative controls over behavior. In both, the bar management is limited in what it can do to influence behavior and to affect drinking and driving. In neither is there a core of regulars who define and direct action.

The Hermitage is located in a large building at the edge of a large shopping center in a northern, suburban part of San Diego, just off an expressway exit. It occupies an entire building which has the appearance of a New England house. Most of the building is taken by the restaurant portion of the Hermitage. The bar is a separate area, occupying a distinct room in the building but connected to the restaurant by a short corridor.

The decor at the Hermitage is patterned after a version of a home of wealth, perhaps a movie version of a British drawing room or a Southern mansion. The entrance to both the restaurant and bar rooms is carpeted and set with large, upholstered furniture. The bar is itself well-lit (no need to adjust the eyes to dim light) and the wall paneled in attractive wood. There are ten to twelve tables as well as a well-polished wooden bar. The tables and chairs are arranged as conversational areas. The furniture is upholstered, and includes wing-backed chairs and small sofas. They are not institutional in appearance but rather are the kind that can be found in living rooms of homes. The walls are hung with prints of sport scenes (horses, hunting) and landscapes, and the floor is hard wood. The atmosphere is one of moderate expensiveness and decorum. The restaurant caters to a dinner crowd, with prices that are moderate to expensive for

San Diego (eight to twelve dollars for dinner in 1977). It is not a sand-wich or "quick food" outlet. The bar services its own crowd and, through waitresses, the restaurant.

Clientele

The clientele is part of the atmosphere at The Hermitage. As one of the bartenders put it, "This is a real nice place, here. Nice customers, nice at-mosphere."

The observer described it as "a fairly fashionable watering hole." Its clientele, more so than that of the other bars observed, appear to be established people of good income and occupational placement. The women are dressier than in any of the three other bars. Pantsuits are fancier and blue jeans conspicuous by their infrequent appearance. A number of the men wear suits and ties. At lunch and in the early evening the dominant crowd is young adult to middle-aged. The setting attracts couples or single-sex groups that have come for lunch or dinner or for a drink en route to some other place or event. While some "regulars" and loners sit at the bar, the bulk of the bartender's work is serving cus-tomers—those at the tables and those in the restaurant. The regulars are not as constant in attendance nor do they stay till closing as the regulars do at the Club and Friendly Al's. While the bar is clearly visible to the bartender, there is very little interaction with the customers at the tables. Al's heartiness and sociability to all in "his place" would be out of char-acter in the Hermitage.

The relatively tangential relation of customer to place continues even as the clientele changes in age and activities. During the lunch hour and afternoon, businessmen and housewives make up much of the crowd. Weeknights the after-dinner group and the transient are much in evi-dence, and the bar closes early. On the weekends there is a band and the crowd, younger and somewhat more single, arrives later, after 10:00 P.M. Then people stand around at the bar. Nevertheless, the appeal is still largely to couples, who spend their time talking to each other. Few seem younger than late twenties or early thirties. The lack of dancing space at the Hermitage further restricts its appeal to youth.

The Four Bars as Social Settings

It is possible to conceive of these drinking establishments as different sites of social influence and control. Patrons may, and generally do, drive to and from them. Each type of bar is a different kind of context within which the self, the peers, and the management affect behavior. The Club is a place in which a group of friends spend a great deal of their leisure; they *are* the setting and the management is one of them. At Friendly Al's, either Al or his hired bartender is central to the setting. That Place and The Hermitage are less active sources of potential influence. There the management provides a setting for the patrons to do "their own thing," serves drinks, and gets out of the way. How do these conditions affect the connection between drinking and driving?

COMPETENT DRINKING: THE DEFENSE OF THE SELF

Self-Presentation and Exculpatory Defenses: A Theoretical Perspective

Studies of drinking patterns usually distinguish between quantities consumed, identifying drinkers by some typology of heavy, moderate, light, and abstaining (Cahalan, Cisin, and Crossley 1969). We have found it more useful to utilize a classification that has emerged from our observations. It points not to the amounts that drinkers consume but to how they behave in response to their drinking. This distinction—between competent and incompetent drinkers—first came to the attention of one of us in observing blue-collar workers in Chicago bars and was also apparent to us in the San Diego observations (Kotarba 1977). It is a distinction essential to understanding how the people we observed conceived the drinking and driving event in relation to the investment of the self in that phenomena.

The underlying perspective of this study is derived from a general theoretical perspective in use among sociologists and social psychologists. In part it has arisen during the perusal and discussion of our materials; in part it emerges as I type these words.

The notion of the human self as reflexive, as an object to itself, is an old idea in sociology, captured and elucidated in the "old masters" George Herbert Mead (1934) and Charles Cooley (1902). It has also been given more recent implication in the rising interest in reflexivity discussed in the work of Alfred Schutz (1967). The root idea is that one's self is an object about which the human being can think and feel. One can experience self-love, self-hate, embarrassment, or pride in the imagination of the responses and interpretations of one's behavior as perceived by others. This interactive and reflexive aspect of human life emerges in a web of interpretations of the meaning of events for the maintenance, enhancement, or derogation of the self-conception of the social members involved.

In the 1950s and 1960s sociologists and social psychologists gave this orientation considerable attention by examining how it is that members attempt to control and influence the conceptions that others have about them and how external events impinge on such self-conceptions. The primary influence on both study and thought has been the work of Erving Goffman. The title of his first major work, *The Presentation of the Self in Everyday Life,* indicates the primary thrust of the interest in modes by which social members attempt to manage the self-impressions conveyed by their actions (Goffman 1956): "I shall consider the way in which the individual in ordinary work situations presents himself and his activity to others, the ways in which he guides and controls the impression they form of him, and the kinds of things he may and may not do while sustaining his performance before them" (Goffman 1956, preface).

This general perspective is linked to the drinking-driving phenomena and the instant study by the concepts of "ordinary risk" and "exculpatory defenses." These provide the theoretical and methodological underpinnings of our study of the bars described earlier.

Drinking—including drinking in bars—is part of the ordinary life situation of many Americans and for almost all of the people we observed. It is not an unusual or exotic event. Neither is driving an automobile, although some of our observees either could not or did not do so. Both drinking and driving, thought about separately, are customarily seen as behaviors involving risk. The drinker may lose control of himself, may embarrass himself or others, may insult others, may endanger health or livelihood. The driver may cause accidents and possibly death and, similarly, may be the victim of another driver's "faulty" driving or the dangers of adverse weather or environment. The fact that action is risk does not deter the competent person from engaging in it. Rather, one determination of the competence of people in American society is their ability to undertake "ordinary risks." The adult American who cannot or does not drive an automobile displays a lack of competence to cope adequately with ordinary risk. The member of a drinking group who refuses drinks displays incompetence in drinking. So too, however, do those who engage in the ordinary risks and fail to deal with the risks competently, who cause accidents, create embarrassment, hurt themselves or others, or are unable to perform the needed and expected routine acts of the daily agenda. It is in how the individual handles the risks of drinking and driving and of drinking-driving that the self is presented and one's moral status performed.

It is evident to me and to those we observed that many people at many times fail at the tasks of social assignments. "To err is human." The self swims in dangerous waters where sharks are ready to destroy it. People drink "too much" and make trouble for themselves and others. People drive "badly" and create accidents. All of us must face a world of audiences before whom we forget our lines, appear unclothed, and miss cues. We must deal with the fact of "fucking up." It too is a part of the normal and ordinary routines of life.

It is also the case, however, that the self is protected from the onus of incompetence by a series of acceptable excuses for poor performance. Borrowing a legal term, I will call these "exculpatory defenses," defenses which excuse an otherwise illegal act from punishment (Hart 1968, ch. 2). Among these are self-defense, insanity, duress, and, most recently, alcohol addiction. To be able to say, "I wasn't myself" is a normal and ordinary defense against the opprobrium of being labeled an incompetent and unworthy person. Illness in this society is (one form of) acceptable defense against the label of incompetence for not being at work or for performing poorly (Parsons and Fox 1952).

It is essential to recognize at the outset that the combination of drinking and driving is a normal event in our observations and, I assert, in American society. Roadside stop studies indicate that for every motorist arrested for driving under the influence of alcohol there are two thousand others on the road with blood alcohol level scores above the legal limit (U.S. Department of Transportation 1974, 2). In our observations most bar customers, whatever the amount they had consumed or their state of intoxication, drove to and from the site without occasioning comment by themselves, other patrons, or the bartenders. It is a normal event in the lives of bar patrons. The failure to drive after drinking is the event that needs to be explained. The competent drinker faces the risk of drinking *and* driving with safety. It is the failure to do so that needs to be excused.

Listening to excuses is an important methodological "device." It is the nature of norms that, being understood and "taken for granted," they are not verbalized. Excuses are necessarily ways of accounting for behavior as unusual. Therefore they indicate, by inference, what is seen as usual as not needing comment.

Understanding how the self is presented and defended is not only important in its own but is also a needed prelude to understanding how these systems of self-presentation operate in the different settings engendered by the bar types described in the earlier portion of this chapter.

The Presentation of Competent Drinking

Our observations of tavern patrons have led me to posit a dual system in the display of competence in drinking. The model of the competent drinker is the person who can drink in accordance with the standards of the setting and the group of which he is a part; he can "hold his own." Having done so he does not create trouble, provide embarrassment for himself or others, and will be able to manage himself and his transportation without causing accident or arrest. But drinking is inherently a risky and even unpredictable action. The drinker gets drunk and risks the loss of his competence. Competent people know when they have become incompetent and display their control and competence by that recognition. It is *not* imcompetent to limit drinking, to avoid driving, or to be drunk as long as the drinker can indicate that the determination of the state of incompetence is *his* self-recognition, that it is not forced upon him. Displaying self-understanding of incompetence is a display of competence. To "know enough to come in out of the rain" is a mark of adequacy of intelligence, just as knowing that one is ill and unable to meet usual obligations is a sign of a capable person in this society.

Drinking is itself evidence of meeting the demands of social membership. The amount and kind of alcohol used testifies to the social adequacy of the member. George is a central figure in the heavy-drinking group that frequents the Club. George comes into the Club almost every night and stays for between three and four hours. Ordinarily a heavy drinker of beer, whiskey, or both, sometimes he leaves early or drinks less than is usual. He says then that he must go to work early the next day. This "excuse" indicates that his norm demands keeping up as the mark of adequacy. George is part of the regulars at the Club who buy drinks by the "round," taking turns ordering and paying for drinks for the whole group. In one case, a "kid," aged twenty-four, enters into the round-buying. The observer reports:

> I was drinking a gin and tonic and George was drinking a screwdriver (orange juice and gin). The kid was getting drunk—it was pretty obvious by his slouching in the chair; he started slurring words and turning beet red. I was getting a backlog of drinks since we were buying rounds and this guy was drinking so fast. My drinks were two-deep and George had one-deep. George noticed the guy was getting drunk and commented that he had better slow down because he was getting drunk and to sort of space it out more. The guy continued to

drink although he did slow down and mostly talked about his past in
the military and working as a horse trainer.

George sees himself as a person who has the ability to drink a lot and
yet "hold his liquor." On another occasion, when the observer fell behind
in drinking, George took it as a sign that Paul was getting drunk. It was
the occasion for George to insist that he drive Paul's car.

Drinking at the level of the "crowd" without incurring more trouble
than your peers is the mark of competence, of "manhood." It is not the
total amount consumed but the ability to meet the norm without displaying incompetence that is essential. This consideration makes the issue
of the bartender's refusal to serve drinks to a customer a significant source
of antagonism and conflict.

Behavior after drinking is another sign of adequacy. Not the fact of
drunkenness but the nature of comportment and its possible interpretation as improper drunken behavior constitutes the delinquency. On one
occasion a young man came into the Club looking as if he'd slept in his
clothes. George said, "Oh, shit. This guy is drunk." He explained that
when sober this guy was "the nicest guy you'd ever want to meet" but
when drunk he was rude, offensive, and "very embarrassing to the management." Ed, the bartender, talked to him, and he left. Ed then explained
that they had an understanding. The customer was allowed to stay for
short periods of time as long as he didn't drink. Here is clearly the incompetent drinker. Jim, George's roommate, had decided not to go into
the Club again. One night the previous week he had gotten extremely
drunk and "made an ass of himself."

Driving after drinking is a part of the test of competence. I have already shown this in the way in which George interpreted Paul's slow
drinking as a sign of drunkenness and then "decided" to drive Paul's car.
The same condition applied in all the bars we observed. We were struck
by the limited discussion of drinking-driving and the normal occurrence
of it. The issue arose only in certain situations. When bluntly told that he
is in no condition to drive, the drinker is held up to an audience as incompetent. At Friendly Al's one night a couple in their late fifties were
leaving at about 1:55 A.M. "The man was making a lot of noise, laughing
and hollering on his way out. The young bartender hollered over to him
to be careful and to take it easy. The man stoically said that he was okay,
that *he 'can take care of himself'* [italics mine]. In hearing this, his wife
laughed loudly and said that her husband was okay because she was

doing the driving. The husband gave her a stern look as if embarrassed at her statement about his condition."

On another occasion at Al's, a customer appeared to people at the bar who knew him as too drunk to drive. He got up to leave. As he staggered off the barstool, one of the women hollered out that he should call a taxi. "Jim insisted that he was okay and able to drive home." The two women at the bar laughed and said that he "was really drunker than he figured." The female bartender entered the conversation and laughingly said that he was "too young a man to take a cab home." Here age appears as related to norms of competence. As we see later, older people can excuse incompetence in ways younger people cannot; the self is undamaged by that act (or perhaps the self is already damaged by age).

The Recognition of Incompetence

In saying that Jim was drunker than he claimed to be, the women at the bar were also derogating Jim's capacity for self-recognition of his incompetence, declaring him incompetent to recognize risks. The oft-repeated statement, "I know when I've had enough" is the drinker insisting on his ability to manage the risks, to distinguish between health and illness.

The following conversation, overheard in Friendly Al's one night, contains both the ingredient of the norm of competent drinking and the self-recognition that the drinker is in too risky a state to drive and can admit it. Notice how the state of incompetence is used to present the drinker as competent in reaching that state:

> First man: You're sure as shit driving home tonight.
> Second man: No, I ain't . . . You're the one who's drinking Seven-up. You gotta take care of your buddy, even when you don't have the balls to take care of him by drinking with him.
> First man: Don't worry, I'll get you home. I wouldn't strand you on the street at this time of night, would I?

The bartender at the Hermitage used a similar typology of competence to distinguish inabilities for risk. He differentiated between those customers for whom he feels he has to call cabs and "good customers who know when to quit drinking or know when to call a cab for themselves." In the first case he, the bartender, had to decide on their incompetence. The second are the "cool customers." They can "control their drinking and be aware of their incapacities."

We had expected that the Breathalyzer machine at Friendly Al's would be used extensively to provide self-evaluation of the drinker's risk. That was not so. Several evenings it was not used at all. In three- and four-hour observational periods, we never saw it used more than three or four times. Never did we see it used at closing time. Our understanding of the rejection of the machine is that it threatens the image of self-knowledge by which the drinker presents himself as adequate.

In steering conversation at Al's toward discussion of the Breathalyzer machine, our observer met with a discounting of its value. The machine undermined the display of adequacy self-recognition presents. "I asked Marty if he had ever used the Breathalyzer machine. He laughed at my question. He said that *he doesn't need a machine like that to tell him how much he's had*" [italics mine]. A little later the observer used the machine after his fourth drink. It registered a .11, and the machine displayed a large skull and crossbones in red, accompanied by a loud noise. The observer was embarrassed: "As I sat back down, Frank, a customer, laughed and said to me, 'Well, it looks like you'd better stay off the booze for a while.' Then he told me not to worry about it; that it's only a machine and that I looked as if I could handle a lot more booze than he saw me drink that afternoon."

The machine embarrasses. It contradicts the drinker's self-judgment of his state of risk-acceptance. Here it is important to repeat what I have asserted earlier. Drinking and driving is the normal way in which drinkers deal with the issue of getting to and from sites—from bar to bar or bar to a home. Experience shows the individual that almost all the times he has driven after drinking he has had neither an accident nor an arrest—the two risks that the drinking driver heightens by his action. He demonstrates his competence by recognizing his ability to drive and to know when he is in danger, when he ought not to drive or ought to take special precautions. Even George, at the Club, whose pride in his ability to hold his liquor has been stated, did ask the observer to do the driving one night, admitting that he had had too much. As one informant at That Place put it, "guys who get themselves in trouble while they're drinking and driving are just plain dumb and don't know how to handle themselves."

Are the studies of drinking and driving on which legislation is based really incorrect? Is drinking and driving not dangerous? In part the distinction must be made between risky events and riskier events. While increased amounts of alcohol, after a point, raise the risks of accident as compared to sobreity, the possibility of any single event ending in accident remains small (Borkenstein et al. 1964; Cameron 1978; Zylman 1975).

Faced with practical contingencies, which I will discuss later, the drinker's attitude is not without a rational basis. Faced with the practical problem of getting from one place to another, his experience tells him that most of the time he will make it without adverse outcomes. He displays his competence in showing that he has not gone beyond the state of drunkenness in which the risk is no longer reasonable and that when he has, he can recognize it and act like a reasonably drunken man should in a situation of greatly heightened risk.

There is also another aspect, however. Riding with the San Diego Police Department's drinking-driver squad several years ago, I became aware that one rule of thumb used by some police to "spot" drinking-drivers was to look for the overly careful driver. The premise here is that drivers who know they are "under the influence" adjust their driving to take account of their state of insobriety. This exists among those we observed. In conversations about drinking-driving some maintained that they were good drivers and did nothing special, although one said that he did drive particularly carefully because he is driving his buddy's car. Some take great pride in the ability to drive while under the influence. The bouncer at That Place commented on his customers: he said that he had never called a cab for a customer. ". . . most of the guys who come into That Place pride themselves on being good drivers, even when they're totally loaded . . . you just have to look at their 'wheels' . . . some of them do a lot of racing, on and off the road . . . it's kind of a touchy thing to talk to a customer about his ability to drive home, whether or not he's drunk or sober . . ." He thought that even some of the customers who are really drunked up have very little trouble driving home because of their expertise behind the wheel.

In his observations of blue-collar bars in Chicago, Joseph Kotarba had found a great deal of discussion of how to drive after drinking and how to avoid police. We had hoped in the San Diego study to gain knowledge of how the drinker adjusts his or her driving to the self-recognition of being under the influence and how it is that the drinker can recognize when he is competent to drive, when he needs to adjust his driving, and when he is in such danger as to avoid driving. "Taking care" is the term that is in frequent use, but its operational meaning is seldom specified. Minimizing "normal" risks appears in occasional references to driving slower and attending to rules. If there is a culture of the art of drinking-driving we were unable to find it in this study. It is ironic that in all the vast research and writing on drinking-driving, there is no study that has attempted to find out how people *do* drive after drinking.

There is one exception to our failure. We did find some mention of techniques for avoiding police arrest. Given the belief that competent people can "handle" the drinking-driver problem, arrest is a comment on competence. The implicit assumption is that adequate drinkers don't get caught. Driving along side streets, for example, is noted as one way of avoiding detection if the drinker sees himself as "under the influence." Driving slow on streets where traffic makes the presence of police difficult to spot is another. Avoiding "jerkiness" in driving and staying inside the lanes are others.

Throughout our observations we were struck by the general lack of comment about drinking-driving. When it emerges in conversation it does so in response to a particular occasion—a person who is thought to be in an especially dangerous state, a history of arrests, a group (women, aged, handicapped) who require special consideration. Drinking-driving is considered a normal event and adjunct to other activities. The risk is understood, but it is the risk that normal, adequate people cope with.

In the following colloquy between the observer and a twenty-one-year-old sailor at That Place the elements of drinking-driving are subordinated and set within a frame of other activities. To this sailor trouble with driving after drinking is a gross display of incompetence; it is the self derogated:

> (Bill comes into That Place once or so a week. He says that he also spends a lot of time at other, smaller bars in the general area. He uses a friend's car.)
> Bill said that the sailors are regularly briefed by the brass about problems with police and bars and so forth. He said that very few of the sailors really pay much mind to these briefings . . . the sailors don't really have much choice in either drinking or not drinking or driving or not driving . . . most of the guys had one thing on their minds— pussy. He said that there is really not much else to do around San Diego besides hopefully looking for women and drinking . . . the guys just won't give that up . . . he later said that its no big deal to be concerned about drinking and driving while being stationed in San Diego . . . you just have to be smart and look out for yourself like you have to do in all other places in San Diego . . . a sailor will get ripped off he just stays down on Broadway [main downtown street] and that the same guy who gets ripped off by the whores on Broadway and the shopkeepers on Broadway are the guys who are going to be stopped by the police for something as dumb as drunk-driving.

Exculpatory Defenses: Protecting the Competent Self

Our method is the reverse of the traditional question in drinking and driving studies. Why do people drink and drive? is not my question. That formulation makes the illegal act the deviant and problematic one. Instead I am operating from the premise which our observations support: *not* driving after drinking is the deviant and problematic act. What is to be explained is: Why *don't* people drink and drive? Action that accords with law and public, official norms is the problem, the behavior that in this case cries for explanation.

It is the problem which those we observed see in the bar interactions. The drinker, his friends, the bartender never were observed explaining their driving unless challenged not to, unless advised to forgo driving. It is the "abnormal" act that has to be defended, the threat to being presented as incompetent that must be coped with. It is here that exculpatory defenses, legitimate excuses, come into use. They permit the user to avoid the drinking-driving situation and yet display himself as an adequate drinker, able to cope with the responsibilities entailed by engaging in the risk of drinking in a sober world.

I want to be clear about the status of our data. We are not presenting behavior. My interest is in the typologies by which those we observe themselves understand and observe behavior, what I refer to as Schutz's first-order typologies, those in use by the actors themselves. In examining excuses I am not concerned with exhaustively describing or counting the situations in which drinkers drive. My interest is in answering the question: Are there ways in which the drinker can avoid driving and yet retain the display of adequate drinking ability? Such ways indicate the existence of typologies within the culture and available to persons. It does not indicate either the range of availability—to whom and where—nor the incidence of the use of such typologies. For example, we found that past arrest for drinking-driving was a legitimate excuse for not driving or for calling a taxi or for allowing others to drive. This does not mean that past offenders do not drink and drive or that past offenders customarily avoid driving. We did observe several situations in which drinkers we knew to be past offenders did drink and drive. What it does mean is that the past offender can preserve the display of self-competence even though he avoids driving.

Some of this discussion of exculpatory defenses has already been presented, and more of it will be presented in the discussion of how intimates and bartenders act to control the drinking-driving situation. Here I present some general types of excuses in use.

In one model case—the competent self—the drinker demonstrates that he can both drink and drive. The bartender at the Hermitage summed it up in explaining why he doesn't have much concern for an older customer who drinks heavily throughout the day: "Men must be responsible for their own drinking." In the second case the drinker recognizes his drinking has made him incompetent and admits it. Samuel is a frequent customer at the Club. He is not a chronic drunk, but when he does get drunk he is close to passing out. He allows himself to be driven home by others and puts up no resistance.

The second model, however, has several difficulties as a display of self and as a practical way of behavior. It depends on self-recognition, and thus ambiguity, and it does lessen the display of competence. It is a second level of competence. Other excuses also exist and are in use.

Responsible people, in the cultures we observed, are able to meet their self-responsibilities in assuming risk. When they are responsible to others, however, the degree of risk to be undertaken changes. The issue of drinking-driving when children are passengers did not, of course, arise in our data. However, within the general culture and within our experience with drinking-driving cases in court, in the mass media, and in the literature of publicity about it, the drinking-driver who takes risks with children is more heinous than one who risks only himself or other adults.

Responsibility to an abstract "society" or to others is too vague and unsituated a concept to emerge in conversation or action. What the drinker owes to others to avoid risk is more specific than that.

One repeated situation in which responsibility is stated is in the relations of men toward women. One of the bartenders at Friendly Al's reports an instance in which the Breathalyzer machine changed behavior. One late Saturday afternoon two young men, in their twenties, tried the Breathalyzer machine in a spirit of fun. Scoring .12 and .14 respectively, one said to the other, "Boy, we've got dates tonight. We'd better cool it." The date as control appears in several other places. The responsibility of wives for husbands and husbands for wives makes the inability of the drinker to carry out that responsibility a particularly notable dereliction of duty. At about 1:45 A.M. a wife was observed trying to get her reluctant husband to go home. She threatened to go home with someone else if he would not let her drive. At the end of their argument she shouted: "You fucking drunk! You're the one who forces me to have to take care of myself."

Another available exculpatory defense is the responsibility to work. It is often unclear whether it is a responsibility to self to avoid unemployment or to others to perform cooperative duties. I have already discussed this as an excuse for minimizing drinking. It also appeared as an excuse for shifting the driving responsibility. A wife was observed to get her husband to let her drive on the grounds that though they are both tired and have been drinking he must get up early the next morning for work. Using a similar logic one of the bartenders at the Hermitage, in describing the daytime and lunchtime drinkers, points out that afternoon work keeps them from drinking too much and can excuse some others because even though they drive they are marvelously able to handle heavy drinking. "Mark said that most of the men do not drink too much during the day because they have to drive, especially the salesmen."

There are special categories of people for whom the norms of competent driving demanded of drinkers are less pressing. Women, the elderly, past convicted offenders for drinking-driving, the "problem drinker" all receive special consideration and can be excused from displaying the level of competence expected of others.

Several such problem drinkers were observed at the Club. These were known to the bartender and to a number of the customers as people who came and drank to the point of passing out, woke up, and drank again. These problem drinkers called a taxi and made no effort to drive. In calling them "problem drinkers" I am using the sense of those in the bar that these people were incompetent, accepted their incompetence, and were given special consideration. Harold illustrates how the display of this persona permits him to handle the drinking-driving problem in a way which maintains his esteem in the eyes of his audience:

> Harold is a guy who's been described as worth several million dollars in property . . . according to what I'd heard he was pretty powerful in local politics . . .
>
> Harold claimed that he'd had five arrests on 502s. What he usually does is get drunk in the morning, passes out in the car or takes a taxi home, wakes up and starts drinking until he passes out again . . . tonight he only had five drinks . . . by the time he left he was totally drunk. (There was much joking about how Harold would buy the bar and fire the bartender if he refused to serve him.)
>
> After Harold left I was the only one in the bar and talked to Frank, the bartender, about Harold, confirming that much of what Harold said was true. I asked him about how he handled Harold's drinking. Frank's attitude was that Harold was basically *a harmless drunk*

[italics mine]. He always knew that Harold would not go out and drive
drunk but that he would either sleep it off in the car or take a taxi or
have a friend drive.

On one evening we observed that Harold drove to the Club in his
camper, got drunk as usual, and then slept in the camper parked on the
parking lot in front of the bar.

It is also the case that drinkers can use past arrests for drinking-driving
as explanations for their concern with the problem in a given situation.
It can make their avoidance of driving understandable and reasonable.
The principle here appears to be that where the risk is greater or the consequences more detrimental, the competent person recognizes it and acts
with greater circumspection than the norm.

Whether or not this principle "explains" the special position of women
and older people is not clear. But what is clear is that both groups constitute categories that are excused for the avoidance of driving and that can
entail special responsibility on others. Bartenders were observed asking
other customers to take an older person or a woman home when they appeared too drunk to drive safely, a less "touchy" situation than suggesting
similar help to a young man. Women in the Club have greater license to
"choose" how much they want to drink. Both in the Club and in Friendly
Al's women received a special status. (That Place was more patently a
"pickup" bar and presented a very different kind of status for women.)

An observation at Al's illustrates how categorical differences can operate. One night an "old man" staggered over to the bar from the back of
the room and said something to one of the women which caused her
anger. Some of the men at the bar told her to ignore him "because he's
old and drunked up." A few minutes later the bartender did something
that the observer had not seen before. He told the old man he thought
he's had enough and should make his way home. The old man did not object, and the bartender said he was going to call a cab, which he did. It
was also typical at Friendly Al's for some of the young women not to
drive but to take taxis.

In one sense the special status of women is observed in instances of
departure from the special role of women drinkers. This is seen in the observation of two women who entered the Club late one evening, one in
her late twenties and the other around fifty. They had been drinking elsewhere and had come to the Club when the Shack closed. (One of them
said that she'd been "loaded" for the last several nights, would get
"loaded" again tonight and call in sick tomorrow.) They annoyed the

bartender by their abrasiveness and by demanding that he keep the bar open after 2:00 A.M. Though the men at the Club do not swear in front of women, these women often used words like *fuck* in their conversation. In a bar ordinarily solicitous of women driving when they were drunk, they were permitted to leave without any warning, remarks of concern, or offer of help.

The same independent status of women is seen in That Place. There an offer by a male to drive a woman home is interpreted as a sexual proposal and acceptance considered an assent.

Women and older men constitute major groups toward whom customers and bartenders display a special solicitousness. Children, of course, would probably also be included in such categories, but the prohibition against serving minors (strongly enforced and strongly obeyed by the bars we observed) finesses that problem. There is some hint of a norm of greater solicitousness of men toward young men ("kids") or women toward younger women, in references to the "kid" character of a youngish drinker in explaining his incompetence or in the remark of one woman at That Place about her younger sister. Told that she was in the back throwing up, Jenny laughed at this information and said her sister was "too young to mix in cheap dope with booze." Nonownership or use of cars was seen among older men and women, not among the other men. Harry, a regular bartender at Friendly Al's, worries about the older customers who live nearby and have a long way to walk or are walking along the street at night. Sometimes, he says, he drives them home after closing time.

I want to remark that I have described the display of the competent self without much reference to what the audience of other patrons and bar employees do to structure, or control, the stage of action. Nor have I indicated the shape, size, or limits and opportunities afforded by different kinds of settings. The idea of the competent self, the ways in which display is affected and incompetence excused is not set aside. I will carry it along in the further description of the stage of action and the way in which the self acts in relationship with others.

The Furnished Stage: Practical Contingencies in Drinking-Driving

The self does not display itself on an empty stage. All of us live in a world of practical contingencies which constrain and limit what we can and cannot do, which make for costs in attempts to achieve benefits. "There is no free lunch" has become the watchword of the economics-minded who daily point us toward a world of scarcities. Some of these are matters of the interpretive world of the drinkers we observed, as in the demands of norms of competence. Some of these are the hard facts of environment, aspects of life at an institutional or physical character seen by the individual and his friends as beyond their control. Some are not even perceived. It is these aspects of the institutional and physical environment which the drinker sees as elements beyond control or taken for granted that occupy my attention here. To some extent these do emerge in what we observed, but in many cases they are conspicuous by their absence.

For example, one alternative to driving after drinking is to stay in the barroom—sleeping, talking, or doing anything but continuing to drink. In all of our observations of bars at closing time this never occurred for more than a few minutes. No one was heard to request it, and the only resistance to closing the bar was couched in demands for continued drinking service. In American life, bars are never in use without service of alcohol available nor are they permitted to remain available to customers after a legal closing time. Historically the congruence of bars and inns has occurred and still does in some societies. It is a practical contingency of drinking in the American bar that the drinker will have to leave at some time during the night. He cannot stay there and "sleep it off." That is clearly recognized by everyone we observed.

San Diego is an automobile city. Distances are far, and many facilities located on the premise that patrons will drive to them. Three of the four observation sites were located next to parking lots. (Friendly Al's was the exception.) Customers engage in a good deal of barhopping and go from one bar to another in the course of an evening. Even the clublike group at the Club shuttle back and forth between the Shack and the Club, using cars most of the time, although the Shack is within walking distance. Even at Friendly Al's, the one bar without a parking lot, most customers drive. The neighborhood pub of hallowed British fame is not the southern California bar for whose customers the automobile is the essential way to get from one place to another, from home to bar and bar to home, although some bar patrons do end the evening with an early breakfast. Here too driving is necessary. Few restaurants are open beyond eleven o'clock or midnight. Only in one site (That Place) was there a restaurant open after midnight and within close walking distance.

In some cases barhopping is used to maintain a widened set of social networks. George always buys a round of drinks when he comes into the Club, and he does the same elsewhere. Frequently he left the Club, went to the Shack, bought a round there, stayed a while, and either returned to the Club or went home. He has at least two "homes away from home." Without "wheels" his social life is greatly narrowed.

In other cases barhopping reflects the specialization of bars. That Place has a particular appeal to young singles. One young man told us that he lives in Chula Vista (approximately twenty miles away) but comes to That Place and nearby similar bars about three or four times a week because the bars in Chula Vista and National City haven't too many girls in them. One of the bouncers told us that, as he observes it, women seldom drive alone. They leave with one or more girls or with a man.

The ecology of San Diego is then one in which the walker in the city is an image of another time and another place. The auto is to southern California as the horse was to the cowboy of American folklore. Here are two excerpts from protocols of observations at the Hermitage. Both involve driving distances of at least thirty miles, not including the drive to and from initial starting points:

> As they were talking they mentioned that they began the evening at Mission Valley. While they were at Mission Valley they "hit" all of the bars there, in hopes of meeting some women . . . The bartender suggested that, after they leave The Hermitage, that they move over to the Winery in Solana Beach . . . much more of a singles, pick-up kind of bar.
>
> I asked Joe if he often goes out cabareting on a weekend. He said that dancing and drinking is a regular activity for him and Shirlee . . . I then asked him if the Hermitage was his first stop for the evening. He said no; that he and Shirlee had already been at the Winery. I asked if they were planning on going on to any other places after the Hermitage. Joe said that they would probably go to the Smooth Kitten in Encinitas and then probably to the Hermitage in Clairmont, where they have disco and dancing.

The couple in the above excerpt planned to go to four different bars in one evening, sampling the different entertainers, and, of course, drinking at each and driving between them.

Even at the Club and at Friendly Al's, where barhopping may be less frequent, observations of what customers did at closing time and occasionally at other times showed that most got into cars after leaving.

Alternatives to Driving

What are the alternatives to driving an automobile oneself as a way of transportation other than walking? Taxis, besides being considered a sign of incompetent drinking, are costly. Distances are far in a physical environment of low density where many facilities are predicated on automobile travel. If the drinker has driven to the bar by himself, he must arrange a return the next day to recover the car, thus doubling the cost. The individuality of financing taxis is a fundamental fact of transportation. The total cost is born by the drinker, and there is no institutional arrangement for pooling groups. With some definite exceptions, transportation is the responsibility of the drinker. At no time in our observations or in our experiences as members of this society was transportation considered a public responsibility, nor did any of our observees ever suggest it might be otherwise.

One of the other practical contingencies of transportation for drinkers is the total absence of mass transportation in the late evening or early morning in the areas of all the bars studied. Never in our observations did anyone suggest or contemplate taking a city bus to get home. The lack of mass transportation as an alternative to self-motoring is taken for granted.

Taxis also possess the practical disadvantage of risking the public display of incompetence. While it may be possible to phone for a taxi without calling attention to oneself, the drinker's condition of drunkenness often requires the aid of others, especially the bartender, to place the call. The practical conditions of meeting the cabdriver accentuates the display of incompetence. The driver customarily enters the bar and loudly announces that Mr. X has called for a cab or loudly asks, "Who called a cab?"

There is one exception to the individual character of responsibility for transportation. During our observational period, both the Club and Friendly Al's arranged outings for their customers—one to Ensenada (a Mexican town about two hours away) and the other to a sports event. Similar outings are held several times a year. Customers joining the outings were taken by bus to and from the bar. A bartender at Al's describes it and indicates how it relates to drinking-driving and to the economy of the bar:

> I told Gabe that I figure the drinkers would really appreciate not
> having to hassle with driving themselves to and from the park. Gabe
> said that this is the exact reason that they get the bus, so that a guy
> does not have to worry about getting too stiffed up before, during and
> after the game. He said that most of the time the bus will not only
> carry the drinker but will be well fortified with several cases of beer
> and some sandwiches for the ride. He said that at the end of the game
> everybody will return to Al's and will sit and drink some more.

A fuller treatment of the alternatives to drinking-driving is beyond the scope of this report. It would have to examine the sources of the risk of accident which drinking-driving entails. For example, as the remarks of the bartender at the Hermitage suggest, the fact that the bulk of heavy drinking in bars occurs at night is important. Given the lighter traffic than in the day, the riskiness is reduced. More important, the extent to which the automobile is designed and constructed to withstand collisions and to be safely driven by fools and drunkards is itself crucial to the contingencies faced by the drinker.

The practical contingencies which are recognized and which vary for the drinker constitute another category of excuses. They affect the degree of risk or the alternatives available. The drinker who does not own a car or cannot drive has a legitimate (competent) excuse for not driving or for using a taxi. This is qualified by the importance of driving as a sign of competence.

There were two classes of these practical contingencies observed. In one class an unusual or nonordinary event is pointed to as explanation for failure to drive. In at least two cases, men were seen as ill. In both cases they had just recovered from surgery. This fact was used by them or by others at the bar to explain their nondriving that evening. In another case, the automobile was itself "sick." George, who prided himself on his drinking and driving abilities, asked Paul to drive him home one night, explaining that he had "auto trouble."

The second class are those special categories of people who do not own a car or cannot drive one. Again, this was only displayed by the same groups who had special exemption from the norms of group drinking levels and self-responsibility for driving: women, old men, and "problem-drinkers." These constituted the only classes who admitted or about whom others mentioned that they did not drive or did not own an automobile. The bartender at Friendly Al's told us some of the young women used taxis because they were alone and their husbands had the car for the evening. These categories, as we have seen, are also the ones for whom intervention by the bartender, in advising the avoidance of driving, is easiest.

Law as a Practical Contingency

Does the fear of arrest deter drinkers from driving? There are two ways in which we tried to answer this question through observations and conversations. In one form, we looked for instances in which the possibility of arrest was discussed—in the abstract, as a reason, or excuse, for not drinking or driving, in relation to a past offense or pending legal action. In a second way of asking the question we looked for instances in which the fear of arrest was accompanied by discussion of ways of avoiding it without curtailing driving.

In general, the police do represent a potential source of trouble for the drinker, but it is a vague and general one, part of the expected risks of drinking and not a matter of great comment or advice. (This is less so where past offenders are involved.) The drinkers we observed live in a world of risk. The police who patrol the roads are an enemy to be watched for but not an especially feared one.

We were surprised by this lack of attentiveness to the possibility of arrest and potential fine or even jail or loss of license to drive. In his study of Chicago bars, Kotarba had found the prospects of arrest for drinking-driving an active part of bar conversations. There was a distinctive subculture that transmitted information about the police, the courts, lawyers, and drinking-driving. Drinkers passed on lore about how to avoid getting caught, how to con police, what lawyers to hire if caught, how to get off if the case got to court.

No such lore and legend were found in the bars we observed. Almost all of the discussion of the law came to us by initiation of the topic into conversations by the observer. As pointed out earlier, even then none of the drinkers gave any indication of knowledge that San Diego had special police cars assigned to the detection and apprehension of drinking drivers, despite the fact that two of our sites, Friendly Al's and That Place, were regularly patrolled by the drinking-drivers squad every night. In discussing the special squad with a sailor, one of us was told that the recruits are warned to look out for the police when they go into town, as well as the prostitutes, pimps, and rip-off artists always on the lookout for sailors. But they are not told about the drinking-driving squads.

As a practical contingency the drinkers with whom we discussed the police see themselves as involved in a game of wits and luck. Harold, the "harmless drunk" at the Club, described with glee how the police waited for him to leave the parking lot as they saw him stumble and stagger to his camper. (He went to sleep in the camper.) He says that the police were there at 2:00 A.M. when he left the bar and were still at the parking lot at 6:00 A.M. He wasn't about to budge because he feared he'd get a ticket. He also bragged about his political pull, claiming that though he had been cited twice for DUI, both times it was *null prossed*. Harold said in another context, however, that he'd been arrested five times for drinking-driving. This was the only instance we saw or heard about in which fear of arrest directly deterred the drinker from driving.

Past arrest does make for an adequate excuse to advise the drinker to change habits or avoid driving. Jenny was overheard at That Place telling her friend that she'd been fined sixty dollars for the ticket she'd received two weeks before. She said that she was really drunk that night and was lucky the cop didn't make her get out of the car so that she was only ticketed for a "Hollywood stop" (not coming to a complete stop at the stop sign). Wrote the observer: "Her friend laughingly told Jenny that she should 'lay off the sauce' before she finds herself in jail on one of her partying nights."

Jenny seemed to have no inclination to respect that advice but was trying to fight the ticket because it would make her third that year and she was afraid of losing her license. Talking about it to one of us, she attributed her record to "bad luck" but explained her avoidance of a drinking-driving charge as her skill: "Jenny said that really has her act down pat in dealing with cops, and that she really knows how to act sober when she gets stopped."

Except for the formal suggestion of naval officials to recruits to watch out for the cops and to hire a lawyer if arrested for drinking-driving, very little information about drinking-driving is processed through informal social organization before the offender finds himself in the arms of the law. Where it arises the people to whom we talked in the bar study attributed arrests either to bad luck or to incompetence—a first order of incompetence in not driving well and a second order of incompetence in not knowing how to avoid arrest. Jenny "explained" her arrest for a traffic offense as "bad luck" but her avoidance of a DUI charge as a result of knowing how to appear sober. A sailor employed at the Naval Recruitment Training Center told us that the recruits run into the most problems with the cops because they know too little about the cops in San Diego or about driving around in San Diego to keep them out of trouble.

Law is a risk which the drinker faces, not much more qualitatively risky than the other viccissitudes the average person faces. It is a world of risk which the average competent person navigates safely with a little bit of luck. Even if luck or competence fail, the consequences are annoying but not grossly different from normal events of risk within the law. It is usually not sufficient to force the drinker into behavior which entails great cost, inconvenience, embarrassment, or changes in living styles of central significance to him.

Such matters of practical contingency exist in interaction with existent structure by which the self is enacted. Of all the practical contingencies the one that emerged as most salient is the existence of other people whose relation to the drinker makes their intervention in his actions possible, feasible and acceptable. This is what I turn to next.

THE SOCIETY OF INTIMATES

It has been an axiom of the dramaturgical analysis of human behavior that "front stage" actions differ from those "backstage" (Goffman 1956, 66–86). Because behavior is oriented toward an audience it takes on a public display considerably different from the private; the housewife prepares the living room for company, the sergeant gets the platoon in order before inspection, the drinker displays competence before the audience of the barroom. "Stage" however is itself a metaphorical expression—a site for appearing in public. Much depends on who constitute the audience and their relation to the actor. Intimacy is a quality of openness to embarrassment more than a matter of physical closeness. As the many accounts of the shyness and strain of the wedding night constantly attest, the man and woman who make love for the first time to each other are as much acting "front stage" and in public as the theatrical performer. Between human beings there are layers of defensiveness and performance—orientation which can be shed between intimates as the Victorian woman shed her petticoats on retiring.

The disposition to play a role of competence has its most compelling impact where the drinker confronts an audience whose judgment of him depends to some degree on their view of his competence. The intimacy of friends, lovers, spouses, or other significant people is complicated by the degrees of intimacy between them. They may be part of the audience before whom the driver wishes to display competence; yet as they are close to the drinker—peers, friends, intimates—they can, and even should, feel the responsibility to intervene when they judge the drinker to have passed the point of competence.

The more intimate the relationship, the more it can accept the drinker as incompetent and tear down the front of competence with no regard for the tissue of exceptions, excuses, and defenses by which the self is dramatized as competent to cope with the world of drinking and driving. It is the essential character of family and primary relationships not only that the person is loved unconditionally, the self unbounded by defenses, but also that the person can be hated, excoriated, embarrassed, and insulted without the relationship being necessarily destroyed. Husbands and wives, lovers and mates, close associates can say things to each other that would make other relationships shrivel and die. That is also what it means to be "backstage" rather than "on stage."

Both aspects of the staging of the self—its being "on stage" and "off-stage"—must be perceived if our account of how the peer group operates is to be understood. Despite the modal norm of the self-competent drinker and driver responsible for his own actions, there *is* intervention; there *is* criticism; there *is* advice and embarrassment; the self is not permitted to exist in a world of its own script.

Borrowing two terms first used by Everett Hughes to describe the rights and responsibilities of professions, I am saying that when the drinker is in a society of his intimates, that group has the *mandate* to preserve his display of competence but also the *license* to destroy it where it seems to threaten him or themselves (Hughes 1958). Mandates imply obligations; licenses imply liberties.

I use the term *intimate* rather than *peer* in order to emphasize the character of the relationship rather than the status of the parties involved. However, below I will refer the general process by which others attempt to influence or control the drinker as "peer intervention." In this section, however, I do not include the bartender, except where his intervention appears in the guise of an intimate. The basis of legitimate right or duty rests on the degree of intimacy between the two people involved, rather than an official, legal, or managerial one. The test is a practical one: imagine what the interaction would signify were it between two "strangers."

The Bar as Creator of Intimacy

In one sense the bar is itself an arena within which relations between customers are defined in terms of closer intimacy than exists in nondrinking situations in American society. The major reason I selected the bar as a research site was the easy availability of people to each other, the lack of strong restraints against engaging each other in conversation and the role of alcohol in dissolving reserve between strangers. It is a place where self-expressiveness is quicker to reach action and display than in soberer places. It is a place where friendliness can be fostered; it is also a place where hostility and antipathy are closer to expression. Both help and abuse are there as tangible possibilities. It is the presence of other people formed into a social group that sets the scene for possible interventions. As one customer at the Hermitage put it, in discussing the helpful constraints on his drinking and his driving when with a date or when alone:

"just having someone there to tell you when to stop and having someone there to do the driving at the end of an evening [is helpful]."

Bars like the Club and Friendly Al's encourage and develop groups of "regulars"—people who come into the bar several times during the week and come to constitute a recurrent group. One of us estimated that at most times Al's customers were 50 percent regulars. The group of regulars at the Club were the base of much of the observations there and have already been described. At the Club the pattern of each member buying rounds not only acted to control the amount of drinking and put pressure on members to drink but also was the means by which the drinker created the solidarity with others that defined him as "in" the group. "Rounds" are tangible obligations to stay and to uphold one's duties to others.

Peer Intervention: The Mandate to Help

In the vernacular of American language the incompetence of the drunk is a test of the charity of his intimates. It is noteworthy that people bolster their claim to intimacy with others by statements such as "I diapered you" and "I held your head when you'd too much to drink." George's roommate, embarrassed by the behavior he displayed when drunk at the Club, was "even sort of mad at George for letting him get that drunk."

The mandate to help your buddies is twofold: a mandate to help with the driving and a mandate to help preserve the display of self as competent. George's roommate was embarrassed by his behavior when drunk and felt his buddy, George, should have helped to prevent it. We saw friends help drinkers protest they were not too drunk to be served, to define the situation as bartender's obstinacy. We saw three regulars help a drunken fourth by carrying him to his car to sleep it off.

The canon of mutual aid can be called upon by the drinker, by his intimates, and even by bartenders to help one of "their bunch." One of us recorded an incident at the Club in which five men came in, already visibly drunk. The oldest was about thirty-five. There was a younger man with him, about twenty-seven or twenty-eight. Both were obviously "smashed" but the younger one even more so. The five men were buying rounds, the first by one of the soberer of the group. The young one wanted to buy the next round, but the bartender wouldn't let him because he'd had too much to drink.

> It was one of the few times I'd seen Frank actually refuse drinks.
> The older guy, who was a little bit soberer but not a whole lot,

> claimed that he would take care of the "kid" and drive him home. . . .
> Frank then allowed him to buy a round of drinks for everyone. The
> direct quote from Frank earlier was "You already have enough to
> drink. Let it ride for a while. Besides, you're always drunk on your
> ass." His friend's direct quote was "Frank, I'll take care of him, Lord
> knows he has taken care of me often enough."

The "kid" (note how he has been turned into an object of obligation
and legitimately lessened competence) was not only permitted to continue drinking but also to preserve his display of competence by holding
up his end of the rounds-buying obligation. Further, he is to be helped in
getting home.

Bartenders can utilize the mandate to help by calling on customers to
help transport fellow regulars. This was pointed out earlier in the ways in
which women and old people are special obligations. Bartenders at Al's
have been observed to ask fellow patrons to take someone home. Frank
did this with George one night:

> Richard (age about 50) came in, sat down at the bar and kind of
> went into a sleep, would occasionally wake up but go back into his
> sleep. Frank served him a beer but commented about how he'd had
> enough to drink and definitely would not drive home. . . . "He's not a
> chronic drunk but when he does get drunk he drinks heavily to the
> point of passing out." Near the end of the evening when George and I
> were leaving, Frank asked George if he would be willing to drive
> Richard home. George said that of course he wouldn't allow his good
> friend Richard to drive home in his present condition. Richard put up
> no fight at all. He knew George quite well and gave him the keys. We
> carried Richard out of the bar, got him in the car and George and he
> drove back to his place. I followed in my car to pick up George and
> we left the car there with the keys under the seat so that Richard
> would not drive off.

Richard's incompetence is displayable to George, but similar incompetence, as we have seen, is not so readily to be shown to everyone. (Note
how George defines Richard as "my good friend.") One's friends and intimates have also to attempt to preserve the display of competence where
possible, as the older man did for the "kid" above. Two incidents at
Friendly Al's show the complexity of actors operating on different stages
at the same time. One occurred at closing time as a couple probably in
their late fifties got up to leave. They had been drinking all night, and the
man was making a lot of noise, laughing and hollering on his way out.

"The young bartender hollered over to him to be careful and to take it easy. The man very stoically said that he was okay; he can take care of himself. In hearing this his wife laughed quite loudly and said that her husband was okay because she was doing the driving. The man looked at her kind of sternly as if embarrassed at her statement about his condition. The couple then quietly walked out." His embarrassment and "stern look" is the sign of his wife's breaking her mandate to support, or at least not undermine, his display of competence.

In another incident the temporary bartender acted to preserve the "front" of a regular customer through handling the display of the customer toward other patrons yet intervening in a "backstage" interaction:

> At about 1:30 A.M. Tim actually began mentioning that he should really be getting on, because his wife would start to worry about him at this point. As he was speaking, both Harriet and Amy grabbed onto his arms and told him that he should stick around a little bit longer. Harriet joked about how Tim could not possibly leave the presence of such beautiful women. It was at this point that Dana (the female temporary bartender) bought the last house round for everybody, including myself. Tim actually did sit for another ten minutes or so and finished his house drink quite quickly, but again said that he really had to get going. As Tim staggered up off his bar stool, Harriet hollered out that Tim should call a cab to get him home. Tim insisted that he was okay and able to drive home. Amy and Harriet both started laughing at how Tim was really drunker than he figured. At this point Dana entered into the conversation and laughingly said that Tim was too young of a man to take a cab home. Dana said that Tim could take care of himself but would probably have a better ride home if one of the two ladies would take him home with her. We all laughed at this.

Having saved Tim's face in front of the two fellow-customers, the bartender now treats him in a different fashion, on a different stage: "When Tim did stand up and began saying his goodbyes to everyone at the bar, Dana did go up to him and quite seriously and quietly asked him if he wanted her to call a cab for him. Tim quite soberly answered that he appreciated the offer but thought that he was really okay. Dana did not pursue the topic further but simply told Tim to be careful and to come back soon."

Tim was not a new or transient customer. Dana knew him well enough to be able to comment on his marital problems after Tim had left.

Peer Intervention: The License to Abuse

In the incident cited earlier, in which the wife embarrassed the husband by contradicting his "front," she was considered to be acting abusively. It is a mark of intimate relationships that between the parties there is both love and hate; both help and abuse. Abusive relations did occur among strangers and slight acquaintances during our observations, but they always meant trouble—violence or the threat of violence. Abuse occurs, in the framework of this study, where the "front" of the drinker is directly attacked and his competence impugned. Intimates are people to whom incompetence can be displayed and insult accepted without impairing the self irreparably. Mel, a customer at Al's, tells us that his present girlfriend, Maureen, once locked him in his car and drove off in her car, carrying his car keys. She had tried to keep him from driving because she felt, over his protests, that he was too drunk to drive.

The following scene illustrates how the mix of the mandate to help and license to abuse can operate:

> At approximately 1:45 A.M. Fern mentioned to Alex: "Let's go Alex, I want to get out of here." Alex did not respond immediately to her request, for he was again down with his head on the bar. Fern then shook Alex and told him again that she wanted to go home. I noticed that Alex's keys were sitting on the bar along with his money and his change. The following is a close reconstruction of the rest of their conversation before leaving Al's:
>
> Alex: "Yeah, let's go home now."
> Fern: "Oh no, you're not driving. Give me the keys."
> Alex: "Bullshit, it's my car, lady, and I'm gonna get us home."
> Fern: "I'm not riding with you. If you drive, I swear I'll go home with someone else, and you can bet that it will probably be a long ride home."
> Alex: "Why you cheap whore. . . . ."
> Fern: "You fucking drunk! You're the one who forces me to have to take care of myself."
>
> By this time the argument was getting quite loud and the bartender came over to quiet them down. (He talked very quietly to them and I couldn't hear what was said.) In any event they got up to leave, I noticed that Fern grabbed the keys just before they got up and that Alex didn't object.

The observer followed them out to the street and watched Fern lead Alex to the car, although he insisted it was parked elsewhere. She unlocked the passenger side and opened it for Alex. He stumbled on getting in, and she had to hold the door for him. She got in on the driver's side, they discussed something too faintly for the observer to overhear, and then Fern drove the car away.

Wives, Lovers, and the Place of Women

I have repeatedly drawn attention to the special significance of the male-female intimacy in defining mandates and licenses around drinking and driving. The woman with whom the man has an intimate relationship is a source of responsibility for the male. He should be competent to drive her home. But the protest against her intervention is often a sham, a display to the bar audience. It is contradicted by the behavior in which she takes the keys and drives. The expectation of the greater sobriety of the female remains a folk belief in this segment of American society.

The case of Dave and Debra will serve as illustrative of the relationship frequently observed. Dave and Debra are regulars at Friendly Al's. Dave is a pool player by avocation and spends much of his time at Al's drinking and shooting pool, while Debra, who is with him, usually sits nearby also drinking but neither as much nor as frequently as Dave. Dave also represents Al's as part of the pool team in competition with other bars.

Debra acts as a kind of "mascot" for the pool team, arranging schedules and taking care of equipment. The observer asked her if her duties ever involve her in having to drive the guys around:

> Debra said that she often drives home after an evening of shooting pool because the men tend to get carried away with each other, mostly in their post-game celebrations. . . . I later noticed that Dave simply allows Debra to drive him home after leaving Al's, without any apparent negotiation between them.
>
> I asked Debra if she ever felt any responsibility for Dave and his driving home after a date with her. Debra says that Dave is a very strong man and can take care of himself . . . I mentioned that I remembered seeing her drive Dave home on several occasions. She said that sometimes she will drive Dave back to her apartment because he has a long ride after he leaves her. On this particular evening Dave did the driving. He appeared quite sober after drinking only two or three drinks the entire evening. The only times I have seen Debra drive Dave are when he gets drunk, which is never while he is playing (competitive) pool. I have seen her drive when they stop at Al's after playing pool at another bar.

At the Club, Al's, and the Hermitage, women driving men passengers was by no means unusual. Counts of driving at closing times showed that among couples, women drove anywhere from one-quarter to one-half of the time. The display of competence and responsibility inside the bar was belied by the behavior inside the automobile.

The Singles Bar

That Place is a contrast to the social order developed at the Club and Friendly Al's and observed among the patrons at the Hermitage. There are regulars at That Place, people who are seen several times, but the absence of a bar atmosphere makes the setting one in which patrons are thrown to their own resources. The sense of fluidity, chaos, and open space mitigates the physical closeness through which the bar can create quasi-intimacy over time. Above all, the relations between men and women are decidedly different. As observed earlier, the single character of That Place means that mixed couples are unlikely to arrive in That Place. Women do arrive in twos and threes and men in small groups, as well as alone. The observer had the impression that men and women who "connected" for the evening drank considerably less than those who did not. For one thing, they left earlier.

An analysis of this and chapter seven are found at the conclusion to chapter seven.

Chapter Seven

The Bar as a Context of Social Control

Joseph A. Kotarba and
Paul K. Rasmussen, co-authors

A fundamental fact about the bar in American life is that it is an economic establishment. It operates in a market economy in which budgets, expenses, profits, and losses are essential considerations. Barowners are in the business of buying and selling liquor.

If the bar is a business enterprise it is not only that. If it operates in a market economy it does so in a limited and special manner. Liquor stores are also in the business of buying and selling liquor. Clothing stores also sell goods. The bar is a particular kind of setting for the sale and use of alcohol. Alcohol is a particular kind of commodity. Bars operate in a legal environment considerably different from the sale of most goods and services in the United States. Their service is everywhere in the United States limited in time to particular hours and in clientele to adults.

In this chapter I will emphasize three aspects of bar life as crucial to an understanding of how bars and bartenders affect the drinking-driving phenomenon. The character of the bar as a business investment, the setting of the bar as a place of public leisure, and the perception of alcohol as a potentially "dangerous" substance combine in particular fashion to make the relation of dispenser to client unlike such relations in other segments of service industries or retail establishments. The problems of social control are magnified in the legal and behavioral climate which the use of alcohol produces.

THE BAR AS A CREATOR OF INTERACTIONS

Bars, as Sherri Cavan suggests, are particular kinds of settings in which some behavior prohibited elsewhere is permissible. Public bars are, in Erving Goffman's phrase, "open regions" (Goffman 1963a, 132). Using this concept, Cavan describes public drinking places as places of greater sociability than is found in other public areas: "those who are present, acquainted or not, have the right to engage others in conversational interaction and the duty to accept the overtures of sociability proffered to them . . . sociability is the general rule in the public drinking place . . . interaction is available to all who choose to enter" (Cavan 1966, 49).

Cavan's description is perhaps too broad. The regulars are not so "open" to the transients or the loners as the quote suggests. Those who sit at tables at the Club or at Al's (described in the previous chapter) are not drawn into interaction with others as readily as those who sit at the bar. The arrangement of seats and the nature of the stuffed furniture at the Hermitage impede rather than promote eye contact or conversation. Nevertheless, the standards of propriety between strangers and casual acquaintances do permit and promote an openness distinct from other public gathering places. All the bars described in the previous chapter have been shown to be places where people regularly meet and make friends. They are all, to some extent, places where people can "hang out" and spend time in each other's company. They are places to drink, but they are also places in which to talk, shoot pool, look for sex, gain friendship, cash checks, and receive messages. They are stages on which interaction occurs.

The bar "sells" more than a commodity. It provides a setting for leisure. I have shown how the regulars at the Club create a social network through the buying of rounds, how at Al's customers and bartender respond and react to each other and have developed a knowledge which constitutes a social organization. At That Place and the Hermitage this is less evident, as the interaction is between customers, and the bar plays a minor role. Both kinds of bars—the clublike and the anonymous—are sites of interaction, but in the former the bartender is a crucial element in creating and maintaining the interaction.

Friendly Al's is the most vivid example of this in our study. Al provides the sociability of the host at a private party:

> His presence is known to all customers in the bar regularly because Al makes a habit of talking to everyone in the bar personally. Al talks fairly loudly and often kids and jokes around with the customers . . . he will almost always make a sarcastic remark of some kind . . . to a

customer when the customer first arrives . . . Al almost always knows the regular drink of the customers who are in the bar and he quickly learned what I was drinking after the first order . . . Al has a way of instantly making the customer feel part of the bar milieu as soon as he enters.

While the bartender also plays a significant part in the Club, there the group of regulars has a certain self-creation in which the bartender is a part but not as central a figure as at Al's.

The phenomena of "rounds" is a key part of the pattern of informal social relationships generated at Friendly Al's:

> The rounds continued until 1:00 A.M. Ed was drinking very heavily and became the pacesetter. I brought up a discussion of rounds and Ed was explaining how it was offensive if I didn't accept the drink although it wasn't all that offensive if I didn't drink it. This is sort of what I've always thought. There's sort of a favor obligation; a you-owe-me relationship that goes on with the rounds, and its very important in establishing friendship. . . . Not only are you helping the bartender out by buying rounds, but you're also establishing friendship.

The phenomenon of drinking and driving is affected by the character of the bar and its impact on interaction between the customers and between customers and bartenders. A customer at the Hermitage suggested it is valuable "just having someone there to tell you when to stop or having someone there to do the driving."

THE ECONOMY OF THE BAR

Competition between bars at the same price range is not a matter of quality of the commodity but of the form of intimacy and loyalty created among customers and with the bartender. The investment of the bartender in his or her property or job is, in bars like the Club and Friendly Al's, a matter of the kind of intimacy and camaraderie he can create and sustain. One of the bartenders at Al's brought a number of customers from his former place of employment to Al's when he left to take his present place. Here is the observer's account of this process of market control:

> The bartenders at Al's appear to be quite competitive with each other. This competition is related to me in terms of how well they control the bar, keep the customers entertained and in general are "good bartenders." The bartenders at That Place or The Hermitage never

talk about how they compare with each other. The comparisons made in jealousy and competition at Al's appear to be a result of the relationship between customers and bartenders in a neighborhood bar like this. Joe for example, mentioned to me that he promised Al that he would increase his business at least 50% when he was hired. The clientele are attracted to a neighborhood bar more because of the presentation of self of the bartender than they are at classier bars like The Hermitage where the customer is generally attracted more by the general atmosphere of the bar than to any particular personality.

This economic interest in loyalty and camaraderie is displayed in the occurrence of "free drinks" both at the Club and at Al's. The customer who buys the bartender a drink, or the bartender who buys the customer a drink, is creating an atmosphere of closeness and a relationship seemingly symbolizing a noneconomic attitude. At the Club, the observer feels that he is now one of the regulars when Frank, the bartender, offers him a free drink. Such dispensations are a regular occurrence there: "The Club was especially slow that day . . . The group by the door was drinking really fast and heavy, obviously drunk, singing songs and getting rowdy. According to Terry, the bartender, they made the bar that night in amounts spent. There was some question of whether or not he should give them a free round, but he did."

George, a regular customer at the Club, keeps up his barhopping activities in part to widen his network of friends, in case he should return to bartending. Both he and the observer find that knowing a number of bartenders increases their access to free drinks and free rounds.

The free drink is also connected, at Al's and other bars observed, with the "last call." It appears to be a necessity at Al's. The customer is not expected to leave the bar without "one for the road." This final drink at Al's is usually "on the house." It offers the bartender a chance to catch up on the "rebound" drinks with those customers for whom he has not bought a drink that evening. Often it is the strongest drink of the evening.

> At about 1:45 A.M. Joe returned to me to ask if I wanted a last drink for the evening. I hesitated but he proceeded to go ahead and mix me another drink. He brought it over and told me that it was 'on the house' and to enjoy it. I noticed that Glenn, the other bartender on duty, also bought a last drink 'on the house' for several of the customers down on their drinks at these few minutes before closing. . . . I also noticed that the drink Joe mixed for me was extremely strong, so strong that I was unable to taste any 7-up in it, as I'd ordered. It was the strongest drink by far mixed by Joe for me that entire evening.

The "last call," with its implicit demand to order another, and the dispensation of "free drinks" may mean that the customer is given more alcohol in a shorter period of time just before he leaves the bar and drives than at any other time in the evening. As the observer points out: "A final big gulp of alcohol is, of course, not the best way to send a customer out on the streets where he is to manage driving home. But like other situations and occasions within the neighborhood bar, the relevance of drinking-driving does not really enter into the situation. The more immediate and overriding relevance is the necessity of the bartender to always maintain the facade of intimacy and cameraderie with customers. At closing time this is demonstrated by buying a last drink."

The development of intimacy ties between customer and bartender operates in conflicting ways for attention to the drinking-driving welfare of the customer. The necessities of selling alcohol along with the surface demonstration of concern for the customer make the bartender sensitive to the displays of competence which customers utilize. He cannot tear down the "front stage" drama of the competent drinker without risking loss of the tie and threatening the other customers as well. Since the bartender represents a recurrent feature of the bar, the customer who is, or wants to be, a regular patron must grant the bartender an even greater significance as audience than he would other patrons.

Two considerations pull against each other. The show of intimacy is double-faced. The peer group is an audience before whom it is important for the patron to display competence, but insofar as it is an audience of intimates, it is both capable and at times able to intervene without the damage to ego incurred from strangers. The bartender is then in a bind; to intervene is to risk being the source of embarrassment as well as diminishing the customer's purchase of alcohol. Both considerations are contrary to rational economic behavior for a seller who depends on the loyalty of the customer based on personal ties (Hirschmann 1970.) Yet if he is indeed displaying his intimacy with the customer, he must act like an intimate, and this often calls for intervention. On the one hand he must cooperate with the customer in the drama of being a competent drinker. On the other hand he must show concern for the welfare of a friend. Either way he risks incurring the "ill will" and future patronage of the customer.

There is a second pull in the direction of intervention that should not be ignored. That is the development of friendship and intimacy ties that exist in conflict with and despite economic considerations. Reading motivations is extremely difficult for observers. One can only recognize when the behavior "fits" a logical explanation based on economic considerations and when it does not. Economic institutions create pressures which demand compliance under penalty of consequences. They do not force compliance, at all times and in all circumstances. People may prefer bankruptcy to illegal or immoral behavior. Nor is any single economically irrational act likely to result in business ruin.

THE MANAGEMENT OF TROUBLE

The concern for maintaining setting has another aspect to it peculiar to the social establishment of public drinking places. Any social establishment is faced with issues of social control. Even in the best regulated of institutions someone may go berserk and threaten the life, property, or well-being of members. In most establishments that risk is limited. In places where people consume alcohol it is not limited; it is a "normal" risk, and special measures must be taken to meet it. The problem of control is a major one for bars and provides an important spot on the agenda of bartender and bouncer action.

The bar represents an area of greater permissibility of behavior in action and language than is the case in other public settings. Access to sociability, assertiveness of language, sexual attention and behavior is in marked distinction from behavior in other establishments (Cavan 1966, ch. 4; Roebuck and Frese 1976, 123–25). Yet it is a moral order with the limitations and restrictions implied in that term. Much goes but not everything. Breaches of the moral order threaten bar settings even more than they do other public areas because the use of alcohol is defined as a precarious activity. The threat of impropriety and disruptive behavior is constant, and bartenders are aware of it. It forms a part of the instruction that one bartender gives to another, as one of the bartenders at the Hermitage tells us. Asked what he tells new bartenders, the bar manager says that he always tells them to reach for the tall Galliano bottle if he gets into a position of having to fight with a customer.

The always present threat of trouble means that the bartender and the patrons are mindful of danger and attempt to manage the scene so as to avoid it. One major source of potential trouble arises from the legal environment. In all our observations, two rules appear to be strictly enforced, and bartenders showed great concern for their enforcement. These are the prohibition against selling to persons under the age of twenty-one and the requirement of closing the bar by 2:00 A.M. One of the major duties of the bouncers at That Place is to check all entering customers for their identification, with concern only for age. The bouncers are stationed at the entrances rather than patrolling the interior of the establishment. Given the youth of the clientele served, and especially the naval recruit population drawn on, the threat of selling to "minors" spells a trouble the management goes to considerable length to avoid. Although less of an issue at the other bars, there was a constant check whenever someone appeared doubtfully over the age limit. Nor, despite protestations from patrons, did any of us observe a bar failing to close by the legal time. The closing time is known to patrons, and the management's desire to avoid trouble with police is accepted.

Bartenders attempt to manage situations which may create trouble in a variety of ways. As arguments erupt among patrons, the bartender frequently tries to head off fights by intervening to "cool off" the parties. Frank, the bartender at the Club uses the institution of "rounds" in an effort to define who he wants to see return. By not serving one customer in a group drinking rounds, he tried to discourage the customer from taking his turn. His knowledge that a particular man is a "mean drunk" led him to try to get someone to take him home as he approached drunkenness. Frank also acted with hostility toward two women, who were not regulars, who came into the bar and swore like men. Thus he discouraged a situation which clashed with the local taboo against men swearing in the presence of women and against women swearing at all.

This analysis of trouble is important for the study of drinking-driving. From it I draw conclusions about what is and what is *not* defined as trouble. Trouble is something that can happen inside the bar and not outside. Things that happen external to the bar, no matter whether or not they originated in the bar, are not troublesome. This is shown in an incident at Al's and in the accounts of bouncers at That Place.

The observer witnessed a fight at Friendly Al's. Two young white males came in, with signs of having had a great deal to drink. One of them, Tom, engaged a young Mexican-American, who was playing at the pool table, in several games of pool. They had some arguments about Tom's criticism of Raoul's manner of pool-playing. Hostility grew as Tom referred to Raoul's "shitty play." At the end of another game, "they began shouting back and forth at each other, while each was holding very stiffly to their pool sticks." At this point the observer himself intervened and told them to get back with the game so he could play. Again they hassled over the rules and, inadvertently swinging his stick, Tom hit the observer. Both Tom and Raoul began to apologize to the observer, and things seemed quiet. Tom even shook hands with Raoul after he, Tom, had lost another game and told Raoul it was a good game.

Tom's friend, Fred, had meanwhile acted to fire the antagonism. After Tom's show of reconciliation, Fred remarked, in Raoul's hearing: "don't kiss that Mex's ass." A little later Tom and Raoul again got into an argument over the pool-playing and began to shove at each other. Again the observer moved between them and tried to cool them. Raoul, who had been indignant at Fred's remark, was mad at this point.

> He kept saying that he will no longer take any shit from that gringo and that he expected the bartender to have more control over the bar but that the bartender, Glenn, was doing nothing. At this point Glenn came over and told Fred and Tom to leave the bar because they were drinking too much. They were swearing and cursing Glenn but they did leave, calling Glenn a "jag-off" for defending the Mexican against them. [The observer tried to keep Raoul in the bar but he got away.] As Raoul left, I followed him out and the three of them were shouting at each other and threatening a fight on the spot as well as a threat to call friends and have a "gang bang."

The observer went back into the bar and told Glenn what was happening, but "Glenn did not seem too excited about the whole thing and simply said that he's *glad that all of the bums are out of the bar* so *that there would be no trouble inside the bar*" when the cops come" [italics mine]. Glenn had called the cops, and, after they came and tried to cool the "fighters" on the sidewalk, Glenn told them he did not know the men and would never serve them again. The observer continued to watch the scene after the cops left and threats of violence continued. The observer reported this to Glenn, but he was unconcerned about the possibility of gang warfare outside the bar.

This same distinction between the internal and the external is found in the two bouncers talked to at That Place. They look out for trouble and try to stop problems before they start, judging by the loudness and rowdy behavior of the customer. As one put it, "I will go up to potential troublemakers and try to quiet them down, and throw them out if necessary." On our first visit to That Place we did see several customers, threatening to fight, hustled out to the parking lot but no effort made to prevent any occurrence outside the bar.

In discussing drinking-driving with the other bouncer, the observer asked if cops had ever entered That Place: "The bouncer said that during his time at That Place he had never seen a cop come into it, at least in uniform. He said that his job was to control the customers at That Place and to keep the lid on things enough to eliminate the need for police. Having the cops come into a bar like That Place for any reason would be very disruptive for business, for a lot of customers get freaked out if they think that they hang around at a place where cops come in all the time."

Drinking-driving is not trouble for bars or bartenders. It does not disrupt the setting. Its occurrence has no economic effect on the public drinking place. There is no legal prohibition violated by the bar when its patron is arrested for drinking-driving or involved in an accident. Police do not enter.

Yet it remains an understood element of danger to customers. Bartenders do intervene and do attempt to manage the drinking-driving situation. Asked about the responsibility or obligation of the drinking place toward the patron, the bouncers at That Place and the bartender at the Hermitage absolve themselves of concern by using what I call "the ideology of adulthood." While they maintain that most drinkers can manage themselves at drinking with competence, they also assert the license and liberty of adults. It is not the responsibility of the management because, as the bouncers at That Place put it, the customers are adults and "a person who is old enough to drink is old enough to take care of himself after he stops drinking."

It is evident from the intervention of the bar at the Club and Friendly Al's that, despite its lack of institutional support, bartenders do, under some circumstances, define drinking-driving as something to be avoided and themselves as responsible to control it. Al is troubled by the issue, and it appears that was one reason for his installing a Breathalyzer machine: "When Al returned with my drink, I mentioned to him that he must be getting a lot of notariety because of the breathtesting machine. Al said he was happy that he first installed the machine in the bar and said, 'If it saves one life then its worth it.'"

THE MANAGEMENT OF DRINKING AND DRIVING

Much of the work of tending bar and serving drinks is the management of drinking behavior. Our observations were directed by our interest in drinking-driving and not in the study of the bar per se. We were surprised by how little the topic of drinking-driving appeared in conversation unless initiated by the observer. Unless the drinker had a specific responsibility for another, as on a date, the necessity to drive was not an excuse for limiting one's drinking. There was little lore about avoiding accidents or arrests that was transmitted through conversation. As a topic of conversation, drinking-driving occurred in the context of specific situations, not as an abstract or rehearsed matter. Perhaps it is too serious a matter for the superficiality of barroom talk.

Our observations were directed toward the ways in which bartenders attended to drinking-driving as an occurrence to be prevented. This did not rule out instances of the opposite—where bartenders or bouncers either did not intervene or, through their talk, supported the drinker in his efforts to assume control of the auto. The very consumption of alcohol is, of course, a requisite to driving while under the influence of alcohol, and serving and even encouraging drink is *the* major activity of the bar. Regretfully, our observations gave too little attention to how the bartender encouraged drinking and thus abetted driving while under the influence of alcohol.

In our observations, four ways were seen by which bartenders tried to limit or control customer's drinking: discouraging the drinker from reordering drinks; manipulating the drinking pattern; manipulating the content of the drink; and, as the most extreme, refusing to serve the customer. These are, however, far from specific to the driving situation. They may appear as general control measures to prevent trouble or they may occur in the context of intimate relations which bind the customer and bartender in ties of mutual loyalty. At times, I even suspect that drinking-driving is used as an explanation of attempts to limit customer drinking while the bartender is more concerned with avoiding trouble in the bar.

In many cases, the bartender may suggest to the drinker that he has had enough but will not refuse service. Tim, an auxiliary bartender at the Club wanted one of the regular customers to stop drinking and commented on the customer's concern about a TV program, asking why the customer cared about what was on TV since he'd be going home soon and going to bed. After serving him another drink, Tim said to the customer that he'd had enough and asked whether he shouldn't go home. In this instance it did not succeed; the customer continued to order and was served. On another occasion at the Club, Frank the bartender suggested to Pete, one of the regulars, that he ought to go home. Pete said, "You know best. Send me home if you think I'm too drunk." But Frank continued to serve. On the same occasion Frank tried to get George to go home and get some sleep so he'd be able to go to work the next morning. Frank stopped short of actually refusing to serve Pete. Refusals are interpreted as hostile, "face-destroying" acts.

However, the bartender can play a role in initiating, encouraging, and activating the circle of intimates to intervene in the drinking or driving of the customer. In general, based on our observations, driving seldom appears as a clear element in limiting drinking by the bartender.

The bartender has two other ways of limiting the drinking of the patron. In these the audience of other customers and the patron himself may be unaware of the control being exerted. In one, where possible, the pattern of drinking is manipulated so as to limit and exclude the one patron about whom the bartender is concerned. This control was used when Frank at the Club used the "rounds" system to try to exclude one patron. He served the others when one of them ordered a round but simply did not put a drink in front of the customer under concern. Another device used at both the Club and Al's was the "short shot" or "dummy drink."

> George's roommate, Jack, came in an hour and a half early. He'd had a bad day and left work. He didn't come over and talk. He sat by himself and had a drink. Then he left for about a half-hour and returned and had another drink. From what George said he was drunk. . . . This is when Frank gave him a "short shot" trying to keep him sober. I asked George about it and he said it was an uncommon kind of thing for a bartender especially Frank to do but that if he did notice someone drinking too much he would pour just one shot. The way they mix drinks in The Club is that they have a shot glass and they have a bottle with a little metal stem on the top of it. They pour the bottle into the shot glass held over a glass with ice in it. They fill the shot glass and let it over-flow into the glass by continuing to pour for a short time after it is filled. With a "short shot" they just do the shot itself and don't even fill it up all the way.

That such gestures can be seen as a mark of the bartender's loyalty to his customer was evidenced by a regular customer at Al's who explained that both Joe and Al use the "dummy drink" (mix with no or little alcohol), which is a sign of their concern for the welfare of the customer as well as a face-saving device. (Customers are not charged for "dummy drinks.")

The refusal to serve was a rare event and a "touchy" matter. Where we did see it, as in one of the other bars observed in our preliminary observations, it almost occasioned a fight between the bartender and a group of patrons, one of whom was refused service. In other cases, as in a fight at Al's, it was clearly interpreted as implying that the customers were no longer welcome to return. Joe, the bartender at Al's, said that he didn't distinguish potential driving problems from other troubles a customer may be having in the bar, with other customers or with the bartender himself. He said he tried to deal with such problems as they came up by cutting off a guy who has been drinking too much, or refusing him when he comes in already too loaded.

This general reluctance to intervene in the name of avoiding a dangerous driving situation is not mirrored in the driving situation per se. Bartenders in several instances attempted to persuade customers not to drive; sought to get friends, buddies, or other customers to drive them home; or limited service to customers they worried were unable to drive. The control or intervention of the bartender in the driving of his customers is selective; it depends to a great extent on the network of close expectations of friendship existing between the customer and the bartender. This excludes transient, sporadic, and hostile customers from the concern of the bartender and from his influence. Also, the "role" of the bartender is only partially institutionalized. It is far from recurrent or homogeneous even for all bartenders in the same place. It follows the situated character of drinking-driving. Nevertheless it does occur and is one element in the system of influences and controls that bear upon the drinking-driving phenomenon.

Frank, the bartender at the Club, persuaded George to drive another customer, Richard, home. Here the network of peers and friendships is used by the bartender to provide an alternative to Richard's driving after he is quite drunk. In a more complex fashion, Manny, one of the regular customers at Al's, explained to the observer how Al "controls" him:

> He said that Al is a real good bartender because he really controls
> what's going on in the bar when he is on duty. (Here Manny
> distinguishes Al and Dana from Glenn.) Manny said that on two
> occasions Al had stopped serving him. On both occasions Al had
> noticed that Manny had been drinking an awful lot and really was not
> up for drinking any more. On both occasions Al came up to Manny
> and asked him "You're driving tonight, aren't you?" When Manny
> agreed, Al would then put a drink in front of him that was all mix and
> no booze (the "dummy drink"). . . . He did all this, said Manny,
> "because he is a good friend and knows me personally, not just as a
> customer." He went on to say that Joe and Al are very concerned
> about the customers in the bar, so that it's "cool" when they do things
> like this that not only help you out but save you from embarrassment
> at the bar.

Although bartenders were observed to intervene in the case of specific customers with whom there was a personal tie or the expectancy of one, they did not function in a public or highly visible fashion to bring the topic of driving into the notice of the customers or to set up a general consideration of it. A typical account of the closing-time situation at Al's is the following from the observer's field notes:

> At the 2 o'clock closing time there were seven customers left in the bar. Of these (excluding myself) four were in couples and three were loner males. All three of the loner males drove off without any apparent incident in their own cars. Of the two couples leaving at closing time both males did the driving also without incident. In fact, one of the two couples mentioned to Joe, the bartender, that they were thinking of looking for a place to grab some quick breakfast on their way home. During the entire closing procedure no mention was made by Joe to any of the customers present about their condition to drive home, the advisability of calling a cab or having a partner drive them home. No mention was made of these contingencies by the customers either.

Old people were one of the special categories whose accepted incompetence made for greater responsibility of the bartender toward them. Al has been known to drive old people home when he thinks them too drunk, and on several occasions we witnessed his efforts to call cabs for them. The following account shows the openness with which it can be done for older customers:

> At about 1:15 A.M. an old woman (around 70) entered Al's . . . She had obviously been drinking already for she made no sense when talking, slurred her words and staggered around. Several customers started shouting, whistling and laughing. Joe, the bartender, came over and asked her, "Now what does a drunk old broad like you want to have right now?" This old woman took about 20 minutes to finish her beer and then got up. As she was about to leave Al's, Glenn, the other bartender hollered out to her to be careful on her way out because they don't need any drunk broads spread across the sidewalk in front of the bar. About two minutes later there was a loud screech of tires . . . the old woman had just missed getting hit by a car. One customer said that woman should not even be allowed to walk, let alone drive.

Later the observer found out that she doesn't drive but lives nearby and is known to the bartenders as "an old alky broad."

Bars and bartenders perform many services for customers. Customers can cash checks, get mail and phone calls, and watch television at bars. The bartender may act as a "broker" in introducing men and women or may direct men to local prostitutes. Sometimes bartenders act in response to customers' requests; sometimes they offer a service unrequested. Telephoning for a taxi is among the services bartenders expect to perform. Whether the customer will request the service or even resist it when requested depends a great deal on their relationship with the bartender. It is seen as a favor, not as a requirement.

Two considerations make the bartender a frequently needed aid in the customer's self-initiated attempt to avoid driving by using a taxi. First of all, the telephone is often, as at Al's and the Club, located behind the bar, and the bartender's permission is needed for its use. Even when there is a phone or phone booth nearby, it is often outside the barroom, and strangers have to be directed to it. Perhaps more important, the customer may be too drunk to locate the number of the cab company, place a call, and accurately direct the cabdriver to the bar.

It is largely among regulars then that the bartender can most clearly play a role in intervening and calling a cab. A patron who is self-initiating the process is less dependent upon the bar. A patron who has engendered hostility between himself and the bartender may find it difficult to enlist aid in what is seen as a favor rather than a right. One evening at Al's, a man about eighty years old hollered to Glenn the bartender to get him a cab. Glenn seemed upset by this and told him to walk down about half a block and get the cab waiting there. Finally Glenn said that he'd do it if the old man promised to take it. Apparently in the past the old man, who lives in the neighborhood but doesn't drive, had Glenn call a cab, and when the driver appeared, the man had refused to take it. He is an annoyance as a customer, often creating "hassles."

Calling a cab is also used as a mode of control, especially with special-category customers. Al called a cab for an old man who had been annoying some of the women one night. He told the customer that he'd had enough and that he was going to call him a cab. Al does the same, sometimes initiating the cab call himself for several young women who come into the bar alone, become quite drunk, and do not drive or have not taken a car.

The bartender at the Hermitage maintained that he does call cabs when he feels customers are not able to drive home safely. However, we never observed him doing this. He stressed that the Hermitage has "nice customers, nice atmosphere. We don't have a lot of hassles." Most of his customers, he insisted, know when they've had enough and quit or call a cab for themselves. In the same context of describing how he calls cabs, he said that he refuses to get physically involved with rowdy customers and, if necessary, will call the police to take them away. I am uncertain how much he uses cabs to aid driving or to control trouble at the bar.

In general calling a cab, especially without the self-initiation of the patron, is looked upon more as a favor than an obligation of the bartender. On many occasions, when the customer was clearly "under the influence of alcohol" the bartender neither called a cab nor suggested it to the customer, even when he advised the customer that he'd "had enough." "Bad customers" will certainly not be granted favors.

The relation between the bartender and the patron in respect to his intervention to protect them from driving danger is dependent on a mutuality of social interactions rather than a unilateral right of the customer to the concern of the bartender. Two women who came into the Club late one night illustrate this:

> Then Betty and Eileen came in. Both of them were definitely drunk . . . Betty had to ask Frank, the bartender, to go into her purse to find her change and, later, her cigarettes because she couldn't find them. They had been bar-hopping and the last place they had hit was The Shack, which was closed so they came over to The Club to continue drinking. The two of them started attacking Frank, getting more and more abrasive as the evening wore on. Frank attacked them in return. First he told them that he didn't like them coming in after all the other bars had closed and then having spent all of their money and gotten drunk at other bars and expect him to entertain them. They certainly were half-in-the-bag and he was getting fed up with them. In addition to the fact that they had come in late and wanted the bar kept open until 2:00 A.M. there were a couple of things that weren't stated. They were calling Frank "a male chauvinist pig" and giving a hard Women's Lib rap. I think that offended Frank. Also they were swearing, using words like "fuck" a lot. Frank never uses words like that in front of other women, although he will use them with men when they're alone . . .
>
> The drinking was slow until about ten minutes to 2:00 A.M. and then Betty had a ten minute beer. The two of them drove off with Eileen driving. The interior light of the car had been left on, another sign of their drunkenness.

Here Frank refuses to grant these two women the protective attitude given to other women. No effort is made to suggest not driving, to enlist others to drive them home, or to call a cab.

THE ABSENCE OF MANAGEMENT

At That Place there is an entrance by a group or single person every three or four minutes during the peak of the evening. People congregate and move around through the several rooms and two levels that constitute the premises. The scene is fluid, crowded, and noisy. The bartenders have little contact, if any at all, with the customers. "Management," in the sense of social control and interaction, is absent.

> I suppose the most noticeable feature of the bar is that it's very disorganized. People walk around in a very fluid kind of environment. It does appear that people know each other, that there are regulars.
>
> As I approached That Place from the street I noticed by the noise and the large number of people coming and going that this would probably be a typically crowded Friday night in the bar. . . . There must have been well over 150 customers on both levels of the bar this evening. In the dance area at the rear of the bar there were about 18 young women either dancing or talking with men back there. It was impossible at this point to determine what proportion of the customers were in couples and what proportion were singles. They were simply talking or dancing with each other. Typically, the male crowd were about half civilian and half sailor types, judging by hair styles.

What does not appear, however, is the informal, social network of relations between the management and the customers observed at the Club and Al's. Much of the area of the bar is not visible to either the bartenders or the bouncers. The entire impression is that of a large warehouse to which people are invited and then left to themselves on condition that they buy drinks when approached by waiters.

The relation between management and customers is marked by the routinization of control. Unlike at the Club or Friendly Al's, there is no mass exodus at closing time. That Place is not a club. There are no free drinks.

> That Place is a kind of bar where the bartenders will turn on all the lights, turn off the music and clear the tables at five minutes to two. The bouncer and the bartenders will circulate among the crowd at closing and take the drinks away from them and loudly announce that it's closing time and everybody has to leave. As a matter of fact the call for last drinks at That Place is made over the P.A. system and is made at approximately twenty minutes to two. . . . This is understandable due to the logistics problem of having to clear such a large crowd.

A good deal of interaction occurs in the parking lots adjacent to the bar; men and women continue conversations, arguments occur, men try to get in a last-minute "hustle" with some woman they've met. This "external" life of That Place, however, goes on without either the watchful eyes or intervention of bouncers or bartenders.

The bouncers at That Place are physically large and strong-appearing. Stationed at the entrances to the bar, their major activity is the prevention of underage persons from being customers. They routinely check identification cards for age and refuse permission if identification of legal age cannot be proven to the bouncer's satisfaction. In addition, they do attempt to control situations when they reach the point of visibility. They neither watch for incipient trouble nor intervene until it has reached considerable visibility within the bar. They do not attempt to manage situations nor to act in aid of customers. The following discussion with one of the bouncers is indicative of the detachment of "management":

> The observer then talked with the bouncer Paul and asked him if any unusual incidents had occurred since they talked last, especially involving customers driving home. Paul said that about a week ago they had had "some trouble" with a customer driving out of the parking lot about 1:15 A.M. Three young men (in their 20s) who had been drinking for 2 1/2 hours in That Place left through the front door. Paul said that he remembered them because he always tries to keep an eye on the male drinkers who are in groups because they are the ones who tend to get the rowdiest. Several minutes later one of the bartenders working toward the rear of the bar ran up to Paul and told him there was a fight brewing out in the back lot. Paul then had the bartender temporarily take his place at the front entrance while he went out the back door to see what the *trouble* was [italics mine].

It turned out that two cars had backed up against each other in the lot. The three men he had just seen leaving the bar were confronting the driver of the other car, and all were shouting at each other. As he had left the bar, Paul had asked the bartender to call the police. They arrived shortly after he was out on the lot. The lone driver seemed drunk enough, according to Paul, to take on the other three, whom he accused of being drunk and causing the accident. When the police arrived Paul quickly left and returned to his spot as bouncer:

> Paul said that whenever an incident like this occurs outside the bar, they always try to call the police first and let the police take care of the incident. He said that they do this because any trouble that occurs outside the bar is really none of the bar's responsibility, but is a police

responsibility because it happens outside. . . . Again, as during our
first conversation Paul told me that he doesn't feel, nor do the other
personnel at That Place feel, that it is their responsibility to look out
for the customers after they leave the bar. He again told me that the
customers who are old enough to drink are old enough to pay the
price for what happens after they drink.

The bouncers do try to keep out potential patrons who appear at the
entrance already quite drunk and, in this way, to avoid trouble. They do
sometimes suggest that a buddy drive when they see a patron leaving visibly quite drunk. No special attention is given to women driving. In part,
as one bouncer explained, they feel less sure of a diagnosis of drunkenness where women are concerned. Women, says one of the bouncers, almost always come to That Place in groups. If they are drunk, they are
quite likely to be taken home by a male. The pattern of free drinks, of concern for the "good will" between the bartenders or bouncers and customers, is absent. The economic basis of That Place is very different from
the Club and Friendly Al's.

The absence of management also characterizes the Hermitage, but it
has a distinctively different character. Here the entire bar is open to the
observation of the bartender. He is aware of and concerned with possibilities of "trouble." His relation to customers is almost exclusively that
of service tinged with control. His job is to mix drinks and occasionally
talk to the "loners" at the bar. As compared to the more intimate kind of
bar represented by the Club and Friendly Al's, the management of drinking and driving at the Hermitage is almost exclusively a product of the
setting and the customers themselves. The bartender has no stable set of
social interactions either emergent from his relation to customers or supported by an economic need to create the setting of a small club. As the
regular bartender at The Hermitage put it, "a bartender can't keep track
of what his customers do after they leave the bar. The bartender's only
real responsibility to the customers is to cut them off when the bartender
feels that the customer has been drinking too much."

In the several observations made at the Hermitage we never saw a
group of regulars akin to the groups at the Club and Al's. We never saw
any customer on more than one occasion. Nor did we see the bartender
cut off any customer, suggest that he not drive, try to arrange another
ride, or suggest that he call a taxi. More than at any of the three other
sites, we were dependent on the bartender for much information about
the bar. Much about the setting and the customers was considerably
different from the neighborhood bar or the singles bar. For one thing, a

number of customers used the bar on the way to something else. Few customers were there for most of the evening. Some customers came to the bar before or after eating in the restaurant which was part of the establishment. There was very little movement from spot to spot within the bar or evidence of people meeting friends in the casual fashion of regulars. Couples stayed to themselves. Even on Saturday night, when the Hermitage became a "night spot," it was one of several places on the circuit. On weeknights it closed early, often before midnight.

The setting of the Hermitage further mitigated against the closeness of a neighborhood bar or the loose, casual disorganization of the singles bar. The upholstered furniture and the paneled wood walls had the mark of taste and age that befits the bar's name. The dress of many of the men was more formal, more often suited businessmen than blue-jeaned Californian youth. In age, the Hermitage clientele was at least two levels above that of That Place; in class, one or two levels above both the Club and Al's.

These two aspects of setting and clientele at the Hermitage help explain the limited role of the bartender and the absence of management. As the bartender maintained on several occasions, his way of handling trouble is to call the police. His management of drinking is to refuse further service. He gives no recognition of an ability to mobilize the peers of the drinker or to utilize his own personal knowledge or attachment as a device to influence the drinker. But, as he also maintained on two occasions, the kind of people who come into the Hermitage are not likely to give him much trouble. They are "nice people, cool people." "The Hermitage is a nice place attracting nice customers." "They know when to quit drinking or know when to call a cab for themselves. . . . The cool customers . . . can control their drinking and be aware of their incapacities." They are, in fact, most gracious when he suggests a cab. Again they are the kind of customers attracted by the atmosphere of The Hermitage.

Here the bartender is neither the center of interaction nor the source of the atmosphere. As at That Place, he tries to control but not to manage.

AFTERWORD, 1994

Social Control

In the 1970s and 1980s there was a tendency to use the term "social control" as descriptive of political and legal controls. Yet sociologists earlier confined it to distinguish it from those institutional controls of legal and political sources. It is in that sense that the concept is used in this section. The description of bar behavior in this chapter is focused on the social controls that are utilized in bar behavior and which affect the drinking-driving event. Much drinking-driving and drinking problems research concentrates on attributes of the person, and in this fashion ignores any form of influence or control between the coercion of law and the self-control of the individual.

The relations between law and behavior are more complex than the direct interaction of law and deterrence. In this study of bars there was both interaction between legal and social controls and observance of social controls with indifference to law. Law operates, or fails to operate, as one element in a complex of elements. In this study, that complex has included the relations among the self, peers or intimates, the institutional establishment (in this case the bar), and the practical contingencies, of which the laws governing bars and drinking-driving are pertinent.

The description and analysis of how the self is implicated in aspects of bar behavior related to drinking-driving owes much to the seminal work of Erving Goffman (1956). The self is not an enclosed, contained entity. The person is conscious of his or her self as on display before an audience and on a stage. The bar represents a specific type of stage, and behavior in it is a mode of self-display before an audience. From the standpoint of an audience, drinking can be performed competently or incompetently. The idea of competence is complex and includes as well the ability to display self-knowledge of incompetence. As evidence of competence, the adult males described here are expected to be able to drink and drive.

Within the concept of competent drinking, there are exceptions to the display of incompetence by not drinking and driving. Women, old men, past DUI offenders, chronic alcoholics—all have accepted excuses, "exculpatory defenses." Under specific exceptions adult males may also have acceptable excuses.

Any concept of social control needs to include the importance of peers, especially intimates, as agents of social control. Through help in driving, through suggestion, and through insult, wives, husbands, lovers, and friends have a special mandate and license to assume influence and quasi-coercion over the drinker. The importance of this relationship as a form of social control is especially significant in the drinking-driving event. The relation between men and women forms a crucial part of this mode of control.

The bartender is a final link in the system of social controls we observed in the San Diego bars. He or she can play a variety of roles in intervening in the actions and decision of drinkers. Some aspects of that intervention are discussed below but here I am emphasizing those controls which operate in the bartender's relationship to customers whom he or she knows, especially "regulars." There are a number of ways the bartender was observed to intervene—through mobilizing friends or intimates; through direct help, such as calling a taxi; through suggestions; through manipulating or increasing the drinks; through continuing or refusing continuance of service.

Context

An emphasis on the person and his or her attributes as the focus of drinking behavior, and drinking-driving as well, treats the act of drinking and drinking-driving as unrelated to the milieu of other people and the context of place in which it occurs. In studying drinking-driving as it emerges in bars, my focus is on the event, involving the triad of person, interaction with others, and the context of the bar. Interaction is not with a generalized "other" but with people in specific roles—as spouse, friend, stranger, bartender. A concern for context is also complex, involving different dimensions of place.

One dimension of context is institutional—the ongoing and recurrent aspects of rules that control or permit particular kinds of action. Certainly the legality of the bar as a place of on-premise drinking is so taken for granted that it never enters observation or conversation. The laws against sale to minors and hour of closing are significant in placing boundaries on to whom and when the bar is available. Drinking in homes is a different context in these regards.

I have noted how the lack of responsibility for events occurring outside the bar makes the bartender less concerned about controlling such events. "Trouble" is defined as that which occurs within the premises. This is an aspect of institutional context, the laws which define and enforce responsibility and liability.

The distinction between "regulars" and "transients" is a facet of the context influencing the intervention of management. Here the relationship of the bartender to customers has both interactional and institutional features. The institutional features involve the economics of the bar, both the need to sell drinks and the need to form and maintain good will and a congenial, protective relationship with customers, especially regulars. These influence the interaction, but they should not blind us to the interpersonal influences that flow from relationships of friendliness and human concern.

Central to our observations was the differences in the character of the four bars studied. Each bar catered to somewhat different and distinct types of customers. Each was different in its architecture. Each had material props and locations which impinged on the opportunities and resistances to particular action. The character of the management of drinking and drinking-driving was sharply affected by these differences.

This triad of person-interaction and context is essential to understanding the behaviors observed on this study. Above all, the conception of drinking as an event in which action emerges within that event remains in my judgment the major contribution and value of the study irrespective of its time and place.

Within circles of alcohol policymakers there has recently been a move toward a focus on the bar and other sites of drinking. Especially in taverns and tavern associations, the issue of how much and what kind of intervention management should practice has become a practical matter. One facet of this which has gained much attention in the media and elsewhere has been the designated driver movement. This was one recommendation of the 1989 Surgeon General's Conference on Drinking-Driving (Office of the Surgeon General 1989). To the best of my knowledge, the degree of use or the impact on outcomes of drinking-driving has not yet been well-tested. Nor have there been studies of the drinking contexts which promote or impede the use of the designated driver. (For further description and analysis see Saltz 1989; Ross 1992, ch. 5, 7.)

Part 4

The Creation and Entitlement of Stigma

Chapter Eight

Moral Passage
The Symbolic Process in Public Designation of Deviance

Recent perspectives on deviant behavior have focused attention away from the actor and his acts and placed it on the analysis of public reactions in labeling deviants as "outsiders."[1] This perspective forms the background for this chapter. The symbolic import of different forms of deviance leads to different public responses toward the deviant and helps account for the historical changes often found in treatment of such delinquents as alcoholics, drug addicts, and other "criminals," changes which involve a passage from one moral status to another.

INSTRUMENTAL AND SYMBOLIC FUNCTIONS OF LAW[2]

Agents of government are the only persons in modern societies who can legitimately claim to represent the total society. In support of their acts, limited and specific group interests are denied while a public and societal interest is claimed.[3] Acts of government "commit the group to action or to perform coordinated acts for general welfare."[4] This representational character of governmental officials and their acts makes it possible for them not only to influence the allocation of resources but also to define the public norms of morality and to designate which acts violate them. In a pluralistic society these defining and designating acts can become matters of political issue because they support or reject one or another of the competing and conflicting cultural groups in the society.

Let us begin with a distinction between *instrumental* and *symbolic* functions of legal and governmental acts. We readily perceive that acts of officials, legislative enactments, and court decisions often affect behavior in an instrumental manner through a direct influence on the actions of people. The Wagner Labor Relations Act and the Taft-Hartley Act have had considerable impact on the conditions of collective bargaining in the United States. Tariff legislation directly affects the prices of import commodities. The instrumental function of such laws lies in their enforcement; unenforced they have little effect.

Symbolic aspects of law and government do not depend on enforcement for their effect. They are symbolic in a sense close to that used in literary analysis. The symbolic act "invites consideration rather than overt reaction" (Wheelwright 1964, 23). There is a dimension of meaning in symbolic behavior which is given not in its immediate and manifest significance but in what the action connotes for the audience that views it. The symbol "has acquired a meaning which is added to its immediate intrinsic significance" (Parsons 1951, 386). The use of the wine and wafer in the Mass or the importance of the national flag cannot be appreciated without knowing their symbolic meaning for the users. In analyzing law as symbolic we are oriented less to behavioral consequences as a means to a fixed end, more to meaning as an act, a decision, a gesture important in itself.

An action of a governmental agent takes on symbolic import as it affects the designation of public norms. A courtroom decision or a legislative act is a gesture which often glorifies the values of one group and demeans those of another. In their representational character, governmental actions can be seen as ceremonial and ritual performances, designating the content of public morality. They are the statement of what is acceptable in the public interest. Law can thus be seen as symbolizing the public affirmation of social ideals and norms as well as a means of direct social control. This symbolic dimension is given in the statement, promulgation, or announcement of law unrelated to its function in influencing behavior through enforcement.

It has long been evident to students of government and law that these two functions, instrumental and symbolic, may often be separated in more than an analytical sense. Many laws are honored as much in the breach as in performance.[5] Robin Williams has labeled such institutionalized yet illegal and deviant behavior the "patterned evasion of norms." Such evasion occurs when law proscribes behavior which nevertheless occurs in a recurrent socially organized manner and is seldom punished.[6] The kinds of crimes we are concerned with here quite clearly fall into this category. Gambling, prostitution, abortion, and public drunkenness are all common modes of behavior although laws exist designating them as prohibited. It is possible to see such systematic evasion as functioning to minimize conflicts between cultures by utilizing law to proclaim one set of norms as public morality and to use another set of norms in actually controlling that behavior.

While patterned evasion may perform such harmonizing functions, the passage of legislation, the acts of officials, and decisions of judges nevertheless have a significance as gestures of public affirmation. First, the act of public affirmation of a norm often persuades listeners that behavior and norm are consistent. The existence of law quiets and comforts those whose interests and sentiments are embodied in it.[7] Second, public affirmation of a moral norm directs the major institutions of the society to its support. Despite patterned practices of abortion in the United States, obtaining abortions does require access to a subterranean social structure and is much more difficult than obtaining an appendectomy. There are instrumental functions to law even where there is patterned evasion.

A third impact of public affirmation is the one that most interests us here. The fact of affirmation through acts of law and government expresses the public worth of one set of norms, of one subculture vis-à-vis those of others. It demonstrates which cultures have legitimacy and public domination, and which do not. Accordingly it enhances the social status of groups carrying the affirmed culture and degrades groups carrying that which is condemned as deviant. I have argued elsewhere that the significance of Prohibition in the United States lay less in its enforcement than in the fact that it occurred (Gusfield 1963, 117–26). Analysis of the enforcement of Prohibition law indicates that it was often limited by the unwillingness of dry forces to utilize all their political strength for fear of stirring intensive opposition. Great satisfaction was gained from the passage and maintenance of the legislation itself (Gusfield 1963; Sinclair 1964, ch. 10, pp. 13–14).

Irrespective of its instrumental effects, public designation of morality is itself an issue generative of deep conflict. The designating gestures are dramatistic events, "since it invites one to consider the matter of motives in a perspective that, being developed in the analysis of drama, treats language and thought primarily as modes of action."[8] For this reason the designation of a way of behavior as violating public norms confers status and honor on those groups whose cultures are followed as the standard of conventionality, and derogates those whose cultures are considered deviant. My analysis of the American temperance movement has shown how the issue of drinking and abstinence became a politically significant focus for the conflicts between Protestant and Catholic, rural and urban, native and immigrant, middle class and lower class in American society. The political conflict lay in the efforts of an abstinent Protestant middle class to control the public affirmation of morality in drinking. Victory or defeat were consequently symbolic of the status and power of the cultures opposing each other (Gusfield 1963, ch. 5). Legal affirmation or rejection is thus important in what it symbolizes as well or instead of what it controls. Even if the law was broken, it was clear whose law it was.

DEVIANT NONCONFORMITY AND DESIGNATOR REACTION

In Durkheim's analysis of the indignant and hostile response to norm-violation, all proscribed actions are threats to the existence of the norm.[9] Once we separate the instrumental from the symbolic functions of legal and governmental designation of deviants, however, we can question this assumption. We can look at norm-violation from the standpoint of its effects on the symbolic rather than the instrumental character of the norm. Our analysis of patterned evasion of norms has suggested that a law weak in its instrumental functions may nevertheless perform significant symbolic functions. Unlike human limbs, norms do not necessarily atrophy through disuse. Standards of charity, mercy, and justice may be dishonored every day yet remain important statements of what is publicly approved as virtue. The sexual behavior of the human male and the human female need not be a copy of the socially sanctioned rules. Those rules remain as important affirmations of an acceptable code, even though they are regularly breached. Their roles as ideals are not threatened by daily behavior. In analyzing the violation of norms we will look at the implications of different forms of deviance on the symbolic character of the norm itself. *The point here is that the designators of deviant behavior react differently to different norm-sustaining implications of an act.* We can classify deviant behavior from this standpoint.

The Repentant Deviant

The reckless motorist often admits the legitimacy of traffic laws, even though he has broken them. The chronic alcoholic may well agree that both he and his society would be better if he could stay sober. In both cases the norm they have violated is itself unquestioned. Their deviation is a moral lapse, a fall from a grace to which they aspire. The homosexual who seeks a psychiatrist to rid himself of his habit has defined his actions similarly to those who have designated him as a deviant. There is a consensus between the designator and the deviant; his repentance confirms the norm.

Repentance and redemption seem to go hand in hand in court and church. Gresham Sykes and David Matza have described techniques of neutralization which juvenile delinquents often use with enforcement agencies: "The juvenile delinquent would appear to be at least partially committed to the dominant social order in that he frequently exhibits guilt or shame when he violates its proscriptions, accords approval to certain conforming figures and distinguishes between appropriate and inappropriate targets for his deviance" (1957, 666). A show of repentance is also used, say Sykes and Matza, to soften the indignation of law enforcement agents. A recent study of police behavior lends support to this. Juveniles apprehended by the police received more lenient treatment, including dismissal, if they appeared contrite and remorseful about their violations than if they did not. This difference in the posture of the deviant accounted for much of the differential treatment favoring middle-class "youngsters" over lower-class "delinquents" (Piliavin and Blair 1964).

The Sick Deviant

Acts which represent an attack upon a norm are neutralized by repentance. The open admission of repentance confirms the sinner's belief in the sin. His threat to the norm is removed and his violation has left the norm intact. Acts which we can perceive as those of sick and diseased people are irrelevant to the norm; they neither attack nor defend it. The use of morphine by hospital patients in severe pain is not designated as deviant behavior. Sentiments of public hostility and the apparatus of enforcement agencies are not mobilized toward the morphine-user. His use is not perceived as a violation of the norm against drug use, but as an uncontrolled act, not likely to be recurrent.[10]

While designations of action resulting from sickness do not threaten the norm, significant consequences flow from such definitions. Talcott Parsons and Renée Fox have pointed out that the designation of a person as ill changes the obligations which others have toward the person and his obligations toward them (1952). The authors' description sensitizes us to the way in which the sick person is a different social object than the healthy one. He has now become an object of welfare, a person to be helped rather than punished. Hostile sentiments toward sick people are not legitimate. The sick person is not responsible for his acts. He is excused from the consequences which attend the healthy who act the same way.[11]

Deviance designations, as we shall show below, are not fixed. They may shift from one form to another over time. Defining a behavior pattern as one caused by illness makes a hostile response toward the actor illegitimate and inappropriate. "Illness" is a social designation, by no means given in the nature of medical fact. Even lefthandedness is still seen as morally deviant in many countries. Hence the effort to define a practice as a consequence of illness is itself a matter of conflict and a political issue.

The Enemy Deviant

Writing about a Boston slum in the 1930s, William F. Whyte remarks: "The policeman is subject to sharply conflicting pressures. On one side are the 'good people' of Eastern City, who have written their moral judgments into law and demand through their newspapers that the law be enforced. On the other side are the people of Cornerville, who have different standards and have built up an organization whose perpetuation depends upon the freedom to violate the law" (1955, 138).

Whyte's is one of several studies that have pointed out the discrepancies between middle-class moralities embodied in law and lower-class moralities which differ sharply from them.[12] In Cornerville, gambling was seen as a "respectable" crime, just as antitrust behavior may be in other levels of the social structure. In American society, conflicts between social classes are often also cultural conflicts reflecting moral differences. Coincidence of ethnic and religious distinctions with class differences accentuates such conflicts between group values.

In these cases, the validity of the public designation is itself at issue. The publicly defined deviant is neither repentant nor sick, but is instead an upholder of an opposite norm. He accepts his behavior as proper and derogates the public norm as illegitimate. He refuses to internalize the public norm into his self-definition. This is especially likely to occur in instances of "business crimes." The buyer sees his action as legitimate economic behavior and resists a definition of it as immoral and thus prohibitable. The issue of "off-track" betting illustrates one area in which clashes of culture have been salient.

The designation of culturally legitimate behavior as deviant depends upon the superior power and organization of the designators. The concept of convention in this area, as Thrasymachus defined Justice for Socrates, is the will of the stronger. If the deviant is the politically weaker group, then the designation is open to the changes and contingencies of political fortunes. It becomes an issue of political conflict, ranging group against group and culture against culture, in the effort to determine whose morals are to be designated as deserving of public affirmation.

It is when the deviant is also an enemy and his deviance is an aspect of group culture that the conventional norm is most explicitly and energetically attacked. When those once designated as deviant have achieved enough political power they may shift from disobedience to an effort to change the designation itself. This has certainly happened in the civil rights movement. Behavior viewed as deviant in the segregationist society has in many instances been moved into the realm of the problematic, now subject to political processes of conflict and compromise.

When the deviant and the designator perceive each other as enemies, and the designator's power is superior to that of the deviant, we have domination without a corresponding legitimacy. Anything which increases the power of the deviant to organize and attack the norm is thus a threat to the social dominance symbolized in the affirmation of the norm. Under such conditions the need of the designators to strengthen and enforce the norms is great. The struggle over the symbol of social power and status is focused on the question of the maintenance or change of the legal norm. The threat to the middle class in the increased political power of Cornerville is not that the Cornerville resident will gamble more; he already does gamble with great frequency. The threat is that the law will come to accept the morality of gambling and treat it as a legitimate business. If this happens, Boston is no longer a city dominated by middle-class Yankees but becomes one dominated by lower-class immigrants, as many think has actually happened in Boston. The maintenance of a norm which defines gambling as deviant behavior thus symbolizes the maintenance of Yankee social and political superiority. Its disappearance as a public commitment would symbolize the loss of that superiority.

The Cynical Deviant

The professional criminal commits acts whose designation as deviant is supported by wide social consensus. The burglar, the hired murderer, the arsonist, the kidnapper all prey on victims. While they may use repentance or illness as strategies to manage the impressions of enforcers, their basic orientation is self-seeking, to get around the rules. It is for this reason that their behavior is not a great threat to the norms although it calls for social management and repression. It does not threaten the legitimacy of the normative order.

DRINKING AS A CHANGING FORM OF DEVIANCE

Analysis of efforts to define drinking as deviant in the United States will illustrate the process by which designations shift. The legal embodiment of attitudes toward drinking shows how cultural conflicts find their expression in the symbolic functions of law. In the 160 years since 1800, we see all our suggested types of nonconforming behavior and all the forms of reaction among the conventional segments of the society.

The movement to limit and control personal consumption of alcohol began in the early nineteenth century, although some scattered attempts were made earlier.[13] Colonial legislation was aimed mainly at controlling the inn through licensing systems. While drunkenness occurred, and drinking was frequent, the rigid nature of the colonial society, in both north and south, kept drinking from becoming an important social issue.[14]

The Repentant Drinker

The definition of the drinker as an object of social shame begins in the early nineteenth century and reaches full development in the late 1820s and early 1830s. A wave of growth in temperance organizations in this period was sparked by the conversion of drinking men to abstinence under the stimulus of evangelical revivalism (Gusfield 1963, 44–51). Through drinking men joining together to take the pledge, a norm of abstinence and sobriety emerged as a definition of conventional respectability. They sought to control themselves and their neighbors.

The norm of abstinence and sobriety replaced the accepted patterns of heavy drinking countenanced in the late eighteenth and early nineteenth centuries. By the 1870s rural and small-town America had defined middle-class morals to include the dry attitude. This definition had little need for legal embodiment. It could be enunciated in attacks on the drunkard which assumed that he shared the normative pattern of those who exhorted him to be better and to do better. He was a repentant deviant, someone to be brought back into the fold by moral persuasion and the techniques of religious revivalism (Gusfield 1963, 69–86). His error was the sin of lapse from a shared standard of virtue. "The Holy Spirit will not visit, much less will He dwell within he who is under the polluting, debasing effects of intoxicating drink. The state of heart and mind which this occasions to him is loathsome and an abomination" (*Temperance Manual* 1836, 46).

Moral persuasion thus rests on the conviction of a consensus between the deviant and the designators. As long as the object of attack and conversion is isolated in individual terms, rather than perceived as a group, there is no sense of his deviant act as part of a shared culture. What is shared is the norm of conventionality; the appeal to the drinker and the chronic alcoholic is to repent. When the Woman's Anti-Whiskey Crusade of 1873–74 broke out in Ohio, church women placed their attention on the taverns. In many Ohio towns these respectable ladies set up vigils in front of the tavern and attempted to prevent men from entering just by the fear that they would be observed.[15] In keeping with the evangelical motif in the temperance movement, the Washingtonians, founded in 1848, appealed to drinkers and chronic alcoholics with the emotional trappings and oratory of religious meetings, even though devoid of pastors (Krout 1925, ch. 9).

Moral persuasion, rather than legislation, has been one persistent theme in the designation of the drinker as deviant and the alcoholic as depraved. Even in the depictions of the miseries and poverty of the chronic alcoholic, there is a decided moral condemnation which has been the hallmark of the American temperance movement. Moral persuasion was ineffective as a device to wipe out drinking and drunkenness. Heavy drinking persisted through the nineteenth century and the organized attempts to convert the drunkard experienced much backsliding.[16] Nevertheless, defections from the standard did not threaten the standard. The public definition of respectability matched the ideals of the sober and abstaining people who dominated those parts of the society where moral suasion was effective. In the late nineteenth century those areas in which temperance sentiment was strongest were also those in which legislation was most easily enforceable.[17]

The Enemy Drinker

The demand for laws to limit alcoholic consumption appears to arise from situations in which the drinkers possess power as a definitive social and political group and, in their customary habits and beliefs, deny the validity of abstinence norms. The persistence of areas in which temperance norms were least controlling led to the emergence of attempts to embody control in legal measures. The drinker as enemy seems to be the greatest stimulus to efforts to designate his act as publicly defined deviance.

In its early phase the American temperance movement was committed chiefly to moral persuasion. Efforts to achieve legislation governing the sale and use of alcohol do not appear until the 1840s. This legislative movement had a close relationship to the immigration of Irish Catholics and German Lutherans into the United States in this period. These nonevangelical and/or non-Protestant peoples made up a large proportion of the urban poor in the 1840s and 1850s. They brought with them a far more accepting evaluation of drinking than had yet existed in the United States. The tavern and the beer parlor had a distinct place in the leisure of the Germans and the Irish. The prominence of this place was intensified by the stark character of the developing American slum.[18] These immigrant cultures did not contain a strong tradition of temperance norms which might have made an effective appeal to a sense of sin. To be sure, excessive drunkenness was scorned, but neither abstinence nor constant sobriety were supported by the cultural codes.

Between these two groups—the native American, middle-class evangelical Protestant and the immigrant European Catholic or Lutheran occupying the urban lower class—there was little room for repentance. By the 1850s the issue of drinking reflected a general clash over cultural values. The temperance movement found allies in its political efforts among the nativist movements (Billington 1938, ch. 15; Gusfield 1963, 55–57). The force and power of the anti-alcohol movements, however, were limited greatly by the political composition of the urban electorate, with its high proportion of immigrants. Thus the movement to develop legislation emerged in reaction to the appearance of cultural groups least responsive to the norms of abstinence and sobriety. The very effort to turn such informal norms into legal standards polarized the opposing forces and accentuated the symbolic import of the movement. Now that the issue had been joined, defeat or victory was a clear-cut statement of public dominance.

It is a paradox that the most successful move to eradicate alcohol emerged in a period when America was shifting from a heavy-drinking society, in which whiskey was the leading form of alcohol, to a moderate one, in which beer was replacing whiskey. Prohibition came as the culmination of the movement to reform the immigrant cultures and at the height of the immigrant influx into the United States.

Following the Civil War, moral persuasion and legislative goals were both parts of the movement against alcohol. By the 1880s an appeal was made to the urban, immigrant lower classes to repent and to imitate the habits of the American middle class as a route to economic and social mobility. Norms of abstinence were presented to the nonabstainer both as virtue and as expedience.[19] This effort failed. The new, and larger, immigration of 1890–1915 increased still further the threat of the urban lower class to the native American.

The symbolic effect of Prohibition legislation must be kept analytically separate from its instrumental, enforcement side. While the urban middle class did provide much of the organizational leadership to the temperance and Prohibition movements, the political strength of the movement in its legislative drives was in the rural areas of the United States. Here, where the problems of drinking were most under control, where the norm was relatively intact, the appeal to a struggle against foreign invasion was the most potent. In these areas, passage of legislation was likely to make small difference in behavior. The continuing polarization of political forces into those of cultural opposition and cultural acceptance during the Prohibition campaigns (1906–1919), and during the drive for Repeal (1926–1933), greatly intensified the symbolic significance of victory and defeat.[20] Even if the Prohibition measures were limited in their enforceability in the metropolis there was no doubt about whose law was public and what way of life was being labeled as opprobrious.

After Repeal, as dry power in American politics subsided, the designation of the drinker as deviant also receded. Public affirmation of the temperance norm had changed and with it the definition of the deviant had changed. Abstinence was itself less acceptable. In the 1950s the temperance movement, faced with this change in public norms, even introduced a series of placards with the slogan, "It's Smart *Not* to Drink."

Despite this normative change in the public designation of drinking deviance, there has not been much change in American drinking patterns. Following the Prohibition period the consumption of alcohol has not returned to its pre-1915 high. Beer has continued to occupy a more important place as a source of alcohol consumption. "Hard drinkers" are not as common in America today as they were in the nineteenth century. While there has been some increase in moderate drinking, the percentage of adults who are abstainers has remained approximately the same (one-third) for the past thirty years. Similarly, dry sentiment has remained stable, as measured by local opinion results.[21] In short, the argument over deviance designation has been largely one of normative dominance, not of instrumental social control. The process of deviance designation in drinking needs to be understood in terms of symbols of cultural dominance rather than in the activities of social control.

The Sick Drinker

For most of the nineteenth century, the chronic alcoholic as well as the less compulsive drinker was viewed as a sinner. It was not until after Repeal (1933) that chronic alcoholism became defined as illness in the United States. Earlier actions taken toward promotion of the welfare of drinkers and alcoholics through temperance measures rested on the moral supremacy of abstinence and the demand for repentance. The user of alcohol could be an object of sympathy, but his social salvation depended on a willingness to embrace the norm of his exhorters. The designation of alcoholism as sickness has a different bearing on the question of normative superiority. It renders the behavior of the deviant indifferent to the status of norms enforcing abstinence.

This realization appears to have made supporters of temperance and Prohibition hostile to efforts to redefine the deviant character of alcoholism. They deeply opposed the reports of the Committee of Fifty in the late nineteenth century.[22] These volumes of reports by scholars and prominent men took a less moralistic and a more sociological and functional view of the saloon and drinking than did the temperance movement.

The soundness of these fears is shown by what did happen to the temperance movement with the rise of the view that alcoholism is illness. It led to new agencies concerned with drinking problems. These excluded temperance people from the circle of those who now define what is deviant in drinking habits. The National Commission on Alcoholism was formed in 1941 and the Yale School of Alcoholic Studies formed in 1940. They were manned by medical personnel, social workers, and social scientists, people now alien to the spirit of the abstainer. Problems of drinking were removed from the church and placed in the hands of the universities and the medical clinics. The tendency to handle drinkers through protective and welfare agencies rather than through police or clergy has become more frequent.

"The bare statement that 'alcoholism is a disease' is most misleading since . . . it conceals what is essential—that a step in public policy is being recommended, not a scientific discovery announced."[23] John Seeley's remark is an apt one. Replacement of the norm of sin and repentance by that of illness and therapy removes the onus of guilt and immorality from the act of drinking and the state of chronic alcoholism. It replaces the image of the sinner with that of a patient, a person to be helped rather than to be exhorted. No wonder that the temperance movement has found the work of the Yale School, and often even the work of Alcoholics

Anonymous, a threat to its own movement. It has been most limited in its cooperation with these organizations and has attempted to set up other organizations which might provide the face of Science in league with the tone of the movement.[24]

The redefinition of the alcoholic as sick thus brought into power both ideas and organizations antithetical to the temperance movement. The norm protected by law and government was no longer the one held by the people who had supported temperance and Prohibition. The hostility of temperance people is readily understandable; their relative political unimportance is crucial to their present inability to make that hostility effective.

MOVEMENTS OF MORAL PASSAGE

In this chapter I have called attention to the fact that deviance designations have histories; the public definition of behavior as deviant is itself changeable. It is open to reversals of political power, twists of public opinion, and the development of social movements and moral crusades. What is attacked as criminal today may be seen as sick next year and fought over as possibly legitimate by the next generation.

Movements to redefine behavior may eventuate in a moral passage, a transition of the behavior from one moral status to another. In analyzing movements toward the redefinition of alcohol use, we have dealt with moral crusades which were restrictive and others which were permissive toward drinking and toward "drunkards." (We might have also used the word "alcoholics," suggesting a less disapproving and more medical perspective.) In both cases, however, the movements sought to change the public designation. While we are familiar with the restrictive or enforcing movements, the permissive or legitimizing movement must also be seen as a prevalent way in which deviants throw off the onus of their actions and avoid the sanctions associated with immoral activities.

Even where the deviants are a small and politically powerless group they may nevertheless attempt to protect themselves by influence over the process of designation. The effort to define themselves as ill is one plausible means to this end. Drug addiction as well as drunkenness is partially undergoing a change toward such definition.[25] This occurs in league with powerful groups in society, such as social workers, medical professionals, or university professors. The moral passage achieved here reduces the sanctions imposed by criminal law and the public acceptance of the deviant designation.

The "lifting" of a deviant activity to the level of a political, public issue is thus a sign that its moral status is at stake, that legitimacy is a possibility. Today the moral acceptance of drinking, marijuana and LSD use, homosexuality, abortion, and other "vices" is being publicly discussed, and movements championing them have emerged. Such movements draw into them far more than the deviants themselves. Because they become symbols of general cultural attitudes they call out partisans for both repression and permission. The present debate over drug addiction laws in the United States, for example, is carried out between defenders and opposers of the norm rather than between users and nonusers of the drugs involved.

As the movement for redefinition of the addict as sick has grown, the movement to strengthen the definition of addiction as criminal has responded with increased legal severity. To classify drug users as sick and the victims or clients as suffering from "disease" would mean a change in the agencies responsible for reaction from police enforcement to medical authorities. Further, it might diminish the moral disapproval with which drug use, and the reputed euphoric effects connected with it, are viewed by supporters of present legislation. Commenting on the clinic plan to permit medical dispensing of narcotics to licensed addicts, U.S. Commissioner of Narcotics Anslinger wrote: "This plan would elevate a most despicable trade to the avowed status of an honorable business, nay, to the status of practice of a time-honored profession; and drug addicts would multiply unrestrained, to the irrevocable impairment of the moral fiber and physical welfare of the American people" (Anslinger and Tompkins 1953, 186). Redefining moral crusades tends to generate strong countermovements. The deviant as a cultural opponent is a more potent threat to the norm than is the repentant, or even the sick deviant. The threat to the legitimacy of the norm is a spur to the need for symbolic restatement in legal terms. In these instances of "crimes without victims" the legal norm is *not* the enunciator of a consensus within the community. On the contrary, it is when consensus is least attainable that the pressure to establish legal norms appears to be greatest.

Chapter Nine

Deviance in the Welfare State
The Alcoholism Profession and the Entitlements of Stigma

A major perspective in sociological thought has led many to view social problems as the reflections of the disorganization and malaise of modern societies (Merton 1976). The emergence of concern about social conditions is then judged to be a consequence of phenomena to which a public responds. That perspective often ignores the constant and even greater persistence of ills and troubles in preindustrial and/or precapitalistic periods. Such "problems" lacked the social organization or the ideologies that might have led to sustained attempts to produce resolutions through social mechanisms. Problems of family strife, of crime, of poverty cannot be approached as social issues without a requisite set of ideas and social structures for stating them and making solutions operative. Even revolutions require a state against which to rebel (Walzer 1969, ch. 1). The definition of problems as conditions to be changed, alleviated, or ameliorated is not only a response to conditions. It is also a cultural invention of modern societies—a characteristic way of ordering and organizing phenomena into objects of public attention and collective action.

In his classic paper, "Social Problems That Are No More," the late Ian Weinberg succinctly described this process of turning private troubles into public problems: "In a modern society it is accepted that the family has not the human, material or organizational resources to deal with problems such as illness or crime. The educable, the sick, the criminal are quickly removed from the family. Modernization means that private family problems should quickly become public and social problems" (Weinberg 1974, 657).

It is certainly not that preindustrial and pre-nineteenth-century societies lacked troubles. Destitution, poverty, physical handicap, social strife, and familial trauma were hardly unknown. The development of whole areas of life and entire groups as "social problems," however, implies also that such phenomena have become public responsibilities—objects of amelioration and change for public agencies and agents of reform. The rise and enhancement of social problems is thus part of the development of the state as an agent of public goals and of the emergence of professions dedicated to the solution of such problems. I shall argue in particular, that the development of the mix of political ideals and governmental facilities labeled the "Welfare State" has a profound impact on which phenomena have become public problems and the responses made to them. The very concept of "social policy" implies a social organization committed to problem resolution.

The concept of "deviance" seems paradoxical to be coupled in my title with the welfare state. Characteristically sociologists have described deviance as a condition to be eradicated or controlled. Thus Edwin Lemert entitled his collection of papers *Human Deviance, Social Problems, and Social Control* (Lemert 1967). Even where sociologists have presented the deviant with sympathy they have also portrayed him or her as embattled, in conflict with authority (Becker 1963), an outsider. Yet, I shall argue, the assumptions of welfare ideas and the interests and missionary zeal of emergent professions serve to create entitlements in deviance and vested interests in their existence and continuation.

The ease of mobilizing politically those whose stigma creates solidarity, is enhanced by the emergence of "referral agents" whose very mission and livelihood exist in being their champions. As recent social problems theory suggests, sociological conceptions of deviance that emphasize the action of authorities toward stigmatized and weak outsiders will miss the interaction and the political environment within which social problems are constantly being defined and redefined (Spector and Kitsuse 1977).

The origins and the assumptions of welfare policies are multiple and vary from country to country (Wilensky 1975). Nevertheless there is a common distinction, especially in capitalistic economies, that separates welfare orientations from the attitudes of state and society within the conception of a free market. Whether the extension of services and perquisites to larger and larger segments of the public in such measures as old age assistance, medical insurance, or social security and unemployment compensation are seen as ways to quiet protesting classes or outcroppings of new political ideals, certain consequences of the welfare-system idea are apparent (Piven and Cloward 1971; Bendix 1964).

One of these is the provision of a floor beneath which the contingencies of a market economy are not to be tolerated. Orphans must not be left to starve although they have little productive contribution. Old people, the handicapped, and the poor are not to be left to the vagaries of a laissez faire economy in which they are too weak to compete (Briggs 1961; Marshall 1965). In this sense the orientation to provide for the welfare of the disadvantaged is a limitation placed on the market society, but only a limit. It is what James O'Connor refers to as the "social costs" of conducting a politically stable capitalist economy within the confines of twentieth-century corporate and state capitalism (O'Connor 1973).

Alvin Gouldner has expressed a similar thought in analyzing a utilitarian basis for welfare perspectives; especially where the "deviant" is the case: "A central problem confronting a society organized around utilitarian values is the disposal and control of 'useless' men and useless traits. . . . Increasingly the Welfare State's strategy is to transform the sick, the deviant, and the unskilled into 'useless' citizens and to return them to 'society' only after periods of hospitalization, treatment, counselling, training or retraining" (Gouldner 1970, 76).

Both O'Connor's and Gouldner's formulations see the welfare state largely as a social control mechanism, whose gains are reaped by political extraction from an unwilling elite of controllers. They miss another significant aspect of welfare ideology, one which Bendix and Marshall have stressed; the collectivist conception of common citizenship (Bendix 1964; Marshall 1965). This ideal seeks not minimum conditions of life for all members of the polity but equivalence of conditions. Social security legislation and public education are examples. In these cases the services are provided without a means test, irrespective of need.

Deviance presents an anomaly. If deviants suffer from a stigma, as in the case of the mentally disturbed, or from a defect of character, as in criminality, then they lie outside the society, and are something less than citizens. Toward such deviants it is possible to take a social control orientation in order to prevent deviance from impinging on the total society. Such has not been the welfare stance toward alcoholics, no less than toward the mentally disturbed, the physically handicapped, or the old and destitute. Reform, restoration, and rehabilitation have marked the designs of welfare, increasingly so in recent decades.

Nor can it be argued that such measures as rehabilitative programs directed at reforming the criminal are strategies to maximize the labor force. Such cost-benefit calculations are seldom made or introduced into public or legislative arguments in other than an abstract fashion. Indeed, it can be more cogently argued that taking people, especially unskilled labor, off the labor market, is a sounder mode of social control than curing them and increasing the labor force and the politically troublesome possibilities of unemployed workers.

This thrust toward citizenship, which I will detail in this paper in the instance of the chronic alcoholic, develops along with the occupations and associations which come into being with the very idea that the deviant is both treatable and reformable. Once the state undertakes responsibility, others can undertake to shape and effect that responsibility.

My argument is illustrated by the case of alcoholics and public policy toward alcoholism. In the development of public commitments to the poor, the disabled, the criminal, the sick and other groups, such as alcoholics, people are defined as in trouble and with a just claim to public help. It is crucial to the understanding of my argument to recognize the growth of occupations and professions that exist to help the troubled persons. Such "troubled-persons" industries are of major importance in understanding the political role of their constituencies in the formulation and implementation of policy toward deviants. In the past two decades, alcohol problems have been significantly influenced by the emergence and proliferation of the professional pursuits of "the alcoholism industry."

THE SOCIAL PROBLEMS PROFESSIONS

The emergence of an aggregation of social problems, including alcohol use, is a piece of the historical development of public commitments to the poor, the disabled, the criminal, the sick and other groups that come to be defined as people in trouble with a claim to public help (Wilensky and LeBeaux 1958). The provision of welfare to the needy has become a major function of contemporary governments in Europe and the United States (Wilensky 1975; Janowitz 1978, ch. 5). By 1975 the United States was spending approximately 20 percent of its gross national product on welfare expenditures—for health, education, income maintenance, and community development (Janowitz 1978, 138–40).

The increase in welfare function by public agencies brought with it a new and significant occupational force—the "troubled persons" professions. As the United States moved from an economy geared to primary and secondary production and into one more heavily oriented toward services, the segments of the labor force in professional and semiprofessional work sharply increased (Singelmann 1978; Gartner and Reissman 1974). In 1950 the ratio of goods production to service provision in the American economy was 51 to 49. By 1968 it was 36 to 64 (Gartner and

Reissman 1974, 19). Occupations developed through welfare functions and social problems are a phase of this diminution of agriculture and manufacturing in the labor force.

Not even an approximate count exists of the numbers of the service sector involved in serving "troubled persons." Given the diversity of job classifications, such a census would be difficult to conduct. The National Center for Health Statistics reported in 1971 that full-time employees of in-patient health facilities for the mentally retarded, orphans and dependent children, the emotionally disturbed, unwed mothers, alcoholics and drug abusers, the deaf and blind, and physically handicapped together numbered approximately 250,000 people (U.S. National Center for Health Statistics 1973). A list of occupations concerned with the solution of social problems would certainly include such specialties as city planners, urban renewal specialists, social workers, guidance counselors, probation officers, psychologists, safety consultants, and alcohol rehabilitation workers. A much longer list can be made but the boundaries are at present hard to define. The same person may devote only part of his or her time to "troubled persons." He or she may shift from one field to another as funds dry up and/or flow from different directions (Helfgot 1977). Frequently nomenclature has not yet caught up with activities.

In whatever organized form or however specialized, the public attention to social problems has created an environment in which new occupations have emerged for which the designation "problem-solving professions" is apt (Gold 1976, 512–26). These occupations are professional in making a claim to a body of knowledge and skill resulting from specialized training and education. Some, like social work, are highly organized with a long history of professional credentials and licensure. Others have training facilities and opportunities which define the field but do not develop exclusive jurisdiction for control of conditions or recruitment. Examples here are child guidance or community organizations for which baccalaureate programs exist in colleges but do not control occupational entry. Others are in a more nascent period of professional development, just beginning self-definition and systems of control. Drug abuse and alcohol abuse specialists are among these.

Such professions are by no means in a static relationship to their existing or potential clientele. The development of problem-solving professionals has produced a body of people who possess the skills, interests, time, mission, and resources to articulate and organize the groups whom they serve or seek to serve (McCarthy and Zald 1974). They innovate programs and policies and frequently assume leading roles in reformist movements to alleviate the problems of their clientele or newly discovered clientele. Reflecting on the origin of the American antipoverty programs of the 1960, Daniel Moynihan maintained that reform has become professionalized. "War on poverty was not declared at the behest of the poor. Just the opposite" (Moynihan 1965, 248). Pressures were placed by paid staff members within one wing of government on other wings of government.

CHAMPIONS AND THEIR DEVIANTS

The example of the antipoverty programs of the 1960s are by no means typical of all social problems approaches by government. Yet the discussion in Moynihan, as in McCarthy and Zald, emphasizes the reforming, articulating, and mobilizing leadership that professional social-problems solvers supply to the construction of a problem, its theory of explanation, and its policies to alleviate the problem. The popular imagery of how professionals relate to the social groups they serve is generally a one-way analysis; the professionals minister to needs and to needful people; they do not create or generate such needs. That popular model minimizes the interaction between clientele and professionals. In that interaction the stigmatized group, mobilized with and through the support and action of those who provide their needs, enter the areas of power and politics. Such considerations of what Schur calls "the politics of deviance" contrast sharply with the traditional sociological imagery of the deviant as necessarily powerless (Schur 1980). Illustrated here in the growing claims of alcoholics to public assistance for treatment and protection, these considerations introduce a newer conception which contradicts the passive, dependent, and stigmatized symbolism inherent in the analytical uses to which even labeling theory was put.[1]

There is a considerable difference between deviance or stigma viewed as deprivational and the same condition viewed as entitlement. The first gives rise to public hostility toward deviants and enforcement or conformity. The second creates a demand for services that enhance the stigmatized, even if it maintains the stigma.

An illustration drawn from an Indian experience may make the point about the public consequences of what Ralph Turner calls deviance avowal, using Alcoholics Anonymous as illustrative (Turner 1972). In his last years B. R. Ambedkar, the leader of India's untouchable caste (or outcastes), converted to Buddhism and advised his followers to do likewise, convinced as he was that Untouchables could never achieve justice within

Hinduism. Being non-Hindu, the three and one-half million who followed Ambedkar's advice claimed they were no longer Untouchables. As non-Hindus, they were now outside of caste definitions or caste rules. After independence, however, the new Indian constitution granted Untouchables and other "scheduled Castes" certain advantages, such as quotas to insure admission to schools and governmental employment and extra points in civil service exams. The former Untouchables, now Buddhists, tried to gain these advantages of stigma by declaring themselves Untouchables for purposes and in areas of advantage. They still retained their new status as Buddhists and non-Untouchables for other purposes. In a famous decision in the early 1960s the Indian Supreme Court upheld their right to do so (Harrison 1960).

The model of the Indian case suggests that stigmatized, deviant, and "troubled" groups may possess a stake in their infirm status. They may mobilize for purposes of obtaining and retaining the interests in services that are or can become attached to their condition rather than resist the definition of themselves as stigmatized people. Stigmatized groups can become organized publics as a means to gain welfare services, to defend themselves against political deprivations, to be helped with their problems, and even, as in the case of homosexuals, to protest their status as stigmatized and "troubled persons." In this process the problem-solving professionals may function in interaction with the clientele, operating to mobilize them in achieving the very services the professionals provide. The social worker who organizes the aged, or the lawyer who works for increased treatment for alcoholics are all in the business of mobilizing deviant or stigmatized people and being their champions in promoting the entitlement of "troubled persons" to service.

The division between the clientele and the professional is perhaps too finite. As the case of alcoholism suggests, both mobilization of stigmatized groups and the problem-solving professionals contain significant components of persons who are, or have been, members of the stigmatized clientele. People can find capital in their troubles and use them to provide access to leadership, livelihood in the clientele organizations or entrée into the profession that services the group. The homosexual employed by the Gay Rights Union, the recovered alcoholic serving as a county alcoholism agent, the former or intermittent mental patient who becomes a counselor or clinical psychologist are all instances of a prevalent tendency for people to develop interests and missions out of troubles and to capitalize their stigmas as sources of occupational income. The same is true of minorities and ethnic groups in general (Wiley 1967).

THE INVENTION OF ALCOHOLISM AND THE
RISE OF SERVICES

The idea that there exists a specific segment of the population of drinkers who suffer from the use of alcohol, that they cannot be helped without special procedures of intervention, and that a specialized referral structure of organizations and professionals is needed to help them is not an old one. It is a product of the mid-twentieth century. Its occurrence is predicated on two primary events: (1) the dominance of the chronic alcoholic as the problem of alcohol in American society, and (2) the invention of the disease concept of alcoholism.

While excessive use of alcohol was often observed as a matter of concern before the nineteenth century, it was not organized as a problem— as a demand that public organizations attempt resolutions to alleviate the problems of troubled people (MacAndrew 1969). When alcohol did emerge as a public issue, after 1826 in the United States, the concern of the temperance movement was with drinking, and not only with a special segment of drinkers. "Habitual drunkards" were, of course, recognized, but only as a part of the problem of drinking. The general incapacities of alcohol were given dominance in thought and policies of the movement (Gusfield 1963; Levine 1978b; Schneider 1978; Conrad and Schneider 1980, ch. 4). The alcohol problem was not encapsulated, nor was the remedying of the "habitual drunkard" a primary, or even major, aim. Only in the Washingtonian movement of the late 1840s and the 1850s was there an attempt to direct attention specifically toward the drunkard as the target of an anti-alcohol movement.[2]

The religious orientation of the temperance movement was consistent with the view that acts of will were the solution to personal issues of alcohol excess. The political bias of the movement was toward prohibition of sales as the solution to diminishing alcohol problems. Neither special attention nor special personnel were called upon by the then current definition and understanding of alcohol problems. In fact, the development of hospitals and other medical institutions and services as specialized units was itself a matter of evolution through the nineteenth century (Rothman 1970, ch. 6; Weinberg 1974).

There were some "straws in the wind" in the late nineteenth and early twentieth century. A group of physicians working in mental institutions became aware of alcohol patients as presenting a unique kind of mental illness. In the 1870s these doctors established the *Quarterly Journal of Inebriety* and also championed the creation of special clinics, hospitals, and other facilities specifically for the inebriate (Wilkerson 1966). The physicians and the *Journal* had little evident impact on either the temperance movement or the general public.

The demise of Prohibition in 1933 made a new conception of alcohol problems and their resolution possible. As alcohol problems receded from the arenas of political conflict between cultural groups, they were transformed into medical and scientific problems of helping the suffering chronic alcoholic. In this transformation the concept that alcoholism is a disease was a crucial change in the consciousness of Americans. The term "alcoholism" is itself not in common use in the United States until after the second decade of the twentieth century. It was not until the 1940s that alcohol research became a part of university activities and that a body of work began to appear in which the condition of alcoholism was described and defined, and in which it was referred to as a "disease" and hence a medical problem to be treated (Jellinek 1960; Wilkerson 1966; Paredes 1976; Bynum 1968; McCarthy 1958).

The view that alcohol problems are confined to a special group of deviant drinkers and that the condition is a medical one resulting from external influences rather than the "will" of the alcoholic is part of a turn away from seeking solutions to these problems through direct political conflicts. It is also a turn toward the provision of services of treatment for a special group whose stigma entitles them to consideration and help. It is also the basis for development of a corps of specialists in treatment, cure, and service.

The field, or subdiscipline, of "alcohology" is an instance of expertise in motion. The physicians who founded the *Journal of Inebriety* in 1870 may be seen as its precursors, but the proliferation, organization, and increasing specialization of the alcohol problem and alcohol specialists dates from the 1940s. It is since then, and especially in the past twenty years, that an array of subprofessions have developed through which persons earn their livelihood by treating alcoholic patients, administering facilities for alcoholics, counseling people with alcohol problems, conducting research about alcohol and alcohol problems, and teaching others about alcohol and alcohol problems.

The rise of the alcohol expert has been accompanied by the increase in specialized facilities for the alcohol abuser—detoxification centers, half-way houses, hospital wards, alcohol outpatient clinics, alcohol hospitals, and the public facility for personal transformation, Alcoholics Anonymous.

The development of the alcohol therapist is part of the process of evolution of the human services economy. It includes speech therapists, occupational therapists, physical therapists, family therapists, drug abuse therapists, sex-development therapists, and, of course, pyschotherapists. It is a period whose growth is captured in the title of Phillip Rieff's book, *The Triumph of the Therapeutic* (1966).

THE ALCOHOLISM INDUSTRY

The period from the Repeal of Prohibition to the early 1970s has been one of the withdrawal of alcohol issues from high priority on the agenda of public issues and its reemergence as a problem of public welfare and service. This shift from "drinking" as the center of attention to "alcoholism" as the central preoccupation of public associations and government is what I refer to as the "alcoholism movement."

The movement that redefined the character of the alcohol problem in America may be described in the activities and development of three major groups. These are the sufferers from alcohol problems; the academic scientists; and the medical and quasi-medical personnel, especially psychiatrists and quasi-psychiatrists, such as clinical psychologists, social workers, and counselors. While there is much divergence in outlook, belief, and activity between these three, they have all shared a common perception of the alcoholic as an object of care and of alcoholism as a disease which must be accorded the same nonjudgmental status as other illnesses (Seeley 1962). It is not drinking or the commodity of alcohol that is the object of attention. The "abnormal," "deviant," "excessive," or "addictive drinker" and his or her recovery has now taken the public stage.

With the establishment of Alcoholics Anonymous in 1935, the clientele, the sufferers, organized to effectuate their own salvations (Maxwell 1962; Leach 1973; Norris 1976; Cahn 1970). Although AA has explicitly refrained from professional and political action, it has emphasized the deviant character of the alcoholic and made his or her recovery a major aim of the solution of alcohol problems. Although AA has made its appeal to personal transformation through spiritual and interpersonal relationships, it has also perceived the condition of alcoholism as one of disease and as something that cannot be helped without intervention.

Another way in which AA contributed to the change in the nature of alcohol problems in the United States was through the emergence of a corps of people—"recovered alcoholics"—who represented an important source of political pressure, financial and moral resources, and organizational mobilization.[3] These people have contributed greatly to the political and publicity activities of the movement, and have made up an important part of the treatment arm as well.

The appearance of an academic science interested in alcohol brought into play a knowledge and established authority that provided training and skill to a nascent profession. Beginning in the mid-1930s, in the wake of Prohibition repeal, this effort came largely from the development of the Center for Alcohol Studies at Yale (now at Rutgers University). It was followed in later years by an expansion of courses, institutes, and summer schools elsewhere. Mark Keller, who witnessed the founding of the precursor of the Yale Center, the Research Council on Problems of Alcohol, has written: "A small group of thoughtful people had a brilliant idea. Drinking and the associated problems had been around for a long time and neither legislation nor compulsory inculcation of the fear of disease or hellfire had been effective in preventing or ameliorating them. Were we not in the age of science? Could not the power of science be brought to bear on these problems?" (Keller 1976, 20).

Through its staff's publications, especially the highly influential *The Disease Concept of Alcoholism* (Jellinek 1960), the Yale Center laid the foundation for the profession of alcohologists. It made alcohol and alcohol treatment valid objects of scientific study. It was the leading agent in creating a body of knowledge that could serve as a basis for the claim of practitioners to know something and practice a skill that justified their legitimate mandate to practice a profession.

In casting a clinical eye at the alcoholic, the scientists were in tandem, if not in league, with Alcoholics Anonymous. Both groups visualized the alcoholic as "victim" of something beyond his ready control. He or she became an object of commiseration and help instead of indifference, exhortation, or condemnation; a victim, instead of a villain; a patient instead of a sinner. Alcoholics Anonymous "helped the Center on Alcohol Studies by reinforcing the teaching that alcoholics were not all Skid Row bums, that they could be rehabilitated. That, in turn, helped the Center in reinforcing the teaching that there were other things to do about alcohol problems than just fight alcohol—for example we would help the victims" (Keller 1976, 22).

Both Alcoholics Anonymous and the academics focused attention on the deviant drinker—the chronic alcoholic—as the object of public policy and concern. Operating within a medical framework of disease, they made the transformation or "cure" of the alcoholic the major task of the alcohol issue. This framework of thought and action was reinforced in the development of programs of treatment and treatment personnel. A new occupation of alcohol therapy came into existence. It forms the backbone of what I call "the alcoholism industry."

The treatment establishment takes the form of clinics, hospitals, and other facilities devoted in whole or part to the alcoholic. In 1973–1974, a partial list of such clinics and facilities numbered 2,565 in the United States (*Alcohol and Drug Problems Association of North America, 1973–74*), a great increase over the 1940s (Corwin and Cunningham 1974; Kahn 1970, 70). In the past two or three decades a large number of organizations, associations, treatment centers, detoxification units, journals, and local councils have come into existence to find, screen, treat, and rehabilitate the chronic alcoholic. Beginning with the Yale Center in the 1940s, many training institutes in the fields of alcohol studies and alcoholism have been established to provide training for personnel in these fields.[4]

Defining alcoholism as a medical problem requiring treatment is the basis for the intervention of skilled personnel into alcohol work. Although the American Medical Association declared alcohol to be a medical problem in 1956, it has remained largely a psychiatric and psychological field (Kahn 1970). A network of psychiatrists, psychologists, social workers, counselors, guidance persons, and other quasi-medical persons have been drawn into alcoholism treatment as a source of livelihood. Often the recovered alcoholic has made up a significant component of the occupational population. Sometimes the occupation includes research workers and clinical personnel who move from one problem to another— drugs, alcohol, suicide, child abuse—as fashion and funds dictate.

AA and the treatment establishment have often been in conflict. A major assumption of treatment occupations has been that skills in treatment can be learned, "that personal experience is not a prerequisite for helping others with a given condition" (Cahn 1970, 141). Between the professional outlook of the alcohologists and the spiritual emphasis of AA, suspicion and contempt has often existed. Nevertheless, all three groups, including the academic scientists, have helped create a climate of thought that has made the chronic alcoholic the center of alcohol problems and the intervention of others essential to his or her recovery. In that fashion they have laid the foundation for the professions and welfare programs which have emerged in recent years as a part of the "problem-solving" professions.

THE ALCOHOLISM MOVEMENT AND THE
POST-REPEAL PERIOD

The temperance and Prohibition movements in the United States had set one segment of the population against another (Gusfield 1963). In making the activity of alcohol drinking the target of policy, these movements politicized American lifestyles. With the diminution in the power and passion of the anti-alcohol movements after 1933, the target of policy was narrowed to a "victim"—the chronic alcoholic. This transformation enabled both welfare policy to emerge and professions to arise that could service such problem people. There were four major characteristics of the cultural beliefs which provided a source of validity for the new service professions.

1. *The acceptance of alcohol as a legitimate commodity.* All of the groups described above were agreed on the legitimacy of alcohol in the lives of most of the American population. It was only the chronic alcoholic—the deviant drinker—who constituted a problem. In this they broke with the dominant emphasis of temperance on alcohol and on drinking. In its slogan, "The fault is not in the bottle. It's in the man," the liquor industry indicated the belief that alcohol problems are only found in a special segment of the drinking population—those who have lost control over their capacity to control their drinking. That segment is not simply a different culture, people with different values, but a set of people who need help.[5]

2. *Alcoholism is a disease and should be accorded the same status as other medical ailments.* The medical definition of alcoholism puts the "condition" into a class of conditions that are not solely a result of the will of the sufferer. As a medical ailment it can be a target of "treatment." Like mental illness, cancer, and drug addiction, the person is "sick" and amenable to intervention and "cure." Even AA, though it retains part of a spiritual definition, sees alcoholism as a disease. This cultural meaning of the status of a chronic alcoholic is largely a product of the past thirty-five years (Jellinek 1960). It makes the emergence of specialized personnel in treatment a possibility. Furthermore, it legitimates the existence of the "health" policies of government welfare.

3. *The location of responsibility for the problem of alcoholism in personal reconstruction through institutional help.* From the standpoint of development of the services sector, the significant impact of the changed meanings of alcohol abuse in American life is precisely in the rise of institutions to help alcoholics and/or problem drinkers toward

rehabilitation. As this becomes the goal of alcohol policy, personal change is a public charge. It is the welfare of the "victim" that is the object of public attention. While other considerations, such as utilizing valuable labor supplies or preventing public disorder, may exist, the manifest goal of public policy is now directed at the improvement and rehabilitation of a special category of deviant people.

4. *Redefinition of the alcohol problem as one of welfare rather than political conflict.* Defining the problem of alcohol as that of the alcoholic was a great change from the century of agitation and conflict over the sale and distribution of alcohol as the major issue in alcohol policy. That conflict, represented by Prohibition and Repeal, made the "liquor question" a center of intense political struggle over the status and legitimacy of diverse lifestyles and segments of population. The alcoholism movement helped to defuse the controversial character of alcohol policy. The issues became statable as those of "How much should we help alcoholics?" They were no longer clearly issues of control and authority of the state over lifestyles.

For at least seventy-five years, issues of liquor control had been salient in American politics; a constant issue before legislatures and in elections. Alcohol questions had polarized American electorates along lines of religious, urban-rural, and immigrant-native memberships. It was a potent differentiator of cultures and lifestyles and leisure in America (Gusfield 1963). Drinkers versus abstainers, wets versus drys were engaged in political disputes over the moral status of drinking. With Repeal, the legitimacy of drinking was established, although alcohol remained a "special commodity" to be accorded restrictions in its use that distinguished it from most other salable goods. In coming to define *the* problems of alcohol as those of a deviant group whose lack of control was distinctive and abnormal, the alcohol problem no longer contained the sources of political conflict. Both wets and drys, the church and the liquor industry could easily agree that alcoholism was a disease that should be eliminated and alcoholics people who merited sympathy and help. The more conflict-producing questions were now finessed.

THE EXPANSION OF THE "TROUBLED PERSONS"
INDUSTRIES

By the mid-1960s the alcoholism movement had become the major source of alcohol activities in the United States. Largely voluntary rather than governmental, it had nevertheless brought into being an active group of recovered alcoholics and a set of new specialties and professions occupied in the care and treatment of alcoholics. The mobilization of these groups significantly affected the pressing of new claims on government. These new claims, in turn, produced even greater expansion of the alcoholism industry.

The two major achievements of the alcoholism movement have been the establishment of the National Institute for Alcohol Abuse and Alcoholism and the increasing decriminalization of public drunkenness. The first of these, the establishment of the NIAAA, occurred in 1970 and is the more instructive of the two in its implications for professional growth. In 1970, Congress passed the Comprehensive Alcohol Abuse and Alcoholism Prevention, Treatment and Rehabilitation Act. It established the NIAAA as a unit within the National Institute for Mental Health. (Since then, Mental Health, Drugs, and Alcohol have become separate institutes making up a new agency, the Alcohol, Drugs and Mental Health Administration.) The legislation also provided for grants-in-aid to states in the amount of $180 million over a three-year period to assist state and local programs. Among its other provisions, it also forbade discrimination in federal employment on the basis of prior alcoholism and prohibited hospitals receiving federal funds from refusing admission to patients because of alcoholic condition (U.S. Title 42, 4551–4593; U. W. Code, 1970: 10690–10693). The 1970 Act has meant a major expansion in alcoholic treatment and prevention facilities and programs.

The passage of the act owes a great deal to the support and activity of the major alcohol groups and associations. The National Council on Alcoholism—an organization of recovered alcoholics, interested persons, and professionals—has chapters in most counties in the United States. The Alcohol and Drug Problems Association of North America represents the professional and governmental personnel in alcohol work in Canada and the United States. These two, and other organizations, were effective lobbyists and campaigners for the 1970 act. Their efforts were immeasurably enhanced by the congressional leadership of Democratic Senator Harold Hughes of Iowa, a publicly declared "recovered alcoholic" and a strong proponent of treatment programs and government aid.

The crux of the role of these groups in pressing claims on government is seen in the resistance the movement encountered to passage of the legislation. The major opposition came from the White House and the Department of Health, Education and Welfare (based on interviews with informed persons who were party to the passage of the act). They feared that establishment of units around a category of disease, such as alcoholism, would provide an avenue by which the mobilization of political pressure in favor of alcohol treatment would be increased.

The decriminalization of public drunkenness was by no means solely the work of the alcoholism movement. It also coincided with a great concern over the increasing costs of incarceration (Pittman 1967). However, the organized efforts of the alcoholism movement to depict the alcoholic as "victim" had implications for the decriminalization movement and included decriminalization in its goals. Through mass-media campaigns and through state and federal lobbying, the movement sought a basic change in the concept of the alcoholic as Skid Row bum and as able to achieve his own salvation through will alone. The development of the Cooperative Commission on Alcohol Problems was a significant step in public agitation and constituency-building especially through the publication and dissemination of an influential report on alcohol problems (Plaut 1967).

Each step in provision of new services in turn created a body of personnel who become the source of a mission to expand as well as defend services. The decriminalization of public drunkenness led to the development of detoxification centers in many cities and the expansion of alcohol recovery treatment centers funded by state, county, and federal auspices (Regier 1979). The professions thus come to constitute a group at several levels of public welfare in the United States.

STIGMA, ENTITLEMENT, AND OCCUPATIONAL GROWTH

The treatment model, whatever its other implications for medical, professional power and authority, legitimates its intervention in the name of client as victim. A consequence of defining the client as someone to be helped rather than punished is that he or she shares in whatever are the general entitlements to health in the society. Increasingly the insurance coverage for alcohol and alcohol-related "illnesses" has been expanded; the right to medical and quasi-medical treatment service provided through governmental funds increased. The alcoholics and recovered alcoholics have been mobilized to use political power in defending themselves against possible stigma and its consequences. This process, which Renee Fox aptly calls "conditionally legitimate deviance" (Fox 1977), is predicated on his or her assumption of the illness role working to effect cure by cooperation with the defined system of medical authority. Alcoholics seek treatment rather than resist and disavow the stigmata of alcoholism.

An example of the growing entitlement character of deviance is shown by the Rehabilitation Act of 1973 which protects handicapped people against job discrimination. In July 1977 the Labor Department used this act as a basis for directing employers with federal contracts to take "affirmative action" to hire drug abusers and alcoholics if they are able to perform the work. The assistant secretary of labor for employment standards compared the drug abuser and the alcoholic to Blacks, Hispanics and other minorities. In his press release, the assistant secretary made an interesting comment: "'Our government spends a considerable amount of money each year to rehabilitate alcoholics and drug abusers, to help them again become employable, productive citizens. It would be incongruous to turn around and deny them protection under the antidiscrimination law'" (*New York Times*, pt. 1, July 6, 1977, 14).

Here is outlined how the cognitive structures that represent the alcoholic as ill and thus handicapped make him the logical candidate for political measures to help the helpless.

The same process of entitlement to services occurs as well in private industry. In the past, labor-management contracts gave management the right to fire workers who were alcoholic—being drunk at work or absent. Increasingly such contracts prohibit firings in these cases unless management has first made adequate programs for treatment and rehabilitation available.

The growth of the "troubled-persons industries" is a significant part of service economy development of the welfare state. This paper on the alcoholism industry of the past three decades has illustrated the importance of the organization and cultural symbols created by the "troubled persons" and their professional helpers. It suggests that professions do not arise in response to abstract functions for abstract clients. They are products of human intervention and activity in which cause and effect are interactive. In the political economy of a welfare society, troubles are also opportunities and service is also reward.

Those who label and define others as "social problems" are by no means simply "agents of social control." Somebody's trouble, in an open polity and a welfare economy, is somebody else's job. The interplay between the two is a necessary ingredient in understanding the character and political status of deviance in contemporary American life. The alcoholism movement is one example of this process. It can also be duplicated, I suggest, in the instances of mental health, minority rights, and physically handicapped, to name three other areas. This interplay between problems and those charged with their resolution suggests as well the political component which deviance now necessarily includes in understanding its forms and its history. Even the relationship described here between alcoholism treatment and the alcoholic may be in process of change. As the medical commitments of the welfare state have grown, the costs of a treatment model have become increasingly apparent. The current movement toward prevention in medical circles and in alcohol policy is one such indication (Gusfield 1984b).

Nevertheless, the interdependence of occupation, welfare policies and deviance continues. The considerations examined here indicate how problem-solving occupations are sources of their own expansion. In serving others, the welfare state serves itself. What was said of the American missionaries in Hawaii is overly cynical, yet captures a side of the analysis. It makes the paradox of mission and reward a pointed one: "They came to do good. They stayed and did well."

AFTERWORD, 1994

In the past several decades, and especially since the 1960s there has occurred in the United States what is being referred to an explosion of rights or, in legal terms, the "due process" revolution. The legal historian Lawrence Friedman has described the phenomenon clearly in *Total Justice:*

> The end result, from the vantage point of 1984, is a radically
> altered legal culture. Specifically, two new social principles, or
> superprinciples, appeared as part of American legal culture . . .
> The first is what we can call *a general expectation of justice;* the
> second is *a general expectation of recompense.* The first, in brief,
> is the citizen's expectation of fair treatment everywhere and in every
> circumstance. . . .
> The second general expectation . . . that somebody will pay for any
> and all calamities that happen to a person, provided only that it is not
> the victim's "fault" or at least not solely his fault. (Friedman 1985, 43)

The "revolution of rights" is best exemplified in the civil rights and in the women's movements but it goes far beyond those two categories. It includes many groups who, before the changing culture of new laws and new social principles, were excluded from entitlement claims. Among these are prisoners, children, students (at all levels of education), the physically handicapped, employees, homosexuals, immigrants, patients, and animals. We can even speak, though in a limited sense, of prostitutes' rights (Jenness 1993; Weitzer 1991). What is significant about these new claims to fairness, equality, and treatment is that, in a number of cases, they are developed in movements of people in their and about their special statuses. Though stigmatized or deviant, their claims are to persons of that status. Thus prisoners' rights refer to the rights of prisoners in relation to required goods and services and the facilities of their punishment.

The trends in the proliferation of entitlements for the mentally disturbed, the alcoholic, and the drug addict described in this chapter and the growth of the professional "champions" of them have continued in the years since this was originally written. In general, federal and state funds for treatment of all three increased in the period 1984–1991, despite the alleged antipathy of the Reagan administration toward the welfare state. In 1973–74, as stated in the chapter, there were 2,565 facilities for treatment of alcoholics funded by the federal and state governments. In 1984 this had grown to 3,943, an increase of 53.7 percent (Butynski, Record, and Yates 1984). By 1991 this had increased to 900 alcohol treatment units and 5,572 alcohol and drug combined units, an increase of 64.1 percent in seven years (Butynski et al. 1991). In the same period, admissions for alcohol problems had also increased but by a lesser amount, 33 percent. In the years 1986–1991, total expenditures for alcohol and drug programs by state and federal sources had increased by 97.9 percent. For all these years, approximately 75 percent of all funds went to treatment.

The right of the problem drinker to treatment for his or her stigma was furthered by the changes in health insurance policy which made for coverage of chemical dependencies. This marked a distinct change from the earlier policies of noncoverage for alcoholism and drug addictions.

The entitlement of alcoholics and recovering alcoholics to security of employment was further enhanced by the federal vocational rehabilitation acts and handicapped persons acts which prevented dismissal where no evidence of incompetence at work could be shown. Even where alcoholism is shown to be related to poor work performance a body of Workman's Compensation law is beginning to grow which, in some cases, treats alcoholism as a medical condition and prevents dismissal without employer provision of opportunities for treatment (Sonnenstuhl and Trice 1991; Scanlon 1986, ch. 11; Staudenmeier 1987).

The prevailing image of alcohol problems as those of alcoholism lost a great deal of its power during the 1970s and 1980s (as I indicate in chapters 11 and 12). The medicalization of the alcoholic inherent in the disease concept of alcoholism came into conflict with the criminalizing image, especially in the image of the drinking-driver. Nevertheless the compassionate and entitling image of the alcoholic continued to be influential in legal and governmental policies. The changes in the status of public drunkenness is indicative of this shift.

Although far from uniform, in the United States to a considerable extent the public drunk has been in process of change from a criminal status, involving arrest and incarceration, to a medical one, involving detoxification centers and access to treatment (Pittman 1991). Legal decisions have given added protection to the chronic alcoholic and supported a decriminalized status for the public drunk.

All of this is by no means a disappearance of stigma or deviant status. What it implies however is the continuance of the trend recognized in the chapter, published in 1982, of the proliferation of the professional champions of the stigmatized and the growing proliferation of rights and entitlements accruing to their clients.

Chapter Ten

Persuasion to Deviance
Stigma and Redemption
in Law and Medicine

The medicalization of alcohol problems exemplified in the disease concept of alcoholism was much more than a revision of scientific theories. It was at the same time a bid for revision of the public image of the troubled and troublesome drinker. Earlier conventional wisdom about drinking had attributed chronic drunkenness to a flaw in the character of the drinker. The "habitual drunkard," the "chronic inebriate," or the "alcoholic" was that way because he lacked the willpower, the personal capacity or the discipline to be otherwise. In a profound sense, he "chose" his malady. The disease concept shifted the explanation of alcoholism from the internal, inherent nature of the drinker to the external nature of a disease. For the nineteenth century and the first third of the twentieth the habitual drunkard was someone to be condemned as a sinner and pitied for his moral limitations. He bore the stigma of the sinner. With the disease theory of alcoholism, he was a victim of illness and beyond judgment by moral criteria. He was an object of help, not condemnation.

Some of the research papers studying alcoholism as an attribute of drinking-drivers were clear in drawing the implications of their research for legal sanctions on drinking-driving offenders (Waller 1967). They saw the legal policies of fines and jail as futile attempts to deter many drinking-drivers. The deterrence theory of legal compliance has been based on the assumption that potential offenders were able to control their drinking and were therefore responsible for their acts. Once seen as addicted and sick the opposite conclusion is drawn. The problem is not legal but medical.

At first sight it would seem that the two institutions—Law and Medicine—operate with two very different conceptions of their objects. For law the offender is a criminal, an offender. For medicine he is a patient.

The terminology points to different attitudes. The basic question of Anglo-Saxon law, Who is at fault?, presupposes a theory of causality imputing intentionality and will to the defendant (Hart 1968, ch. 2; Packer 1968, pt. 1). While doctrines of strict or absolute liability have existed and have been increasingly used, the imputation of individual fault has been a central feature of both criminal and civil law. Guilt at law carries the stigma of moral lapse, of sin or incompetence or both.

Medicine, and especially the concept of disease, seems exempt from the threat of stigmatizing the patient (Conrad and Schneider 1980; Siegler and Osmond 1974). The patient is protected against the attribution of social deviance. His illness is not self-caused but the result of extrinsic processes. Since these are beyond his control, they present no basis for disapproval of the person. They are not flaws in his character. Illness is not a result of sin or incompetent living (Parsons 1951, ch. 10).

This chapter is a report of two studies of diversionary programs an American court used in sentencing convicted drinking-drivers in 1973. In it I analyze some implications of the attempted transformation of legal problems into medical ones. Each of the programs described here was presented to the defendant as an alternative to a jail sentence or, in some cases, to a fine and/or license suspensions.[1] One was a class called The Drinking Driver, mandated at the discretion of some judges in lieu of other "punishments" for drinking and driving. The other was a special program of presentencing probation interviews completed with convicted DUI offenders. The interviews were conducted by a probation officer preliminary to his sentencing recommendation to the court. These programs posed some of the issues of legal versus medical dispositions and the varying ways of conceiving of alcohol problems in the United States.

The distinctions that I have drawn between the legal and the medical view of an offense are able to be dissolved into each other. That is a theme in the material presented here. While fault carries with it an implication of sin and viciousness, the existence of punishment may also, under some circumstances, play a redemptive role. It restores the person to his social roles intact and, in this sense, removes the stigma of moral delict. The act, and not the person, is at stake. If the act is presumed to be the result of will and purpose then the person is capable of reformation, of being law-abiding and sinless. Punishment returns him to square zero, to a new life, so to speak. It "wipes out" the offense. In the language of exchange, the offender has "paid for it." Appealing to a theory of the offender as rational person, it establishes his commonness with the lawful. He has committed a deviant act but he is not, in his character, a deviant person. In this sense, the law may not stigmatize; it may redeem.

What appears as the removal of stigma in the medical approach also contains the ambiguity of its opposite. From one perspective, the imputation of being someone who needs treatment is an indulgence, a way of escaping the stigma of law. From another perspective, however, it entails the description of the offender as a flawed person. His actions are not matters of choice but of necessity, a part of his self (Sontag 1978). The self is out of control, and only medical treatment can help him. The offender has not committed an incompetent, deviant act. He *is* incompetent and deviant (Packer 1968, ch. 2). He is stigmatized but not redeemed.

Both programs described here operated to convince the offenders of their flawed character, of their deviance as possible alcoholics. They were efforts to bring the offender to avow his deviance, the flaw in his self. How this was done, the practical contingencies that occurred within this quasi-medical and quasi-legal setting and the resistance of many offenders to the attempted definitions of themselves comprise the subject matter of this chapter.

THE SCHOOL FOR THE SCANDALOUS

Over the past decade, with the highly accentuated public campaigns against drinking-driving, both enforcement and punishment of drinking-driving has risen (Ross 1992; see chapter 13 in this volume). States, both in legislation and in court dispositions have found it useful to utilize diversionary programs to minimize the load on jails and to diminish the potential pressure of an offender class whose finances and political power are above that of the usual offender for petty or serious crimes. As a condition of a lesser sentence, many offenders are "sentenced" to specially designed classes on drinking and driving. In 1988, approximately 17,000 offenders were ordered to attend such classes by judges in Sunland City as a condition of receiving minimum sentences. (Sunland is a cover name used in the vain attempt not to disclose the identity of a major city of approximately one million in a county of close to three million people close to the Mexican border.) These classes are financed by the tuition of the offenders and are taught, in Sun County, under contracts between the county and a variety of agencies, including local universities and colleges, counseling and therapy organizations, and religious organizations. In Sun County they were supervised by the Alcohol Programs Office of the Department of Health Services, which is an arm of the Board of

County Supervisors. (As of 1991 the alcohol and drug abuse offices are combined.) At present there is a division between classes for first and for multiple offenders.

In the summer of 1973, when I observed the court-directed course, "The Impact of Drinking on Driving," its use was entirely at the discretion of the judge. In Sunland, some judges hardly ever used it; others prescribed it for almost all convicted of DUI in their court. In Eastland, a much smaller city contiguous to Sunland, the four judges in that jurisdiction made extensive use of it. In both cities the course was organized and taught under contract with local universities, through their extension divisions.[2]

I attended all sessions of a six-session course. One session was in a course held for convicted offenders in Sunland and the other five were held for convicted offenders in Eastland. Each course was held on Monday night over six weeks. I attended similar courses in 1979 and again in 1982. This report covers only the 1973 classes, although the later observations do not clash with these.

The city of Eastland is a suburban city east of Sunland and contiguous with it. It had at that time a population of 52,000. DUI offenders in the Sunland courts were almost entirely apprehended by special DUI squads of the Sunland Police Department or by the California Highway Patrol (CHP). Eastland's police had no such special squads so that almost all the offenders were apprehended by the CHP. There were some significant differences between the two jurisdictions that made for a comparatively smaller number of offenders in Eastland than in Sunland and a higher mean blood alcohol count on Eastland offenders than on Sunland's (Gusfield 1972).

I received permission from the extension division and from the instructors to attend classes unobtrusively. Sitting in the class I attracted no more attention from the "students" (the term used by the instructor) than any other one present. Since several people took notes it was easy for me to do so. Immediately after the class I sat in my car and expanded my notes into a tape recorder, including general observations. The notes were later transcribed and constitute the data for this section of the chapter.

The Contents of the Course

I examined the contents of the course and came to two significant conclusions about the definition it projected of the drinking-driver problem and of the offenders who made up the student body.

1. *The problem of drinking and driving was posed exclusively as that of excessive drinking by drivers.* The drinking-driving situation involves a set of multiple elements (Gusfield 1981a, ch. 3; 1985). Among these are alternative systems of transportation, institutions of manufacture and distribution of alcoholic beverages, group supports and interventions, and the technology of the automobile, and the road. The course was exclusively focused on diminishing the changes in drinking habits as the sole solution to decreasing accidents and deaths from automobile use. The attention of the course was directed to diminishing their consumption of alcohol. Although there were admonitions not to drive after drinking, these were not explored with any detail.

2. *Driving while under the influence of alcohol is described as abnormal and arrest for it as a sign of potential or existing alcohol abuse or alcoholism.* Much of the course conveyed information on the assumption that the students were excessive drinkers, many of whom probably had a drinking problem or were alcoholic. The intent of the course appeared to be that of changing the habits of the students, of convincing them that they were deviant drinkers and a danger to themselves and others.

Before I describe details of the course, an overall, quick description of the contents is necessary.

Session #1: In the introductory session, the instructor repeated the public fact that "30,000 of the 56,000 auto deaths last year were due to alcohol or involved alcohol." The instructor's manner was matter-of-fact, and the course was described as primarily educational and non-punitive. The history of the course was reviewed, and it was presented as an alternative to other possible dispositions, such as honor camp, suspension of driver's license, and jail. Attempts were made to stimulate discussion on the folklore of drinking beliefs the students had. One discussion dealt with the impact of drinking on driving. We also watched a traffic safety film on the dangers of falling asleep at the wheel and the advantages of using seat belts. The compulsory nature of the course was muted, although attendance was carefully taken.

Session #2: This class was focused on the physiology and psychology of alcohol use. The instructor introduced himself and a toxicologist and chemist from the Sunland Police Department, saying, "We will impart information which, if you'd had it, you wouldn't be here." The presentation was a straightforward account of the chemical properties of alcoholic beverages and their effects on the human body and psychology. The class asked questions, and the "expert" answered them.

Session #3: The topic of this session was the impact of alcohol on driving. The instructor "lectured" on the effect of alcohol on motor skills and especially on driving. This included information on the blood alcohol level, the Breathalyzer, and some other material overlapping the first session. It also included a movie on experiments with driving over an artificial course after drinking. There was also material on the pressure to drink in American society. As at all sessions, considerable questions and discussion occurred.

Session #4: This was on alcoholism and alcohol abuse. The lecture by the instructor was on alcoholism and problem-drinking. Much of his effort was concerned with how the individual decided that he had a drinking problem. A movie was shown on the hidden drinking of housewives. There was a discussion of the disease concept of alcoholism.

Session #5: This session was entirely given over to a presentation by a husband and wife, both of whom, like the instructor, were recovering alcoholics and members of Alcoholic Anonymous. They recounted their experiences as alcoholics and how AA had helped them.

Session #6: This was graduation day. The students received a diploma. The presiding judge of the Eastland court talked about the DUI law, recent changes in it and the nature of probation. After he left the head instructor of the programs talked about the DUI legislation and the impact of a record on the individual. There was a general discussion.

Attention to drinking dominated the course. Illustrative of this was the showing of the movie, *One for the Road,* at the introductory session. It told the story of a suburban, junior executive depicted as a law-abiding citizen who had a concern about the consequences of drinking and driving. He and his wife are shown drinking at a cocktail party. Knowing that they were not going home until much later, they believed that there would be ample time to "sober up" before driving home. An emergency occurs. The babysitter has been taken ill, and they must return home immediately. On the way home, influenced by the cocktails, he runs a stop sign, hits and injures a girl pedestrian and is sentenced to prison for a year.

What was the message of the film? What should the man have done? Neither in the film nor in the instructor's comments was there any directive about how the situation might have been avoided. Should he not have been drinking? Should he have called a taxi? Should he have left the children alone at home? Should he have called a neighbor? The problem was narrowed to a preoccupation with drinking, and other possible, even institutional, solutions were ignored, unstated, or unexamined. In the six sessions I attended there were few instances in which the instructor examined alternatives to less drinking as a means of avoiding the dangers of drinking and driving. The problem of drinking and driving was not conceptualized as a problem of transportation as well or as an alternative to consumption. Perhaps a representative of the taxi industry might be as "meaningful" as a toxicologist.

The DUI Offender as Deviant Drinker

The bulk of the course, in its presentation, may be thought of as an effort to persuade the arrested and convicted offender that his is a problem of unhealthy drinking and to think of himself as a patient in need of medical or psychological attention and possibly treatment for alcoholism. The course can be seen as an effort to change the self-conception of the class member from one of health to one of sickness.

The instructor presented his argument in three stages. In the first, he attempted to convince the class of the seriousness of the offense and therefore the soundness of the legislation. They were not, he suggested, victims of a law unjustly interfering with their liberties. In analyzing the physiology of alcohol effects, the guest toxicologist stressed the greater risk of an accident associated with a higher blood alcohol level (BAL). He pointed out that even though a defendant may not have a drink for a few hours before driving, if he had been drinking heavily, he might still be influenced hours later. If a drinker had reached a BAL of .31, given the normal oxidization rate of .015 per hour, his BAL after thirteen hours would be .12, still above the then legal limit of .10. (Since 1990, the legal limit in California has been .08.)

Several times the instructor defended the students' arrests and the value of the school by reference to the defendants' welfare. At the "graduation" the instructor said: "Last year five thousand people were killed in California on the road. Twenty-five hundred were due to drinking-driving. The legislature wants to get the drinking driver off the road . . . The judge did you a favor. You might have been in an accident and lost your life or someone else's if you had not been stopped. This is what [the judge] will remind you of when you ask why you were arrested when there are so many others."

It should be remembered that in 1973 people arrested for drinking-driving were not the usual array of arrestees for other misdemeanors and felonies. They were less likely to have a prior arrest record. They were older, employed, and more stable in family and finances. They were not accustomed to thinking of themselves as deviant or even as "problems."

Trying to persuade them that they were "flawed persons" was a major part of the rhetoric of the class.

A central part of the process of medicalizing the alcohol problem for this group of offenders was to convince them that their individual arrest was an appropriate and necessary occasion to review their drinking habits. They must look at their drinking as quite possibly, and probably excessive, not within the "normal" range, and productive of danger. They are probably deviant drinkers.

There were two kinds of evidence that students were exhorted to look at in deciding their classification. One was the fact of arrest and the high BAL it represented.[3] The other is the examination of the defendant's drinking styles as evidence of possible problem-drinking or alcoholism.

Several times, and especially in the lecture on the physiological effects of alcohol, it was stressed that it takes a lot of drinking to reach a BAL of .15-.20, which is most common among DUI arrestees. What the defendants' levels indicated were more than casual, moderate drinking. Most people, the instructor maintained, couldn't even drive at such a BAL, indicating that excessive drinking is a customary experience for these defendants. Drinking-drivers are people used to drinking a lot.

Do the defendant-students have a problem with alcohol? This was the central question of the fourth session. The instructor began the class saying that they would discuss a "very serious problem," that of alcoholism. With a note of sacredness and heaviness in his voice, he said, "I don't mean to refer to anyone here." He talked about both "problem-drinkers" and "alcoholics" and asserted that in this room he would use the two terms synonomously.

The class discussion during the first half seemed intended to give the class ways of determining if they were problem-drinkers. Nine signs of alcoholism were presented, combined from several sources and tests:

1. Increased tolerance for alcohol
2. Occasional memory lapses
3. Drinking beyond one's intentions
4. Increased dependence on alcohol
5. Sneaking drinks
6. Preoccupation with alcohol
7. Resentment when one's drinking is discovered
8. Futile attempts to go on the "water wagon"
9. Rationalizing loss of control

After presenting these signs the instructor said: "How many of these would you need to think of yourself as a problem drinker? If you have *one or more* of these symptoms you *may* need help and should seek guidance." (Italics mine.)

The instructor also used the test called "20 Questions" to see how many of the students would answer "Yes" to questions. The class administered these to themselves, after which the instructor said: "If you answered 'yes' to any one you may be an alcoholic. If you answered 'yes' to two, the chances are that you are. If you answered 'yes' to three, you should definitely seek help."[4]

Later in the session he offered a different kind of definition, less operative and less descriptive of content. "If your activities interfere with your drinking, then your drinking interferes with your activities."

Another stage in the process of persuasion involved convincing the defendant that alcoholics are not mostly Skid Row "bums." Judging by their clothing, automobiles, and references to their jobs, the class members were being far from "bums" or even unemployed. It was largely a middle-class and stable working-class group. With a stereotype of the alcoholic or problem drinker as someone who has "hit bottom" of the social scale, it remained easy for the defendant to separate himself from the alcoholic. This the instructor attempted to counteract: "Only 3 percent of alcoholics in the United States are of the Skid Row type." In showing the movie *The Secret Life of Sandra Blaine,* he underlined the message that middle-class, stable citizens are also potential victims of alcohol.

The session devoted to Alcoholics Anonymous carried the same message. Both the husband and wife who spoke that night held good, professional jobs and had held them throughout their drinking "careers." In the fourth session, before the AA members appeared, the instructor described the couple, saying: "You ought to see that they're not Skid Row bums. One is in management, is in an executive position with public utilities and his wife is the vice-president in a savings and loan bank. They're reasonable people, educated people."

The final stage in the course involved persuading the defendants to seek treatment for their drinking problem. This was also the conclusion of the AA members in their presentation to the class. They ended a tragic account of their drinking experiences with an upbeat account of their "victory" through admitting that they were, and still are, alcoholics who needed help. In an earlier session the instructor had said that while alcoholism carried a stigma, it didn't do so if you were doing something about it.

In his discussion of alcoholism the instructor used the four stages of how alcoholism develops described by Jellinek in the early 1940s. Even though medicine has no cure for alcoholism, it can be treated. At one point, becoming emotional, he said: "You crossed the line between social drinking and heavy drinking or you were close to crossing it. Don't kid yourself. Go to meetings of the AA. They have had the most successful treatment so far. There's no such thing as a little bit alcoholic."

The instructor vacillated between such general characterizations of the class as a group of problem-drinkers and demurrers. In introducing the AA members, he entered a disclaimer: "I have no intention of pointing a finger of accusation at anyone in the room. Instead I intend to plant a seed so that you know where to go. They'll tell you what happened to them. The majority of you probably don't have a drinking problem."

A tone of combativeness began to emerge in the class during the second session. The instructor seemed to be fighting an uphill battle to convince the class that they were anything other than victims of chance. Many felt they were among the few offenders unlucky enough to have been caught.

Resistance to Persuasion: The Disavowal of Deviance

The concept of "deviance disavowel" was coined by Fred Davis to describe victims of infantile paralysis who, in their behavior and in their self-presentation, denied and disavowed a status as "crippled" (Davis 1961). These people admitted the illness but denied its consequences.[5]

The members of the class I observed were not uniformly avowers or disavowers. Nevertheless there was a considerable amount of vocal opposition to what was assumed to be the attempt of the instructor to persaude them of their deviance. It was enough to lead the instructor into a defensive posture.

Resistance could be seen in two parallel yet distinct actions. One was in a persistent effort to question, deny, and disavow the validity of the contents, the materials presented. The other was observed in the shifting dynamics of the classroom. Over the several sessions it shifted from the neutral tones of a lecturer confidently transmitting information to a receptive audience to that of moralistic preaching in which the claim to authority had to be made legitimate against a doubting and resistant group.[6]

Conflict over the Sick Role

A basic part of the argument made to the class was that they were arrested because they were drinking heavily and thus endangering others as well as themselves. People who drink as much as they did are drinking excessively and need help. This argument was attacked by a number of vocal student-offenders.

A focal point of this conflict was the "meaning" or significance of a high BAL or its equivalent on the Breathalyzer. Consider this byplay between the guest toxicologist and a class member at the second session:

> [The toxicologist] had made the point that many very heavy drinkers and alcoholics may never reach a normal 0.00 count in their normal functioning, given the oxidation rates for blood alcohol. In discussing drinking and its impact on driving, he referred to studies showing that, beginning in cold sobriety, the heavy drinker might be able to function as well at a .15 as a light drinker might at .05. One class member, whose remarks identified him as naval personnel, then made the point that a study which got heavy drinkers down to 0.00 may not be getting them to the point at which they normally functioned best. They might function much better at a higher level of alcohol usage. The norm comparing them with cold sober might be illusory, given the oxidation rates. This man went on to say that he, and apparently others, are frequently involved in heavy exercises, in football, baseball when they are normally drinking heavily. They could well be playing ball, he said, with BALs of .25. The toxicologist replied that heavy drinkers would drive worse at a BAL of .15 than at .00. The navy man replied: Wasn't he being discriminated against for being a normal .20 when he might indeed be driving better than an 80-year-old at .00? The toxicologist kept coming back to the comparison between the heavy drinker at a high BAL and the same drinker at a low BAL. He went on to talk about the extent to which it was driving in a defective manner that brings the subject to the attention of the police and not drinking per se.[7]

Here the antagonists had touched on a matter of considerable ambiguity and significance. It reflects the situation that the relation of drinking to driving operates in a complex situation of multiple variables interacting with each other, including age, general health, and drinking experience as well as other aspects of the environment (Gusfeld 1981a; 1984b). The objection to the instruction was not without some foundation. The uniform BAL adopted by the legislators made administrative sense, but it was not uniform in its operation. The driving abilities of some motorists are affected by alcohol with BALs under the legal limit, and some are unaffected with BALs over the limit. The physical health of the driver and his or her driving experience are among elements influencing the relation between driving and alcohol use. The legal boundary is set high enough to attempt to "catch" all affected drivers but runs the risk of excluding some "guilty" and including some "innocents." Nevertheless, for any personal drinking and driving history, increased consumption increases risk to some extent.

The same resistance was produced by members of the class over the question: How much is too much to drink? In one of the sessions a student told of having lost the quarter-panel of his truck after he had had three cans of beer and suffered a "blow-out" on the road. This was volunteered in discussion after the instructor had analyzed the impact of drinking on motor skills. Several of the other students resisted the student's interpretation of the incident. One insisted that it was fear that slowed the reaction time, not the beer. Another student, who frequently objected to many of the instructor's statements, loudly maintained that three cans of beer could never have done that.

Here, and throughout the sessions, the instructors were caught in the dilemma of stress on the high BAL as evidence of heavy drinking. What is heavy drinking for some is not for others. To focus on the "abnormal" amount of drinking necessary to attain the legal limit leaves the less frequent drinker with a belief that what is heavy drinking for him is safe. Small amounts, by the standards of the heavy drinker, may be much greater in their effect on the light drinker. The instructor vacillated between these two emphases, and the resistant students seized on the "weak" spots. One of the students, responding to the statement about the high amount needed to reach the legal limit, objected to the determination in his case saying that he only had two martinis and a can of beer and couldn't possibly have reached the .14 level indicated by the Breathalyzer.

The Shifting Dynamics of the Classroom

Although I observed two different instructors and a guest lecturer during the first two sessions, all presented themselves and the course in tones of educational neutrality and objectivity. They made references to the educational goals of the course. The instructors were there to give the students information, not to condemn or to punish. "We will impart information which, if you had had it, you wouldn't be here," said the instructor at the second session, suggesting they were rational men talking to other rational men and women who could be helped through knowledge and self-examination. The instructors referred often to research; charts and drawings were used. There was an air of science and inquiry.

As time wore on, and as the instructor met resistence, the tone changed. Instructional neutrality was replaced by a defensiveness displaying antagonism and moral condemnation. The compulsive character of the class, a probationary requirement of the court, became more noticeable. The class members began as students; they ended a defendants.

I first began to notice signs of antagonism just before the "break" at the third session. The instructor had passed back papers which the class had written between the first and second sessions recounting the experiences that had led to their arrests on DUI. During the class, one of the students was quite angry, claiming that the instructor had written "derogatory" remarks on his paper. Those angry remarks seemed to have set a new tone.

A movie, *.08*, was shown at this session. It described experiments on the effect of alcohol on driving. The instructor commented on the small amount of drinking that may lead to deterioration in driving skills. The same navy man who had been so critical at the last session said that he noticed that one of the professional drivers in the movie had driven with his feet on both the brake and the gas pedal at the same time. He concluded that this was bad driving form. The instructor seemed to feel "needled" by this question coming from this student. In responding he talked about the irrelevance of the question to the subject of drinking and driving. The class would not let the question drop, however. One woman asked if this way of driving was illegal. The instructor's tone became angry, and he "lectured" the class about the possibilities of accidents resulting from drinking and driving.

As the session continued, there were more and more references by students to their own particular case. These took the form of "Why was *I* caught?" In discussing the amount of drinking necessary to reach the presumptive limits, one of the students said that he knew a guy who had "gotten off" because the policeman was his relative. The instructor was now clearly angered at the apparent efforts of the class to neutralize the contents of the course. He stressed the help that arrest would bring, that it would help them prevent possible future accidents or death. There are two types of people taking this course, he said. There were those who decided that since they had to take the course, they might as well learn something out of it. Then there were those who didn't want to learn anything from it. He repeated the results of an earlier study in Eastland showing that the DUI school was associated with a reduction in DUI recidivism.[8]

The course culminated in the graduation session. The presiding judge of the Eastland court spoke, explaining the terms of probation and the revised DUI law that had just passed the state legislature. His tone was legalistic. He distinguished the DUI school from punishment. There were questions, but they were couched respectfully and without a display of antagonism.

After the judge left, the class was taken over by the instructor in charge of the entire instructional staff. He was a professor of safety education and, like the other instructor, a recovering alcoholic. His remarks were a warning about future accidents. He said: "You're not everyone else when you get behind the wheel. You have this probation on your head. The judge did you a favor. You might have been in an accident and lost your life or someone else's if you had not been stopped."

In the course of his remarks, he described the then (1973) recent decision of the U.S. Supreme Court making searches of automobiles by police more permissive. One of the students, who had been raising objections in most of the sessions, angrily interrupted saying: "It's Communism. The judge telling you how you have to live. The majority also has rights."

The persisting and mounting conflict between instructor and class was evident. The DUI legislation, the physiological effects of alcohol on driving, police enforcement practices, and the definition of excessive drinking were all called into question.

THE AMBIGUITY OF THE MEDICAL ALTERNATIVE TO PUNISHMENT

What accounts for the students' resistance and hostility toward the class? It seemed a less harsh alternative to jail or loss of license or even a larger fine. True, the particular class I observed took place on a Monday night at the beginning of professional football season, but football did not enter significantly into the talk between students during the class "break." An answer to this question lies at the center of the analysis of medicalization as an alternative strategy to law as a policy toward DUI offenders.

DUI as a Degradation Ritual

A magistrate in one of the county's justice courts explained his philosophy of punishment for DUI cases to me. He said that for most of the people involved in these cases the process of arrest and court appearance was itself highly degrading and punishing. That is why, he said, he always gives them a very severe lecture but light sentences.

The magistrate's view of the enforcement proceedings is akin to what Harold Garfinkel, in an insightful paper, has referred to as "degradation ceremonies" (Garfinkel 1956). These are acts of public denunciation in which the ceremony degrades and denounces the individual. Metaphorically it is as if the person were being cursed: "I call upon all men to bear witness that he is not as he appears but is otherwise and *in essence* of a lower species" (Garfinkel 1956, 421). The magistrate has described his courtroom as just such a ritual site. The DUI school can be conceived in analogous fashion. Beginning in an air of educational inquiry the class increasingly became moralistic and condemnatory. It became a punishing process.

I have already described the changes in the instructor's attitude, as he became assertive and moralistic toward the resisting students. Two other aspects of the process added to its stigmatizing and punishing character. Both involve assertions about the character of the DUI offender and the student-defendant.

First, the supposition that the student may be a problem-drinker or alcoholic was not consistently treated as a morally neutral, medical description. Consider the manner in which the instructor introduced the AA representatives: "I have no intention of pointing a finger of *accusation* at anyone in this room." While maintaining that there was no stigma in recognizing problems with alcohol he consistently disowned the implication that he was calling anyone a problem drinker or alcoholic. He used the terms "problem-drinker" and "alcoholic" interchangeably. Given the lists of symptoms and the "loose" way in which it was interpreted, a derogatory assertion about any kind of heavy drinking or heavy drinker was evident. The content of the resistance I have described above reflects the hostility of people who seem to view themselves as drinkers but not as people of less than adequate capacity for life's activities, including driving an automobile. What is called into question is their character. They are not people who have committed an illegal act. They are flawed people, deviant in essence. The acceptance of this judgment is the acceptance of stigma unlike that of other medical judgments.

A second element in the stigmatizing process of deviance-construction lay in equating the student-defendant with the stereotyped portrait of the "killer drunk" (Gusfield 1981a, 151ff.). This is the irresponsible, drunken driver careening wildly across the road. Oblivious to the dangers he poses for innocent people, he thoughtlessly destroys the lives of children. Most of the students voicing opinions, as well as others described below, did not see themselves in this image. They are ordinary drinking people who happened to have been caught. There are many more in the community just like them but lucky not to have been caught. Whatever the illegality which established a probable cause for police to have stopped them, it was far from that of the "killer drunk." They had not been involved in an accident.[9]

In conducting the DUI class the instructor was constructing a script in which he attempted to persuade the student-defendant to identify himself in the part of the social deviant. When, at the final session, a student objected, saying "It's Communism. The judge telling you how you have to live. The majority also has rights," the head of the instructor's staff replied: "When you're doing fifty miles an hour on a Sunday afternoon and some drunken driver hits your car, what protection do we offer the innocents?" He then related his experience as a court reporter, describing murders: "You have to see trials and executions and feel sorry for the murderer. And somebody said to me, 'Who speaks for the dead?' When you're driving under the influence of alcohol it's vehicular homicide like the same we saw in the paper the other night, the twenty-one-year-old girl who killed two people."

Law and Medicine: Stigma and Redemption

At the same final session, a student-defendant muttered, at one point, "Why don't they give us our fines and just let us go home?" In this phrase is contained a distinction between the stigmatizing and the redemptive processes of punishment. Although the legal process can, and often is, a ritual of degradation, it also contains the possibility of an alternative and redemptive process. The distinction is that of punishment for an act and punishment for being a person with a criminal or deviant character. In the former case, the act is the basis of the designation. Having paid the fine or served the sentence the offender has redeemed his personal character. From the very beginning he is judged to be redeemable. In the latter case, the offender cannot erase the blight of his act without a change of self.

In this sense, the medicalization of the DUI offender was stigmatizing. It was an effort to affect drinking-driving through constructing the deviance of the DUI offender as a person. It became punitive in its effort to prevent further occurrences. The redemptive forms of punishment enable the defendant to achieve closure. It is not his self that is condemned but his deed. Having absolved the deed through punishment, having "learned his lesson," he can now once again be a respectable citizen. Paraphrasing Garfinkel, "He is as he appears and not in essence of a lower species."

THE CONSTRUCTION OF THE DUI AS ALCOHOLIC

It should be evident to the reader, as it was to the staff of the DUI classes, that not all offenders suffered from alcohol problems. The assumption that they might operated as a basis for the class emphasis on alcohol problems and treatment as a solution to their possible future arrest for the same offense. In 1975, the possibility emerged for me to study the process of defining the individual "problem-drinker" or alcoholic for court disposition.[10]

Four years earlier, under state and federal grants, Eastland had begun the course on "The Impact of Drinking and Driving" described above. Further grants had enabled the court in that jurisdiction to conduct presentence investigations through interviews between probation officers and offenders. These interviews were the bases for the probation officers' recommendations for sentencing, including conditions of probation under which sentences might be suspended. In practice this meant that the probation officer determined the possible existence of a drinking problem and recommended solutions to it as a condition of suspending the sentence.

The probation officers had two general questions to answer. First, did the offender have a "drinking problem"? Second, in light of the answer to the first question, what sentence and/or conditions of probation should he or she recommend? The recommendations had considerable force since they were followed by the judges in most cases.

I attended eighteen probation interviews and afterwards discussed them with the probation officer who conducted them. I also talked with several other probation officers, either severally or together. I took notes on the interviews as they occurred and supplemented them soon after with comments on a tape recorder. I recorded notes on other conversations with probation officers soon after their occurrence.

The Work Culture of Probation Officers

The Sun County Probation Department had its Eastland offices in a small, two-story building about half a block from the Eastland court. At the time that I studied them, there were six probation officers plus a supervisor responsible for the drinking-driver program. One of these worked only with convicted DUI offenders on formal probation who were mandated to meet with him on a regular basis. Four of them met with repeating offenders for presentence interviews. These were defendants who had a prior DUI on their record. One of the probation officers met only with first offenders.

None of the probation officers had had any previous experience in alcohol counseling, treatment, or other work related to alcohol problems or drinking. Neither had they been trained as social workers. They came to probation through a variety of routes. They all had B.A.s or M.A.s or their equivalents in one of the liberal arts, chiefly psychology. One had been a Catholic priest and had counseled parishoners. One had been in survey research work and hadn't liked it. Of the five presentence probation officers, one had been in DUI work for more than a year. Three had been in this work for less than a month. Their formal exposure to knowledge about drinking and drinking problems had come from attending other sessions of the DUI school described above. As a group, and singly, they were not part of the world of alcohol counseling or research. In at least ten visits to the offices, I never saw a journal or other publication devoted to alcohol studies, programs, or treatment.

The probation officers were not enthusiastic about their work with DUIs. They were industrious and concerned about the problems of drinking and driving and often referred to the importance of the problem and that "half of all auto deaths involved alcohol." Nevertheless, they displayed little affect for the work, compared to that expressed by three of them about their past probation work with children or with juvenile delinquents. The jobs had opened up for them with the appearance of the grants and the sudden need for an expanded staff. The supervisor reported little difficulty in getting people to work in the program. Some wanted the job because it put them closer to homes in Eastland or nearby communities. However, after the first grant ended, people did leave, wanting to go somewhere else.

The drinking-driver program also had certain career values for the probation officers. It helped promotions if their record could show that they had worked in a variety of places and had diverse work experiences. The opening of the DUI program provided another opportunity for diversity.

Although they called themselves "the drunk healers" their work was set in the constraints of the legal system. "I feel like a cog in the wheel of justice," said one. "There's no counseling to be done, and you see people only for an hour and with adults their styles are already fixed." He had worked with juveniles in an honors camp and much preferred that kind of work.

Unlike some social workers, they could not be seen as spokespersons for the people they interviewed. It was clear that their clients were the judges and not the offenders. In conversations at lunches and coffee breaks the probation officers expressed both indignation at and wariness of those they interviewed. Similar expressions occurred before and after the interviews in my conversation with probation officers. Significantly the probation officers never referred to those they interviewed as clients, patients, or, as in the DUI School, students. They always used the legal term of "defendants" and never a medical language. Jackson, the officer interviewing first offenders, remarked that defendants often maintain that they hadn't murdered anyone, but he declared that when you know what happens and realize thirty thousand people die in auto deaths every year due to drinking, you look at it otherwise. He, and others in the same conversation, suggested that the probation officers possessed greater knowledge about the impact of alcohol, and this differentiated them from the defendants.

The probationary activity was set in a rationale of medicine, a means of determining possible treatment for alcohol problems or alcoholism. Nevertheless, the legal realities of compulsion never remain dimly in the background. The probation officers do not identify with the defendants. They are part of the culture of alcohol professionals, but they are part of the criminal justice system and an agency of the court. The DUI offender, the interviewee, is someone to be watched suspiciously. The interview is a phase of the legal process; it is not a clinic on alcoholism.

The Interview as Interaction: Conflict and Negotiation

The interview of the defendant by the probation officer is one part of the story of crime and punishment which began when the driver was stopped by police. It is part of the process by which the court decides what to do with the drinking-driver. Is he to be "disposed of" by the usual stock of punishments—fines, license removal, jail? Or is he best dealt with by treatment for an illness?

There were several possible recommendations available to the P.O. (probation officer). These are listed below in ascending order of restrictiveness, from the least severe to the most, as both P.O. and defendant appeared to classify them.

1. Simple levy of a fine. Here the P.O. adds nothing to the court's actions.
2. The Living Sober course. This was an "advanced course" to "The Impact of Drinking on Driving" described above. Also offered by university extension it operated explicitly on the premise that students had a drinking problem and needed help.
3. Alcoholics Anonymous. Some AA chapters held special meetings for court-mandated people, but that was not always the case. In all meetings, procedures were developed to report on attendance.

4. Antabuse. This was a chemical compound which the probation department had been recommending in some cases for more than a year in Eastland. Antabuse was the trade name for a medical preparation in the form of tablets which, when ingested, will cause nausea and vomiting if alcohol is consumed while the user is under its administration. (This was the prognosis for 95 percent of cases.) To complete the treatment, now known as adverse conditioning, the user needed to continue use for a year. Since Antabuse could be dangerous to people with heart problems, it could only be prescribed if an examining physician endorsed its use for specific defendants.

These were recommendations for conditions under which suspended sentences would be granted. The P.O. might suggest all or only one or any combination. Additional recommendations were possible. At the time of my observations there were no treatment clinics available and connected with the court. One P.O. was using biofeedback as an alternative. While custody (jail) was not part of the P.O.'s possible recommendations, he or she could recommend that custody time be spent on weekends and/or consist of voluntary work, such as serving for a community organization. In practice the more evident the drinking problems, the more "severe" the recommendation.

The Centrality of the Record

On what basis can the P.O. make a judgment about the drinking of the defendant? The P.O. has before him or her a file on each offender to be interviewed. It details his or her past arrests and convictions and the police accounts of each offense. The file also contains general demographic information such as age, residence, and occupation. The arrest records are supplied by the FBI, the Criminal Investigation Inventory (CII), and the local police. A summary of the offender's driving record is supplied by the Department of Motor Vehicles (DMV). There might be P.O. reports from past arrests. Most important, and among the first items P.O.s looked at, is the blood alcohol level determined in the instant case and, sometimes, in past cases of DUI as well.

The file is the central object in the interview. It is crucial to the eventual diagnosis and decision of the P.O. He or she almost always has read the file before the interview. If not it will be read while the interview proceeds. Customarily the P.O. holds it in his or her hands or keeps it close on the desk and refers to it often during the interview. In a world of doubt and ambiguity the record in the file is the one incontrovertible "fact." In a significant sense, the record is what the P.O. sought to explain.

The Interview: Disavowing Deviance

People who work with alcoholics or others whom they see as possible "problem drinkers" frequently report the difficulties of convincing the potential patient that he or she has a problem. We have seen the attempt to convince the student-defendants of their status as problem-drinkers in the DUI course. The phrase "I don't have a drinking problem" is by now almost a parody of the problem drinker or the alcoholic. For the P.O., the defendant's resistance to admitting he or she has a problem with alcohol makes the task of obtaining information from the defendant a difficult one. Information from the defendant that presents a picture of himself or herself as devoid of alcohol problems is already suspect. Like the resisting student-defendants in the DUI course, the defendants rise to the P.O.'s questions to disavow their deviance.

Riding with the drinking-driving squads of the Sun City Police Department I was often aware that arrestees disavowed that alcohol was at work in their driving or that they had a problem with it in their lives. Arresting officers were frequently given what I called a "cover story" by which the motorist counters the conclusion that his or her faulty driving resulted from the influence of alcohol. This was also at work in many of the interviews. The defendant "explains away" the arrest, accounting for it in some fashion other than the influence of alcohol. Here is one such account from an interview between the P.O. and a middle-aged female offender:

> P.O.: Did you feel "tight" when you were driving?
>   D.: I was driving my son's car and it was strange to me.
> P.O.: Why did the police stop you?
>   D.: I don't know. They didn't tell me. I knew I wouldn't take the walking test because it was out on the roadway and I have a great fear of it. I can't do that test well anyway even if I'm sober.[11]
> P.O.: (Looking at the record as he speaks) They say you were weaving.
>   D.: I know they had a reason, cause my son's car was strange to me but I can't use that as a reason.

Later in the same interview she told a long story about being given the field test much earlier by a police friend as a stunt and not being able to pass while sober. Still later she explained the event of the arrest by saying that if she had had dinner that night or not driven her son's car she wouldn't have been arrested. The car is a stick shift rather than an automatic transmission, and she wasn't familiar with that type. It was raining and the combination of hunger, her son's car, and the rain led her to drive poorly. The event that brought her there was thus, she implied, not a result of her characteristic drinking.

Throughout the interview she maintained the self-presentation of an occasional drinker, "seldom more than a few beers or Champales a day, and not every day." She said "no" to every standard test item for behavior associated with chronic alcoholism, such as memory lapse, morning drinking, hiding drinks, or other indicia. She asserted that she had never been worried about her drinking and that she did not have a drinking problem.

The arrest is the dominating "fact" for the P.O. He cannot accept her "story." The P.O. must begin with an assumption of doubt and suspicion about anything the defendant tells him that is not in the record. From the outset this interaction is one between adversaries, one of whom is trying to hide what the other, the P.O., wants to learn. The metaphor of cross-examination is closer to a description of this interview than is that of client and servicer or patient and doctor. There is little analogy to a patient bringing a complaint of respiratory difficulty to a doctor.

The assumption of resistance makes the record central to the conduct of the interview. When the P.O. pointed to the police assertion in the record that she had been weaving, he did so in a tone contravening her claims about the event.

The Interview: Negotiating the Recommendation

The interview was not, however, an empty gesture. Throughout the time (usually fifteen minutes with first offenders, forty-five to sixty minutes with multiple offenders) the P.O. tested his or her initial hypothesis while the defendant presented his or her case. The hypothesis is proposed to the defendant in the light of the record. The reaction of the P.O. may lead to change or revision by either party.

Through his power to recommend, the P.O. holds valuable cards, but they are not complete. The cooperation of the defendant is needed to ease the process and to help if treatment is recommended. There is an effort made to convince the defendant of the soundness of the recommendation. The threat of prison lurks in the background, but it is an alternative that is not preferred by either party.

The problem in the administration of Antabuse illustrates some of the difficulties. When Antabuse was mandated, the defendant could not be given the tablets and expected to take them as required. Instead, offenders were required to come to the office and be given their tablets at periods specified. The sign on the cart containing the Antabuse tablets read, "Take your Antabuse tablets. By order of Judge Devlin." Frequently the staff were too preoccupied to see that the offenders did take them. Even so, it was hard to supervise an offender who failed to swallow.

Here are three cases. In each the interview leads one or both parties, the P.O. or the offender, to change his or her attitude.

> 1. D. (defendant), a male in his mid-twenties, has a long arrest record, both as a juvenile and as an adult, including one prior DUI, several accidents, a hit and run and other criminal charges. He was stopped for speeding and had a BAL of .20. His record indicated that he had been going to a community mental health center, and a letter from an official there indicated that he would probably come to the interview "heavy-shouldered" (presumably a sign of drunkenness). He didn't. Instead he talked incessantly. D. carried a scrapbook with him which showed that he'd gained the status of journeyman carpenter after four years in the training program; one of 188 to do so out of the 3,000 that started. He claimed that since the offense he'd been attending a community health center, undergoing therapy, and also taking Antabuse himself. He did have a drinking problem, but no longer. He spoke with anger about the drinking at a recent community dinner and maintained that he'll continue Antabuse. "When I go back to work I'm around a lot of drunks and drinkers, and I might backslide. No, thank you."
>
> The P.O. recommended that he pay his fine through volunteer carpentry work and also recommended the Living Sober class. He also recommended Antabuse but through the same monitoring system D. now has his common-law wife administer it to him every morning. Later the P.O. decided to drop the Living Sober class since D. is attending the community mental health center. He was impressed with D.'s accomplishment in becoming a journeyman carpenter.
>
> 2. D. (male, thirtysomething) presents a "story" to account for his arrest. He accounted for the redness of his eyes saying that he has worked long hours and seven days without stop. He insists that he has no problem of excessive drinking. He was stopped by the police for speeding.
>
> D.: "With all these tickets it may seem as if I have a drinking problem but it's that I drive fast even when I'm sober."

P.O.: We need guarantees. You have several DUIs over the past nine years. Eighty percent of the people do it again. You did well on probation and I'll recommend a year of probation and recommend Antabuse.

D.: I took that before on my own.

P.O.: Have you been to AA?

D.: I was there on my own, too.

P.O.: (In an ironic tone) Do you have a problem with alcohol?

D.: I'm going to tell you yeah. I can't tell you not. I never get in trouble when I'm sober. Some people are different. Take my father. He drinks all day and never gets in trouble. My brother and uncle, too.

P.O.: It might have to do with the time. Friday nights, for example, the Sun City PD and the CHP (California Highway Patrol) are looking for drinking-drivers.

D.: You're not going to let them send me to jail and lose my job? If you do, let me know and I'll get things squared away.

P.O.: There is a mandatory 48 hours which can be served on weekends and since you're close to the end of the five-year period since the last arrest for DUI it might not count. I will not recommend any time at all. But I see there is a third offense, one within seven years, so I'll have to recommend hours. The license loss is also mandatory for six months.

Here the P.O. brings D. to admit his drinking problem. He uses the record both to establish the recommendation and to challenge the initial self-definition of D. as someone without a drinking problem.

3. D. is a multiple offender, male, in early twenties. Here the interview results in a less restrictive recommendation as D. shows a strong resistance. D.'s case reads like that of a "real loser." He was cited for revocation of an earlier probation for a prior DUI. He had a long string of arrests over the past five years including public drunkenness, two DUIs and several criminal charges. There was a warrant for his arrest on child support charges when he was arrested for DUI currently. Also he has a long DMV record of moving violations and one accident. Currently his license is revoked. In the present case his BAL was .23. In the two prior cases it was .20 and .32. When stopped, after four times failing to dim his bright lights, he gave a false name to police.

The record showed that he's only attended three AA meetings. In explanation he said that he just didn't like it and that he didn't think it (not attending) would cause any trouble. (The P.O. pointed out to me that the $1,000 fine for revocation of probation was senseless since D. didn't have the money.) He also has several unpaid moving violation

fines as well as the child support. The alternative is custody which
P.O. will recommend but D. can make it in five weekends.

   In response to questioning D. said that he didn't like AA because
there were "too many winos and drunks. I don't like winos and
drunks." The P.O. told D. that he wouldn't recommend AA since D.
obviously doesn't want it. P.O. will recommend the Living Sober class
and Antabuse. D. balks at Antabuse and tells an elaborate story about
working for the sheriff's office in a confidential capacity and being
unable to take a medication which might endanger his confidentiality.
Says it is too confidential to tell the P.O. D. does not succeed in
"lifting" the Antabuse, although its use remains problematic since D.
says he'll bring a lawyer to challenge it.

   P.O. is outraged by D. in this case and by his efforts to avoid
Antabuse. Nevertheless, D. did emerge from the interview without
fines or AA attendance mandated. P.O. felt that he wouldn't pay the
fine and that he wouldn't benefit from AA anyway. It is notable that
with three DUI convictions in three and one-half years, D. has yet to
pay any more than $10 in fines or to receive any more inconvenience
than three AA meetings.

In many ways these interviews are another form of plea bargaining
(Mather 1979). The negotiation over the definition of the defendant as
problem-drinker is connected to the negotiation over the recommended
"sentence." The P.O. attempts to challenge the defendant's disavowal of
deviance and to get him or her to avow it. Considerable care was taken to
avoid punishment which will interfere with employment. Jail was avoided
as much as possible. If custody was meted out, it was servable on weekends and with community service rather than imprisonment. The result
was a negotiated settlement.

Diagnosis: *The Importance of the Record*

In much of the research on DUI and its relation to problem-drinking, researchers have tried to explain the record—the acts of DUI for which the
offender is tried—by a pattern of drinking that is more recurrent than the
instant case. At the time of these observations the heavy and excessive
drinker and the chronic alcoholic were seen as more frequent sources of
DUI than is presently the conventional wisdom (Waller 1967). Problem-
drinkers were seen as major sources of DUI.

   The problem posed for the P.O. is to determine if the offender has a
medical problem, if his or her drinking is of such a character as to call
for treatment. If not, it is solely a legal issue and not to be construed as a

medical situation. Is the DUI to be explained as an outcome of pathological drinking or as "normal" drinking as controllable as any other traffic
offense?

Logically one of two kinds of evidence would seem needed to explain
the DUI as a case of pathological drinking requiring some form of medicalization: (1) The existence of a pattern approximating one or another
model of addictive and excessive drinking, or (2) A pattern of other "troubles" resulting from excessive drinking such as loss of job, arrests for public drunkenness, marital discord or dissolution, or health problems.

The record of DUI arrests is the variable to be explained. What I found
in the interviews was that the record became both the object to be explained and the source of explanation as well. It was both topic and resource. The record was used to determine the drinking pattern of the offender, which was used to explain the record.

In the morass of the defendant's lies, anticipated lies, and suspicions of
lies, the one beacon of certainty the P.O. has is the file on the offender.
Again and again, in interviews and in discussion of the interviews with
me, he or she came back to the record to substantiate and justify a judgment and a recommendation, to support the conclusion that the offender
was or was not a "problem-drinker" or chronic alcoholic.

The case of the woman who drove her son's car, mentioned earlier, is
instructive in how the record was the touchstone of diagnosis. At the conclusion of the interview the P.O. informed her that he would recommend
the usual fine plus attendance at AA meetings once a week for three
months. This seemed "light" to me. I did not believe her "story" about
her limited drinking and lack of any other problems with alcohol. After
D. left I asked the P.O. "Why did you believe her?" He seemed surprised
at my question. "I don't believe her. She probably drinks much more but
I need much firmer evidence to recommend Antabuse. The court would-
n't accept it. If the blood count were higher [it was .15, not considered a
high count] it could be done. Still two violations in three and a half years
is gross. Most people don't have that."

Three aspects of the file are of particular consequence for diagnosis
and recommendation: the blood alcohol level, the number of prior DUI
convictions, and the recency of them. Of these the most significant, as the
P.O. used them, was the blood alcohol level. The closer the BAL to the
minimal BAL constituting a legal judgment of DUI, the less likely that
the P.O. would recommend restrictions on the offender's activities and
the less likely he or she would be considered a chronic alcoholic or someone requiring a form of treatment.[12] That reasoning was based on a belief

that a high BAL represents a higher threshold of drunkenness and evidence of chronic alcohol problems. The heavy drinker, it was presumed, can walk and operate a vehicle, though dangerously, at levels which would lead the "normal" drinker to pass out or render him/her unable to operate a vehicle at all. A "rule of thumb" used at the time was that a BAL of .20 was evidence of "problem-drinking."

When the record showed a past conviction or arrest for DUI or for reckless driving it added support for a conclusion of drinking problems.[13] In one case the defendant had a long record of arrests on criminal charges and many vehicle code citations for moving violations. The only DUI conviction was the present one. His BAL was .10, the legal minimum for a DUI offense without additional evidence of intoxication. Nevertheless, the defendant was interviewed as if he were a prior offender. However, the P.O. told him that he would recommend "only the standard fine." In his recommendation the P.O. treated the defendant as a first offender and did not diagnose a drinking problem. The record was used to defend the conclusion and the recommendation rather than any direct information on the defendant's drinking.

In conversations with me several of the P.O.s were explicit about their dependence on the file. They maintained that they depended more upon the written, established, and reliable record than upon the interview or telephone conversations with relatives or friends of the defendant. They felt that these latter sources were also unreliable, although if they did uncover work or family problems it strengthened the assumption that the DUI offense was a sign of other drinking problems.

Recidivism, and recent recidivism more so, made the presumption of problem-drinking even stronger. At the time of my observations there was a move to dispense with reports and interviews with second offenders and go directly to "treatment" recommendations.

In a previous study of Sun County sentencing practices in DUI cases the plea bargaining negotiations between prosecuting and defense attorneys depended heavily on the record of prior offenses and the BALs (Gusfield 1972). In the probation process discussed in this chapter the file is again the dominating set of "facts." Having a "clean" or a "bad" record is the significant step in the diagnostic process. That initial categorization has multiplier or spiraling effects.

Where the defendant was caught becomes significant because it has a bearing on the record. A court, like that of Sun City, engaged in plea bargaining; hence, the record was not as close to the event creating the arrest as it was in Eastland. A different character profile would result.

In the midst of this legal and quasi-medical process, what has happened to the disease conception of alcoholism? The P.O. has before him or her a defendant whose arrest and conviction for DUI is to be explained. Is he or she someone who should be treated for alcoholism or other problems with the use of alcohol? Is he or she someone whose drinking is "normal," whose act of DUI does not stem from an illness or character flaw any more than other traffic offenders?

The P.O. is in a cognitively difficult situation. He or she cannot rely on information given by the offender in the interview. Even the defendant's account of his or her own record is not reliable. In this situation the record becomes its own explanation. The existence of a drinking problem becomes an inference from the record and not the other way around: the record substantiated as an outcome of a drinking problem established independently of the record. Behavioral evidence such as blackouts, memory lapses, and loss of control depend on information supplied by the offender and are thus unreliable. Even a measure of quantity and frequency of alcohol intake compared to a "normal" measure does not exist. That too would depend on offender information. What the P.O. can observe independently of the offender is his or her physical appearance (not a reliable index either) and the existence of "trouble" connected with alcohol use. That, of course, is the record.

In practice, the observation of "trouble" is itself a sign of an alcohol problem. The existence of a medical or quasi-medical problem is unobservable for the P.O. In the confrontation between the offender and the P.O, it is the record which the P.O. uses to convince the offender of a problem. In one case, mentioned earlier in another connection, the offender says that he does not have a drinking problem; he has a driving problem. The only time his drinking gets him in trouble is when he drives because he drives too fast even when sober. His record does show many tickets for speeding but also a number for DUI, which enabled the P.O. to get the offender to admit to a drinking problem.

Regularly the interview included the Michigan Alcohol Screening Test, which consists of twenty-three questions about the drinking behavior of the respondent. The P.O.s discount the information obtained because it, too, is tainted by being based on self-reported behavior. Only if it is exceptionally high or if the offender appeared very defensive in taking it does it become at all useful to the P.O. In none of the interviews I observed was it more than an additional item, used in conjunction with the file.

The physical appearance of the defendant is another datum which the P.O. took into consideration. What was observed and commented upon to me was the physical appearance of the offenders, especially the women. The P.O. took into consideration such items as puffiness of the face, redness of the nose and eyes, and differences between recorded and apparent age where the recorded age was younger than the apparent age. The offender's "story" and his or her claims were more or less believable as they met the P.O.'s view of what someone having alcohol problems did or did not look like.

Stigma and Punishment

This has been a description of the process by which drinking drivers were screened into those who do and those who do not have a drinking problem for which help should be required. Alongside the legal language of the court there is the medical language of alcoholism treatment. The language of evidence and the vehicle code is supplemented by the perspective of the disease concept of alcoholism. Stigma and punishment, which seem antithetical to medicalization, nevertheless characterize the recommendations which the P.O. makes to the court.

Defendants do not come into the interviews in the role of patients seeking help in defining their illnesses. Their "stories" about the arrest and about their drinking are often protections of the self and defenses against the accusation of being "abnormal." They protest that they are not "deviant drinkers" for whom using alcohol constitutes a serious problem. They try to explain away their arrests as untypical events, as something other than the result of recurrent and frequent drinking patterns. They and the P.O. treat each other as adversaries. The recommendation has the aura of punishment and several of the interviewees stated their preference for heavier fines and no probationary conditions.

Enrollment in the Living Sober course, attendance at Alcoholics Anonymous, and mandated use of Antabuse are stigmata of being a "problem drinker," an incipient alcoholic, or a chronic alcoholic. To accept one of these is, as the interviewees express it, to accept a moral designation of themselves as flawed in character, as being deviant people. They do not express it as medical advice, as a medical condition for which they are not responsible. They are judged to lack an ability for self-control which "normal" people possess. The more constraining the recommendation, the greater the stigma. Like mental illness and venereal diseases, alcohol problems remain sharply distinguished from less morally toned conditions as cancer, high blood pressure, or the common cold.

This is also apparent in the P.O.'s style during the interview. He or she tries to bring the offender to admit the status of someone with a drinking problem. In a number of interviews he or she met the offender's objections to the Living Sober Course or Alcoholics Anonymous by indicating that the defendant had been done a favor; the offender had not been given a more constraining recommendation such as AA rather than the Living Sober course or Antabuse rather than AA. What is at stake is the judgment of the moral status of the offender entailed in the cognitive question: How much is excessive drinking? Is the offender an excessive drinker?

The issues raised in this chapter and in these observations are deeply set in the operations by which the event of drinking and driving serves as a sign of possible recurrent problems with alcohol. How much is too much? These questions of stigma and punishment, of moderate or heavy drinking are crystallized in the following interview with a naval career man. A large portion of it is reprinted here as taken from my notes on the interview, produced at the time of the interview and placed on tape shortly after.

Interview Between Probation Officer and
DUI Convicted Offender, "John Short"

Short had failed to appear for the first appointment and the P.O. did not expect him to appear today although scheduled. However, in the event that he might show I read the record before the scheduled time. Short is twenty-nine, married and living in Eastland. He had a prior DUI six years ago in another state and in 1972 (three years before) he failed to appear on a traffic violation. The record also indicated that he had had a criminal charge dismissed, also several years ago. Short is a sailor, a naval career man who is stationed aboard a warship in Sun City. He was arrested while driving his own car, a 1972 Mazda. Short had only recently returned after thirty days at sea, and in the instant case he was driving home from a retirement party with his wife in the car. Neither the police report nor the BAL was in the record. When I pointed this out to the P.O. he phoned the court and got the BAL—.14.

Before Short appeared I talked with the P.O. and asked if he/she handled all of the DUI first offenders referred by the Eastland court. He/she did. They used to spread them around but now found it more efficient to have one person doing one kind of thing. I asked for the ratio of first to second offenders referred by the court but the P.O. talked about the total number of arrests. They used to get about 120 a month but now it's up. When they began they were getting about thirty percent to one-third of all first offenders, ones on whom there would be some

kind of action, such as AA or something more than just the DUI
school. Surprisingly, this ratio has remained the same; sometimes
more, sometimes less.

At this point, the offender, Short, came in. He was casually dressed
in blue jeans, an open shirt and boots. He wore glasses. The shirt
was a long-sleeved, dress shirt with a pattern. It turned out to be a
long interview—45 minutes. (At one point during the interview a
woman came into the room and talked for some time with the clerk
administering the Antabuse. She had two small children with her and
they became curious about me and kept talking to me, wanting to
know what I was doing, what I was writing, etc. It made it difficult to
follow all of the interview at various points. Such are the vicissitudes
of field work!)

P.O.: (beginning in usual fashion) Have you ever had any car accidents?
Short: I had one in (another state), but not in California. That was six or
seven years ago.
P.O.: Were you cited for DUI?
Short: No.
P.O.: Had you been drinking in that accident?
Short: No.
P.O.: Were you ever arrested other than the two times listed?
Short: No.
P.O.: How would you describe your drinking problem or don't you
think you have one?
Short: No, I don't. If I had, I'd of had to get out of the Navy. I worked
for (missed) and drive (missed). An important job. Sometimes we
go over to the club and have one or two at lunch time or at slack
time. I have a beer when I'm not working, but I wouldn't say I've
got a drinking problem.
P.O.: Has your wife ever asked you to cut down?
Short: No. I don't do too much drinking. When I drink, I drink at
home—have one or two beers with my wife. When we go out we
may have one or two. I'd been to a retirement party and just got
nailed, I guess.
P.O.: What shape do you think you were in?
Short: I thought I was in pretty good shape. My wife did, too. Usually,
sometimes when I'm not in good shape, she'll ask to drive and I'll
let her drive. She certainly didn't do it this time.
P.O.: Have you signed up for the drinking-driver school?
Short: Yes. I missed two classes last week—I had to work late. The judge
put down on that piece of paper there that my obligations to the
Navy come first.

(The P.O. then went over the probation grant. This was the point at
which the two girls entered and I missed all of the recommendations.
From the context that followed, later verified in conversation with the
P.O., he had suggested that Short attend AA meetings as a condition of
probation. Short objected strenuously, saying that his last DUI, prior
to the present, had been more than five years ago.)

P.O.: No doubt in my mind, though, that you drink too much. You're
       not an alcoholic, but you could go that way.

Short: If a person goes out to sea and he has no problems, he's able to do
       that; he's not addicted.

P.O.: Of course not at sea and you're not addicted.

Short: (speaking with some heat) You say if I go home and have five or
       six beers I'm getting addicted?

P.O.: Well, it's a damned good way to get there. It'll build your toler-
       ance up if you keep drinking like that.

Short: I understand but like my father, well, he's sixty now; he'd
       come home and have four, five or six beers and he still does.
       He might have a few at lunch, at dinner or after dinner and he
       doesn't have any problems with drinking. How can you say
       that I'm like that, that I have problems just because I've been
       arrested?

P.O.: (interrupting Short) Twice arrested. The normal drinker is never
       arrested for DUI.

Short: Maybe if you're arrested every two years or so, but mine was five
       years ago.

P.O.: Anyway, what I think isn't important. It's what the judge thinks
       and normally on a second time around he'll want to see more.

Short: (now quite heated) How can they judge me on what happened in
       another state? I've already suffered my consequence for it. But I
       happened to go to a retirement party and happened to get stopped.
       If I hadn't told you about that past 502 (Former vehicle code
       designation for DUI) it wouldn't mean a thing.

P.O.: (also getting heated) Christ, we know about that. We're not
       stupid; we got records on everyone. If I had a prior arrest I'd be
       damn sure to avoid it again.

Short: What does it show about my ability to control drinking, that I
       can't avoid it?

P.O.: The judge has the final say and he'd modify my order if I didn't
       make it.

Short: I'm going out of the country at the end of the month. I'll be gone
       three or four months.

P.O.: He'll certainly take that into consideration, and certainly will have to let you out to sea. But he'd require attendance on your return and might require you to report to the Alcohol Control Officer on board ship.

Short: I'm going to reenlist next month. That might hurt me.

P.O.: Do they know about it?

Short: People I work with sure know about the 502.

P.O.: If you were referred to the Naval Rehabilitation Center, that would go on your record.

Short: Why should I hide it? When I go to reenlist I'd be accused of hiding it. This could hurt my reenlistment.

P.O.: I'm just trying to let you know so that you might prefer not to inform the Naval ARTC (Alcohol Rehabilitation Training Center). We won't.

Short: If they say I have to go to AA meetings and I have orders to go somewhere or be transferred, what then?

P.O.: Just write a letter to the court telling them and they'll probably modify the order.

(P.O. asked Short to supply a name and number where he could verify that Short will leave for six months. Somewhere in the interview, probably when I was interrupted, Short had escalated the coming time at sea from three to six months.)

P.O.: I would like to refer you to the Naval ARC. Your drinking now is not a great problem but it could become such and you have no insight into your problem. You are not a normal drinker. All the information, all the statistics indicate that you are developing a problem. If you continue you may get into trouble with the police, may kill someone, have trouble at work.

Short: (indignantly) Trouble at work! If I had problems, I would not have that job if I wasn't squared away performance-wise, knowledge-wise, behavior-wise. My performance is very high.

P.O.: Your drinking hasn't affected your efficiency yet. When it does you won't know it. However I'll explain the situation to the court and consider the alternatives. Nothing I can tell you as to what will happen.

Short: A couple of times I had traffic violations and didn't appear. The judge made me feel like that (makes the sign with his fingers to signify a degrading event). The way he put it was that I was irresponsible, because he said, "You're not reliable." I don't remember exactly what it was; a taillight out or something, but he looks at his papers and suggests that I'm a total fuck-up. If I was irresponsible, I wouldn't be in the Navy doing what I'm doing.

(According to the record, he was actually convicted on reckless driving in this last offense.) But he's supposed to have an open mind. I started with two strikes against me.

P.O.: You feel the deck is stacked against you?

Short: Yeah.

P.O.: The judge is fair and consistent. Failure to appear isn't good, but he isn't going to persecute you for it.

Short: When he called me irresponsible he's saying that I'm a fuck-up. That was three years ago that happened. I've been back on active duty for two and a half years and I had to submit letters to do that.

P.O.: If you don't have a problem, there's no harm in your drinking. If you do, then you ought to quit your drinking.

Short: (A sentence in my notes is illegible). I think he has a biased mind himself.

P.O.: What the court wants is for you to quit before you have trouble.

(The interview came to an end at this point. I asked the P.O. if he/she was going to recommend that the Naval ARC be informed. The P.O. said. "I'll call his officer to verify that he's really going to sea for several months, and I'll ask about his drinking. I'd like to avoid ARC, and we'll try to if he's a career Navy man. I'll recommend that he be given attendance at AA when he gets back to port. The judge may even say, 'To hell with it.' But if he's having one or two beers at lunch and five or six beers at night, he's drinking too much.")

CONCLUDING REMARKS

The two case studies described above were part of a diversionary process in many jurisdictions. Various forms of the DUI school are presently in wide use. The presentencing procedures are not uniformly found in most courts. In Eastland they were in place on a special federal grant at the time.[14] Both programs studied operated from a framework in which drinking and driving was viewed as a problem of alcohol abuse. Attention to the offender was sharply colored by a perspective which defined alcohol problems in medical terms—as a consequence of a special class of people who suffer from an infirmity in controlling drink. They either suffered from a disease—alcoholism—or were in an early stage of its development. Both programs can be viewed as efforts to persuade the offender that he or she is a person of particular, unusual kind and not one of the "normal" population of drinkers.

In his historical study, *Discipline and Punishment*, Michel Foucault suggests that punishment and incarceration are means by which authorities define what is normal by creating what is delinquent: "The delinquent is to be distinguished from the offender by the fact that it is not so much the act as his life that is relevant in characterizing him . . . The legal punishment bears upon an act; the punitive technique on a life" (Foucault 1977, 253–54).

At the time data was collected for this study (1975) the drinking driver was an object of public condemnation, but his or her delinquency was low on the public agenda of social problems. Since, during the 1980s, drinking-driving has come to occupy a higher place on that agenda (Gusfield 1986; McCarthy et al. 1988; Ross 1992). Under the impetus of Mothers Against Drunk Driving (MADD), Remove Intoxicated Drivers (RID), and other agents of the victims' movement against the drinking-driver, and supported by federal agencies, state legislation governing DUI has mandated more severe punishments. At the same time much has continued to substantiate an earlier view of the status of the drinking-driver as that of a high-level traffic offender. DUI classes have become an increasingly prescribed adjunct of sentencing. Although jail is mandated in many states, sentences are frequently served on weekends or in "volunteer" community service. While not a "folk-crime" neither is DUI a "serious" crime. Implicitly, the legal treatment of DUI is not unambiguously a process of constructing deviants or delinquents. Not the drinking-driver but the act of drinking and driving is the object of legal sanctions. In the process, however, the self of the offender cannot help being part of the enforcement programs.

In an etymological sense, excluding the diversionary processes described above, the legal career of the convicted DUI offender is a true example of the penitentiary: it evokes penance. In doing penance, the offender is restored to the world of the law-abiding from which his acts and not his person have removed him or her. He or she is outside the pale, but acts of penance—fines, jail, loss of driving license—can restore the offender to communal membership. It is this recognition of the restorative process that leads me to refer to the redemptive element in the legal process. "He served his time; he paid his debt."

This is in clear contrast to the rehabilitative perspective toward punishment which, though under current criticism, has underlain a great deal of modern penal thought. Here the source of crime lies in the intrinsic character of the person; his or her mode of living, personality, and style of life. Personal habits are so implicated in his or her illegality that, before redemption is at all possible, the person must change and the stigma be removed before there can be a return to normality and community membership. He or she is in essence of another species. His or her actions define and construct a class of deviants who cannot do penance because the crime is an expression of the person. The action that constituted the cause of arrest is a function of the person.

Here lies the ambiguity in the idea of medicalizing as a means of minimizing stigma. Jellinek and the Yale School thought that defining alcoholism as a disease would eradicate the stigma and embarrassment of chronic inebriety (Jellinek 1960; Keller 1976). The intense resistance of the DUI offenders in the DUI school and the probation interviews to becoming defined as "deviant" suggests that this is by no means certain. As the naval career man put it, "You're calling me a fuck-up." Within the context of a legal offense, DUI, the evil becomes located, whether disease or not, as an emanation from the flawed character of the person.

Being defined as a "problem drinker" or alcoholic is part of the potential self-transformation from a competent drinker who has committed an incompetent act into an incompetent drinker whose DUI act was "natural," in keeping with his or her character. Doing penance for an act may be capable of achieving redemption for a sin but it cannot change fundamental character. Whatever the eventual career of the drinking offender—treatment, recovered alcoholic status, or other—the initial image of the self as flawed and deviant is stigmatizing.

There is another side of the coin of the diversionary programs as modes of deviance construction. Driving while under the influence of alcohol is a common occurrence in American life.[15] Even in this period when DUI is high on the public agenda, it still remains a commonly experienced event in the lives of a great many Americans. In many circles, as we saw in the chapters on the bar studies, the opposite—not driving after drinking—is also problematic and unusual. Unlike many "crimes," arrests for DUI is less class-related or group-related, other than age and gender. Where people drink and people drive they also drink and drive. How, then, can the law treat normal behavior as the action of deviant people, as something more than a high-level traffic offense?

This question is at the center of the resistance of offenders to the deviance-construction process in the DUI class and in the probation interviews. The instructor and the P.O. try to convince the offender that he or she is not like others, that DUI is a "serious" offense. The offenders insist that they, as one put it, "just happened to get caught." Their offense is no different in kind from that of the speeding motorist or the driver who made a left turn against the lights. They made a moral or mental error, but they are not flawed persons.

The use of theological vocabulary—stigma and redemption—was chosen originally for its metaphoric, surprise value. Yet the problem uncovered is itself theological. If evil acts are defined as sinful, the evildoer is charged with having been capable of choosing good and able to do so in the future. If evil is defined as expressive of a character deficiency, even an addiction, the evildoer is declared beyond redemption until transformed as a person.

In one bit of advice found in a guide to DUI defense attorneys, the author suggests that attorneys will be successful in DUI cases if they can get the jury to think, "There but for the grace of God go I." In the day-to-day process of administering justice, police, attorneys, and judges often make a distinction between "real" criminals and others. The imposition of social controls and the legitimacy of authorities would seem to depend on a belief that a wide gulf separates the law-abiding from the law-rebelling. How to accomplish this in the realm of DUI is filled with obstacles. In the kingdom of the one-eyed men, the blind are different.

Part 5

Cultural Perspectives and Public Policy

Chapter Eleven

The Prevention of Drinking Problems

The progress of medical science has been one of the glories of the modern world. Discovery of the bacterial basis of many diseases has made it possible to use sanitation, vaccines, and antisepsis in the prevention of epidemics. Through medical knowledge, sicknesses that in the past laid waste to large segments of the population have been brought under control. The problems of diphtheria, typhoid, smallpox, malaria, and poliomyelitis have been "solved" as their epidemic outbreak has been prevented. Problems associated with human behavior and not readily perceived as chiefly biological in origin have proven less amenable to resolution. Despite much research, much organized effort, the expenditure of large sums of money, and even much political agitation, problems of poverty, crime, mental abnormality, suicide, family conflict, drug addiction, and harm-causing drinking are far from disappearing. This volume is testimony to the attention that modern industrialized societies have given to the troublesome aspects of alcohol use in a variety of life areas. Work, family, crime, automobile driving, and health are just a few of the arenas in which some users of alcohol find that "excess" has produced painful consequences for the self, the family, the operation of major institutions.

The history of progress in health has had a profound effect on many fields where solutions to human ills are sought through the application of knowledge. In the applications of medical science to health problems, prevention can be distinguished from treatment. Even though we possess effective "cures" for diphtheria and smallpox, treatment is an unwieldy, cruel, and costly way of dealing with the problems of those diseases. Preventive medicine engages in activities that forestall or reduce the occurrence of the events that constitute the problem of illness or, if not

245

forestalled, reduce their intensity. The inoculation of dogs with antirabies serum is a preventive for the occurrence of rabies in both dogs and humans.

It is, of course, always possible to respond to any problem solely through treatment, even when prevention might be possible. Expensive methods of preventing the common cold or the ordinary headache may not be as practical as equally expensive methods of preventing cancer or suicide. In these cases, the severity of the "illness" must be weighed against the costs of its prevention.

The argument for attempts to prevent problem drinking as an alternative or in addition to treatment rests on the following three propositions, the data for which are spelled out in the essays in this volume: (1) treatment for the various problems of alcohol misuse is expensive and not consistently effective; (2) the suffering and economic loss to both person and society are themselves painful and expensive (and their occurrence and recurrence thus need to be avoided); (3) under present conditions, treatment is available or acceptable to only a small percentage of those whose alcohol misuse creates pain for themselves or others. To increase treatment facilities to cover this target population would be immensely expensive, if at all possible.

In this chapter I will examine a variety of past and present attempts, largely but not exclusively in the United States, to prevent the occurrence of problems associated with drinking. It is my thesis that these have involved a common mode of conceptualizing the relation between drinking and drinking problems which has unwisely curtailed the development of new approaches and restricted the reemergence of useful past approaches. Methods of prevention used in the field of public alcohol policy have depended chiefly upon the character of the problem as it has been perceived by those devising the policies. The perception of the problem, I maintain, has been closely related to the prevention solutions suggested. The distinction between problem and solution has been blurred.

This chapter presumes an audience interested in public, not private, policies. The issues are not posed to influence individual action but to affect public agencies and institutions. The chapter presupposes that it is public policy, as enunciated in laws, institutional actions, educational campaigns, and so forth that is being analyzed, although such public actions *may* have individual policy as their objectives.

THE CHARACTER OF DRINKING PROBLEMS
AND SOLUTIONS

Human problems, including medical ones, do not spring full-blown into human consciousness. Even to recognize a situation as painful requires a system of categorizing and defining events. To perceive the event as requiring a solution and to search for that solution is not given by the event but is the product of a social and historical process. There is a long history, for example, to the events we today label "mental disorder." In that history much of what are now seen as abnormalities that cry out for remediation went unnoticed as special actions requiring alleviation or were seen as unique behavior, often of a valued rather than devalued nature (Rosen 1968; Scheff 1966).

Phenomena become problematic when their continued existence and attributes are no longer taken for granted, but are selected for investigation, explanation and possible correction. Thus the change of seasons is not problematic; however people may think of it, the cycle of weather is not yet seen as capable of being changed by human control. Neither is the aging process, except in Faustian fantasies. Crime and juvenile delinquency are problematic in this society. Efforts are made to understand their occurrence and to eradicate or limit their frequency.

At least two aspects of problem formation follow from this reasoning. First, problems involve both a cognitive and a moral judgment. The moral judgment is entailed in the conclusion that this phenomenon is painful, that it should be eradicated. Medical conceptions of illness also contain this moral element. Many would certainly view the aging process as unwelcome as many have for long viewed the position of black people in the American social structure as painful, from a moral concern with human equality. But problems are also cognitive; they involve a belief that the situation need not be, that it is capable of alteration toward a less painful or better state. Many do not believe this about the aging process today and it is only very recently that it has become an active subject of biological research.

A second aspect of this perspective toward problem formation is that what is problematic to A need not be so to B. The aphorism, "One man's moral turpitude is another man's innocent pleasure," sums up the implications of a pluralistic society. The difference may be moral or cognitive or both. Many social issues involve just such disagreements about whether or not a given state of affairs should be altered. Racial disputes, pornography, sexual equality are but three examples where moral diversities are

at work. While cognitive disagreements are less productive of social conflict, they are also at work and the shifts in the agenda of issues from one
historical period to another testify that one generation may define as
problematic situations that another has ignored. Poverty, for example,
has a history of diverse attitudes across generations and historical periods
ranging from positive acceptance, through resignation, to positive rejection (Matza 1966).

An analysis of drinking problems must then include the stance from
which the situation is seen as problematic, both in moral and cognitive
terms. It must include the standers from whose perspective this is a problem. It should also include those from whose perspective the situation is
not a problem.

The cognitive element, however, contains a further feature in the development of the reality of the problem. What, exactly, constitutes the
problem? Here we are in the realm of conceptualization, which bears
heavily on the issues of prevention because it deeply affects the character
of proposed solutions. For example, let us consider the implications of
heavy drinking for pedestrian behavior on icy sidewalks. I believe that,
other variables being the same, someone who has been drinking to the
edge of sobriety is less able to navigate an icy sidewalk than someone who
has not been drinking. If I am interested, for humanitarian or economic
reasons, in preventing injury to the drinker from icy sidewalks, am I involved in the prevention of drinking problems? The reader will immediately recognize that there are many ways of conceiving of this situation
which lead to many possible solutions. Deicing sidewalks by an effective
friction-producing substance is one solution. The wearing of specially
constructed shoes is another. Staying inside is still another. Moving to
Florida is still another. Staying sober is yet another. The designation of
injury as a result of drinking is not contained in the situation but is a designation by the observer from among a number of possible interpretations of the problem (Andreasson and Bonnichsen 1966).[1]

The designation of problems as drinking problems is therefore both a
theory of causation and a strategy of attack on them. For example, when
absenteeism in industry caused by alcohol use is designated as a drinking
problem, the process may lead to a strategy aimed at diminishing drinking among employees as the way to reduce and prevent absenteeism.

It is a major thesis of this chapter that the way in which drinking
problems have been conceptualized in the United States has unprofitably
limited the range of potential prevention policies. The relationship has
also operated in reverse: experience with prevention policies has unduly

limited the range of conceptualization of drinking problems. The legacy of past policies and concepts has led to a narrowed focus on the amount of alcohol consumed as the major target of public action and on changing the individual's decision to consume as the major mechanism for preventing problems of alcohol use.

This thesis will be elaborated through the remainder of this chapter as we examine the diverse forms of prevention attempted in the United States and elsewhere.

THE OWNERSHIP OF DRINKING PROBLEMS

For much of the nineteenth and part of the twentieth centuries, the Protestant churches were the major source of agitation and activity in the definition, conceptualization, and development of public strategies toward alcohol use in the United States. As such, they defined the legitimate cognitive and moral approach to alcohol problems, concentrating on the consumption of alcohol as the central problem. The churches played a central role in putting issues of drinking high on the political and public agenda, in publishing persuasional materials, and in developing their personnel as authoritative persons qualified to examine cognitive aspects of drinking. In becoming the legitimate source of public policies toward alcohol use, the churches came to "own" problems of drinking. Other possible sources of ownership were absent or weak. The medical profession was poorly organized in America and unequipped to present an alternative conceptualization until well into the twentieth century. The same was true of the universities, which were less autonomous from religious auspices than has been true in recent decades. Government was less the initiator than the recipient of alcohol policies. In general, the alcohol industry, both beer and spirits, "disowned" the issue, seeking neither to develop strategies toward drinking problems nor to counteract those developed by the churches.

Much of the persuasional literature of the temperance movement (and later the prohibitionists) recites many of the same "problems" detailed in this volume—the relation of alcohol to crime, ill-health, immorality, and low productivity. Implicitly, and often explicitly, however, the theme was sounded that drinking is itself immoral, that it leads to excessive drinking, and that the only effective strategy is one that decreases the total amount of national consumption.

This strategy—the diminution of consumption—was congenial both as a cognitive judgment and a moral one. As a cognitive judgment it focused attention on laws to limit the sale of alcohol, on efforts to persuade users to discontinue use, and on the public appearance of abstinence. To conceive of solutions to alcohol problems that still permitted drinking would be contradicted by cognitive theories and moral disapprobation. While distinctions were drawn between the "alcoholic" and the "normal" drinker, in practice they were both targets of policy. Since drinking per se was a suspect activity and normal drinking led to excessive drinking, the curtailment of consumption was the heart of policy.

With Repeal of the Eighteenth Amendment, the churches receded as the legitimate authority in the area of alcohol problems, and with them prevention receded as a strategy. Both within the churches and in relation to the secular world, religion was no longer of major influence in defining any drinking as a moral failing. The postrepeal period, until the mid-1960s, has been one of low national and political salience for issues of alcohol and problems of drinking. With the development of the Yale Center of Alcohol Studies (now the Rutgers Center) and the gradual development of medical interest in the field, ownership shifted toward the universities, the medical profession, and the growth of a secular occupational group responsible for treatment of alcoholics. All of these activities and their knowledge base led in the direction of treatment for those who defined themselves, or were defined by others, as people in trouble through excessive drinking. Alcoholics Anonymous and the role of the "recovered alcoholic" in the proliferating voluntary organizations devoted to alcoholism added still another group whose interests came from experience and expertise in treatment.

The period in alcohol policy from 1933 to 1968 has seen a strong reaction against the religious and moral conceptions of drinking problems of the temperance movement and Prohibition. The slogan "Alcoholism is a disease," has been a self-conscious attempt to shift the moral character of the drinker toward public acceptance and of the excessive drinker toward that of a sick person. As we shall see, this orientation has had two consequences. First, by attending chiefly to treatment it has eschewed preventive policies. Second, insofar as prevention has been discussed or attempted, the cognitive concern for diminution of drinking has continued as the major strategy in preventing alcohol problems.

Situational and Individualistic Policies

An understanding of past prevention policies in the United States must recognize the primacy given to the act of drinking as the focus of preventive efforts. The temperance movement was concerned with decreasing intake, Prohibition with destroying it. Others have been concerned with preventing only excessive drinking. Some have been concerned with changing the methods, the substances, the settings, or the cultural meanings of alcohol. But the major thrust has been directed at the phenomena of the consumption of alcohol as the place toward which to direct prevention of problems arising from its use.

Within this common focus on drinking, I want to distinguish between two kinds of policies—the situational and the individualistic. Situational policies are directed at the conditions, structures, environmental availabilities, on physical facilities which surround the person. These policies do not attempt to change the drinker but to change the conditions under which he or she is able to drink or act as a consequence of drinking. The regulation of hours when bars and liquor stores may do business is one example of preventive measures that are situational in objective. Such laws make no effort to change the desire or demand for alcohol but only its availability. Individualistic policies attempt to affect or influence the action of the person toward drinking. Television advertising with the message, "If you drive, don't drink," is an example of such a policy. It is an effort to change the demand for alcohol or for driving by an appeal to the user to change his or her actions.

These diverse strategies, by no means inconsistent in their use, nevertheless operate on different assumptions about how change is effected, require different political climates, and raise moral issues of differing sorts. I will first describe the major policies that have been used in prevention of each type and then analyze these assumptions and climates.

Situational Policies

All modern industrial societies have some measures to inhibit and limit the sale of alcohol (Tongue 1962; Wilkinson 1970). Among these are zoning regulations, fixed hours of sale, heavy excise taxes, state-owned monopolies of alcohol, advertising limits, price controls, and the direct prohibition of sale or possession and use. Most of these measures attempt prevention of drinking problems by preventing or diminishing the availability, to potential users, of the substance seen as causing the problem.

Other situational policies, including some of those above, attempt to influence the drinking act in ways that will minimize, or mitigate, its presumed ill effects. These are less concerned with the amount of drinking than with the style of accompanying elements of the drinking act. For example, many states in the United States have laws requiring the availability of food in bars, under the assumption that eating slows the absorption of alcohol into the bloodstream and thus minimizes its ill effects. Other measures, sometimes used and sometimes suggested, are those that substitute beers or wines for distilled spirits, or systems of taxation and price control. Among measures also considered are diminishing the alcohol content of beverages and developing a pattern of sipping rather than gulping drinks. All of these policies attempt to control and decrease the amount or kind of drinking by measures that do not require the deliberate cooperation or assent of the drinker.

Less easily classifiable are strategies to change the cultural meanings of alcohol usage which will be discussed in greater detail below in connection with the influential recommendations of Rupert Wilkinson. Insofar as they attempt to change such aspects of drinking as the availability of alcohol, the settings for alcohol, the alcoholic strength of beverages, and the actions of socializing agencies (parents, teachers, doctors, mass media), they are situational. What distinguishes this strategy from the others described above is that these are not oriented to the diminution of drinking but to the development of new ways and settings for drinking. The objective is to disseminate and influence a conception of drinking that will make excessive use less acceptable for its present functions. One example of such situational policies is the proposal to change licensing so that a wide range of recreational facilities—such as bowling alleys, sports events, theaters, and resorts—will be permitted to serve all types of alcoholic beverages. The proposal is based on the effort to take alcohol out of a drinking-only setting and, by placing it in familial contexts, in controlled contexts, and in a setting of normal leisure, to reduce or eliminate the concept of alcohol as a special, forbidden, and thus particularly appealing substance (Wilkinson 1970, chs. 8 and 9).

Individualistic Policies

Individualistic policies attempt to prevent drinking or behavior connected with it from occurrence by persuading the person to change his individual drinking behavior or the behavior connected with it. Two very different types of effort have been the focus of the majority of such policies—law and education.

Laws against public drunkenness, against driving while impaired by alcohol, against injuries to others while under the influence of alcohol, exist in almost all states. Following Andrenaes (1966), we can distinguish two levels of deterrence as the object of such laws. Specific deterrence refers to the impact of punishment on those who are arrested for violating such regulations. The preventive character of the law is presumed to deter repetition of the action. General deterrence refers to the impact of the law on the general public—those who are not arrested. Here the deterrent effect is in the expectation that fear of detection and punishment will prevent persons from committing acts that, if detected, would lead to arrest and punishment. They are dissuaded from excessive drinking and the punishable acts connected with it.

The impact of laws on drinking problems is more diffuse, in theory, than the situational policies. From the standpoint of the law, being drunk in public is illegal (though in many states no longer a crime), but being drunk in private is not. One can avoid arrest and punishment by changing his drinking habits or by not being seen in public. In any case, however, the law as a preventive measure is an effort to use the threat of punishment as a device to persuade the individual to change.

Information and Education. During the nineteenth century in the United States, the Temperance movement succeeded in getting legislation passed in most states requiring that time be set aside in public schools for classroom teaching of the "evils of alcohol." The movement was also successful in influencing the content of textbooks and other materials used in the schools. Even after Repeal of the Eighteenth Amendment, such mandated teaching has remained in the statutes, although the vigor of its enforcement is much weakened. Such education is only one instance of efforts made by various groups, of widely differing persuasions, to control the drinking of others by methods of persuasion. These run the gamut from advertising to instructional film to informational literature. The recent television campaign prepared by the Office of Alcohol Countermeasures of the National Highway Traffic Safety Administration carries the message that many auto fatalities involve drivers under the influence of alcohol, that many of these are people with drinking problems, and that the audience should try to prevent others from driving while under the influence of alcohol.

At one level or another, such appeals aim at providing information thought to be lacking and to change behavior by appealing to the individual decision-maker who consumes the alcohol. The effects of alcohol abuse are pointed out and the appeal is to the rational concern of the hearer or viewer or reader with the painful consequences of excessive drinking.

Natural Consequences. It must be pointed out that a great deal of prevention occurs without definite public policy or as a consequence of policies unrelated to an objective concerned with drinking. Fear of loss of job, of death or injury in auto accidents, or of loss of respect apparently all operate to curtail drinking and excessive drinking though these may not be embodied in legal punishments, educational campaigns, or other efforts of persuasion. The existence and perception of these consequences are not stable elements. As the general public and dominant classes have become more tolerant of drinking, and even more humane toward problem drinkers, the natural consequences are themselves changing. In similar fashion, without policy or planning, the nation shifted during the latter half of the nineteenth century from hard liquor toward beer, and recently it seems to be shifting toward wine, in response to the impact of immigrants as well as prices. We must not overestimate the percent of the variance that planning and policy can or do influence. Much prevention and treatment occur without public or institutional intervention (Andrenaes 1966).[2]

Policy Assumptions

Because they require institutional changes, situational policies must proceed from a much stronger political base than individualistic ones. Even laws aimed at deterring individuals require less political strength because they are applied to individuals and thus possess much variance in police and courtroom enforcement. The period of Prohibition indicated the great difficulty in maintaining situational policies without a very clear political dominance of those who sought and supported the Eighteenth Amendment. As America became a more plural cultural and political society, it became increasingly difficult to enforce a policy affecting all drinkers.

Situational policies thus apply uniformly to the entire body of drinkers—both those for whom drinking creates problems and those for whom it does not. Prohibition attempted to restrict both the moderate drinker and the alcoholic. Such policies operate on the assumption that individual rationality and foresight are insufficiently dependable for those segments of the society for whom alcohol use has become problematic. Individualistic policies operate on the opposite assumption—that the use of alcohol can be clearly seen as dangerous or punitive by those who have problems with it and that such perceptions will change their behavior.

THE EFFICACY OF PREVENTIVE MEASURES

In this section I shall examine the historical outcomes of measures and suggested measures intended to curtail or influence drinking problems.

Policies Aimed at Levels of Consumption: The Political Variable

To the best of our knowledge, most policies directed at decreasing consumption of alcohol through legal strictures have been aggregate policies, falling like the sober rain from heaven upon the problem and problem-free drinker alike. Although Scandinavian countries have done so, I don't know of any political unit in the United States that has attempted to restrict sale of alcohol only to persons who have had no evidence of any problem connected with alcohol. The question is therefore raised whether or not efforts to decrease the consumption of a nation will affect the occurrence of problems connected with alcohol. Will the heavier drinkers, the "addictive" drinkers, and others highly dependent on alcohol be equally or less affected by such measures than other drinkers?

Evaluating the efficacy of various past measures to prevent the occurrence of drinking problems is a difficult and perhaps impossible task. Few evaluative studies have been conducted with the care and sophistication essential for drawing adequate conclusions. A major deficiency stems from the use of statistical indexes that measure reporting and institutional behavior rather than drinking behavior and the problems connected with it. This is especially the case where such indexes as public drunkenness arrests, drunken driver convictions, and institutionalized alcoholics are used as units by which to measure the amount of problem drinking. Such indexes vary greatly as functions of police policy, reporting procedures, legal definitions, and medical practice. They cannot be used as direct measures by which to evaluate policy results without a considerable amount of direct observation of the activities of the reporting agencies (Berger and Luckmann 1966).[3]

Recent analyses in France and Canada have suggested that there is a constant relationship between gross national consumption of alcohol and the prevalence of alcoholism, evidenced by heavy drinking or deaths from liver cirrhosis (Ledermann 1956; Schmidt and DeLint 1970), and that the lognormal distribution curve can be used to estimate the anticipated increase or decrease in alcoholism produced by an increase or decrease in total national consumption. It would follow that aggregate policies could be effective as measures to diminish that drinking which is associated with problems. The basic difficulty here, as in much of the evidence for and against various aggregative policies, is both conceptual and empirical. The studies supporting this view of the effectiveness of aggregate consumption measures are open to much criticism (Mäkelä 1975; Room 1973; Skog 1973). They rest on dubious assumptions regarding the relation between heavy drinking and drinking problems and between cirrhosis and alcoholism. Further, they limit drinking problems to the restricted model of classic alcoholism. The studies and the debate are recent and the area is still in flux (DeLint 1973).

If we turn to more empirical situations, again the data are far from clear. The Prohibition period in the United States (1919–1933) appears to have affected some decrease in total drinking, largely through increasing the cost of alcohol. Evidence, admittedly sketchy, indicates that while the urban upper middle classes continued to drink, working classes did diminish their use of alcohol (Gusfield 1968). In areas which had been strongly pro-Prohibitionist, the law appeared to operate more effectively.

The Prohibition period, as well as Norwegian experience (Brun-Gulbrandsen, n.d.), put up two great limitations on such aggregative measures: (1) Since they affect problem-free drinkers (the bulk of alcohol users) as well as those with excessive drinking patterns, they attempt to control a very large segment of the population by measures very difficult to enforce. (2) Unlike heavy commodities like automobiles, alcohol is easily and cheaply produced in homes. With prohibitive measures, a "black market" develops and the price of alcohol rises. While this result does decrease drinking, it accentuates the enforcement problem, and its impact on heavy drinkers is uncertain.

Does prohibition decrease problems connected with drinking? The data on the periods before, during, and after the 1920s suggest that it did have some effect in diminishing death from cirrhosis of the liver. However, the relation between that health issue and marital, occupational, and other alcohol-related problems is not clear, nor is the relation between alcoholism (as distinct from heavy drinking) and cirrhosis as direct and clear as once thought.

The Scandinavian countries have often been used as evidence for the view that regulation of sales can reduce problems of drinking. Under the Swedish *motbok* system, in operation from the end of World War I to the mid-1950s, moderate drinking was encouraged and excessive drinking discouraged by imposition of corresponding rations. This system was revised in 1955 to permit free choice, and the total consumption of alcohol rose sharply. Along with this went a rise in public drunkenness that was met by a pricing policy that increased the price gap between light beverages (wines and beer) and spirits. After this change, public drunkenness rates diminished. During the same period there is evidence that Swedish drinking patterns were becoming more moderate, but not as a function of public policy. (For Norway, see Brun-Gulbrandsen, n.d., footnote 4.)

Further evidence is provided by the occurrence of strikes in the state monopoly systems of Sweden and Finland. In 1963 the monthlong shutdown of all liquor stores in Sweden was accompanied by a sharp diminution in arrests for public drunkenness (Andreasson 1966). In Finland a similar recent strike of seven months led to a decrease in arrests for drunken driving. When the strike ended, however, the incidence rose sharply.[4] On the other hand, the end of the prohibition on alcohol sales in rural Finland in 1951 was not marked by an increase in excessive use (Kuusi 1957).

The evaluation of the effectiveness of preventive measures based on total consumption rests on two kinds of evidence. The historical experience with prohibitory and other restrictions on sales in the United States and the Scandinavian countries is especially difficult to assess because it has largely depended on just such data as police and court reports, alcoholism rates, and other indexes discussed above as exceptionally poor sources for evaluation. The studies which seek to correlate total consumption with cirrhosis of the liver in a number of differing cultures seem on stronger ground. Nevertheless, what the recent studies of total consumption have done, as Mäkelä (1975) pointed out, is to focus greater attention on the political variables in alcohol use and less on the cultural patterns of drinking habits.

Policies Aimed at the Consumption Act: The Cultural Variable

Recently, attempts to stress public acceptance of moderate drinking as a deliberate policy in the United States have attracted much attention. The report of the Cooperative Commission on the Study of Alcoholism (Plaut 1967) and Rupert Wilkinson's *The Prevention of Drinking Problems* (1970) have championed limited drinking as the basis of a new public strategy. The same policy has been given governmental support in the National Institute of Alcohol Abuse and Alcoholism's (NIAAA) development of campaigns to promote "responsible drinking."

These policies are responses to the ambivalent attitudes toward alcohol use in the American experience. On the one hand, public norms and laws relegate the display and context of drinking to special settings and adult age groups, which establish drinking as a less than respectable act. In this, the United States continues to treat drinking as not quite moral and legitimate behavior—a belief redolent of the Prohibition period. On the other hand, the sale and use of beer, wine, and liquor are legal and widespread. Drinking is part of the lifestyle of many groups and heavy drinking is far from rare (Cahalan, Cisin, and Crossley 1969). The aim of the newer strategy is to create a public atmosphere that accepts moderate, safe, and responsible drinking and, by so doing, to diminish the cultural significance of heavy drinking as the major pattern of drinking and non-conforming behavior.

The policies suggested by this approach involve presenting alcohol, especially to the young, in "wholesome," respected surroundings that teach Americans how to drink in moderation and in settings in which peer, work, and kin groups operate to constrain alcohol misuse. Wilkinson's proposals (1970, 105–47), for example, include the removal of many present restrictions on alcohol use in such leisure settings as bowling alleys, theaters, resorts, and sports arenas. He would permit adolescent use of alcohol, abolish licensing that prevents sale in many restaurants and in grocery stores, and establish educational and advertising programs that stress and portray moderate use of alcohol. He further advocates the use of tax policies to increase existing differences between beer and wine on the one hand, and distilled spirits on the other. Wilkinson also proposes the development of lighter proof liquors and the establishment of newer, less exclusive taverns.

This attitude toward change in the culture of drinking is derived from a variety of studies of the drinking patterns of American ethnic groups and the socialization experiences of heavy and "normal" drinkers from abstaining and nonabstaining familial backgrounds.[5] Such studies have supported a conclusion that early induction into moderate drinking as a respectable pattern is associated with low rates of problem drinking and alcoholism. They have shown that, among drinkers, childhood backgrounds involving stern abstaining parental attitudes toward drinking may become associated with high levels of problem drinking and alcoholism. These studies have led to the belief that problem drinking can be diminished by associating early drinking experiences with situations in which drinking does not symbolize virility or cultural defiance. Wilkinson has summed up the gist of this approach in describing one aspect of his proposals as promoting "drinking on occasions when drinking itself, being only one of several integrated activities, does not become an overwhelming focus of the group's attention" (1970, 7).

As Mäkelä points out in a recent criticism of these strategies (1975), they assume a substitution rather than an addition effect; moderate drinking will become a substitute for heavy drinking rather than an addition to current practices. His analysis of Finnish consumption patterns, however, leads him to conclude that the increase in beer and wine drinking was not accompanied by a decrease in spirits consumption; patterns of moderate, daily drinking were added to the existing middle-class patterns of episodic hard drinking.

It should also be pointed out that a rigid use of studies of Italian and Jewish cultures as models for drinking patterns ignores the consistency and interrelated character of food patterns and drinking customs with the history, economic position, and religious rituals of specific cultural groups and their patterns of mood-altering behavior. Grafting a device or activity from one culture to another is itself assuming a consistency of meaning from one culture or subculture to another.

Lastly, we need to recognize the resistance of alcohol misuse to control which results precisely from its place in the occasions of mood alteration and irresponsibility associated with leisure in the American and many other cultures. Between the "polite cocktail" and the "hard belt" there is a great gap in attitudes and function. Other areas indicate that the substitution effect is far from assured. There is no evidence that moderate driving has reduced the cultural significance of speeding and racing as symbols of masculinity or approved recklessness.

Policies Aimed at Persuasion: The Legal Variable

One of the most frequently used means to prevent disapproved drinking behavior has been police and court enforcement of legislation, especially in the areas of public drunkenness and of driving an automobile under the influence of alcohol. In most countries and states, drunkenness is not an acceptable excuse in civil wrongs and even increases the degree of negligence. In most, if not all, states in the United States, it is a felony to cause an injury to others in an automobile accident while driving under the influence of alcohol. Driving under the influence of intoxicating beverages is per se an offense punishable by fine, jailing, or license suspension or revocation. Until recently in most American jurisdictions public drunkenness has been punishable by fine or jail or both (U.S. Department of Transportation 1968, ch. 7). Only quite recently have some states decriminalized public drunkenness and substituted detoxification centers for the formerly ubiquitous "drunk tank." However, unlike insanity, drunkenness is not an acceptable defense in prosecutions for crime.

The laws prohibiting public drunkenness and alcohol-impaired driving have had as justification their supposed influence on potential offenders. The fear of an arrest record, of fine or jail or loss of driving license, and the public shame of arrest and a court appearance have been viewed as deterrents to the commission of the offenses and thus to the behavior whose eradication is sought.

In general, the results of such legislation in preventing problem behavior have been disappointing. Over many years the large number of cases of public drunkenness clogging the American courts and the very high recidivism rates of those convicted have been a major source of the agitation to take public drunkenness out of the realm of criminal actions (Pittman 1967).

There is little evidence that laws against drunken driving have been very effective in reducing automobile fatalities. The very careful study by Ross (1973) provides a clear analysis of the aspects involved in such legislation. Ross studied the impact of the widely heralded campaign in Britain in which breath-testing equipment was used by police in patrol cars. Given much publicity, this campaign was successful in sharply curtailing road traffic fatalities during the first year (1967) of its operation. Three years later, however, fatalities had returned to their precampaign levels. Careful examination both of the rates and of police enforcement showed that there had been a limited impact on fatality reduction. The complexities introduced by appellate court decisions in protecting defendants' rights had greatly reduced police incentive to apprehend and arrest on drunken-driving charges.

A recent study of the effect of heavier punishment for alcohol-impaired driving in Finland disclosed a situation much like that in England. As punishment increased, the rate of increase of drunken driving declined, but only temporarily, and was followed by a more permissive attitude of police toward the marginal cases (Jaakola and Takala 1971). Such studies indicate the complex character of preventive legislation, especially when it involves policing and traditional citizen rights.

Certainly the laws against alcohol-affected driving are variously enforced, both by police and by courts. Several studies in the United States have demonstrated that a first offense generally is not punished by license removal or jailing, that rates of recidivism are high (as much as 5 percent), and that severity of punishment has not reduced recidivism appreciably (Blumenthal and Ross 1973; Gusfield 1972; Robertson, Rich, and Ross 1973; Zylman 1970).

The crucial issue, however, is the effect of law in preventing automobile fatalities—the ostensible purpose of the legislation. Under the best of enforcement conditions, police can apprehend only a small portion of offenders. (The Ross study indicated the complexity of the effort.) It has often been said that, because of their heavy punishments of mandatory license revocation and jail sentences, Scandinavian countries have been successful in diminishing drunken driving. However, evidence of the success of such efforts in Finland, Norway, and Sweden is slight; blood alcohol analysis is indifferently conducted even in cases of fatalities.[6] Consequently, the conditions for ascertaining the claimed effectiveness do not exist in these countries. Analysis of traffic fatalities shows much difference between them, however, with Finland having a high rate per automobile owner and per miles driven, while Sweden and Norway are not unusually low compared to other countries with less rigorous legislation.

This discussion leads to a pessimistic attitude toward increased enforcement and harsher sentences as a means of preventing drinking-related problem behavior. Even in Norway, the most restrictive of the three Scandinavian nations, as automobile ownership has increased and the middle class is caught up in it, the populace has forced reconsideration of the mandatory character of their drinking driving laws.[7] Where a large percentage of a population engages in a practice, it is difficult to enforce proscriptive legislation except against a small percentage of offenders. In the absence of strong pressure groups, such laws have dwindling impact as they move from the halls of legislation to the highways of the traffic police and the courtrooms of local judges.

Policies Aimed at Persuasion: The Communication Variable

A great amount of time, effort, and money is spent on programs of advertising, leaflets, television, radio, and campaigns for school curriculum education. Such campaigns, of course, are of various kinds. Some stress dissemination of rational information, aiming at convincing the audience of the harmful effects of alcohol excess or the relation between fatalities and alcohol use. Within this category, some communications disseminate information designed to lead the audience to influence others, as in recent TV advertising concerning problem drinking and drinking drivers. Some are oriented toward a general audience, some toward special audiences such as youth, children, parents, and police. Others utilize more emotional, less rational styles.

It is doubtful that campaigns depending solely or largely on public information and education or even on school education are useful strategies for changing behavior. Most have not been evaluated by careful study. Where they have been, the results have been disappointing to their initiators or, at best, of limited value. Even Wilkinson, who advocates advertising and education programs, sees them as adjuncts to situational changes and ineffective as sole policies (Wilkinson 1970, 43ff.).

The history of seat belt use is a good illustration of the limited effectiveness of advertising and dedication in prescribing behavior. Despite much agitation and education, the use of seat belts, even though required as part of standard automobile equipment, has been low (approximately 20 percent of capacity use). A recent careful study by the Insurance Institute of Traffic Safety laid the basis for a series of special campaigns. Identifying the areas of concern of the population, they were able to use control groups and to conduct a series of TV ads aimed at specific audiences (children, youth, parents, and so forth) over a nine-month period. In spite of many favorable elements and astute methods, the campaign had no discernible impact, as other seat belt studies have found (Fleischer 1973; Haddon 1972). While advertising has at times been successful in switching interest from one brand to another and occasionally in the introduction of a new product, this is very different from preventing the use of a product among those with a high commitment to it. Wilkinson's assertions rest more on faith than on past experience. That information and education *may* be effective in conjunction with other policies is a different question.

Policies Aimed at Screening Individuals

Strictly speaking, efforts to detect people with drinking problems and to persuade them to obtain treatment are not aggregative prevention measures. However, they are a method of preventing one problem from becoming a collection of problems. The use of police and court agencies as possible screening mechanisms is a recent aspect of legal enforcement agency activities in this field. The Alcohol Safety Action Project programs have made the detection of problem drinkers among those arrested and convicted of drunken driving one of the major devices for prevention of recidivism. Similarly, the use of schools for drunken-driving offenders has this as one of its major functions. Research is now in progress to construct a simple, workable test for the detection of problem drinkers which would supplant expensive probationary methods.

Much of the action of detection has been hindered by lack of knowledge or concern among groups that are in especially good positions to observe drinking behavior and to make recommendations that will be taken seriously by the drinker. Police and the courts are in an especially authoritative position, as are employers. The medical profession is a key group. Here ignorance about alcohol problems is a major block to prevention on the case level. In part this is also a reflection of the currently indefinite and diffuse character of the treatment of alcoholism and alcohol misuse. For example, the unwillingness of health insurance underwriters and hospital authorities to accept alcohol misuse on an equal footing with other illnesses is an obstacle to effective case-finding procedures. It leads to an ambiguity which perpetuates the stigma of alcohol as immoral. It corrodes the doctor's interest and willingness to advise patients when their medical problems are closely associated with excess in drinking. In general, physicians are reluctant to accept cases when they see little that can be done to alleviate the patient's condition (Freidson 1970).

PREVENTION: *DRINKING* PROBLEMS OR DRINKING *PROBLEMS?*

This short survey of prevention efforts has shown that past policies have been concentrated either on diminishing the total amount of drinking by a population or on persuading individuals to drink less. Especially in the United States, both discussion and action have displayed the "hang-ups" resulting from a disposition to defend or to attack the moral status of alcohol use rather than the specific issues arising from the problems created by alcohol use.

In the remainder of this chapter I want to set forth two ideas that may facilitate a broader discussion of prevention possibilities. Both follow from the general conclusion that past policies have had limited effectiveness. The first idea is that it is important to view the problem situation as well as the drinking situation. The second, which follows from the first, is that it is necessary to create a political situation, rather than an educational one, in which the search for effective prevention and treatment can be conducted.

The Drinking Problem as Situational

Throughout this chapter I have cast much doubt on the utility of individualistic policies as effective prevention mechanisms. Appeals to punishment and to rational thought have not proved to be very useful means to decrease drinking or alcohol misuse. By an emphasis on the situational, I refer to measures that change the environmental surroundings of behavior, but that do not depend on changing the psychic or consumer values of the alcohol user. Thus, in recommending that colleges provide safe facilities for drinking experiences, Wilkinson (1970) is suggesting a change in a situation within which drinking occurs in the United States, without any attempt to directly change the college student's attitudes toward drinking.

It is also possible to examine the situation as a total environment, concentrating on other aspects of the problems inherent in their definition. Thus, the problem of the relation between alcohol and absenteeism in industry can be conceptualized as a problem of workers being late or absent from work, rather than a problem of drinking. If the "Monday morning hangover" is a severe problem for industrial establishments, possible redesign of the job to provide a greater measure of individual decision as to how to stagger his or her work week may be a solution. The large amount of experiment and analysis of job redesign and work hours now going on in Europe, America, and Japan is not instigated by alcohol misuse and has had little input from alcohol problems experts but represents an important way to approach the problem of job security often associated with excessive drinking (Upjohn Institute for Employment Research 1973).

This mode of reasoning reverses the characteristic way in which we have approached problems of alcohol. Instead of asking, "How do we adjust the individual drinker to his or her social functions?" it asks, "How do we adjust social functions so as to permit 'excessive' drinking?" Put in another form, it asks, "How can we minimize the painful consequences of drinking without minimizing the drinking?"

The case of alcohol-affected driving provides an area in which this mode of conceptualizing a problem of prevention can be illustrated. Objectives of changing the situation need not emphasize drinking alone but can be oriented toward other aspects of the total action, such as the act of driving or the physical characteristics of the automobile. Those interested in the problem of drinking and driving have, with few exceptions, paid little attention to the act of driving. For example, is it possible to provide the drinker with alternative modes of transportation, such as inexpensive taxi or bus service? Is it possible to inspect automobile drivers in areas near bars to prevent those found to have above legal amounts of alcohol from driving? One vital exception to the nonsituational character of current drunken-driving prevention activity is the process of developing an ignition interlock system that would prevent the impaired driver from starting the automobile. All these measures "bypass" the decision-making process of the person, as does the seat belt interlock, without changing the motorist.

The problem of drinking and driving can be looked at from a still wider level, one that has had a profound impact on thinking about automobile injuries and fatalities in the past decade.[8] Research during the 1950s had established that a major source of death and injury in automobile crashes came not from the impact of the crash but from the "second collision" with such dangerously designed equipment as protruding dashboard knobs, noncollapsible steering wheels, noncollapsible telephone poles, breakable windshields, and other objects, as well as the ejection of the occupant because of badly designed door locks. Much concern of legislation and agitation through the past decade has gone into developing more crashworthy vehicles and less dangerous roadside objects. From this standpoint, a more efficient strategy should be taken oriented toward the reduction of injury and death after the crash rather than toward the prevention of the crash itself. Automobiles and roads would then be built with the assumption that drivers, for whatever reason, including drinking, will sometimes be impaired.

Not all actions seen by participants (drinkers) or by others as problems are equally amenable to such situational analysis. If we look at the eleven problem areas used in the public opinion survey by Cahalan and associates in the mid-1960s, some—like "binge drinking"—refer to drinking itself; some—like "job problems"—refer to consequences of drinking; and some—like "problems with spouse, relatives"—are mixed. However, solutions to problems with a new conceptualization cannot be given readily until they have been attempted.

Even the phenomenon of drinking itself may be attacked in a wider scope. One report of preventive action in a remote Alaskan village showed considerable improvement in drinking problems with the opening of a recreation center (Chafetz 1973). It is possible to examine alternatives to drinking, as the Committee of Fifty did in *Substitutes for the Saloon* in 1901. Recent emergence of new forms of drugs used for mood alteration, such as marijuana and LSD, and the use of prescribed tranquilizers raise the need for research and policy toward provision of competitive mood-altering substances that may be less "dangerous" than alcohol.

Drinking Problems as Political

Two significant conclusions follow from the promotion of prevention policies through situational strategy. First, whether the emphasis is on drinking or on problems, it is wiser to attack a series of specific problems, each with its own characteristics and groups, than to concentrate only on *the* problem of drinking. To seek the prevention of drinking problems

largely through prevention of drinking or even through changed drinking patterns unduly narrows the range of potential "solutions." Problems
of alcohol misuse need to be considered as parts of wider problems in
which both alcohol and nonalcohol "experts" are engaged.

This would mean that alcohol problems prevention could play a role
in areas in which it is customarily absent, as well as bringing in nonalcohol specialists in areas that have traditionally been the province of the alcohol expert. An example I frequently use is that of the zoning and construction of hotels, motels, and associated bars along expressways and
other highways. Such places are often highly dependent on the resident as
well as the transient population for sale of entertainment and drink.
Urban planning does not seem to have taken account of the relation between drinking and driving in planning such areas. The drinker has no access other than his automobile or expensive taxis. Similarly, specialists interested in alcoholism in industry could work with job designers to create
occupational contexts where such phenomena as binge drinking are not
inconsistent with the character or scheduling of the work.

The second conclusion is perhaps more significant and involves a more
directed strategy than the first. It is that situational changes frequently involve political conflicts. As I have insisted throughout this chapter, individualistic strategies are not very effective. However, since they involve
little coercion, they do not meet political objections as readily as attempts
to alter the environment. For example, a proposal of Wilkinson's (1970,
158) that all grocery stores be permitted to sell low strength alcohol products associated with eating occasions threatens the economic interests of
soft drink industries, of liquor stores which have invested in license costs,
and of higher strength alcohol products which cannot compete in the
same market. It must face the opposition of moral interests in keeping alcohol away from "respectable" people and activities. This may be compared with another Wilkinson proposal intended, as is the first, to asso-
ciate food with drink—that liquor stores be required to prominently
display light foods and booklets on serving food with alcohol. This move
disturbs no one. Neither does legislation as diffuse and unenforced as
laws against drunken driving and public drunkenness.

The political fallout of situational strategies merits extended analysis
because it bears heavily on the second aspect of strategy—the conditions
of problem solving.

POLITICAL CONSTITUENCIES AND THE PREVENTION
OF DRINKING PROBLEMS

Attempts to change institutions, even on an experimental and limited basis, involve costs and benefits. Especially in areas of behavior where moral and economic interests are deep and intense, the attempt to change situations cannot fail to engender public issues and conflicts. The willingness to seek solutions and to support them in the face of conflicts requires more than a casual commitment. It is this realization which leads to the second point about prevention—the need for an appropriate political climate within which to seek solutions.

Most of this chapter has explored prevention strategies and tactics as possibly effective mechanisms for alleviating the problems associated with alcohol use. That represents one way to discuss the issues of prevention in a more dynamic fashion—seeking for mechanisms of problem solution that may generate the creation and implementation of new strategies and tactics. In one sense, this is analogous to the ways in which solutions to infantile paralysis were implemented—not by picking and choosing from among past programs but by devoting energy and money to establishment of laboratories in which new solutions could be discovered. What is needed in the field of alcohol prevention is the appearance of groups of concerned and committed persons and constituencies for whom the problems associated with drinking have a high priority on the agenda of public issues.

The Repeal of Prohibition removed issues of alcohol from the agenda of the national and state political scene. The constituency of morally concerned persons operating through the structure of organized churches now plays a minor role as an initiating and even as a veto group. For much of the post-Repeal period that has meant an absence of politically relevant constituencies. In recent years, however, new groups have emerged as possible bases for prevention policies as well as treatment programs.

Following the demise of Prohibition the "ownership" of alcohol problems descended on the universities and the medical profession. The universities, notably the Yale (now Rutgers) Center of Alcohol Studies, gave alcohol concerns a legitimacy as scientific and morally neutral interests, in sharp contrast to the long period of church-organized campaigns against Demon Rum. They could not, however, provide either the public pressure or political leadership essential for an atmosphere in which prevention or treatment could assume a high priority among public concerns. Neither did the medical profession accept alcohol as a major health hazard, either in research or teaching or advice to patients.

Two groups have emerged as possible effective sources of prevention programs. One, as has occurred before in the United States, consists of recovered alcoholics, people whose own personal experiences have given them more than a casual interest in this specific set of problems. They have been an active force in organizations, and in the informal roles through which legislation is won, funds raised, and programs implemented.[9] They bring to the alcohol field a moral drive that is lacking in other alcohol activities.

The other element has been the recent appearance of the national government. A number of events, including the public interest occasioned by marijuana, heroin, and LSD use among youth, and also including the work of recovered alcoholics, has brought about the establishment of federal agencies concerned with treatment and prevention. There are now governmental structures dedicated to national policy in the field of alcohol, such as the Office of Alcohol Countermeasures of the National Highway Traffic Safety Administration and the National Institute on Alcohol Abuse and Alcoholism. These are important initiating mechanisms for development of problem solutions and for implementing climates within which new constituencies can be formed.

These agencies, however, are dependent on others. Global campaigns oriented to the decrease of drinking and depending on arousal of a general public are not likely to be effective in building the kinds of constituencies from which new solutions can be expected. While they may lead to a general and diffuse interest in alcohol problems as an aspect of welfare, such programs are not likely to develop organized activities and groups in which the problems of alcohol have a high priority. While moral constituencies are lacking, there are economic groups with potential interests in preventing specific and particular problems. Insurance companies represent one major source of interest in the health and injury aspects of drinking. Police and the courts have a considerable concern for the elimination of impaired driving and public drunkenness, problems they are reluctant to handle through rigorous enforcement. Industries have a vital interest in absenteeism, turnover, and productivity, and the recent surge of concern for problems of work alienation and redesign is a signal of this new atmosphere. The medical profession, increasingly organized into medical insurance programs, has an interest in the development of organized and reliable systems of screening and treatment, an area in which the commitment of medical insurance interests would be vital. Other groups, such as educators or labor unions, cannot be expected to play more than a partial, peripheral role. Their major objectives and skills do not lead to a high level of commitment.

The significance of an adequate political atmosphere is not only that it is necessary to the passage, implementation, and execution of programs. Even more important is the effect of moral and economic interests in unleashing the imagination and energy with which new solutions, concepts, and programs are created and organized. Without interest in achieving a solution, commitment to finding it and to the development of innovative plans, the best policies "on paper" can be poorly carried out. With such concerns, many things become possible and new ideas can emerge.

The development of such creative climates is especially important in the area of prevention. There have been many false starts, and much has been accepted and rejected without adequate test, experiment, or evaluation. Proposals for new programs and for the reappearance of old ones will need the careful assessment that comes with experience, experiment, and controlled research under realistic conditions of actual practice.

AFTERWORD, 1994

In thinking about public problems as social constructs my intent in this chapter was to "free up" alternative ways of conceptualizing the problem of alcohol. Consistent with much of the emphasis in this volume, I wanted to think about alcohol problems in ways that did not focus on eliminating or minimizing drinking, but to separate the consequences of detrimental consequences of drinking from the drinking itself. A contemporary example can be that of public drunkenness. In most Western societies and in Japan, even where public drunkenness is formally outlawed, it is not given the enforcement attention that has occurred in the United States The focus of enforcement is not on the drunkenness but on illegal consequences that may ensue. Public drunkenness per se is not the object of legal enforcement concerns. This is the meaning of my distinction, in this chapter, between *drinking* problems and drinking *problems*.

A similar theme was introduced much earlier by the late William Haddon in his research and writing about automobile safety. (Haddon later became the first director of the National Highway Safety Administration and still later the director of the Insurance Institute for Highway Safety.) Both in his influential book, *Accident Research,* and in a series of papers, he emphasized what came to be called "the second collision" (Haddon,

Suchman, and Klein 1964; Haddon 1970; 1972.) This has meant placing an emphasis on the design of automobiles so as to minimize the consequences of crashes, including improving or providing safety belts, air bags, heavier autos, better locks on doors, safety windows, improved steering mechanisms, and other changes in automobiles designed to lessen the damage and injury consequent to crashes. Many of these have since been incorporated in American automobiles.

In recent years discussion of policies toward illicit drugs have introduced the term *harm reduction* as a way of conveying somewhat similar reconceptualizations (Nadelman et al. 1994; Lewis 1992). Examples of such policies are provision of clean needles to drug users as a means of preventing transmission of HIV; use of methedone with heroin addicts as a means of treatment; "drug parks" as a means of bringing drug users into needed medical attention; changed legal policies toward users convicted of minimal amounts in possession; and partial or complete legalization of sales as a means of eliminating the needs for increased income that may push users to crime, including the selling of drugs.

However, "harm reduction" in the case of drug use differs from the same concept if used in alcohol policies. While in both cases there is a development of alternatives to dominant ways of thinking, the differences largely stem from the illegal character of drugs used in the United States. Much of the arguments over alternatives to present prohibition of use and sale of such psychoactive drugs as marijuana, cocaine, and heroin involve analyses of harms stemming from their illegal staus. For example, the high incomes accompanying the criminal activity of selling large quantities is an important factor in violence and homicide between seller's gangs. To a significant extent common crimes such as burglary, theft, and mugging appear to be motivated by the need for money with which to purchase drugs, although this is only one element in the complex issue of drugs and crime (Inciardi 1986). In the case of alcohol, however, its legal status removes harms of this character.

It is important to recognize, in any discussion of the costs, benefits, harms, and boons of drinking that public discussion is by no means a matter of rational assessment of consequences. Since it became a public concern in the early nineteenth century, drinking has also been a target of disapproval as an action condemnable in its own right, apart from consequences of an economic or social nature. Fear of loss of self-control has been a potent element in the disapproving attitude toward drinking which has been a principal element in understanding the American temperance and Prohibition movements and is also at work in drug policies

(Levine and Reinarman, forthcoming; Gusfield 1975; forthcoming). This analysis and the symbolic character of public policy in these areas has been developed in several past publications of mine (Gusfield 1963; 1975b; 1981a) as well as in chapter 3 of this volume. The diverse meanings that specific alcohol policies have for different groups is also discussed in chapter 13.

Chapter Twelve

Prevention
Rise, Decline, and Renaissance

During the past decade there has been a renaissance of interest in programs, policies, and research for preventing the incidence of alcohol problems. Within the field of alcohol studies there is an awareness of prevention as a developing movement of change in policies toward alcohol problems. The Third Special Report to Congress from the National Institute on Alcohol Abuse and Alcoholism describes that movement and its recognition: "Recent years have seen a considerable increase in interest in prevention programs and a growing recognition of the necessary differences of approach between prevention and treatment programs. Imaginative, realistic, and effective prevention programs are beginning to emerge" (U.S. Department of Health, Education and Welfare 1978, 131).

In this chapter I will examine prevention as a perspective toward alcohol policies during the post-Repeal period and during the past decades, emphasizing the shifting imageries of alcohol problems and the explanatory theories associated with them. Seen as social and cultural movements, these changing conceptions are also related to historical contexts of wider expanse than that of alcohol policies and alcohol studies.

Although I will refer to various studies and reviews of research on prevention, this chapter is not a review of such research.[1] It is instead an analysis of how the movement toward a a revival of interest in the prevention of alcohol problems both contains and generates a new conceptualization of the object—the problem of alcohol. Policies and programs are not only means toward the realization of given goals and ends. They are also embedded in assumptions, perceptions, and theories about the reality of the problem, its nature, and its sources. Such assumptions lead us to attend to some matters and to ignore others. In Kenneth Burke's apt phrase: "Every way of seeing is also a way of not seeing."

Both research and action in the field of alcohol problems operates in a climate of opinion and belief built up around what Robin Room calls "governing images": "A governing image is a summary characterization of the problem organized around a coherent perspective which determines the social rubric and usually the action model for the problem, both for social policy and in terms of the individual cases" (Room 1974). The literature of alcohol studies both shapes and is shaped by such images. So too, prevention as a movement is more than a set of measures. It has come to constitute the symbol for a new image of alcohol problems.

THE CONCEPT OF PREVENTION

To understand the ways in which symbols activate and energize human beings, it is necessary to see them as contrasts to other symbols. Definitions exclude as well as include. They take their meaning from contrast as much as from similarity. Prevention is emerging as a counterconception to treatment. Prevention should be seen as a contrast to treatment, as an alternative, even conflicting orientation toward alcohol and health. For a variety of reasons, to be detailed later in this chapter, it is the changes in governing images of alcohol problems that have given these terms such significant importance as contradictory perspectives and policies. As contrasts they bear important affinities to more general movements in medicine and in politics.

I stress the contrast between prevention and treatment because conventionally alcohol studies have explicitly or implicitly denied this and, as a consequence, have denied certain significant political perceptions. Typically alcohol studies distinguish three forms of prevention: primary, secondary, and tertiary. Primary prevention includes actions to prevent agents from causing disease or injury. Secondary prevention is concerned with the early detection and treatment of alcoholics or potential alcoholics or problem-drinkers. Tertiary is concerned with preventing further deterioration and reducing disability. Put in another fashion, tertiary prevention is aimed at existing "problem-drinkers," secondary at beginning "problem-drinkers" and high-risk persons, and primary prevention at general populations at various levels of risks. It should be noted that this nomenclature is drawn from medical circles and is, especially in secondary and tertiary prevention, primarily oriented toward preventing disease and especially chronic conditions in persons. The governing imagery is that of disease and the vocabulary that of epidemiology—host, agent, environment.

Typologies such as this are always difficult to utilize, and numerous situations, measures, and programs become unclassifiable. The most controversial, and the ones forming the cutting edge of discussion in recent years, have been measures of primary prevention, especially those of legal and economic controls over the availability of alcohol. It is these that are forming new images of alcohol problems.

In generating a conception of prevention in this paper, it is necessary to consider the idea of prevention from a somewhat different standpoint than that in conventional usage. I approach the concept of prevention through analysis of the "medical model" and the idea of prevention at work in recent general discussions of preventive medicine (U.S. Department of Health, Education and Welfare 1979; Knowles 1977). In the annals of medicine, the "medical model" has been a continuous and constant image of activities (Siegler and Osmond 1974). We may imagine medicine as an institution of doctors, patients, and hospitals practicing clinical activities, a matter of diagnosis, treatment and cure. Alternatively we may visualize medical activity in the form of engineers, chemists, and public health workers acting to discover causes of disease, to drain swamps, creat DDT, and educate populations about hygiene as a means to eradicate malaria. A medical model oriented to *treatment* attempts to reduce the *prevalence* of a disease, to achieve health by curing the unhealthy. A medical model of prevention aims at reducing the *incidence* of disease, at eradicating or minimizing its occurrence. The former is necessarily attentive to the sick—those who deviate from normal conditions. The latter is wider in its scope; it is oriented toward those who might become sick. Treatment is necessarily individualistic and remedial; prevention more collective and environmental.

Among alcohol programs, treatment-oriented policies are individualistic and attentive to "problem-drinkers," alcoholics and to those at high-risk of becoming "problem-drinkers" or alcoholics. Such programs involve efforts to provide facilities and materials for curing individuals who suffer, are likely to suffer, or are seen by others to be suffering from problems explainable by consumption of alcohol. The provision of recovery centers, clinics, counseling, peer group intervention (such as Alcoholics Anonymous), case-finding, including early case-finding, and research on the effectiveness of different modes of treatment are all instances of treatment-oriented programs and measures. Measures which locate the source of problems as a condition of the *person* and seek his or her rehabilitation or cure are included in my usage of treatment.

Prevention, as I use it here, is policy directed toward forestalling an occurrence. It operates more collectively than does treatment because the prevention concept directs attention toward environmental conditions, situational opportunities and restraints, normative standards, and legal controls. Since the scope of prevention is less that of individuals than of societies, it takes and attends to events as well as to conditions of persons. Minimum-age drinking laws are instances of preventive measures. They affect all within an age category, whether or not they drink or are at greater or lesser risk of becoming persons with alcohol problems. As a measure directed at drinking-driving such laws are concerned with fore-stalling events—accidents—rather than curing or rehabilitating persons. Educational campaigns promoting moderate drinking or abstinence are also prevention programs. They attempt to control behavior through information or persuasion but without reference to specific persons and through exposure to a wide range of differential risk-levels.

I also find it useful to distinguish between different types of prevention measures: (1) those which attempt to persuade people to do something or refrain from doing something, to deter drinking or behavior associated with it, and (2) those which attempt to shape the *situation* or environment within which drinking or the problematic event can occur or the condition of the person develop (Gusfield 1976a). The first is *persuasional*. Although others may be, and often are, exposed to the form of persuasion, it is not directed at the abstainer, the nontroublesome drinker or those not at risk of being or creating a problem.

The second type is *situational*. It affects environmental conditions which make acts possible and provides alternatives to them or supplies opportunities and deterrences. Alcohol education in the public schools is an example of a persuasional form of prevention, intended to modify attitudes through information and personal clarification of values (Blane 1976). Development of normative standards of moderate drinking through introducing alcohol in previously abstinent situations is an instance of situational measures (Wilkinson 1970). Another illustration of a situational measure is the program introduced at Notre Dame University. Faced with increasing deaths and injuries involving students drinking and driving, buses were introduced to enable students to ride across the state line from Indiana to Michigan, where drinking was legal at lower ages, and thus avoid the coupling of drinking with driving.

In general, with some significant qualifications, the decline of interest in prevention after Repeal has meant a lessening of efforts toward the social control of drinking. Treatment orientation utilized imagery of alcoholism as *the* problem of alcohol use, and alcohol problems as the actions of deviant and diseased persons. The renaissance of prevention foreshadows a return to an imagery of alcohol problems as also problems of normal drinkers and of alcohol policies as implicated in the social control of drinking and drinking situations. The remainder of this chapter is an elaboration of this thesis and its implications.

THE FALL OF PREVENTION: THE ALCOHOLISM MOVEMENT

The year 1933 is a watershed in the history of alcohol policy in the United States. Repeal of the Eighteenth Amendment meant the collapse of the major orientation toward alcohol problems of the nineteenth and early twentieth centuries—the prevention of problems through limitations on the availability of the commodity. Reflecting on the history of the mid-1930s and the development of the Yale (now Rutgers) Center of Alcohol Studies, Mark Keller remarks: "of the four action objectives (research, education treatment and prevention) promulgated by the Center of Alcohol, Studies, three were actively prusued. The fourth—prevention—was given only lip service, as it has by everyone else since" (Keller 1976).

The neglect of prevention which Keller laments is an accurate description of one consequence of the turn away from the definition of alcohol use as a morally suspect form of behavior and its redefinition as a matter of personal taste made problematic only by a group of people whose problem is a form of sickness. This change from the dominance of prevention policies to the dominance of treatment policies is also a change from the dominance of drinking and drunkenness as social problems to alcoholism as the problem. For this reason, following Robin Room's usage, I refer to the activities of alcohol-concerned publics in the post-Repeal era as the "Alcoholism Movement" (Room 1974).

It is important to recognize that a major consensus about alcohol use developed in America during the nineteenth century. Alcohol came to be seen as a dangerous commodity, a substance held responsible for accidents, crimes, and moral lapses (Levine 1978b). A consensus developed that alcohol was no longer proper within the workplace (Gusfield 1963; Levine 1978a; Harrison 1971; Tyrell 1979). This consensus is by no means a simple recognition of fact. It is deeply embedded in the changed character of the workday and the workplace accompanying the rise of industrial organizations. The temperance movement succeeded in defining alcohol as a commodity antithetical to industrial work and the workplace (Harrison 1971; Gutman 1977). Sobriety and inebriety became important symbols of ethical and economic character. Abstinence was viewed as essential to the qualities of self-control needed for an industrial, market economy (Gusfield 1963; Levine 1978a). The use of alcohol was a moral as well as an economic problem. Chronic alcoholism was one of the problems of alcohol, and the alcohol problem was embedded in the total society as a matter of collective significance. The governing images of alcohol use were those of sin, stigma, and choice. Law and religion could be called on to help in resolution.

By focusing attention on the chronic alcoholic, the alcoholism movement conceptualized alcohol problems in a different fashion. Deviance and disease became the governing images. Once alcohol problems are seen primarily as those occurring in the abnormal drinker, the one who has limited control over his or her drinking, a sharp distinction is made between the social or normal drinker and the alcoholic. Deviant drinking and deviant drinkers, not drinking, are the focus of attention.

The disease concept of alcoholism made questions of alcohol abuse those of medicine and health. Accordingly it was felt that scientific research can illuminate solutions as it can in matters of heart disease or diabetes. If the problems of alcohol pertain only to sick people suffering from an external agent—disease—then policies to be pursued are legitimately those of treatment and cure. The deviant is not sinful but sick (Gusfield 1967a). Alcohol problems are not collective, engaging many groups and levels of society. They are those of alcoholics and others interested in their welfare, a matter of sickness rather than morality. If alcoholism is an illness it is also a medical and scientific object. A technology of treatment should then be possible and a profession should be able to be trained to administer it.

The growth of the alcoholism movement has been manifest in the increased attention legislatures and voluntary associations have given to providing funds to make treatment available to chronic alcoholics, to educate the general public to the disease concept of alcoholism and to change the public image of the alcoholic from one of moral stigma to one of accepted illness. The success of Alcoholics Anonymous in capturing public attention has been a major force in directing public actions toward alcoholism.

The focus on alcoholism has not been a simple matter of logical deduction. A number of events and processes made the treatment emphasis in policy more feasible. (1) The alcoholism movement depoliticized the alcohol problem. During the Temperance and Prohibition periods the alcohol question was a focus of significant political conflict not only between generalized culture patterns but between groups carrying differing orientations to the use of alcohol—Protestants vs. Catholics; natives vs. immigrants; rural vs. urban (Gusfield 1963). The medicalization of the alcohol problem defused this source of political tension. Alcohol disappeared from a high place on the agenda of public issues and political controversy. The styles of life supporting drinking or abstinence were not in conflict: the object of attention—the alcoholic—was deviant to both. (2) Nor did the alcohol industry find the alcoholism movement a source of great threat. Coming after a period in which the entire industry had been declared illegal, the emphasis on treatment of the alcoholic was a welcome relief. Implicitly the industry and the movement shared a belief in the slogan of the alcohol beverage manufacturers: "The fault is in the man and not in the bottle." From this perspective what is to be prevented is the incidence of alcoholism. Prevention came to mean early case-finding or education about how to detect alcoholism or early "problem drinking" and where to go for treatment. Drinking was cleansed of restrictions on the behavior of "normal drinkers."

Logically, of course, prevention refers to the attempts to minimize or forestall the occurrence of an event or situation. From that consideration, emphasis on the control of alcohol availability can be directed at prevention of alcoholism from a health perspective as well as from a moral perspective. In its concern for treating alcoholics the alcoholism movement shied away from the political albatross of availability of alcohol as a strategy of prevention. It is quite appropriate to characterize the dominant policy of American society toward prevention of alcohol problems in the period 1933–1970 as one of efforts to persuade individuals with drinking problems to drink less or to undergo treatment for alcoholism.

Nevertheless, in several important ways alcohol persisted in its pre-Repeal conception as a special commodity in American society. Some primary prevention programs were an accepted legacy of prohibition. Following Repeal, all states restricted the sale of alcoholic beverages in one or another fashion, even though Prohibition continued in only a few states (now in none) and in a small proportion of local jurisdictions, now comprising about 3–5 percent of the population (Room et al. 1979, 14). Place and time, and age of customer remain as major restrictions which distinguish the sale of alcohol from other commodities. Minimum-age laws came into widespread existence after Repeal (Mosher 1980). Most states established alcohol beverage control boards, ostensibly to promote temperance. These functioned however to regulate the market and to license sellers, largely on the model of escaping the undesirable effects of the old saloon (Medicine in the Public Interest 1976; Wilkinson 1970). Public drunkenness and driving while intoxicated continued to be illegal. The law against drinking-driving represents one of the clearest measures of a prevention approach to an alcohol-related problem, that of automobile accidents. It aims at persuading potential drinking-drivers to refrain from acts of drinking or driving or both.

What happened during the period of the dominance of the alcoholism movement may be seen as the defusing of the political conflict around alcohol problems. The movement separated the general population and its behavior toward alcohol from that of the alcoholic—a special type of deviant who could not handle alcoholic beverages competently: An emphasis on treatment of the alcoholic defined policies as those which affected only this minority. The "special commodity" status of alcohol was never seriously attacked, however, but alcohol was removed from the agenda of major issues in American society and politics.

IMPLICATIONS OF ALCOHOLISM IMAGERY

Once alcohol problems are placed in the framework of disease, deviance, and the special category of chronic alcoholics, measures to alleviate the problems are directed at the special category. From this standpoint measures that might restrict the behavior of the general population are excessively confining or unneeded. Most people do not drink heavily, and, even if they are drunk occasionally, they manage it competently. With the imagery of the alcoholism movement what is to be prevented is chronic alcoholism. Thus prevention is either minimized as a strategy, in favor of treatment, or attached to treatment as a form of early case-finding or education which will persuade those "suffering" from the disease to seek treatment.

The preoccupation with alcohol problems defined as "alcoholism problems" has two significant implications: (1) it directs public attention to the chronic alcoholic image as the descriptions of all persons who experience difficulties imputed to alcohol use, and (2) it leads public officials to define all alcohol-related problems as those resulting from persons suffering from alcoholism. In both cases policies are aimed at reforming *persons* rather than preventing *events,* at chronic alcoholism rather than instances of drunken behavior and its consequences.

The classic picture of the alcoholic as the Skid Row resident has undergone considerable revision in recent years. The concept of the "problem drinker" has been offered as a way of describing the variety and flexibility of alcohol problems as they affect individuals (Cahalan, Cisin, and Crossley 1969; Cahalan 1970; Cahalan and Room 1974). It is doubtful, however, that this concept has had much impact on the general public which has subsumed the "problem drinker" as another form of "alcoholic" (Gusfield 1981a, ch. 3).

The issues surrounding drinking-driving illustrate the problem of prevention conceived within the framework of alcoholism or conceived within alternative frameworks. Much research on drinking-drivers has been devoted to the questions of whether or not a large segment of drinking-drivers and a large proportion of drinking-driving events are produced by chronic alcoholics, problem drinkers or "normal, social drinkers." The debate has produced the usual rash of research studies and the usual shifts in "fashion" from the consensus of the late 1960s and early 1970s on the problem-drinking or alcoholic character of many drinking-drivers to the more recent criticisms and qualifications of that thesis (U.S. Congress 1968; Waller and Turkel 1966; Waller 1967; Cameron 1978 226–41; U.S. Department of Health, Education and Welfare 1978, 87).

If drinking-drivers are perceived as people who, as a class, have more than the "normal" problems of self-control with alcohol, then legal measures, which hold the threat of punishment, can have little impact on deterring drinking-driving. In recent years many courts have inaugurated courses and other facilities to persuade drinking-driving offenders of their alcohol problems and lead them into treatment and possible cure. If drinking-driving is seen as a problem of the alcoholic/problem drinker, then it is only another form of the general problem of alcoholism. Proper policy then consists of case-finding: discovering the alcoholic and prealcoholic, convincing him or her to accept treatment, and providing treatment.

This monistic view of alcohol problems can be contrasted with a view which stresses the different forms of problems seen as alcohol-related. If the drinking-driving issue is conceptualized as one chiefly involving normal social drinkers or even occasional drinkers then it is an issue of the consequences of drunkenness or even just drinking, an *event* rather than a personal *characteristic;* indeed it is one so ubiquitous in American life that even though social drinkers may be deterred by one conviction, the pool of that population is so large as to constitute a continuous problem (Wolfe 1975; Zylman 1975; Gusfield 1981a). Laws that penalize driving under the influence of alcohol are limited means for preventing the event when the target group consists of alcoholics/problem drinkers but not when the target is the general population of drinkers (Waller 1967; Gusfield 1976a).

Seen as one single problem—that of alcoholism/problem drinking—the prevention of alcohol problems is absorbed into preventing the incidence of alcoholism and reducing its prevalence. Treatment, case-finding, information about the signs and dangers of excessive and continued drinking become expedient and useful measures aimed at a specific portion of the population. If alcohol problems are plural, each requiring its own strategy, then prevention policies need to be specific, different policies for different problems.

In a sense the alcoholism movement has made it more difficult to perceive multiplicity in alcohol problems. By making the problem of alcohol that of the alcoholic, it has minimized the consequences of drinking and drunkenness in the general population of normal, social drinkers and the sources of alcohol problems stemming from the general environment of institutional practices. It has also made the plurality of alcohol problems into a single one of characteristics of the deviant drinker. A wider spectrum of alcohol problems could recognize drinking-driving, diminished work productivity, marital strife, and cirrhosis of the liver as separable. Although they may be discoverable in greater degree in the "problem-drinker" they are by no means exclusively theirs. Events of drunkenness, for example, occur more frequently among problem-drinkers, but they may nevertheless make up only a small part of the total alcohol-related risk-taking events in the society. A recent study of U.S. Air Force personnel found that although the $3^1/2$ percent of the persons defined as very heavy drinkers accounted for 26 percent of drunk days, the remainder of drinkers accounted for 74 percent of the drunk days. A concentration on the *person* in the image of the alcoholic provides a different perspective from a concentration on the *events* (Polich and Orvis 1979).

THE RENAISSANCE OF PREVENTION AND ITS IMAGERY

The sense of a new activism in the field of alcohol is apparent to many who have been working in these groves for a number of years. The commission of conferences, symposia, and working groups on problems of prevention is one sign of activity and interest.[2] Because of the renewed attention to measures that limit the availability of alcohol and other programs and policies to control the uses of alcohol, I refer to this as "the new temperance movement." Richard Bonnie refers to this as well as several other measures "to engineer changes in collective life style as an essential component of the new public health initiatives" as "the new paternalism" (Bonnie 1980, 39). The title of a leading publication frequently cited in contemporary alcohol policy circles, *Alcohol Control Policies in Public Health Perspective* (Bruun et al. 1975), indicates both the social control orientation of the movement and its setting in the imagery of public health.

An important part of that report's orientation builds on research steming from the work of a French statistician, Sully Ledermann, on consumption of alcohol and on the work of the Canadian Addiction Research Foundation (Schmidt and DeLint 1970) on the association between national rates of alcohol consumption and rates of alcohol problems. Briefly put, increases in the national rate of consumption of alcohol are correlated with increases in rates of cirrhosis of the liver, and decreases are related to decreases in such rates. (Some claim that other problems, such as rates of alcoholism, are also so related, although this remains a matter of conjecture and debate at present. The report did not support this contention.)

The importance of this new approach to problems of alcohol is that it shifts attention away from a special group of alcoholics and prealcoholics and points toward general national policies as means of preventing alcohol problems. Such strategies include pricing mechanisms such as taxation as potent measures through which to effect problems through diminishing consumption. Unlike the focus on treatment, this movement is concerned with limiting the availability of alcohol. The prevention of cirrhosis of the liver and, in another facet of recent alcohol campaigns, the prevention of the fetal alcohol syndrome lead to measures applicable to the total population. From the perspective of this chapter, what is significant about the distribution of consumption approach is less its scientific truth or falsity than its historical importance in raising control measures, including alcohol availability, to a point of serious reconsideration.

What has emerged is a growing demand for approaches to alcohol problems through primary prevention rather than treatment or secondary and tertiary prevention. The "new temperance movement" is thus emerging as another form of health movement. The effort to educate a public around the fetal alcohol syndrome, for example, presents information and education in a context of prenatal care (U.S. Department of Health, Education and Welfare 1978 ch. 4). The concern for lowering national rates of consumption is clearest in a focus on the dangers of cirrhosis of the liver.

PREVENTION MEASURES AND THEIR EFFECTIVENESS

In discussing studies of the scope and effectiveness of various types of measures, the limits of such studies should be clearly understood. Specific, isolated events, such as the effect of strike among alcohol beverage employees or a demonstration project to test the effect of advertising on diminishing consumption of alcohol abound in the literature of the field. They should be sharply contrasted with large-scale programs composed of many acts and actions, no one of which may be significant but the entirety of which builds into a climate of attitude and behavior control distinctly different from the sum of its parts.[3]

A second important caveat in the use of individual studies as support or negation of suggested policies is the difficulty in importing studies from one context into another. Differences in social structure, culture, and institutions make it hazardous to reach conclusions about what might happen in the United States based on results taken in Sweden or vice versa. Additionally, studies of one program or commodity cannot, without further study, be applied to another (Katz and Lazarsfeld 1955). Maccoby's study suggests that the use of mass communications alone is ineffective in changing health habits relevant to heart problems but when accompanied by a community organization program could be effective (Maccoby et al. 1977). Whether those results can be applied to alcohol consumption cannot be known without another study.

Since Prohibition represents a prevention program of major scope and national arenas, its impact on alcohol problems is of great concern. Did it lead to diminished consumption? Did it lead to decreased incidence of alcohol problems? Unfortunately the data on the effects of Prohibition in the United States is far from perfect. However, analysis of grains production, of drunkenness arrests, of cirrhosis of the liver rates over Prohibition and post-Prohibition periods all oppose the popular view that the "noble experiment" was ineffective or led to increased drinking and drinking problems (Gusfield 1968; Aaron and Musto 1981). The increase in alcohol consumption that marked the period preceding Prohibition did not continue after Repeal. America was a nation of more drinkers, but more moderate drinkers, after Repeal than it had been before Prohibition.

The Prohibition period suggests other effects, however. What happened during that period was a sharp rise in the price of alcoholic beverages (available only on "black markets") and a shift to the manufacturing of sprits rather than beer. All of this worked to diminish drinking in the lower income classes and to increase the demand for spirits among the middle classes. Prohibition appears to have supported the long-run, over-all trends toward a more moderate drinking pattern in America. Its impact on basic sentiments toward alcohol policy seems slight (Gusfield 1968).

Prevention measures include far more than such sweeping and restrictive legislation as Prohibition entailed. I will discuss six types of measures undertaken or discussed in recent years as part of the emerging new impulse toward prevention and control. In doing so, it is important again to distinguish persuasional from situational measures and those that attempt to change persons from those attempting to control events.

1. *Case-finding*. One frequently encountered meaning of prevention is that of preventing alcoholism, problem-drinking, or cirrhosis of the liver by finding those whose drinking habits have already placed them in a population at greater risk than is normal. Such people can then be targets for persuasion into treatment or habit change. The programs of required classes on alcohol education for convicted drinking-driving offenders is an example. They have operated as mechanisms for detecting and channeling alcoholics or potential alcoholics and leading them into treatment.

What is being prevented by case-finding? One ready answer is that alcoholism and problem-drinking is being discovered before it becomes even more a source of suffering and trouble than already has occurred. In the instance of drinking-driving there is also an additional rationale; a high proportion of drinking-drivers are also problem-drinkers or alcoholics (Waller 1967). From this viewpoint, the event of drinking-driving can be controlled by changing individuals, those who are problem-drinking prone. Whether this explanation of drinking-driving is correct or not, to date the results of such classes as a means of deterring further drinking-driving events among those "students" has not been salutary. Classes for offenders do not appear to have diminished rates of rearrests among those exposed to them (Nichols et al. 1978; Wendling and Kolodji 1977; Michelson 1979), although their implications for reducing alcoholism may have been more effective.

Similarly, the shifts from jail as punishment for public drunkenness to decriminalization, detoxification, and treatment may be useful means for bringing alcoholics into the treatment facilities but their effectiveness as mechanisms for removing drunks from shopping and entertainment areas is much in doubt (Regier 1979).

Here, as in so much of the discussion of alcohol problems, the efficacy of specific measures depends greatly on how the problem is delineated.

2. *Education*. Faith in education and information is almost a cardinal principle of American life. There is a great, almost mystical faith in the

powers of advertising and communications media in the United States. Education through school and especially through the mass media is often surrounded with an almost religious awe at the "power of the press." Providing information about the harmful effects of a behavior in a context of attitudinal approval is presumed to be an assured means of creating change. That such measures persist so continously in the history of alcohol control in the face of so many adverse studies testifies either to the great American belief in the wisdom of the individual or to a great predilection for cheap solutions. It is one of the clearest arguments for the persistence of magic in modern societies.

A growing disappointment with campaigns to control alcohol through dissemination of information has led the advocates of prevention to policies of situational forms. Howard Blane's influential reviews of educational measures have reached the conclusion that while educational programs may affect information and even attitudes, their impact on behavior is slight (Blane 1976). Even Wilkinson, who advocates advertising and education campaigns, sees them as only effective in a context of accompanying situational measures (Wilkinson 1970, 43ff.).

3. *Law-Deterring the Drinker.* The field of alcohol controls is filled with laws aimed at deterring the delinquent behavior of drinkers. The legislation against public drinking and drinking-driving represent two such familiar laws. They operate within a utilitarian philosophy of reward and punishment. Threats of fines, jail, or loss of auto use are expected to deter the individual from the illegal acts (Zimring and Hawkins 1973). Increased punishment is expected to lead to increased conformity.

It is apparent today that such expectations have great limits. Efforts to increase enforcement of drinking-driving laws or to raise the punishment level have not proven effective as measures to diminish alcohol-caused automobile deaths in the United States, although it may have had temporary success in England (U.S. Department of Transportation 1974; Gusfield 1972; 1981a; Zador 1976; Ross 1973; 1977). This is not to say that such laws may not be effective deterrents to even *more* public drunkenness or drinking-driving. No American state has attempted so radical an experiment in the interests of research as to repeal drinking-driving laws. However, it seems doubtful that increasing punishments to the individual will decrease the occurrence of the events. (But see chapter 13, this volume.)

4. *Situational Measures.* Legislation aimed at controlling the situation or environment of the drinker did not disappear with Repeal. As I pointed out earlier, laws restricting sales to minors, zoning regulations, licensing requirements, and other governmental acts have continued to define al-

cohol as a special commodity and to provide a less than fully permissive environment for the purchase of beer, wine, and especially whiskies. Much of the discussion and debate about prevention measures since 1970 has focused on efforts to increase the range, intensity, and salience of further measures to control the availability of alcoholic beverages to the general public or to particular groups. The situational measures are applicable to all types of drinkers—occasional, moderate, and heavy, problem-free, alcoholic, and problem-drinkers.

A major point of debate within alcohol policy and research circles has been the policy of increasing taxation on alcohol beverages espoused by the Addiction Research Foundation of Ontario (Popham, Schmidt, and DeLint 1976; Schmidt and DeLint 1970). This viewpoint was partially supported by *Alcohol Controls in a Public Health Perspective*. It represents a distinctly new approach to problems of alcohol control since Repeal. This policy follows from the work on national consumption patterns described above. Correlations between the incidence of cirrhosis of the liver and national consumption patterns appear convincing evidence that diminutions in total consumption affect problem-drinkers and alcoholics as well as normal drinkers. Both kinds of drinkers appear to be influenced by price, as alcohol now seems to be a more price-elastic commodity than earlier assumed (Bruun et al. 1975, ch. 6). With cirrhosis rates rising in many nations, including the United States, increased taxation has appeared to many to be supportable as a national health measure.

The policy is more debatable in its effects on other alcohol problems, however. Schmidt and DeLint, who have done the major research in this area, posit a constant relation between cirrhosis rates and other alcohol problems, but that ratio is disputable (Schmidt and DeLint 1970). Some recent evidence also suggests a positive relation between auto deaths and alcohol prices (Cook 1981). The policy of increasing taxes has been a major focus of discussion in the NIAAA and in the several recent and influential conferences.

With inflation and a general world-wide increase in consumption of alcohol (since taxes are a high percent of alcohol sales price, the price has declined relative to other commodities), the argument for tax measures has gained greater support. (See the exchange between Parker and Harman 1978 and Schmidt and Popham 1978).

Measures to affect the availability of alcohol have been easier to enforce than measures aimed at individual drinkers. Because they impinge on a relatively small and visible segment of the population—sellers and distributors—the enforcement problem is lessened. They represent the kind of legal sanctions most easily applied-where little discretion is needed in determining dereliction and the sanctions are clear and easily imposed, as in loss of license (Handler 1979). Minimum-age laws and closing-hour laws appear more enforceable than laws that restrict drinkers, such as drinking-driving legislation or public drunkeness laws.

The fact that such laws are readily observed does not necessarily imply their effectiveness in reaching desired goals of preventing or minimizing the occurrence of alcohol problems. Increasing or decreasing the numbers of retail outlets or hours of sale does not appear to have changed rates of consumption or alcohol problems significantly in places where such experiments have been attempted (Popham, Schmidt and De Lint 1976). However, it does appear that lowering or raising the age of permissible sale has some effect in some places on alcohol-involved deaths from auto crashes (Popham, Schmidt, and DeLint 1976, 592–94; Williams et al. 1975).

The minimum-age drinking laws are instructive. In the early 1970s, in the wake of lowering the voting age to eighteen, eighteen American states lowered the minimum drinking age to eighteen or nineteen. Studies of the effects of this move, and of the subsequent raising of the age in six states, indicate that lowering the age was accompanied by an increase in youthful auto accidents and deaths due to drinking, a generally increased amount of drinking, and an increase in sales to formerly minor persons (Wechsler 1980; Douglass 1980). Results of studies investigating the effect of raising the age are not yet available. It should also be pointed out that in the leading study (Douglass 1980), while sharp effects are shown for Michigan and Maine, no changes were found in Vermont.

The minimum-age laws are significant in another sense. In six cases, legislatures, alarmed at perceiving ill effects from lowering the minimum-age law, have raised the minimum age, by 1–3 years. To be able to take away rights shortly after they have been given indicates a high political capacity for control of alcohol problems. The alcohol industry does not appear to have been able to stem the legislative tide for such controls over drinking behavior.

5. Reconceptualization of Problems. The policies discussed above direct public attention to drinking as the central cause of the problem and as the target of policies. Policies attempt to make the world and the person safe *from* drinking and drunkenness. Suppose that framework were reversed and instead policymakers asked, "How can we make the world and the person safe *for* drinking and drunkenness?" As Ralph Nader put it in testimony at the congressional hearing on auto safety: "Let us produce an automobile that will be safe on the assumption that it will be driven by fools and drunkards."

When a problem is defined as an alcohol problem, that formulation directs attention toward drinking as the cause and preventing drinking as the solution to the problem. The "reality" of the problem is thus a capsulated form of theory and policy. It is possible to reconceptualize some such "alcohol-related" problems in ways which diminish the centrality of alcohol. For example, the Monday morning slump in industrial attendance and productivity (the modern equivalent of the "Saint Monday" in industrializing periods of history) is often seen as a problem resulting from weekend drinking. It can also be seen as a problem of the scheduling of work in such a fashion that it conflicts with the individual needs of workers. A number of firms, especially in Europe, have experimented with more individual work schedules, not for purposes of adjusting work to drinking habits but as a means of making the work experience less alienating (Upjohn Institute 1973).

In a similar vein, issues of drinking-driving have placed emphasis on not drinking before driving or not drinking. However, no study has been made of how drinkers do drive or might drive better after drinking. No concerted experimentation has been made into alternative modes of transportation, such as a policy charging taverns with responsibility for transporting its customers home. The technological invention of an automobile unable to be started when the driver is inebriated represents another form of minimizing the prevention of drinking as a basic strategy in favor of a strategy of preventing the problem (Thompson, Tennant, and Repa 1975). Perhaps we might seek a form of alcoholic beverage which was equally disinhibiting but affected motor capacities less strikingly.

Such a reconceptualization operates on a moral premise in which drinking is neutral. The aim is to provide an environment in which it is safe for drinkers to drink and to be drunk. In the landmark Powell case (*Powell v. Texas*, 1968), the majority of the Supreme Court agreed with the dissenting opinion that chronic alcoholics should not be punished for their condition but upheld Powell's conviction on a public drunkenness charge because his crime was not being drunk but being drunk *in public*. A possible "solution" to this boundary problem lies in providing places for homeless men to drink where they will not impinge on such people as merchants and shoppers. Some communities are beginning to experiment with "wet parks" which would accomplish such boundary-maintaining programs.[4]

6. *The Sociocultural Environment.* There has long existed an orienta-

tion toward alcohol problems that has explained them as aspects of larger institutional and historical elements. Marxists may find capitalism and problems of work at the root of personal strains and stresses that produce excessive drinking and alcoholism (Stivers 1976a). An emphasis on the general cultural and social conditions should not be dismissed but, by themselves, are too global for preventive strategies. Measures to deal with such deeply seated institutional elements are beyond the ken of the fundamentally reformist orientation which dominates alcohol studies. Often they rest on nothing more than a series of assertions about the relation between background conditions and alcohol issues. Perhaps Griffith Edwards has summed up what can be best said at present: "Since we are unable to manipulate personality and produce a race with no neurosis, the only realistic method of exerting a benign influence on prevalence of alcohol addiction is by control of environmental conditions of drinking" (Edwards 1971, 424).

Another orientation has been that of efforts at integrated drinking (Wilkinson 1970; Frankel and Whitehead 1979). Here the relation between drinking norms and drinking problems has been the object of scrutiny. In one form or another, proponents of integrated drinking have argued that alcohol problems are accentuated in cultural settings where drinking is proscribed. A more accepting attitude toward drinking would then provide for a learning process in which people are socialized into a more controlled drinking pattern, how to do "responsible drinking." This view is bolstered by reference to research on drinking among American Jews and Italian-Americans, which shows a low rate of alcoholism coupled with a high percentage of nonabstainers. However, as many have pointed out, high rates of nonabstinence do not imply high use of alcohol on any one occasion. Nor is it the case that an increase in the moderate use of alcohol means a diminished use of alcohol excessively on other occasions (Room 1971; Mäkelä 1975).

I have placed this discussion of the sociocultural context at the end of this section because it suggests an important dimension to discussion of preventive measures and programs. In a significant manner, research and policy contribute greatly to the sociocultural climate because they affect the conception of the object, alcohol, and of the alcohol problem. They aid in maintaining or developing new governing images. In turn, they are themselves a part of changing conceptions and institutions which bear on the images and institutional features of alcohol problems and their resolution. They help the development of the very sociocultural environments from which they are drawn.

In considering prevention as a movement, it is this function as an agent in the reconceptualization of alcohol problems that I have emphasized. In the final section I turn my attention to the larger social and cultural environments from which the new prevention movement draws its support and to which it in turn contributes.

SOURCES OF NEW ALCOHOL MOVEMENTS

The new turn toward prevention in the alcohol field draws on a number of sources and resources both inside the arena of alcohol-concerned persons and outside in large social and cultural movements. The 1970s differ from the pre-Repeal eras in several ways significant to an understanding of the changing imagery and programmatic interests relevant to alcohol problems. Of course through the period of the alcoholism movement, America was changing. What I want to analyze here is the significance of some of those changes for the development of prevention strategies and the governing images of alcohol.

Chief among the changes significant for alcohol programs is the greatly increased role of the state, at all levels but especially at the federal, as a provider of human welfare. The welfare state has become a reality far beyond that existing in the nineteenth century and through Prohibition (Wilensky 1975; Wilensky and LeBeaux 1958; Gronbjerg 1977). Increasingly Americans have viewed the state as the central organ for affecting the welfare of the population, including the provision of medical services. In the late 1970s government—federal, state, and local—was the source of two of every five dollars spent on medical services in the United States (Ginzburg 1977, 6).

The entry of the state into the treatment of alcoholism was a major trend during the post-World War II era. At the state level, treatment-oriented agencies were established in the period from 1945 to 1953 in thirty-eight states. With the inauguration of the National Institute on Alcohol Abuse and Alcoholism in 1970 recognition of alcohol problems as national and state concerns had come of age.

The entry of the state into the health provision field has coincided and interacted with two other important developments. One is the greatly increased commitment to health and health provision in the United States. Between 1960 and 1976 the nation's expenditures on medical care rose from 5.2 to 8.6 percent of the gross national product, and estimates put the 1981 figures at 10.2 percent of GNP (Gibson and Mueller 1977, 4).

The second development, perhaps related to the first, is the growing criticism of conventional medicine and the domination of treatment orientations to health. It is out of the criticism of conventional medical practice that a movement toward preventive medicine has evolved in the United States (Ginzburg 1977; Carlson 1975; Knowles 1977; Starr 1978). That criticism has been compounded by many sources: realization of the slim returns in health from large expenditures for new technology, an egalitarian impulse against expertise and expert authority, a demand for a more equitable distribution of medical services.

With a large proportion of elderly in the population and with an expanded commitment to health welfare, the state has become more sensitive to the costs of medicine as well as the quality (U.S. Department of Health, Education, and Welfare 1979; Ginzburg 1977, ch. 2). The search for alternatives to clinical medicine is thus one possible solution to the costs crisis in medicine. So too is the rising importance of various self-help and holistic medicine programs. Campaigns to induce exercise or lifestyle changes emerge in a context of preventive health. The campaign against cigarette smoking, actively led by the Public Health Service, is a good example of one form of preventive medicine that has almost become a model for prevention activities.

It is noteworthy that in these activities, while there have been pressures and movements from within the society, government officials and health researchers have played a leading role. The entry of this echelon of reformers, not themselves in positions of immediate interests, is a salient feature of movements in contemporary America. This is what Daniel P. Moynihan has dubbed "the professionalization of reform" (Moynihan 1965).

The alcohol field has reflected these trends. Since the rise of the alcoholism movement and the emphasis on treatment, alcohol problems have been approached largely as matters of health and medicine. The NIAAA was formed chiefly through the activities of that movement. It is located in the Public Health Service. In recent years it has given greater attention to prevention, both as a term of interest and as program directives (Klerman 1980). In 1973 the NIAAA established a Division of Prevention. Although its initial programs were directed toward youth education, increasingly it has moved into community organization and toward consideration of more primary prevention. Some move in the direction of concern for alcohol problems outside of the health concept is seen in the Alcohol Safety Action Programs conducted by the Department of Transportation to minimize drinking-driving programs which in the main were not clearly successful.

The Cultural Background of Prevention

The growing political importance of health as a public value may be a clue to subtler changes in the American culture that might generate political support for alcohol prevention programs. The old constituencies that formed around the temperance and prohibition battles have lost vibrancy and structural supports. Alcohol use is no longer a symbol which sharply divides religions, classes, or major sociological categories. While differences exist between varying styles of life that sanction or condone drinking and drunkenness, as I have argued elsewhere these are no longer clearly linked to such institutional-communal bases as Protestant/Catholic, urban/rural, or native/immigrant (Gusfield 1963, ch. 6).

The emphasis on the workplace and on self-control, which the nineteenth century made the justificatory values for temperance, contained a dualism and a tension from which polar types emerged. In one orientation, life must be monistic; the same attitudes demanded in work are also demanded in leisure. Self-control, discipline, and a mien of seriousness should pervade both. Alcohol is a constant threat and drunkenness an event of great danger without reward. In a diverse attitude, life is dualistic. Drinking and drunkenness are threats to work and life in its serious side, but leisure permits us "time out"—a clear differentiation from work and an acceptance of play.[5]

The emphasis on health as a value is, perhaps, part of a newer orientation to the self and to the relation between work and leisure. The widespread expression of interest and activity in health and safety campaigns is seen in diet and nutrition programs, in exercise programs, in the styles of life now enjoined in heart disease campaigns, in the various self-improvement and personal potential movements. Health is itself becoming a leisure-time pursuit as well as a prerequisite to work and play. The concern for a variety of illnesses, including not only cirrhosis but also heart disease, cancer, birth defects, general effects on metabolism, and the exposure to risk and illness which drunkenness as well as alcoholism entail put alcohol in a significant place as a topic in discussions of appropriate health lifestyles. The fetal alcohol syndrome is an apt example of how such linkages are being formed. Note that the description of Fetal Alcohol Syndrome (FAS) by the NIAAA emphasizes binge drinking rather than overall consumption (U.S. Department of Health, Education and Welfare 1978, ch. 4). The public information campaigns emphasize the current unsettled state of FAS research and caution moderation or abstinence during pregnancy. Both include a much wider segment of normal drinkers than the population of alcoholics or problem-drinkers.

The import of these concerns and the prevention measures they entail is that they return to an emphasis on the normal drinker, as the concern for auto safety, seen in the minimum-age laws, also does. It is rash to undertake predictions as to the future acceptance and growth of primary prevention programs. Social science is filled with the ghosts of prophecies. By their very appearance, movements of change test the existence of the latent supports and generate new ones. The relative success of the cigarette smoking programs in changing the normative environment for smoking in the United States has given much encouragement to other campaigns to change deeply ingrained habits.

What I am suggesting is that the prevention movement possesses a reconceptualization of alcohol problems and their solutions which represents a distinctively new element in the public attitudes and definitions toward alcohol problems. Unlike the era of the alcoholism movement, such programs necessarily represent controls over environmental conditions and personal choice. As such they become drawn into the arena of political conflict and struggle.

The authors of the original *Alcohol, Science and Society* hoped that Science might rescue us from the disputes and struggles of political conflict that Prohibition had entailed. As alcohol issues become involved in measures of primary prevention, law and public policy are drawn on as mechanisms of control. The higher the place of alcohol on the agenda of public attention, the more that detachment from politics may be dissolved. The issues of personal autonomy versus public health and safety may again be raised in the context of resolving alcohol problems.

AFTERWORD, 1994

During the decade since this paper was published, issues of alcohol and prevention have remained higher on the public agenda than in the heyday of the alcoholism movement of the 1950s and 1960s. It is doubtful that they have possessed the same salience in recent years as they did in the early 1980s when this paper was published. At that time it seemed as if alcohol and alcohol establishments were likely to see increased taxation. Yet that has not occurred, and the issue has receded from the public agenda. In 1990 a California initiative to raise the taxation rate on alcoholic beverages, widely expected to pass, was rejected at the polls. Yet an initiative shortly before had resulted in increases in cigarette taxes. In the early discussions of health reform legislation at the federal level there had been some discussion of "sin taxes," including one on alcohol, as a means of raising revenues. That focus disappeared and was replaced by an anticipated increase in cigarette taxation. With the rejection of health reform legislation, that too has disappeared from the federal agenda.

The health lifestyle movement described in the text of this chapter has continued and with it the general advice to a health-conscious public about the assumed detriments of drinking, now folded into the category of "substance abuse," including tobacco and illicit drugs.

It is difficult to assess the impact of that movement on drinking habits in the American public. However, it is clear that in the past decade the trend toward increased consumption of alcohol has been reversed. During the 1960s and 1970s consumption of alcohol had increased, both in the United States and worldwide. This has often been attributed to the lowered "real" price of alcohol as a consequence of high rates of inflation. Such rates increased the costs of most goods, but the price of alcohol, with its large component of taxes, did not increase correspondingly.

Beginning in the late 1970s, the consumption of alcohol, per capita of the drinking age population (fifteen and over), has been steadily declining (Williams, Clem, and Dufour 1993; Treno, Parker, and Holder 1993; Room 1991). Three aspects of that decline should be noted: (1) Most of the decline has occurred in consumption of hard liquors. The decline in consumption of beer and wine has been modest. (2) While the causes of the decline are not clear, neither the price of alcohol nor declining incomes have been a major factor. The increasing age of the American population does appear to bear some relation, but that too is far from a major explanatory element (Treno, Parker, and Holder 1993). (3) Although the American population has decreased its consumption of alcohol, it is nevertheless still at the then historically high level of the early 1970s (Williams, Clem, and Dufour 1993).

At the time of original publication of this chapter, there were optimistic hopes among many that new methods of communicating public health messages might be effective in diminishing rates of alcohol consumption and, through that, diminishing alcohol problems. The effectiveness of Maccoby's successful experiment in diminishing risky behavior in re heart disease by conbining mass communication with the action of supportive community organizations was widely heralded as the way to reach needed goals in alcohol prevention. An experiment in three California counties, using Maccoby's format of controls and variables, indicated that the procedure was not effective in the area of drinking behavior (Walleck and Barrows 1981).

Two developments of the late 1970s and early 1980s had been signifi- cant in placing alcohol problems other than alcoholism into a higher position on the public agenda. One had been the organization and activ- ity of the National Institute of Alcohol Abuse and Alcoholism. Developed from Congressional action in 1970 it was the first major agency at the federal level devoted to alcohol issues since Prohibition. By the late 1970s its activities had become central to alcohol treatment and prevention across the nation. Second, the emergence of Mothers Against Drunk Driving and similar organizations had dramatized the anti-drinking-driving movement and with it the issue of alcohol control. By 1990, while the movement and the organizations were still in existence, they did not command the same level of public attention. Social problems, like clothing, also has its cycles and careers of fashion and fad. Nevertheless, the concept of prevention of drinking problems remains as a significant addition to and substitute for the treatment orientation of the alcoholism movement.

Chapter Thirteen

The Control of Drinking-Driving in the United States
A Period in Transition?

The story is told that when Adam and Eve were driven out of the Garden of Eden Eve berated her man for their Fall. Having enjoyed the bliss of innocence and plenty they were now suffering the indignities of climate and meager clothing in the environment of a cruel Nature. Adam attempted to assuage her bitterness by remarking, "After all, my dear, we are in a period of transition." Are we now in a period of transition in the control of drinking-driving such that our previous conceptions and conclusions may be passé, and limited in their worth?

This question serves as the focal point for this chapter on American controls on drinking and driving, particularly the movements, policies, and legislation that have emerged in the past six to ten years. It is my contention in this chapter that several trends, both independent of and yet also related to each other and to drinking-driving, have converged in the past decade. Although a definitive assessment of their effects is premature, they are too significant in their potential to be ignored in this discussion.

My interest in alcohol issues began in the early 1950s and my specific interest developed in drinking and driving in the early 1970s. Although alcohol issues and drinking-driving were more noticeable in public discussion in the 1970s than in earlier periods, they continued to have a low priority on the agenda of public issues. The 1980s witnessed a dramatic increase in the salience of alcohol issues, including drinking-driving, in the communications media, in legislatures, and in judicial and law enforcement circles. Drinking-driving has become the focus around which alcohol and traffic safety issues are approached.

Heightened awareness of the drinking-driving problem has been translated into legislation and law enforcement policies. For the first time since repeal of Prohibition (1933) there has been a flood of new legislation placing restrictions on the availability and conditions of sale of alcoholic beverages. Many states have increased the punishment for violating driving under the influence of alcohol (DUI) laws and made apprehension and conviction of offenders easier. A highly visible and active anti-DUI movement has emerged, and the resulting attention to DUI prompted its transition from a minor issue to a major national problem.

The trends and movements responsible for this transition each contributed different perspectives on DUI as a public problem. Public problems can be, and often are, conceptualized in different ways by different groups. These diverse frames or perspectives confer different levels of importance to the condition of DUI, often favor different governmental policies, and represent different attitudes toward the problem and its possible amelioration (Spector and Kitsuse 1977; Gusfield 1981a).

Three of these perspectives will be discussed. First, this chapter addresses the "auto safety" perspective, which considers drinking as one among a number of other elements in controlling traffic. The other factors include the design and construction of roads, the use of seat belts, the number of miles driven, and, especially, the manufacture of safer automobiles. The emphasis of the automobile safety perspective in the past two decades has been on automobile design, rather than on the condition of the motorist. The second perspective views drinking and drunkenness as public health concerns within the more general problem of the use of alcoholic substances. In recent years the focus among alcohol and health professionals has been away from emphasis on the person as a victim of alcoholism who needs medical treatment toward prevention of a variety of alcohol problems through policies that affect institutions and environment.

A third orientation is toward drinking-driving as a specific and unique problem. This perspective largely involves a moral dimension: drivers who were drinking and cause accidents and deaths are viewed as more morally reprehensible than those drivers who for other reasons, such as carelessness, fatigue, defective machinery, or automobile design, cause accidents and deaths. Justice and retribution play a significant role in this perspective. Punishing the drinking driver is essential for justice as well as to deter others. The most notable reason for the acceptance of this approach has been the recent emergence of an organized anti-DUI movement in such associations as MADD (Mothers Against Drunk Driving), RID (Remove Intoxicated Drivers), and SADD (Students Against Drunk Driving).

The important changes in recent years in government policies toward drinking and driving are related to the emergence of a community of professionals who deal with alcohol problems, a community of recovering alcoholics, and the sharply increased role of the federal government in alcohol problems and automobile safety. However, it is my contention that the most significant changes have resulted from the organized movements that believe drinking-driving is a serious criminal act and deserves a more severe punishment.

Each of the perspectives outlined above may be in conflict with others, may support each other, or may be indifferent and unaffected by any other. I contend that, with some qualifications, they have emerged in confluence and cooperation. This chapter first describes each of these in their historical development and then analyzes their influence on drinking and driving by examining recent changes in legislation, patterns of alcohol consumption, and death rates from automobile accidents, and specifically, from DUI-related automobile accidents. This chapter concludes with an assessment of the possible future of the changes that have occurred in the recent decade.

THE LIMITS OF DUI RESEARCH

At the outset of this inquiry several towering impediments to a clear response to my initial question must be addressed. These arise from a number of different sources among which the following are significant: the limited character of the available data; the complex interactions between variables; and the historical period in which this chapter is written, along with the diversity of meanings and perspectives within which the subject is itself characterized and the public problem posed.

The Limited Character of DUI Data

Almost all scholarly DUI studies are dependent, in one way or another, on official records of enforcement agencies, coroners' statistics, and local, state, and federal agencies. This has two consequences. First, the vast amount of behavior constituting the events of drinking and driving goes undetected and unreported and thus is outside the ken of most published studies. This difficulty, which Ross refers to as the "dark figure" problem, must be kept in mind (Ross 1984). There is a cultural and social organization in which the daily events of DUI are situated, to support and/or resist DUI. This unofficial, informal, and interactive "society" may itself be in process of change. Although our meager knowledge of this "dark side" to DUI studies is important, for the purpose of this chapter this problem needs only to be noted.[1]

Second, DUI data is problematic because official records are often misleading or lacking in completeness and methodological utility. They are the outcomes of social organizations for which disinterested research skills and methodological competence are often lacking (Kitsuse and Cicourel 1963; Cicourel 1964; Gusfield 1981a).

The Complex Interaction of the Variables

The key index in determining DUI events is the blood alcohol level (BAL) in connection with some variable that distinguishes an unwelcome event, such as arrest or accident or death. Both the measurement of the BAL and the outcome, the dependent variable, are subject to severe limitations, not only of sampling, but also of the confluence of elements that interact to produce the outcome.

One example of confounding circumstances involves DUI fatalities and young drivers. Young people (aged sixteen to twenty-five) are disproportionately represented among the automobile fatalities who were found to have been drinking above the legal limit, 0.10 in most states. However, among other confounding elements, young people have less experience with drinking or driving, are more likely than older people to drive in the nighttime and on weekends, and are more likely to suffer automobile fatalities when sober than are older people. They are more likely than other older drinking drivers to come to the attention of authorities. The appearance of alcohol is not a complete explanation of the differences between age groups in automobile fatalities or even DUI fatalities (Carlson 1973; Zylman 1968a, 1973; Gusfield 1985).

The Present Historical Period

Whether the trends observed over the past few years will continue and with what results is still uncertain. The reported studies and statistics are one to two years behind the present writing of this chapter (January 1987). By the time this chapter is published it may be so out-of-date as to mar its value as a description or assessment of legal and social controls.

Since the late 1930s, and especially since the 1960s, DUI has been the object of thousands of studies, many aimed at evaluating the effects of official controls or countermeasures. Despite all this sound and fury, the significance is only slightly more than in Shakespeare's time. Our knowledge is meager, incomplete, and often misleading. This chapter cannot produce certainty but it can identify the issues that deter clarity and consistency about the control of DUI.

DUI: THE PERSPECTIVE OF SAFE TRANSPORTATION

At a recent conference on DUI, Frank Haight, editor of the journal *Accident Analysis and Prevention,* summed up one view of automobile safety: "It is probably fair to say that the transportation community now regards accidents as an unfortunate, but unavoidable, price to pay for the enormous benefits of road transportation" (Haight 1985, 14–15).

Whatever the validity of that remark, it does point to a conflict between widespread use of the automobile and traffic safety. In its present form, as in the past, the automobile is an inherently "dangerous instrument." Efforts at establishing control over the automobile by government and others have frequently been torn between the goals of speedier, less expensive traffic flow and interest in preventing the deaths, injuries, and property losses associated with accidents. Haight's statement suggests that there are limits to how much safety we can buy without diminishing automobile use.

Driving is a ubiquitous event in the United States. Most adults have driver's licenses and use them. In 1983, 65 percent of Americans of *all ages* had a license to drive. Widespread use of the automobile and limited availability of public transportation are a necessary background to the problems of DUI. The dependence of the American economy on driving and the relation of the automobile to consumer habits and styles of leisure are also basic data.

In the historical development of the automobile in America the major avenue of traffic control has been the building of more and better roads. Safety was a goal but of less concern than the provision of roads. In the early years of the automobile's emergence, safety did have a prominent position in government policies, particularly in legislation designed to protect nonmotorized road users and pedestrians (Baker 1971). The early development of a mass consumer market in the United States in the 1920s, however, prompted a shift in emphasis toward supporting traffic flow, rather than safety, as a major goal of traffic legislation.

As the automobile became increasingly common in the United States, control of traffic passed from being largely an individual matter under the direction of general rules to being the concern of the states, enforced through specific laws and specialized agencies. Speed limits changed from general principles, such as "reasonable and safe," to specific miles per hour posted along streets and highways. During the 1920s most states utilized local and county police as traffic law enforcers but added to them a new force in the form of state highway patrols (Cressey 1975).

It is comparatively recent that considerable attention has been paid to the design of safer automobiles. In the period between World War I and World War II some of the basic research on traffic safety did focus on the automobile and its design. This research, largely sponsored by the U.S. armed forces, led to such elements of automobile design as the padded dashboard, the collapsible steering wheel, and seat belts. However, the hearings on the National Highway Safety Act of 1966 revealed that the amount spent on research on automobile safety by the automobile industry was less than 0.1 percent of its profits (U.S. Congress 1968).

The reason for this lack of emphasis on automobile design was that, until the 1960s, traffic safety problems were either connected with the building of roads or seen as matters of the individual motorist responding to traffic laws. The development of the federal Department of Transportation in 1960 and the agency within it, the National Highway Traffic Safety Administration (1966), marked the appearance on a national basis of major governmental agencies directed specifically toward automobile safety. NHTSA's primary activities have been to supervise the automobile industry and mandate more safely designed automobiles. Its perspective has been toward the automobile industry rather than toward either laws or education directed at the individual motorist (Gusfield 1981a, ch. 2).

Within this perspective of the safety professional, drinking-driving laws are among a number of possible policies directed toward controlling the motorist. It is debatable that DUI laws should necessarily have primacy as a measure to provide traffic safety. The Insurance Institute for Highway Safety, reflecting the position of the late William Haddon Jr. (its director for many years and the first head of the NHTSA before that), grants much more importance to the design of the automobile and the prevention of injury as the most appropriate safety measures (Insurance Institute for Highway Safety 1986; Haddon 1972).

From this standpoint DUI is seen as a legitimate problem but not as an object for effective countermeasures. From this perspective what is to be prevented and controlled is injury and damage, whatever their source. The effect of the accident is the object of study and concern. All variables affecting safety are equally worthy of being assessed for their relation to that event and for the practicable possibilities of controlling them. The controllers are cast in the role of traffic facilitators. DUI is a facet of the problems produced by the automobile but not necessarily the best object of policies. Ralph Nader, whose writings and experiences helped the passage of the NHTSA act, once said that the aim should be to have the automobile industry produce an automobile that would be safe under the assumption that fools and drunks would drive it.

The entry of the federal government into the field of traffic safety and the attendant controls over the design of automobiles has been a major set of events in traffic safety. Localities and states, however, have jurisdiction over such matters as speed limits. In the 1970s, spurred by the oil crisis, the U.S. Congress passed legislation recommending a fifty-five mile per hour speed limit on highways. Not having direct jurisdiction in this matter, they put "teeth" into it by threatening to diminish highway funds to states that did not comply with the recommendation.

Where the traffic safety perspective and other perspectives converge is in the laws directed at controlling the motorist. Such laws include requiring obedience to posted signs and stoplights, speed limits, driver's licensing, and DUI, as well as the host of statutes that comprise the state vehicle codes. The enforcement of these laws emerged in the 1920s and exists today in substantially the same form: the use of police as agents of laws directed against the person—the motorist. This system, involving local police, traffic squads, and state highway police, operates through mechanisms of detection, arrest or citation, and punishment through fines and, in some instances, loss of license or even imprisonment. This system of deterring the driver through fear of punishment or penalty has, with one major exception (minimum age for alcohol sales), dominated public attempts to limit and control drinking and driving. It is preventive in nature, attempting to diminish the occurrence of accidents. (It should be distinguished from events that involve DUI as a felony, when injury or death has occurred.)

The automobile has become the most frequent source of relationship between police and citizens. Parking regulations are, perhaps, the most often used source of citizen citation for breach of law. There are more than ten million such citations in California alone every year (Judicial Council of California 1985). Although cases involving automobile accidents are among the most frequent source of negligence suits, and automobile theft is the third most frequently committed felony (Thomas and Hepburn 1983, 84), traffic violations remain the most frequently committed "crime" in the United States.

The quotes around crime are placed to indicate that referring to parking and "routine" traffic violations begs a significant question. Are traffic violations criminal acts? Is drinking-driving a criminal act? For the sociologist, as for many citizens, whatever may be the legal designations, the behavior of many persons may not be congruent with the legal definitions. H. Laurence Ross has coined the term "folk crime" to point to the discrepancy between a legal view of acts as crimes and a popular, public view that is opposite (Ross 1960).

No figures exist on the number of Americans who have ever committed a traffic offense or have been cited for an offense. Certainly it would be a large percentage of all drivers. Characteristically, events such as illegal parking, driving above the posted speed limits, or making a turn against posted prohibitions are not regarded by friends, spouses, relatives, or even strangers as moral derelictions in the same category as felonious assault, embezzlement, automobile theft, or even public drunkenness. Applications for employment that ask if the applicant has ever been convicted of a crime usually either specifically exempt traffic offenses or assume such. These are folk crimes, ones committed by many people or viewed by many as human acts that may be dangerous or foolish but not opening the actor to moral disapproval.

In this classification of crimes, where is DUI? In the perspective of traffic safety, laws that attempt to regulate the motorist are judged not by the moral status of the action to be controlled but by the laws' relation to automobile accidents and by their expediency as policy goals for preventing accidents and attendant damage and injury. In the detached perspective of traffic safety, the drinking driver is per se no more or less derelict than drivers who misuse roads, fail to use seat belts, or are fatigued.

DUI: THE PERSPECTIVE OF ALCOHOL USE
AND HEALTH

From the perspective of an interest in public health, DUI is a facet of the problems produced by beverage alcohol. The countermeasures associated with the consumption and distribution of alcohol are central in this concern. As is true of the traffic safety controllers, laws that attempt to deter the motorist from drinking or from driving are only one means among many in developing a policy to minimize drinking problems or to achieve a safer highway. It is just as logical to control the institutions that sell alcohol, to treat chronic alcoholics or "alcohol abusers," and to maintain high prices on alcohol as it is to prohibit and punish DUI as a way of promoting automobile safety. As in the transportation perspective, institutional regulation exists as an alternative to regulation of the person. However, unlike the transportation perspective, the control of alcohol has a history that makes more difficult the consideration of alcohol control policies completely apart from moral perspectives.

Drinking and drunkenness have been a far more salient political issue in American life than in most industrialized countries. With the exception of the Scandinavian nations, the United States is unusual in the degree of public concern and legislation attempting to limit the use of alcohol.[2] It is the only nation to have prohibited the sale of alcoholic beverages entirely, as it did in the passage and maintenance of Prohibition (1917–1933). The American temperance movement has a long history, commencing in the 1820s and never quite disappearing from the American public scene. Its importance for the topic of DUI lies in the meaning which alcohol has come to display among large segments of the American population and in public life.

The conflicting orientations toward alcohol that have dominated American policies since the repeal of the Prohibition amendment (1933) are revealed in two general conclusions that describe the American system until approximately 1980.

The first of these conclusions is the belief that alcohol is a "dangerous commodity." Its use is restricted by laws limiting the time, place, manner, and person of consumption. Consistently, since the early 1940s, one-third of American adults report that they do not use alcohol (Gallup 1985). No state treats alcohol or its sale or use as just another commodity. It has a particular legal status which, in every state, places some restrictions on its availability and use.

The second of these general conclusions is that drinking is an accepted custom in American society. Since Repeal (1933) the public problem of alcohol has been defined largely as that of deviant drinkers who develop personal pathologies and addictions (Gusfield 1982; Beauchamp 1980). Chronic alcoholism has been defined as the major problem caused by the use of alcohol. Until recently, the treatment and prevention of alcoholism has been the primary aim of public alcohol policies. Efforts to restrict the availability of alcohol have not been increased. Neither drinking nor even drunkenness but deviant drinking has been the object of public policy.

With repeal, alcohol policy became a minor issue in American politics. Federal concern was minimal and state governments played a small role. Private organizations, such as Alcoholics Anonymous and the National Council on Alcoholism were the major "owners" of the alcohol problem in the United States. This began to change in the late 1960s with the establishment of the National Institute for Alcohol Abuse and Alcoholism, an agency of the Department of Health and Human Services. During the 1960s, organizations such as the National Council on Alcoholism, largely the outlet for recovering alcoholics, and the North American Association of Alcohol and Drug Professionals, largely the outlet for people engaged in treatment of alcoholics, were active in obtaining federal aid for treatment, research, and other programs concerned with alcohol. Their efforts were capped by the passage of legislation establishing the National Institute for Alcohol Abuse and Alcoholism in 1970. In this fashion alcohol issues became a federal responsibility for public health. Not only did this spur the development of state and county programs for alcoholism treatment, but it brought about a new climate of research and public exposure for the gamut of possible alcohol issues.

A great amount of ambivalence about alcohol exists in the American culture. Not only is there the past legacy of the political battle between "wets" and "drys," there is also the perception of drinking as dangerous and yet accepted and appreciated. Within the movements concerned with "the alcohol problem" these ambivalences have been manifested in conceptions derived from concerns with health and those derived from moral disapproval of drunkenness. Since repeal there has been a sustained effort to define alcoholism as a disease and to bring to it less morally condemnatory attitudes than have existed in the past (Jellinek 1960). The effort to reconceptualize alcoholism as a medical rather than a moral failing has only been partially successful (Schneider 1978; Beauchamp 1980).

From the standpoint of alcohol problems, DUI is one among a variety of concerns, including public drunkenness, alcoholism, and labor force productivity. Where the traffic safety perspective focuses on the automobile, the alcohol perspective focuses on the substance of alcohol and/or the user. Within each, the person—the motorist or the drinker—is one element in the system. In some historical periods such as Prohibition, the substance has been emphasized. In others, the person, as in driver education campaigns, has been emphasized. We can express this set of alternatives as those of substance abuse or abusive substance. In the past decade alcohol policy has been moving away from a concentration on substance abuse toward a conception of abusive substance. The watchword is shifting from treatment to prevention.

During the late 1960s and through the 1970s two federal agencies— the Department of Transportation and the Department of Health, Education and Welfare—became centers of concern for drinking and driving. The problem was now open to two diverse perspectives toward DUI. One was the perspective of traffic control and traffic safety. The other was the concern for alcohol abuse, a facet of public health concerned with accidents but also with a condition of the person—alcoholism. Each represented a different constituency and a different notion of where the DUI problem was located and what significance it possessed. In terms I have used elsewhere, the ownership of the problem of DUI and its conceptualization were differently constructed (Gusfield 1981a, ch. 2).

The countermeasures associated with the consumption and distribution of alcohol are central in a concern for prevention. As is true of the traffic safety controllers, laws that attempt to deter the motorist from drinking or from driving are only one means among many in developing a policy to minimize drinking problems or to achieve a safer highway. It is just as logical to control the institutions that sell alcohol, to treat chronic alcoholics or "alcohol abusers," and to maintain high prices on alcohol as it is to prohibit and punish DUI. During the 1970s these policies, aimed at prevention of a variety of alcohol problems, assumed great importance in the research and policy fields. They came to supplement, and perhaps even supplant, the previous emphasis on alcoholism as the major alcohol problem and treatment as the major recommended policy (Moore and Gerstein 1981; Gusfield 1982).

DUI: THE PERSPECTIVE OF MORALITY AND JUSTICE

In one of his essays on punishment, H. L. A. Hart points out that while different behaviors may result in the same consequences, they do not possess the same moral status and thus do not admit to the justice of similar punishments. The Ming vase, he writes, is just as broken as a result of carelessness as of vandalism but punishing each act equally would be offensive to the moral sense of most people.

From this perspective DUI has the status of a morally condemned act. It differs from other traffic offenses such as speeding, making an illegal turn, or even reckless driving. In most states it is a misdemeanor punishable by a jail sentence. In cases in which an injury has occurred, the DUI motorist is guilty of a felony.

Over the 165 years of antialcohol agitation in the United States, health has by no means been a major concern of the movements. The moral disapproval of drinking and drunkenness has played a major role, especially in the movements led by the Protestant churches that culminated in Prohibition (Gusfield 1963). In much of the research and the public discussion of alcohol there exists what James Collins has called the "malevolent assumption"—the assumption that whenever drinking is associated with an unwelcome event, it is the cause of that event (Collins 1982, 152–206).

The moral condemnation of the drinking driver has achieved a wide consensus in society, and has been translated into DUI legislation. Intuitively the belief has existed widely that drinking and driving is risky. Even though the issue of DUI has had a low place on the agenda of public problems, public discussion has seldom included a pro-DUI position. District attorneys and other public officials have continuously made public statements that supported the unique, moral excoriation of the drinking driver. Drinking-driving has a moral connotation that other sources of traffic danger lack. The image of the drinking driver is that of the "killer drunk" whose intoxication is immoral because he threatens "innocent" individuals. His behavior is villainous and those he puts at risk are his victims: passengers, pedestrians, and other motorists.

Within the drama of the drinking driver, the issue of punishment has been the focus of much public comment. The moral status of the drinking driver and the search for punishment are clear in this typical public statement in a Buffalo, New York, newspaper in 1976: "As a result of a total breakdown in law enforcement and the district attorney's 'game plan' an estimated 6,000 drunk drivers will be poured back onto Erie County streets—the majority of them unpunished and with little incentive for rehabilitation" (quoted in Gusfield 1981a, 139).

I cannot read statements such as these without a sense of the moral indignation in which the image of the drinking driver is enveloped. Such statements are seldom made about speeding or drivers whose autos are in need of repair. This attitude is by no means recent in the public denunciation of the DUI offender. He (most often) is described as drunk, rather than under the influence; as delinquent, rather than careless; and as deserving punishment rather than penalty. In the arenas of public talk and action DUI has had the status of more than a traffic offense, more than a folk crime.

Who is being protected by DUI laws? From some perspectives, especially the transportation safety view, the drinking driver is victim of his actions as is the other driver or pedestrian involved in an accident. From other perspectives, certainly the moral view, it is the "innocent" pedestrian, passenger, or driver whose sobriety gives support to a claim of victimization.

There is a decided contrast between the moral indignation that has been characteristic of public statements about drinking-driving and the detached analysis of the traffic safety or alcohol problems "expert." In a substantial manner these groups talk past each other. They represent different conceptual domains and policy priorities. Although they may agree on DUI legislation, they differ profoundly on the significance they attribute to it and in the emotions that they express.

CONTROL OF THE DRINKING DRIVER IN THE 1970S

After World War II two processes began to develop that provided for a changed climate toward the control of alcohol and drinking-driving in the United States. One was the development of a technology that made police detection of drinking drivers more practicable. The other, occurring in the 1960s, was the growth of a research and policy community concerned with alcohol issues and supported by the federal government. There are sharp limits to the impact of each of these on drinking-and-driving behavior in the United States. Neither has succeeded in placing alcohol problems high on the public agenda.

Quite early in the history of the American automobile DUI was seen as a danger to safety. California passed its first DUI law in 1911. However, this intuitive belief in the danger of mixing driving and drinking was not backed by scientific research nor were such laws capable of ready enforcement until a technology for detection of drinking-driving was perfected.

By the 1930s, methods existed to test the blood alcohol level and, with the invention of the Breathalyzer in the 1930s, a fast and accurate instrument of detection enabled police to substantiate claims. Before that, detecting DUI depended on observational evidence that made prosecution difficult and hazardous (Zylman 1968b). The first scientific research into the effects of alcohol on driving did not occur until the 1930s (Holcomb 1938; Heise 1934). Not until the early 1960s did a body of research emerge to support the intuitive claim that drinking is positively related to automobile accidents and deaths (Gusfield 1981a, chs. 2, 3; U.S. Congress 1968).

As with traffic controls, the entry of the federal government into the drinking-driving arena is of fundamental importance. The first major report on DUI is that of the NHTSA to Congress in 1968 (U.S. Congress 1968). This was mandated under the NHTSA act passed in 1966. Much of the vast research conducted in the United States on DUI in the past two decades is supported by either the Department of Transportation or the National Institute of Alcohol Abuse and Alcoholism.

Since the mid-1960s police units specializing in apprehension of DUI offenders have appeared in a number of American cities. The Department of Transportation underwrote the Alcohol Safety Action Projects (ASAP) to diminish accidents and deaths through an experiment in increased enforcement in the 1970s. The program provided funds to state agencies to increase enforcement of DUI laws. Comparison of deaths involving DUI motorists on a before-after basis were then compared to similar data from non-ASAP states. The results of the ASAP study, though much debated, were at best inconclusive, at worst negative. There was no clear evidence that the projects succeeded in reducing accidents or deaths resulting from DUI (Zador 1976).

The ASAP projects were largely efforts to increase enforcement through more and better trained police. Similar efforts to increase enforcement through special units of police specializing in DUI law enforcement have yielded similar results in studies. Increased arrests for DUI have not been followed by a decrease in automobile deaths nor by a decrease in those deaths resulting from DUI (Zylman 1975; Gusfield 1972).

Prosecuting attorneys and judges have had available to them a repertoire of consequences for DUI from which they might choose in whole or in part. Judges might elect from a stipulated range of fines, might impose a jail sentence to be executed or suspended, or might recommend to the Department of Motor Vehicles that the offender's driving license be suspended or revoked for a period of time. As a stipulation for suspension of sentence, the judge might impose many kinds of conditions on the offender, such as writing the judge a letter every week, not drinking, attending Alcoholics Anonymous meetings, or even performing publicly needed work in lieu of going to jail. One alternative, which is commented on below, has been the practice of requiring attendance at special classes on drinking problems for both first offenders and recidivists.

Again the research results have been both ambiguous and inconclusive. Studies of enforcement in the 1970s have substantiated H. Laurence Ross's results from his study of the British Breathalyzer Act of 1973. In the first flush of publicity, deaths from DUI appear to decrease, but after a while (a year in the Ross study) enforcement becomes marred by legal limitations posed by procedural challenges and enforcement becomes lax. In the American studies, prior to the recent wave of alcohol and DUI concerns in the late 1970s, jail sentences were rarely meted out. Those that were often were suspended. Even license suspension or revocation was not the usual course of sentencing. A fine, approximately $150 to $300, was typical. Even the license suspension or revocation appeared to have limited results. Studies showed that one-third of all licensees affected drove without licenses anyway (Coppin and van Oldenbeek 1965). A study of San Diego County showed no difference between deaths due to DUI before and after establishment of a special DUI squad (Gusfield 1972).

Typically, as with many crimes, courts utilized less restrictive and stringent punishments than were available to them (Feeley 1979). The large amount of DUI arrests and the threat of trial was a perfect setting for plea bargaining. Whatever the public display of a consensus that drinking-driving was a "serious" crime, in the behavior of police, attorneys, and courts it was scarcely more than a traffic offense with a much higher fine.

This discrepancy between the public drama of criminal violation and the routine enforcement of a minor offense characterizes the DUI situation in the United States toward the end of the 1970s (Ross 1982; Gusfield 1981a). There is rationality in the attitude of many drinkers whose experience has indicated that the risk of accident or arrest at any time is not great. Although the chance of an accident has been estimated at about three times greater when DUI than when not, the probability of any single trip being interrupted by accident or arrest has been estimated as less than one in one thousand (Summers and Harris 1978; Beitel, Glanz, and Sharp 1975).

The second process—the growth of an alcohol research and policy community—affected the definition and policy discussion of alcohol issues. In the early 1970s the federal government assumed a role in alcohol issues on a large scale for the first time since Prohibition. Although it did so out of the interest in treatment of alcoholism, the research and policy community began to focus attention on preventive measures using tax policy, communications, and laws governing the sale and availability of alcohol. Spurred by activities and research in other countries as well as the antismoking campaigns, the professional community turned its attention to policies other than treatment of alcoholics and to alcohol problems other than alcoholism (Gusfield 1982; Moore and Gerstein 1981). Such concerns remained in the confines of the professional community of alcohol scholars and agency officials. DUI remained a minor problem in the American public arena. Alcoholism occupied the center of the small stage in the small theater of the public problem of drinking.

MADD: DRAMATIZING THE "KILLER DRUNK" AND HIS VICTIMS

In May of 1980 Cari Lightner, a thirteen-year-old girl, was struck and killed while walking on the sidewalk by an automobile driven by a driver who was DUI and who had been arrested a few days before on a DUI charge. Her mother, Candy Lightner, sought, at first unsuccessfully, to arouse government action for new DUI legislation. She did gain the attention of journalists, however, and by the end of 1980 had brought about a California Governor's Task Force on Drinking-Driving and launched a movement that changed the national climate of attention to public problems of alcohol and drinking-driving. She called her organization MADD, an acronym for Mothers Against Drunk Drivers.

MADD was followed by other organizations directed toward a stricter policy of punishment of drinking drivers. Together they have created a new movement that has given a dramatic form to an issue that had been dormant in American life. The very name, MADD, presents the symbols that carry an expressive imagery. "Mothers" puts the issue in a framework of violence against children. "Against" provides an emotional sense of battle and of enemies. "Drunk drivers" provides an image of the DUI as socially irresponsible and out of self-control. This is the "killer drunk" who constitutes the villain of the story.

MADD has brought to the public arena the emotional and dramatic expression of the public as victim. It drew its membership from many who had either been injured or had family members injured or killed in a DUI event (Reinarman 1988; Weed 1985). In moving the issue of DUI into a higher place of public concern, MADD, RID (Remove Intoxicated Drivers), and SADD (Students Against Drunk Drivers) presented the issue of DUI as one of justice and retribution, of bringing the DUI to a deserved punishment and, through this, deterring others. The materials of the movement are filled with accounts of people killed or injured by drinking drivers and the minor punishment imposed on such drivers. As a MADD newsletter put it in 1982: "MADD is the voice of the victim" (MADD 1982, 1).

This capacity to characterize DUI as a drama of villains and victims has produced a moral fervor that moved the problem from its shadowy existence into the light of public mobilization. Lightner maintained that hers was an effort "to get the dirty secret out." In this the media of communications were influential. A television dramatization of Candy Lightner's tragedy and her efforts to move government and the courts to action gave the movement a great help. It enabled the movement to identify all drinking drivers with the "killer drunk."

Emerging in the late 1970s and early 1980s these organizations have had a catalytic effect on the problem of DUI and, as a by-product, on the public control of alcohol. Much of the effort of this movement has gone into the passage and enforcement of more severe DUI laws. Especially is this the case with per se laws and more determinate sentences. In California, for example, the DUI laws were changed in 1982 to make a BAL of .10 for motorists per se illegal. Prior to that, the BAL was evidence of DUI but was rebuttable. Now a forty-eight-hour jail sentence became mandatory on all convicted DUI offenders. A number of states have passed similar changes in DUI laws.

But the movement has had other consequences. It helped bring about the first National Commission Against Drunk Driving, which sparked a move toward increasing the minimum age of legal sale of alcohol. Many American states had made it illegal to sell alcohol to persons below the age of twenty-one, others to lower ages, but none below eighteen. With the age of voting uniformly dropped to eighteen, many states had lowered the minimum age of drinking (Wechsler 1980). Supported by studies of increased automobile casualties among the young, the commission had recommended a return to a higher minimum age. Again the federal government attached such recommendations to the distribution of state highway funds and many states have raised their minimum age.

The movement has not been without support, from government as well as private sources. The federal government has provided grants to help the anti-DUI organizations (MADD 1982). Although it may have drawn some adherents from the reputed increase in "tough" policies toward crime, the movement has not shown an interest in other areas of law enforcement or in crime in general.

Nor have these organizations displayed great interest in the social control of alcohol. Although they have supported some legislation to control the sale of alcohol, such as limits on price discounts of individual drinks (the "happy hour" custom), they have not embraced the prevention programs that have constituted the "new temperance movement." The drinking-driver and DUI laws have remained the focus of the movement (Ungerleider and Bloch 1987).

With the emergence of the anti-DUI movement, both DUI and the social control of alcohol have undergone a rapid and widespread change. The movement did not emerge in a vacuum. A public consensus about the evil of DUI has existed for several decades in the United States, even though muted and immobilized. The developments of the 1970s had built a research and policy community that, even though relatively limited in power, could be utilized in the new atmosphere of public concern. Nevertheless the ability of the movement to provide a symbolism, an imagery, and a dramatic focus was a potent catalyst.

THE "NEW TEMPERANCE MOVEMENT": A PERIOD IN TRANSITION?

After decades of quiescence, DUI has come out of the cold and is now a "hot" issue, high on the agenda of public attention. In that sense DUI is in process of change in the public consciousness and the political arena. So too is a wide spectrum of anti-alcohol preventive measures. Is it all sound and fury, signifying very little alteration of behavior, by drinkers or by law enforcement agencies or both? New legislation is enacted but its effectiveness is not assured by its passage. Symbolic and ritualistic public acts have an importance but in this chapter my interest is in the more literal implications of the new era, or what I and others have come to call "the new temperance movement."

What is occurring is the effects of several separate trends and movements that have become mutually supportive. The anti-DUI movements have galvanized the activities and provided additional support to efforts of traffic safety policy and anti-alcohol programs. In turn these have affected DUI. Within this general series of actions there are indications of a change in American health habits emerging independently of public control efforts and affecting the use of alcohol. It is too early to pronounce an assessment of these activities on DUI. However, there has been a long-run decline in automobile deaths and a more distinct possibility of a decline in the rate of DUI-involved deaths than has been true of past decades in the United States.

Alcohol Control and Consumption

MADD and other anti-DUI organizations have frequently declared they are not movements to restore Prohibition nor are they opposed to drinking. Their support for measures to raise the minimum age for sale of alcohol has been defended solely as an anti-DUI policy. Yet in raising the issue of DUI, the movement has given an impetus to the turn toward prevention that had been developing in the 1970s.

The emphasis of MADD and the other organizations is on the drinking-driver and punishment as deterrent and as justice. Yet a whole series of measures are under consideration and to some extent passed that involve a wider effort to create a less conducive atmosphere to drinking by the general public. Not only has the minimum age of sale been raised while the voting age has been lowered but other measures to limit the sale and use of alcohol are on the public agenda. Measures to limit the "happy hours" (lowered prices for drinks during the cocktail hours), to shorten hours of sale, to make bars and even hosts liable for DUI damages, to curtail advertising of alcoholic beverages, to provide health warnings on bottled goods, and to limit outlets through zoning are all under active public discussion and, in some instances, have been both the object and the outcome of serious legislative debate.

The model for these efforts, in the discussion circles of alcohol policy groups, is the success of the public health campaign against the use of cigarettes. It unites the moral fervor of the anti-DUI concerns with the public health interests of government agencies and a public seemingly more attuned to health issues than in previous generations.

There is some evidence of a decline in alcohol consumption in recent years in the United States as reported by the beverage alcohol industry (*Jobson's Liquor Handbook* 1986) and on sales tax and receipts (U.S. Department of Health and Human Services 1986). During the decade of the 1970s per capita alcohol consumption of the population aged fourteen and over increased. However, almost all of that increase came from the greater use of beer and wine. Whiskies only increased by 1 percent and, since the late 1970s, have steadily declined in use. The use of wine appears to have hit a plateau. Beer, which accounts for half of the alcohol consumed, had also hit a plateau in use. In the past year for which statistics are available (1985), per capita beer use dropped for the first time in many years. It would appear that the ascending curve of alcohol consumption characteristic in the 1970s is at an end.

Is the United States becoming a nation of more moderate drinkers than was the case two decades ago? It is playful to speculate on the possible reasons for such a trend. The growing health consciousness and the turn of medicine toward prevention rather than treatment may be among the noncontrol sources of such a trend. The grassroots movements may play a role but moderation appeared even before the movement made headlines.

However, a degree of caution must be kept in mind before the funeral of John Barleycorn is arranged. First, the trends are most recent and the bulk of the decline in absolute alcohol consumption has come in the use of whiskies. There have been peaks and troughs in the midst of general trendlines before, and it will take a few more years to indicate if anything long-lasting is at work. But the second caveat is more significant. We do not have any clear conception of the relation between total consumption and alcohol problems other than cirrhosis of the liver. It is not the amount consumed but the clustering of consumption in the form of drunkenness or DUI events that is vital to DUI. There are almost no studies that have attempted to measure the relation of total consumption of alcohol to the number of such events.[3]

Enforcement of DUI Laws

Death from DUI is a conclusion established by a variety of data affected by imperfect systems of records gathering. All automobile fatalities are not routinely tested for BAL in all jurisdictions. Even when the effort is made there are limitations. In some instances there is too great a time gap between the accident and the death; in some the condition of the corpse is such that a BAL is unobtainable. Age and general condition of health and access to emergency hospital services affect the death or recovery of accident victims. The use or nonuse of safety belts affects the event of fatality. Suicides are not always distinguishable from accidental deaths. All of these variables appear differentially related to alcohol involvement. Because all these variables are changing through time the conclusions drawn from before and after DUI death rates are inconclusive about the deterrent or nondeterrent effects of increased punishments.

Records and statistics of DUI deaths are distorted by the differential effectiveness of state and local agencies in gathering such data. The Fatal Accident Reporting Service of the U.S. Department of Transportation represents the most uniform source of data on automobile deaths for the entire country. It came into existence only in 1977. Until last year, only fifteen states in the United States had succeeded in testing more than eighty percent of motorists killed in automobile accidents (Fell 1982). More than 50 percent of all motorist deaths in the United States were unexamined for BAL in 1984. BAL tests of surviving drivers are even less often performed or reported. There is also an analysis of the FARS evidence to suggest that the testing and reporting procedures are biased in a manner that inflates the degree of DUI among automobile fatalities (Voas 1984).

Moreover, it is highly important to recognize the "malevolence assumption" in much of the literature, both academic and popular, about DUI. This is the assumption that the fault of the accident is attributable to the driver, and only to one of the drivers and, if alcohol was present in one of the drivers, his or her driving was responsible for the accident. I know of only one study that made an effort to test this assumption. It found the drinking driver responsible in 60 percent of the cases when one of the drivers was DUI (Boston University School of Law-Medicine Institute 1969). Such studies, of course, necessarily do not take into account such features as road conditions, age and condition of cars, time of day or night. Such features act in combination with other conditions, such as the motorist, in determining the final event.

Consider the high rates of DUI deaths for young males (ages sixteen to twenty-five). Even if other elements were equal, such as drinking amounts, young men would still show high rates of DUI death. First, young men are disproportionately likely to be involved in any kind of automobile accident. Second, young men have less experience with drinking and with driving than older men. Both of these increase the likelihood of young men appearing in the list of DUI automobile fatalities. Third, as discussed above, young men are more likely than older men to drive at night when, for all groups, fatal automobile accidents are more likely.

Despite all the difficulties of obtaining definitive conclusions about the relation between drinking-driving and accidents, one generalization has remained fixed. The conclusion of the classic 1964 study of Grand Rapids by Robert Borkenstein and his associates has been confirmed in many places and in many studies: driving under the influence of alcohol increases the risk of accident and increasing amounts of alcohol increase the risk further. This is the bedrock foundation of DUI policy, whatever the degree of risk involved.

Yet, whatever research may show concerning alcohol use and accident risk, we must place this knowledge in context. Automobile deaths result from a number of considerations, one of which is DUI. They are affected by the total amount of driving, which may fluctuate. They are affected by the general safety of automobile design, which has been changing. For many years, for whatever reasons, the United States had the lowest rate of automobile fatalities per miles driven and per autos owned. At the same time, it had the highest absolute number of automobile deaths in the world and a total number of automobile fatalities that was rising continuously over twenty years (Baker 1971; Baker, O'Neil, and Karpf 1984). The low rates indicated the decreased possibility that any single driving event would result in an accident. The high absolute figures represented the increased driving in the country.

Second, although this is conjectural, DUI appears to have some relation to the total consumption of alcohol. Studies of states in which the minimum age was lowered and then raised compared with control states do indicate that DUI fatalities among the young have declined (Wechsler 1980; Cook 1981; Wagenaar 1981; Williams 1986).

All of these variables—consumption habits, DUI laws, automobile use, and automobile condition—are occurring in a period of heightened public discussion and awareness of DUI to which DUI laws and movements have themselves contributed. It would be a better course to diminish the concern for a causal analysis of the deterrent effects of DUI laws and consider the historical question of the impact of the total set of events on DUI. What has happened to deaths of motorists who were tested at above .10 since the emergence of the new temperance movement?

There have been several studies of the enforcement of new, tougher DUI laws as well as of their effectiveness in diminishing automobile accidents and fatalities. Studies of enforcement do indicate a general increase in arrests for DUI in American states. The very limited use of jail sentences and/or license suspension and revocation does appear to have ended but the new-era approaches to sentencing have also not resulted in a high degree of jail sentences for first offenses. An analysis of the courts of Alameda County, California, found that of every thousand arrests, half were of recidivists. Of 840 charged, 720 were convicted. Very few cases (eight) were convicted by trial. Of the seven hundred sentenced only one hundred actually served a straight weekend jail term. Most were fined; many (385) had their license suspended or revoked. Of the 330 sentenced to jail, 230 were given weekend work for public activities or given a work furlough. The majority were forced to attend a DUI school or given treatment for alcoholism (Klein 1985).

Although these descriptions do indicate an increase in "severity" of punishment, they also indicate the limited character of that increase. While the DUI schools may diminish recidivism they do not appear to have much effect on accident and death occurrences (Speiglman 1985). License suspension or revocation appears to be a more effective measure, even though as much as a third of those whose licenses are restricted may nevertheless continue to drive.

In a careful study of the impact of the new (1982) California DUI law on injury accident and deaths, Hilton reports that the decline in such deaths in 1982 was no greater than the decline in non-alcohol-related automobile deaths. However, not only was the decline in alcohol-related events more marked in injury accidents but the deaths involving DUI were significantly greater in the first nine months of the second year of enforcement of the new law, contrary to earlier experiences and Ross's studies (Hilton 1984). Hilton's study suggests the difficulty in relating an outcome—automobile death—to a specific independent variable—new DUI laws.

Deaths from DUI

From the perspective of traffic safety, do DUI laws ensure a safer traffic environment for the potential drinking driver or for the sober driver? Here we must examine automobile fatalities as the result of a multiplicity of elements, only one of which is contained in DUI. I have pointed out the multicausal character of traffic safety as well as the multiple causes that go into accidents even when DUI is present. Deaths from automobiles increased steadily in the United States since the advent of the mass-produced automobile. With the exception of the war years (1941–45) there was no steady and dramatic decline in numbers of motor vehicle deaths until 1973 and the oil crisis (Baker, O'Neil, and Karpf 1984, 216). During the same period the American rate of automobile fatalities per automobile owned and per miles driven continued to decline (Baker 1971; Baker, O'Neil, and Karpf 1984, 215). The paradox is explained by one of the major features of automobile accidents and deaths—the extent to which they are a function of the amount of driving.

Although 54,589 lives were lost in the United States in 1972, the peak year for traffic death, since then the figure has dropped steadily, despite increases in the total population, in automobile ownership, and in licensed drivers, and during periods of increased travel. In 1985 it was 43,555. Similarly the death rate per one hundred million miles traveled dropped from the 1966 rate of 5.72 to the 1985 rate of 2.47 (Insurance Institute for Highway Safety 1986). While numbers of automobile deaths have fluctuated between 1973 and 1985, the general trend has been that of decline (Fell 1982). The decrease in automobile deaths was especially marked between 1973 and 1974, during the oil crisis, and between 1981 and 1982, during the recession. It rose again in 1983 and 1984, but it has not returned to earlier levels as in 1972. Whatever the implications of the anti-DUI movements on automobile deaths, it cannot be said that they alone have been responsible for a dramatic change in automobile fatalities, since that change began well before the current wave. Have the current waves of DUI legislation had any effect on automobile deaths?

It is difficult to account for the decrease in automobile deaths in the United States in any easy fashion. The diminished driving after the oil crisis and during the recession of 1980–82 appears to have affected total deaths, but it cannot have affected deaths per miles driven. Agencies appear to read into the changes whatever fits their existing missions and perspectives. Organizations like MADD and law enforcement agencies attribute it to law and law enforcement. The Insurance Institute for Highway

Safety attributes it to the National Highway Traffic Safety Administration and concern for better safety standards in automobile design. Public health authorities attribute it to a more health-conscious public.

The Fatal Accident Reporting Service of the U.S. Department of Transportation has been amassing statistics on automobile accidents since 1977. They have also gathered reports on BAL levels of drivers involved in fatal accidents, although the testing of the surviving driver in a fatal accident is both sporadic and sparse. In the latest such study only 14 percent of surviving drivers were tested for BAL. Drivers killed in crashes were tested only in approximately 50 percent of the cases. However, analysis of the fifteen states with "good" reporting (80 percent or more) of fatally injured drivers does show a decrease in the percentage of drivers who tested above .10. During the long-run decline in automobile deaths the DUI percentage had remained fairly stable, but in the past four years it appears to have declined steadily. Until 1984 the decline was small. The last report available, from 1984, indicates a significant decrease, however.

Consider the following data from the Fatal Accident Reporting Service on the percentage of fatalities, tested in the "good" fifteen reporting states, who had a BAL of 0.10 or above.

Percent of Driver Fatalities in Total Automobile
Deaths in Fifteen Selected States, 1980–84

Year	Total Fatalities	Total Driver Fatalities	% Driver Fatalities DUI
1980	51,091	28,816	50
1981	49,301	28,200	49
1982	43,945	24,690	48
1983	42,584	24,138	46
1984	44,241	25,582	43

Whether or not the decline of 1983–84 will continue remains to be seen. So much is happening to improve automobile safety and to diminish consumption of alcohol, especially among the young, that it is too early to have any conclusion about the relative role of increased severity of punishment in affecting a decrease in automobile fatalities. The results of the past few years are suggestive of a diminution in alcohol-involved automobile fatalities greater than the general decrease, whatever the causal mechanisms at work. During this writing, the Insurance Institute for

Highway Safety reported a University of Michigan national roadside survey showing a drop in percent of drivers DUI from 4.9 in 1973 to 3.1 in 1986 (Insurance Institute for Highway Safety 1986, 4). Such roadside surveys, however, have some significant problems in interpretation.[4]

It would appear that whatever are the implications of increased severity of DUI laws they are a part of the total processes affecting the downward trend in automobile deaths. To what degree they are effective through a heightened consciousness about alcohol use or automobile safety or through direct deterrence based on fear of punishment is a question that at present eludes our answering.

The occurence of alcohol-related problem behavior seems to be diminishing, but it is much too early to pronounce that the issue has been settled.

CONCLUSION

The current period of DUI control in the United States is unique in the history of the past fifty years. In intensity, in scope, and in effects, it may be having a decided influence on American behavior. Such an assessment is made with considerable reservation, given the short time the new legislation has existed, the limitations of data, and the few studies completed and available. The DUI movement, although itself of considerable importance, is both affected by and affects the wider new temperance movement. The institutional and cultural context of drinking in America may be undergoing changes in the direction of less consumption of alcohol.

The safety of driving has also undergone change in the past decade. Despite increased use of automobiles, the death rate has been sharply and steadily reduced and many fewer passengers, pedestrians, and drivers, sober or DUI, have died from automobile accidents.

But the reduction in DUI is not simply a reflection of the general control of laws and/or the operation of traffic safety controls. The movement toward severe punishment of drinking drivers has been a leading element in the changing character of the American drinking context, whatever may be the direct effects of such legislation. The expanded and focused attention on the moral drama of drinking-driving has been the most vital force at work in the changed nature of drinking-driving in the United States. How these effects may have been attained is also problematic.

This is not to deny the importance of federal entry into both the traffic safety and the alcohol policy arenas. But alone it was unable to dramatize a situation into fault and blame and victimization. It was unable to add an emotional anger sufficient to offset the long-existing public blandness and apathy toward automobile danger, injury, and death.

It is possible that the drinking public may discover the difficulties police and courts have in enforcing DUI laws. They may assert the validity of H. L. Ross's findings that after an initial period of publicity, DUI behavior will be reasserted at a customary level (Ross 1973; 1982). The difficulties created by expanded court dockets and limited jail facilities have led to greater dependence on diversionary programs of alcohol education and treatment and to voluntary service in lieu of jail (Speiglman 1985). As a group, arrested drinking drivers are a more stable part of the labor force and more "middle class" than other criminal offenders. This too makes "toughness" less politically practicable.

Yet the period since 1980 is not the same as the 1970s. The new temperance movement, itself partially a product of the DUI movement, has given a new saliency to control of drinking in American public life. Perhaps the saliency given to youth as the central actors in the DUI drama is a means of achieving compromise between the organizational and political concerns of the courts and police, on one hand, and the demands of the citizens' movements on the other. Young people have achieved a status as a separate group in American life, a source of both concern and fear, a new form of the "dangerous class" in America (Gusfield 1986, ch. 8). Further, they are also a relatively weak political group. As I noted above, a logical conclusion from the safety studies would extend the minimum drinking age to twenty-five and exclude all women from such legislation. The political impossibility of such measures is evident.

Another possibility for the solution to existing and potential conflicts over DUI remains at the inaugural stage only. For at least fifteen years, Japanese and American technicians have been studying possible ways to control DUI technologically. Such an intervention will be placed in use in several American cities on a trial basis. Used only with recidivists, this device locks the ignition system of an automobile and can only be unlocked when the attached Breathalyzer indicates the driver is sufficiently sober. The device will cost several hundred dollars to be installed, and the offender, in most cases, must bear the cost.

AFTERWORD, 1994

Conventional discourse and research about drinking-driving is dominated by the search for certainty about the facts of drinking-driving and the effectiveness of various countermeasures. Throughout this volume and in my earlier book-length analysis of drinking-driving as a public issue (Gusfield 1981a) I have attempted to point to the diversity of meanings and the fragility of socially constructed facts in such public discussions of policy. In this chapter that has been presented in the analysis of the traffic-safety, alcohol consumption, and moral orientations of different groups—traffic professionals, alcohol policy advocates and scholars, and citizen victims groups. Such diverse meanings often distort consensus about the very assumptions that make the presentation of fact and the discourse of rational, cost-benefit analysis confusing to observers.

The focus of much of public attention in the "new temperance movement" has been on drinking-driving and automobile fatalities. The center of policy under scrutiny and debate has been the movement to increase the severity of laws that might restrict drinking-driving and through them reduce automobile accidents and deaths. In the past decade there has been a considerable increase in the number of states that have passed laws enlarging the age-groups prohibited from buying alcohol, lowering the minimum BAL required for arrest, making the BAL a per se offense and increasing the severity of punishment. In 1993 all states in the United States used twenty-one as the minimum age for purchase of alcohol; forty-seven states had per se laws—forty-two at .10, five (including California) at .08, and one at .13. Thirty-two states use mandated license suspension for all offenders (Hedlund and Fell 1993, 1229). Many states have increased fines and jail sentences, including mandated jail for forty-eight hours for first offenders. All of these represent a sizable increase in severity of response to convicted offenders. Punishment, however, has many possible functions. From the standpoint of the moral perspective toward drinking-driving it may be just retribution for criminal behavior. From the standpoint of traffic safety such punishments are debated in terms of their deterrent effects in preventing a repetition of offender's offense (specific deterrence) and preventing others from drinking-driving (general deterrance). Both specific and general deterrence are also viewed in a cost-benefit analysis assessing traffic accidents and fatalities. Alcohol professionals may also be concerned with deterring drinking per se. Any particular person may, of course, share all three perspectives.

Spurred by the activities of the anti-drinking-driving movement led by MADD, the past decade has been one of increased criminalization and moralization of the problem of automobile accidents and deaths. Despite these general orientations, studies of the deterrent effects of punishment are carried out in a discourse shorn of retribution as an aim of punishment.

As I suggested in this chapter the evidence does appear to support the limited effectiveness of a deterrence strategy despite the general skepticism of many scholars about the general deterrence effect of increasing the severity of punishment. What have the past several years shown? Was it a period in transition or not?

In so many areas of the study of human behavior the student who attempts to review the mass of research finds himself or herself drowning in a sea of studies, knocked by successive waves of positive and negative conclusions, often buttressed by the pollution of flawed data arising from the unavailability of uncontaminated waters. What Ross referred to as the "dark problem" of missing data in the field of drinking-driving meets the reviewer at every turn of the tide (Ross 1984). Data is missing or uncertain; comparisons are unavailable; findings of one study contradict those of another. Explanations are often ad hoc.

Drinking-driving is no exception but for one fact about which there is little dissensus: death. The aphorism "Nothing is certain but death and taxes" expresses a folk-understanding, and the line between life and death, though not clear in some rare instances, is about as clear as anything we know except birth. (In rereading this sentence I realize that when birth occurs is a central matter in the conflicts over abortion.) The "facts" about death rates from auto crashes have a ring of certainty about the causation of fatality. Even here all is not certain since a number of deaths from auto crashes might also have been attributable to suicide and/or heart attack (Tabachnik 1973).

Setting aside such elements of the social construction of death rates, it seems evident that driving an automobile has become safer in the past decade in the United States. According to the U.S. Department of Transportation's Fatal Accident Reporting System total deaths from motor vehicles has declined from 44,525 in 1975 to 40,115 in 1993, a drop of approximately 10 percent. Death rates hit a high in 1980 when 51,091 people were killed by or in motor vehicles, and the number has declined steadily since to its lowest point of 39,235 in 1992, a drop of approximately 23 percent (Insurance Institute for Highway Safety 1993; 1994). This represents a decrease in the rate per 100,000 people, from 21 in 1975, 22 in 1980, to 15 in 1992 and 16 in 1994. The decline is even more remarkable since during this period the number of vehicles, licensed drivers, and miles driven all increased. Thus the decline in deaths per miles driven has been even greater.

I could spend the rest of this chapter speculating on the cause for the decline: better safety standards for autos, better educated public, greater awareness of the consequences of drinking-driving, better medical emergency services, less drinking-driving, to mention a few. There is no consensus among traffic safety experts or others that can give us a definitive answer.

What has happened to the incidence of drinking-driving during this period of decline? Has it remained at the same level, increased in its share of causes of auto fatalities? Decreased? What have been the effects of increasing punishments on the behavior?

We have no accurate or historically comparative data on the degree of drinking-driving. Roadblock tests offer one source of possible data but these are not good samples of all locations or all states and we lack data at various points in time. In her study, Vingilis found 6 percent of drivers stopped in a roadblock to be under the risk of arrest for a BAL over .08. (Vingilis 1991). Percentages increase sharply after midnight. The two most cited studies, dating from the 1970s, suggest that there are between 200 and 2,000 motorists driving legally under the influence of alcohol for every one so arrested (Beitel, Sharp, and Glauz 1975; Borkenstein 1972). What does seem to be established is that there are a lot more drinkers driving than arrest records show.

Researchers turn, however, to the certain fact of death and the physiochemical accuracy of the blood alcohol level to gain a better understanding of drinking-driving as a cause of auto crashes. Accidents that do not eventuate in deaths are too poorly reported and present too difficult a situation for BAL determination to be adequate data. Death is a determined state, must be reported, and, through coroner's offices, is a source of accuracy of data about the fact of death and its circumstances. The Fatal Accident Reporting System (FARS) is an excellent agency that has been keeping records from all states since 1975, including the role of alcohol in auto deaths.

Even with all these resources at work an accurate account of deaths from drinking-driving is plagued by many problems not yet surmounted. I have examined many of them in my earlier book, *The Culture of Public Problems* (1981a, chs. 2 and 3). It is rare to be able to get a BAL test in more than 80 percent of the auto crashes, and even FARS depends now on only eighteen states which report 80 percent or more of their fatalities. In recent years more states have raised their percentage of reported BAL, but it is still only a minority of states that have a high enough return to be reliable and comparative over a decade of reporting.

Despite these imperfections, a number of states have provided a basis for comparison, and, taking the total into consideration, the FARS reports show a steady decline in the percentage of deaths attributed to "involving" a BAL above .10 in the blood of fatally injured drivers, from 46.3 percent in 1982 to 38.5 percent in 1991. During this period the total number of auto fatalities in the United States declined 5.5 percent while the total number of drinking-driving attributed deaths declined by 26.4 percent. In the same period the number of fatalities below .10 actually rose in the same period (U.S. Department of Transportation 1991).

However the data is presented or interpreted it does seem that auto deaths attributed to drinking have declined, although they are still at a minimum of almost one-third of the total. While the decline hit a plateau during the late 1980s it has resumed the decline in the past three years.

The explanation for the decline, as I suggest in this chapter, is hardly definitive (Williams 1992). Both in deterrence theory and in drinking-driving studies, the most common view of the effectiveness of legal measures stresses the significant role of certainty of apprehension and punishment rather than the severity as central to the effectiveness of laws (Nichols and Ross 1990; Ross 1992). A point made by Williams needs to be noted. While laws, medical services, and the citizen's movements have all been at work, the combined set of events, especially the citizen's movements, energizes the relevant agencies into actions that otherwise might not have occurred.

It should also be noted that the role of drinking in auto accidents remains a further "dark problem." As I have pointed out in chapter 3 the "malevolence assumption" leads "was involved" to be transformed into "caused." There are no studies of which I am aware of how drinking-drivers do manage to drive safely. James Hedlund has examined the characteristics of "sober" fatalities and "drinking" fatalities and pointed out the poor driving risks that characterized many both "sober" and "drinking" drivers. Answering the title of his paper, "If They Didn't Drink Would They Crash Anyway," he concludes that some would but that there would still be far fewer fatal crashes if they didn't drink (Hedlund 1994).

Despite the confusion of studies what does remain a point of consensus, uncontradicted by any study, is that the higher the BAL of the driver, the greater the risk of accident and injury in driving an automobile. That risk may vary with many conditions—the age and driving experience of the driver, the drinking experience of the driver, the nature of the road, the marital status of the driver, and many other characteristics of the person and the context. Two persons, at the same BAL, may have different risk levels. But, even given all these considerations, the increased risk exists whether it is viewed as small, moderate, or great.

The phenomenon of drinking-driving remains a point of public attention and policy, like many, that brings into play the diversity of cultural discourses, values, and ideologies which mark political action in the interpretation of events. Such elements of human life continue to bedevil those who would search for ways of bringing human behavior into the realm of utilitarian rationality.

Notes
References
Index

Notes

CHAPTER 2. CONTESTED MEANINGS AND THE
CULTURAL AUTHORITY OF SOCIAL PROBLEMS

This chapter is a revision of a presidential address for the Society of the Study of Social Problems at the annual meeting, Berkeley, California, August 1989. It was published as "Constructing the Ownership of Social Problems: Fun and Profit in the Welfare State," *Social Problems* 36 (Dec. 1989): 431–41, and is reprinted by permission of the University of California Press.

CHAPTER 3. "NO MORE CAKES AND ALE":
THE RHETORIC AND POLITICS OF DRINKING RESEARCH

1. I read these papers for the first time in their entirety while working on one of the last drafts of this chapter. It is reminiscent of an aphorism of one of my mentors, Louis Wirth, who said to his students, "Originality is the result of a faulty memory." He might have added "and an inadequate search of the literature."

2. In my 1981 study, the drinking motorist was responsible in 60 percent of the accidents (Boston University School of Law—Medicine Institute 1969). Recent responsibility studies have found between 74 and 94 percent of drivers at BACs above .10 responsible. (See bibliography and discussion in Headlund 1994).

3. See the further analysis of how social problems designations operate to reinforce a hegemony of moral policy in ch. 3.

4. This view of drinking as one mode of "escape moments" is discussed in Gusfield, forthcoming, "Alcohol in America." For other discussions, see Cohen and Taylor 1992. For analyses of bars in this frame, see Oldenburg 1989.

CHAPTER 4. PASSAGE TO PLAY:
RITUALS OF DRINKING TIME IN AMERICAN SOCIETY

This chapter is a revision of a chapter that appeared in *Constructive Drinking: Perspectives on Drink from Anthropology,* edited by Mary Douglas (New York: Cambridge University Press, 1987) 73–88. Reprinted by permission of Cambridge University Press.

1. This should not be construed to imply that preindustrial Western societies did not recognize a difference between periods of work and periods of not-work. Certainly the ubiquitous holidays, saint days, and recreational events would be inconsistent with that notion (Burke 1978).

2. I realize that the concept of play is also used in more restricted forms in which it refers to concentrated and disciplined activity, as in games. Here the activity is both freely chosen and unrelated to practical, work-oriented goals. As in my usage, it is "not serious" though it may demand attentiveness and absorption (Caillois 1979, ch. 1).

CHAPTER 5. BENEVOLENT REPRESSION:
POPULAR CULTURE, SOCIAL STRUCTURE,
AND THE CONTROL OF DRINKING

This chapter is a revision of a chapter that appeared in *Drinking: Behavior and Belief in Modern History*, edited by Susanna Barrows and Robin Room (Berkeley and Los Angeles: University of California Press, 1991). Reprinted by permission of the University of California Press.

CHAPTER 6. COMPETENCE AND INCOMPETENCE IN
DRINKING AND DRIVING: SITUATED ASPECTS OF
CONTROL AND AUTONOMY

Chapters 6 and 7 are revisions of a chapter prepared for a report to the National Science Foundation, Law and Society Program in 1978. Joseph Kotarba and Paul Rasmussen aided in conducting the original research and preparing the initial report, and Joseph Kotarba first suggested the concept of "competence" in drinking.

1. It might be possible to use a recording method closer to immediate note-taking if the observer had been able to spend a great deal of time—perhaps as much as a year—becoming clearly accepted by the customers. Even that seems doubtful, however. E. E. LeMasters, who was a customer for four years at the bar he studied, used the more casual method used here (LeMasters 1975, 5). In recent years scholars working within the genres of cognitive anthropology and sociology have conducted research of a highly formal character in natural settings. Using videotape and verbatim note-taking they have obtained complete sets of field events. (See the work of Sacks 1972 and Mehan 1980 as examples.) Promising as these are, to date they have been limited to particular situations where complete data retrieval has been possible, such as school classrooms and courtrooms, or to analysis of the properties of language.

2. According to the U.S. Census the population of San Diego County was 1,357,854. (U.S. Department of Commerce 1972, 3).

CHAPTER 8. MORAL PASSAGE: THE SYMBOLIC PROCESS IN
PUBLIC DESIGNATIONS OF DEVIANCE

This chapter is a revision of an article published in *Social Problems* 15 (Fall 1967): 175–88. Reprinted by permission of the University of California Press.

1. Becker 1963, ch. 1. A similar view is presented in Kitsuse 1962; Erikson 1965, 457–64, 458.

2. The material of this section is more fully discussed in Gusfield 1963, esp. ch. 7.

3. See the analysis of power as infused with collective goals in Parsons's criticism of C. Wright Mills, *The Power Elite*, in Parsons, 1957, 123, 144.

4. Sutton 1959. In this paper Sutton shows that in some primitive societies, political officials function chiefly as representatives to other tribes rather than as law enforcers or policymakers.

5. Murray Edelman (1964) has shown this in his analysis of the discrepancy between legislative action and administrative agency operation.

6. Williams 1960, 372–96. Hyman Rodman's analysis (1966) of "lower-class value stretch" suggests yet another ambiguity in the concept of norm. He found that in Trinidad among lower-class respondents that *both* marriage and nonlegal marital union are normatively accepted, although marriage is preferred.

7. Edelman 1964, ch. 2. The author refers to this as a process of political quiescence. While Edelman's symbolic analysis is close to mine, his emphasis is on the reassurance function of symbols in relation to presumed instrumental affects. My analysis stresses the conflict over symbols as a process of importance apart from instrumental effects.

8. Burke 1945, 393. Burke's writings have been the strongest influence on the mode of analysis presented here. Two other writers, whose works have been influential, themselves influenced by Burke, are Erving Goffman and Hugh D. Duncan.

9. Durkheim 1947, esp. 96–103. For a similar view see Coser 1962, 172–82.

10. This of course does not mean that the patient using morphine may not become an addict.

11. A somewhat similar distinction as that presented here can be found in Aubert and Messinger 1965, 25–54.

12. See William Westley's analysis (1953) of the differences between the morality shared by the lower class and the police in contrast to that of the courts over such matters as gambling, prostitution, and sexual perversion. The courts take a sterner view of gamblers and prostitutes than do the police, who take a sterner view of the sexual offender.

13. The best single account of temperance activities before the Civil War is that of Krout 1925.

14. Ibid., ch. 1 and 2; also see Earle 1937, 148–49, 156–65.

15. See the typical account by Mother Stewart, one of the leaders in the 1873–74 Woman's War on Whiskey, in Steward 1889, 139–43; also see *Standard Encyclopedia of the Alcohol Problem*, vol. 6, 1930, 2902–05.

16. See the table of consumption of alcoholic beverages, 1850–1957, in Keller and Efron 1959, 180.

17. Rowntree and Sherwell 1900, using both systematic observation and analysis of Federal tax payments, concluded (p. 253) that "local veto in America has only been found operative outside the larger towns and cities."

18. See the accounts of drinking habits among Irish and German immigrants in Handlin 1941, 191–92, 201–09; Hansen 1940.

19. Whyte 1955, 99. Whyte has shown this as a major attitude of social work and the settlement house toward slum-dwellers he studied in the 1930s. "The community was expected to adapt itself to the standards of the settlement house." The rationale for adaptation lay in its effects in promoting social mobility.

20. Although a well-organized Temperance movement existed among Catholics, it was weakened by the Protestant drive for Prohibition. See Bland 1951.

21. See my analysis of American drinking in the post-Repeal era. Gusfield 1969.

22. The Committee of Fifty, a group of prominent educators, scientists, and clergymen sponsored and directed several studies of drinking and the saloon. Their position as men unaffiliated to temperance organizations was intended to introduce unbiased investigation, often critical of temperance doctrine. For two of the leading volumes see Billing 1903, and Calkins 1901.

23. Seeley 1962, 593. For a description of the variety of definitions of alcoholism and drunkenness, as deviant and nondeviant, see the papers by Lemert and by Tongue in the same volume.

24. The WCTU during the 1950s persistently avoided support to Alcoholics Anonymous. The Yale School of Alcohol Studies was attacked and derogated in Temperance literature. A counter-organization, with several prominent pro-dry scientists, developed, held seminars, and issued statements in opposition to Yale School publications.

25. Many of the writings of sociologists interested in drug addiction have contained explicit demands for such redefinitions. See Becker 1963; Lindesmith 1965; and Ausubel 1958. The recent movement to redefine marijuana and LSD as legitimate is partially supported by such writings but is more saliently a movement of enemy deviants. The activities of Timothy Leary, Allen Ginsberg, and the "hipsters" is the most vocal expression of this movement.

CHAPTER 9. DEVIANCE IN THE WELFARE STATE:
THE ALCOHOLISM PROFESSION AND
THE ENTITLEMENTS OF STIGMA

This chapter is a revision of a paper presented at the International Conference on the Service Sector of the Economy, San Juan, Puerto Rico, June 26-July 1, 1978. It was published in *Research in Social Problems and Public Policy: A Research Annual*, vol. 2, edited by Michael Lewis (Greenwich, Conn.: JAI Press, 1982) 1–20. Reprinted by permission of the JAI Press.

1. Even in Howard Becker's formulation of the emergence of deviance, the

entrepreneurs of morality are crusading reformers who act to suppress the deviants engaging in drinking, vice, gambling, sexual delinquency or other items of nonconformity (Becker 1963, ch. 8, esp. pp. 147–48).

2. The Washingtonians bear much resemblance to the Alcoholics Anonymous of today. They were composed of people attempting to rid themselves of drinking. Leadership was not in the hands of the Protestant clergy (Maxwell 1950; Krout 1925).

3. I realize that in the language and logic of AA, no one is a "recovered alcoholic" any more than the diabetic who arrests his or her disability through insulin is a "cured" diabetic.

4. The National Council on Alcoholism listed thirty-seven such training institutes being held between April 26 and May 15, 1977, in the United States.

5. This also implied that all alcohol problems—industrial absenteeism, marital discord, accidents, and other areas of alcohol concern are symptomatic of chronic alcoholism. There are no drinking problems; there is *a* drinking problem.

CHAPTER 10. PERSUASION TO DEVIANCE:
STIGMA AND REDEMPTION IN LAW AND MEDICINE

1. In recent years, as the attitudes toward drinking-drivers have been increasingly criminalized, punishment has increased. Nevertheless, the programs described above, especially the educational ones, have enormously increased in numbers, often as an addition to the mandated forty-eight-hour jail sentence but in place of license suspension in Sun County.

2. The course was listed in the extension division's catalogue as "You and Alcohol" under the category "Alcohol Studies," which also included courses designed for alcoholism counselors. "You and Alcohol," unlike other courses, was open only to those designated by the courts. It was offered almost continuously throughout the year, often in several places at the same times.

3. The BAL as a sign of problem-drinking also appears as central in the probation decisions and interviews described later in this chapter.

4. The validity of this test is seriously in doubt. It fails to distinguish between the casual and occasional event and the recurrent event.

5. In complementary fashion, Ralph Turner has examined "deviance avowal," especially among AA members. Here the consequences as well as the illness are accepted. Treatment depends on the willingness of the member to admit his illness.

6. Another mode of possible resistance was failure to attend. Despite its court-mandated status, attendance dropped off from the first to the sixth session. This has been a constant problem of these classes, as I learned from serving on the Sun County advisory board on alcohol problems from 1982 to 1991.

7. This was not necessarily the case. Anything which constituted a misdemeanor was probable cause for police stopping an automobile. This could, and sometimes did, include such traffic offenses as a broken taillight (Gusfield 1981a, ch. 5).

8. This was inaccurate. The study did not support the course as associated with reductions in DUI recidivism (Wendling and Kolodji 1977).

9. Very few of those arrested for DUI were charged with felony DWI, which occurs whem the motorist is found DUI in an accident where someone is injured. The ratio of felony DWI to misdemeanor DWI in Sun County has consistently been approximately 1/100.

10. The disposition of DWI cases in Eastland was studied again by Richard Speiglman in the late 1980s, with focus on suspended or lighter sentences conditioned on use of treatment facilities, such as AA. That study and the one described here are described and analyzed in Speiglman and Gusfield forthcoming.

11. She refers here to the test of motor skills, given to possible DUIs before the police decide to arrest or not. It involves walking a straight line, touching a finger to the nose and other such skills.

12. In 1975 a BAL of .10 was presumptive evidence of DUI in California. In 1980 it became per se evidence of DUI and nonrebuttable. In 1990 the legal standard became .08.

13. "Reckless driving" had been frequently used in the negogiations over plea bargaining in DUI cases. Under the legislation of the time, prior DUI convictions within the past seven years increased the maximum sentence possible. "Reckless driving" was not considered a prior DUI offense. Recent California legislation has changed that, and it is now considered a prior offense for these purposes.

14. Similar programs are now (1994) in operation in Eastland under another special grant for assessing DUI offenders.

15. There is no accurate count of DUI events. Various estimates, based on survey and other sources, have indicated 200–2,000 DUI events for every arrest. Whatever the actual occurrences, the data are in agreement with our bar study (chapters 3 and 4 of this volume) that DUI, even in the present context of a high-agenda status, is a common occurrence.

CHAPTER 11. THE PREVENTION OF DRINKING PROBLEMS

This chapter is a revision of one that appeared in *Alcohol and Alcohol Problems: New Thinking and New Directions,* edited by William J. Filstead, Jean J. Rossi, and Mark Keller (Cambridge, Mass.: Ballinger, 1976). Copyright © 1976 William J. Filstead. Reprinted by permission.

1. In reading an earlier draft of this paper, Mark Keller pointed out a similar example used by a Greek orator at the funeral of Polyxenos, who had fallen off a cliff while coming home from a country feast. The orator did not know whether to blame the wine or Bacchus or the rains of Jupiter, but he warned topers to beware of slippery paths.

2. An important example of the operation of such private processes is presented by Cahalan and Room (1974) in their study of male problem drinkers. A high degree of problem drinking appeared in the reports of young men (aged twenty-one to twenty-five) and of older nonproblem drinkers about their youthful

drinking. There appears to be a process of "maturing out" of much problem drinking.

3. The use of drunken driver arrests or convictions to measure change in that behavior is a case in point. My experience with police and court procedures indicate that such arrests and ultimate convictions vary with the specific policies of the policy agency, plea-bargaining court practices, and the decision of the individual police to arrest on one of several available charges.

4. Based on personal communication of relevant studies from staff of the Finnish Foundation for Alcohol Studies, September 1973, supplemented by Mäkelä 1974.

5. Wilkinson's book (1970) discusses the major studies on which this view is based. For an example of such studies, see those by Snyder 1958 and Ullman 1953.

6. Studies of blood alcohol level among automobile fatalities in Scandinavian countries are not found in the translated literature. Discussions in September 1973 with staff members at the following research centers failed to uncover reports of studies in Norwegian, Swedish, or Finnish: State Institute for Alcohol Research, Oslo; Institute of Criminology and Criminal Law, Oslo; Department of Sociology, University of Lund, Sweden; Department of Alcohol Research, Karolinska Institute, Stockholm; Finnish Foundation for Alcohol Studies. I am grateful to the following for their aid in arranging meetings: Hans Klette, Nils Christie, Leonard Goldberg, Erik Allardt, and Klaus Mäkelä.

7. This was an issue in the September 1973 elections.

8. The work of William Haddon, Jr., has been seminal in this area and in accident research in general. See especially Haddon 1970, 1972.

9. The role of Senator Harold Hughes was monumental in the passage of the 1970 Alcohol Abuse and Alcoholism Prevention, Treatment and Rehabilitation Act. His own public testimony as a recovering alcoholic has been illustrative of the role this group has played in keeping the issue alive before the public and in creating a positive legislative and executive atmosphere.

CHAPTER 12. PREVENTION: RISE, DECLINE, AND RENAISSANCE

This chapter is a revision of one that appeared in *Alcohol, Science, and Society Revisited*, edited by Edith Gomberg, Helen R. White, and John A. Carpenter (Ann Arbor: University of Michigan Press, 1982). Reprinted by permission of the University of Michigan Press.

1. By now there are a number of excellent, up-to-date reviews of the literature in this field. The reader who wishes to gain a knowledge of the corpus of such studies or parts of it, is referred to the following: Wilkinson 1970; Lau 1975; Blane 1976; Popham, Schmidt, and DeLint 1976: Gusfield 1976; Wechsler 1980; and especially Gomberg, et al. 1980.

2. See especially the report of the conference sponsored by the California Office of Alcoholism in 1974 (Room and Sheffield 1974). The National Institute on Alcohol Abuse and Alcoholism (NIAAA) covened several task forces to prepare

position papers, and the Alcohol Drug and Mental Health Administration (ADAMHA) prepared a position paper on prevention (Klerman 1980). Of particular significance is the commission by ADAMHA of a panel of the National Academy of Sciences on prevention, including a subgroup on alcoholism. Their report and the papers commissioned for it are important in prevention policy (Moore and Gerstein 1981).

3. I am indebted to Nils Christie for pointing this out during the 1974 California conference on prevention.

4. Sacramento, California, has experimented with such a park, and it is under consideration in other cities.

5. In this analysis of "time out" behavior I draw on the work of MacAndrew and Edgerton (1969) and the study of bars by Cavan (1966) as well as my own work on ritual and drinking (chapter 4 of this volume). The analysis of competence and incompetence in drinking owes much to the ideas of Joseph Kotarba and is elaborated in our NSF report (chapters 6 and 7 of this volume).

CHAPTER 13. THE CONTROL OF DRINKING-DRIVING
IN THE UNITED STATES: A PERIOD IN TRANSITION?

This chapter originally appeared in *Social Control of the Drinking Driver,* edited by Michael D. Laurence, John R. Snortum, and Franklin E. Zimring (Chicago: University of Chicago Press, 1988). Reprinted by permission of the University of Chicago Press.

1. My associates and I have analyzed and studied the informal and interactive elements in the social organization of DUI, described in my review of social and cultural contexts of drinking-driving (Chapters 6 and 7 of this volume).

2. Bibliographies on American drinking and alcohol control movements can be found in Jessup 1979, and Gusfield 1986, ch. 8.

3. For one of the very few studies that attempted to count drunkenness events, see Polich and Orvis 1979.

4. But see the critique of methods used in these studies in Vingilis and De Genova 1984.

References

Aaron, P., and D. Musto 1981. Temperance and prohibition in America: A historical overview. In *Alcohol and public policy,* edited by M. Moore and Dean Gerstein. Washington, D.C.: National Academy Press.

Alcohol and Drug Problems Association of North America. 1976. *Alcoholism Treatment Programs Directory—U.S. and Canada, 1973–74.* Rockville, Md.: Information Planning Association.

Andreasson, R., and J. Bonnichsen. 1966. The frequency of drunken driving in Sweden during a period when the supply of alcoholic drink was restricted. Proc. 4th International Conference for Alcohol Traffic Safety, Bloomington, Indiana, Department of Police Administration.

Andrenaes, J. 1966. The general preventive effects of punishment. *University of Pennsylvania Law Review* 114:949–83.

Anslinger, H., and W. Tompkins. 1953. *The traffic in narcotics.* New York: Funk and Wagnall's.

Aubert, V., and S. Messinger. 1965. The criminal and the sick. In *The hidden society,* edited by V. Aubert, New York: Bedminster Press.

Ausubel, D. 1958. *Drug Addiction.* New York: Random House.

Bacon, S. 1943. Sociology and the problems of alcohol: Foundations for a sociologic study of drinking behavior. *Quarterly Journal of Studies on Alcohol* 4:402–45.

Bacon, S. 1969. Introduction. In *American drinking practices: A national study of drinking behavior and attitudes,* edited by D. Cahalan, I. Cisin, and H. Crossley. New Brunswick, N.J.: Rutgers University Center of Alcohol Studies.

Bacon, S. 1976. Concepts. In *Alcohol and alcohol problems: New thinking and new directions,* edited by W. J. Filstead, J. J. Rossi and M. Keller. Cambridge, Mass.: Ballinger/Lippincott.

Bacon, S. 1979. Alcohol research policy: The need for an independent, phenomenologically oriented field of study. *Journal of Studies on Alcohol,* supp. no. 8:2–26.

Baker, R. F. 1971. *The highway risk problem: Policy issues in highway safety.* New York: Wiley-Interscience.

Baker, S., B. O'Neil, and R. Karpf. 1984. *The injury fact book*. Lexington, Mass.: Lexington Books.

Barrows, S. 1979. *Distorting mirrors: Visions of the crowd in late nineteenth-century France*. New Haven: Yale University Press.

Barrows, S. 1983. The uncharted revolution: Drink and café life in nineteenth century France. Paper presented at the annual meeting of the Alcohol Epidemiology Section, International Council on Alcohol and Addictions, June 22-July 2.

Barrows, S., and R. Room, eds. 1991. *Drinking: Behavior and belief in modern history*. Berkeley and Los Angeles: University of California Press.

Barth, G. 1980. *City people: The rise of modern city culture in nineteenth century America*. New York: Oxford University Press.

Barthes, R. 1973. *Mythologies*. London: Paladin.

Barthes, R. 1979. Towards a psychosociology of contemporary food consumption. In *Food and drink in history*, edited by R. Forster and O. Ranum. Baltimore: Johns Hopkins University Press.

Bateson, G. 1972. A theory of play and fantasy. In *Steps towards an ecology of mind*, edited by G. Bateson. New York: Ballantine.

Bayer, R. 1981. *Homosexuality and American psychiatry: The politics of diagnosis*. New York: Holt, Rinehart and Winston.

Bayley, D. 1976. *Forces of order: Police behavior in Japan and the United States*. Berkeley and Los Angeles: University of California Press.

Bazerman, C. 1989. *Shaping written knowledge: The genre and activity of the experimental article in science*. Madison: University of Wisconsin Press.

Beauchamp, D. 1980. *Beyond alcoholism: Alcohol and public health policy*. Philadelphia: Temple University Press

Beauchamp, D. 1988. *The health of the republic: Epidemics, medicine, and moralism as challenges to democracy*. Philadelphia: Temple University Press.

Beck, B. 1978. The politics of speaking in the name of society. *Social Problems* 25:353–60.

Becker, H. S. 1958. Problems of inference and proof in participant observation. *American Sociological Review* 23:652–59.

Becker, H. S. 1963. *Outsiders: Studies in the sociology of deviance*. Glencoe, Ill.: Free Press.

Beitel, G. A., W. D. Glanz, and M. C. Sharp. 1975. Probability of arrest while driving under the influence of alcohol. *Journal of Studies on Alcohol* 36:870–76.

Bell, D. 1976. *The cultural contradictions of capitalism*. New York: Basic Books.

Bendix, R. 1954. *Work and authority in industry: Ideologies of management in the course of industrialization*. New York: John Wiley.

Bendix, R. 1964. *Nation-building and citizenship: Studies of our changing social order*. New York: John Wiley.

Berger, P., and T. Luckmann. 1966. *The social construction of reality: A treatise in the sociology of knowledge*. New York: Doubleday.

Berry, R. E., and J. P. Boland. 1977. *The economic cost of alcohol abuse*. New York: Free Press.

Billing, J. S. 1903. *The physiological aspects of the liquor problem*. Boston: Houghton Mifflin.

Billington, R. A. 1938. *The Protestant crusade, 1800–1860: A study of the origins of American nativism*. New York: Macmillan.

Black, D. 1980. *The manners and customs of the police*. New York: Academic Press.

Blake, J. B. 1974. Health reform. In *The rise of adventism*, edited by E. S. Gaustad. New York: Harper and Row.

Bland, J. 1951. *Hibernian crusade*. Washington, D.C.: Catholic University Press.

Blane, H. 1976. Education and the prevention of alcoholism. In *Social aspects of alcoholism*, edited by B. Kissin and H. Begleiter. New York: Plenum.

Blocker, J. S. Jr. 1989. *American temperance movements: Cycles of reform*. Boston: Twayne.

Blumenthal, M., and H. L. Ross. 1973. Two experimental studies of traffic law. Vol. 1. The effect of legal sanctions on DUI offenders. DOT publ. no. HS-800, 825. Washington, D.C.: U.S. National Traffic Safety Administration.

Bø, O. 1972. *Road accidents: An epidemiological investigation*. Oslo: Universitetsforlaget.

Bonnie, R. 1980. Discouraging unhealthy personal choices through government regulation: Some thoughts about the minimum drinking age. In *Minimum-age drinking laws*, edited by H. Wechsler. Lexington, Mass.: Lexington Books.

Borkenstein, R. F. 1972. A panoramic view of alcohol, drugs and traffic safety. *Police* 16:6–15.

Borkenstein, R. F., et al. 1964. *The role of the drinking driver in traffic accidents*. Department of Police Administration, Indiana University, Bloomington, Indiana.

Boston University School of Law-Medicine Institute. 1969. *Investigation of thirty-one fatal automobile accidents*. Washington, D.C.: Department of Transportation, Bureau of Highway Safety.

Bourdieu, P. 1984. *Distinction: A social critique of the judgment of taste*. Cambridge, Mass.: Harvard University Press.

Boyer, P. 1978. *Urban masses and moral order in America, 1820–1920*. Cambridge, Mass.: Harvard University Press.

Braudel, F. 1973. *Capitalism and material life, 1400–1800*. New York: Harper Torchbooks.

Briggs, A. 1961. The welfare state in historical perspective. *Archives of European Sociology* 11:221–58.

Brown, R. 1970. *Strain of violence: Historical studies of American violence and vigilantism*. New York: Oxford University Press.

Brun-Gulbrandsen, S. N.d. A study of Norweigian alcohol policy. Unpublished. Oslo National Institute for Alcohol Research.

Bruun, K. et al. 1975. *Alcohol control policies in public health perspective.* Helsinki: Finnish Foundation for Alcohol Studies; New Brunswick, N.J.: Rutgers Center of Alcohol Studies.

Burke, K. 1945. *A grammar of motives.* New York: Prentice-Hall.

Burke, P. 1978. *Popular culture in early modern europe.* New York: Harper Torchbooks.

Butynski, W., N. Record, and J. Yates. 1984. *State resources and services for alcohol and drug abuse problems, fiscal year 1984: An analysis of state alcohol and drug abuse profile data.* Rockville, Md.: U.S. Department of Health and Human Services.

Butynski, W., et al. 1991. *State resources and services for alcohol and drug abuse problems, fiscal year 1991: An analysis of state alcohol and drug abuse profile data.* Washington, D.C.: National Association of State Alcohol and Drug Abuse Directors.

Bynum. W. F. 1968. Chronic alcoholism in the first half of the nineteenth century. *Bulletin of the History of Medicine* 42:160–85.

Cahalan, D. 1970. *Problem drinkers: A national survey.* San Francisco: Jossey-Bass.

Cahalan, D. 1973. Drinking practices and problems; research perspectives on remedial measures. Public Affairs Report 14, no. 2:1–6.

Cahalan, D., I. H. Cisin, and H. M. Crossley. 1969. *American drinking practices: A national study of drinking behavior and attitudes.* New Brunswick, N.J.: Rutgers Center of Alcohol Studies.

Cahalan, D., and R. Room. 1974. *Problem drinking among american men.* New Brunswick, N.J.: Rutgers Center of Alcohol Studies.

Cahn, S. 1970. *The treatment of alcoholics: An evaluative study.* New York: Oxford University Press.

Caillois, R. 1979. *Man, play and games.* New York: Schocken.

Calkins, R. 1901. *Substitutes for the saloon.* Boston: Houghton Mifflin.

Cameron, T. 1978. Alcohol and traffic. In *Alcohol, casualties and crime: Report C-18,* edited by M. Arrens, et al. Berkeley: Social Research Group.

Cameron, T. 1982. Drinking and driving among american youth: Beliefs and behaviors. *Drug and Alcohol Dependence* 2:1–33.

Cameron, T., and R. Room. 1978. Alcohol and traffic. Report to the National Institute of Alcohol Abuse and Alcohol. Social Research Group, School of Public Health, University of California, Berkeley.

Carlson, R. 1975. *The end of medicine.* New York: Wiley-Interscience.

Carlson, W. L. 1973. Age, exposure and alcohol involvement in night crashes. *Journal of Safety Research* 5:247–59.

Cavan, S. 1966. *Liquor license: An ethnography of bar behavior.* Chicago: Aldine.

Chafetz, M. E. 1973. Unpublished remarks at Conference of Task Force on Alcohol Abuse and Alcoholism, Education Commission of the States, December 17.

Cicourel, A. 1964. *Method and measurement in sociology.* New York: Free Press.

Clark, B. R. 1960. *The open door college: A case study.* New York: McGraw-Hill.

Clark, W., and M. Hilton, eds. 1991. *Alcohol in America: Drinking practices and problems.* Albany: State University of New York Press.

Clifford, J., and G. E. Marcus, eds. 1986. *Writing culture: The poetics and politics of ethnography.* Berkeley and Los Angeles: University of California Press.

Cohen, S., and A. Scull, eds. 1983. *Social control and the state.* Oxford: Martin Robertson.

Cohen, S., and L. Taylor. 1992. *Escape attempts: The theory and practice of resistance to everyday life.* London: Routledge.

Collins, J. J., Jr. 1982. Alcohol careers and criminal careers. In *Drinking and crime: Perspectives on the relationship between alcohol consumption and criminal behavior,* edited by J. J. Collins, Jr. London: Tavistock.

Conrad, P., and J. W. Schneider. 1980. *Deviance and medicalization: From badness to sickness.* St. Louis: C. V. Mosby.

Cooley, C. H. 1902. *Human Nature and the social order.* New York: Charles Scribner's Sons

Cook, P. 1981. The effect of liquor taxes on drinking, cirrhosis and auto accidents. In *Alcohol and public policy: Beyond the shadow of prohibition,* edited by M. Moore and D. Gerstein. Washington, D.C.: National Academy Press.

Coppin, R., and G. van Oldenbeek. 1965. *Driving under suspension and revocation.* Sacramento: Calif. Department of Motor Vehicles.

Corwin, E., and E. Cunningham. 1974. Institutional facilities for the treatment of alcoholism. *Quarterly Journal of Studies in Alcohol* 5:9–85.

Coser, L. 1962. Some functions of deviant behavior and normative flexibility. *American Journal of Sociology* 68:172–82.

Cramton, R. 1969. Driver behavior and legal sanctions. *Michigan Law Review* 67:421.

Crenson, M. A. 1971. *The un-politics of air pollution: A study of non-decision-making in the cities.* Baltimore: Johns Hopkins University Press.

Cressey, D. 1975. Law, order and the motorist. In *Crime, criminality and public policy: Essays in honor of Sir Leon Radzinowicz,* edited by R. Hood. New York: Free Press.

Davis, F. 1961. Deviance disavowal: The management of strained interaction by the visibly handicapped. *Social Problems* 9:120–32.

Dawley, A., and P. Faler. 1976. Working class culture and politics in the industrial revolution: Sources of loyalism and rebellion. *Journal of Social History* 9 (Summer): 466–80.

DeLint, J. 1973. The validity of the theory that the distribution of alcohol consumption in a population approximates a logarithmic normal curve of the type proposed by Sully Ledermann; a brief note. *Drinking and Drug Practice Surveyor* 7: 15–17.

DeLint, J., and W. Schmidt. 1971. Consumption averages and alcoholism prevalence; a brief review of epidemiological investigations. *British Journal of Addiction* 97–107.

Denzin, N. K. 1970. *The research act: A theoretical introduction to sociological methods.* Chicago: Aldine.

Deutscher I. 1973. *What we say/What we do: Sentiments and acts.* Glenview, Ill.: Scott, Foresman.

Douglas, M. 1966. *Purity and danger: An analysis of the concepts of pollution and taboo.* London: Routledge and Kegan Paul.

Douglas, M. 1974. Deciphering a meal. In *Myth, symbol, and culture,* edited by C. Geertz. New York: Norton.

Douglas, M., ed. 1984. *Food and the social order: Studies of food and festivities in three American communities.* New York: Russell Sage Foundation.

Douglas, M., ed. 1987. *Constructive drinking: Perspectives on drink from anthropology.* New York: Cambridge University Press.

Douglass, R. 1980. The legal age and traffic casualties: A special case of changing alcohol availability in a public health context. In *Minimum drinking-age laws,* edited by H. Wechsler. Lexington, Mass.: Lexington Books.

Duis, P. 1983. *The saloon: Public drinking in Chicago and Boston, 1880–1920.* Urbana: University of Illinois Press.

Dumazedier, J. 1968. *Leisure.* In *Encyclopedia of the Social Sciences,* vol. 9, edited by D. Sills. New York: Macmillan.

Durkheim, E. 1947. *The division of labor in society.* Translated by G. Simpson. Glencoe, Ill.: Free Press.

Earle, A. 1937. *Home life in colonial days.* New York: Macmillan.

Edelman, M. 1964. *The symbolic uses of politics.* Urbana: University of Illinois Press.

Edelman, M. 1977. *Political language: Words that succeed and policies that fail.* New York: Academic Press.

Edwards, G. 1971. Public health implications of liquor control. *Lancet,* 21 August, 424–25.

Ehrenreich, J. H. 1985. *The altruistic imagination: A history of social work and social policy in the United States.* Ithaca, N.Y.: Cornell University Press.

Erikson, K. 1965. Sociology of deviance. In *Social problems: Persistent challenges,* edited by E. C. McDonagh and J. E. Simpson. New York: Holt, Rinehart and Winston.

Farb, P., and G. Armelagos. 1980. *Consuming passions: The anthropology of eating.* New York: Pocket.

Feeley, M. 1979. *The process is the punishment: Handling cases in a lower criminal court.* New York: Russell Sage Foundation.

Fell, J. 1982. Alcohol involvement in traffic crashes. *Quarterly Journal of the American Association for Automotive Medicine* 4:31–38.

Fitzgerald, E. 1928. The Rubáiyát of Omar Khayyám. In *Twelve Centuries of English Poetry and Prose,* edited by A. Newcomer, A. Andrews, and H. Hall. Chicago: Scott, Foresman, and Co.

Fleischer, G. A. 1973. A study of the effectiveness of a radio/TV campaign on safety belt use. *Journal of Safety Research* 5:3–11.

Foucault, M. 1974. *Birth of the Clinic: An Archaeology of Medical Perception.* New York: Pantheon.

Foucault, M. 1977. *Discipline and punish: The birth of the prison.* New York: Pantheon.

Fox. R. 1977. The medicalization and demedicalization of American society. In *Doing better and feeling worse: Health in the United States,* edited by J. H. Knowles. New York: Norton.

Frake, C. 1969. Notes on queries in ethnography. In *Cognitive Anthropology,* edited by S. A. Tyler. New York: Holt, Rinehart and Winston.

Frankel, G., and P. Whitehead. 1979. Sociological perspectives on drinking and damage. In *Alcohol, reform and society: The liquor issue in social context,* edited by J. S. Blocker. Westport, Conn.: Greenwood.

Freidson, E. 1970. *The profession of medicine: A study of the sociology of applied medicine.* New York: Dodd and Mead.

Friedman, L. M. 1985. *Total justice.* New York: Russell Sage Foundation.

Galanter, Marc, 1981. Justice in many rooms. In *Access to justice and the welfare state,* edited by M. Cuppelletti. Rijn: Sijthoff.

Gallup, G., Jr. 1985. Alcohol use and abuse in America. *Gallup Report* (Nov.): no. 242.

Garfinkel, H. 1956. Conditions of successful degradation ceremonies. *American Journal of Sociology* 61:420–24.

Gartner, A., and F. Reissman. 1974. *The service society and the common vanguard.* New York: Harper and Row.

Geertz, C. 1973. *The interpretation of cultures.* New York: Basic Books.

Gibson, R., and M. Mueller. 1977. National health expenditures, FX 1976. *Social Security Bulletin* 40.

Gillis, J. R.. 1981. *Youth and history: Tradition and change in European age relations, 1770 to the present.* New York: Oxford University Press.

Ginzburg, E. 1977. *The limits of health reform.* New York: Basic Books.

Glaser, B.G., and A. L. Strauss. 1967. *The discovery of grounded theory: Strategies for qualitative research.* Chicago: Aldine.

Goffman, E. 1952. On cooling the mark out: Some aspects on adaptation to failure. *Psychiatry* 15:451–63.

Goffman, E. 1956. *The presentation of the self in everyday life.* Edinburgh: University of Edinburgh Social Sciences Research Centre.

Goffman, E. 1963a. *Behavior in public places: Notes on the social organization of gatherings.* Glencoe, Ill.: Free Press.

Goffman, E. 1963b. *Stigma: Notes on the management of spoiled identity.* Englewood Cliffs, N.J.: Prentice-Hall.

Goffman, E. 1974. *Frame analysis: An essay on the organization of experience.* New York: Basic Books.

Gold, H. 1976. The professionalization of problem-solving. In *Combatting social problems: Techniques of intervention,* edited by H. Gold and A. Scarpitti. New York: Holt, Rinehart and Winston.

Gomberg, E., et al., 1980. Issues in the prevention of alcohol problems: A review. In *Alcoholism, alcohol abuse and related problems: Opportunities for research.* Washington, D.C.: National Academy Press.

Gouldner, A. W. 1970. *The coming crisis in western sociology.* New York: Basic Books.

Gouldner, A. W. 1980. *The two Marxisms: Contradictions and anomalies in the development of theory.* New York: Oxford University Press.

Greenberg, D. F. 1988. *The construction of homosexuality.* Chicago: University of Chicago Press.

Gronbjerg, K. A. 1977. *Mass society and the extension of welfare, 1960–1970.* Chicago: University of Chicago Press.

Gurr, T. R. 1976. *Rogues, rebels and reformers: A political history of urban crime and conflict.* Beverly Hills: Sage.

Gusfield, J. 1963. *Symbolic crusade: Status politics and the American temperance movement.* Urbana: University of Illinois Press.

Gusfield, J. 1967a. Moral passage: The symbolic process in public designations of deviance. *Social Problems* 15:175–83.

Gusfield, J. 1967b. Tradition and modernity: Misplaced polarities in the study of social change. *American Journal of Sociology* 72:351–62.

Gusfield, J. 1968. Prohibition: The impact of political utopianism. In *Change and Continuity in Twentieth-Century America: The 1920s,* edited by J. Braeman, R. Bremmer, and D. Brody. Columbus: Ohio State University Press.

Gusfield, J. 1972. A study of drinking drivers in San Diego County. San Diego: Urban Observatory. Report to Department of Health, San Diego County.

Gusfield, J. 1973. Utopian myths and movements in modern societies. Morristown, N.J.: General Learning Press Modular Studies.

Gusfield, J. 1975a. Categories of ownership and responsibility in social issues: Alcohol abuse and automobile use. *Journal of Drug Issues* 5:285–303.

Gusfield, J. 1975b. The (f)utility of knowledge? The relation of social science to public policy toward drugs. *Annals of the American Academy of Political and Social Sciences* 417:1–15.

Gusfield, J. 1976a. The literary rhetoric of science: Comedy and pathos in drinking-driver research. *American Sociological Review* 41:16–34.

Gusfield, J. 1976b. The prevention of drinking problems. In *Alcohol and alcohol problems,* edited by W. Filstead, J. J. Rossi, and M. Keller. Cambridge, Mass.: Ballinger.

Gusfield, J. 1981a. *The culture of public problems: Drinking, driving and the symbolic order.* Chicago: University of Chicago Press.

Gusfield, J. 1981b. Managing competence: An ethnographic study of drinking-driving and barroom behavior. In *Social drinking contexts,* edited by T. Harford. Washington, D.C.: Department of Health and Human Services.

Gusfield, J. 1982. Social movements and social change: Perspectives of Linearity and Fluidity. In *Research in social movements, conflict and change,* vol. 3, edited by L. Kreisburg. Greenwich, Conn.: JAI.

Gusfield, J. 1984a. On the side: Practical action and social constructivism in social problems theory. In *Studies in the sociology of social problems,* edited by J. Schneider and J. I. Kitsuse. Norwood, N.J.: Ablex.

Gusfield, J. 1984b. Prevention: Rise, decline and renaissance. In *Alcohol and society revisited,* edited by E. Gomberg, H. White, and J. Carpenter. Ann Arbor: University of Michigan Press.

Gusfield, J. 1985. Social and cultural contexts of the drinking-driving event. *Journal of Studies on Alcohol* supp. no. 10.

Gusfield, J. 1986. *Symbolic crusade: Status politics and the American temperance movement,* 2nd ed. Urbana: University of Illinois Press.

Gusfield, J. 1993. The social symbolism of smoking. In *Smoking policy: Law, politics, and culture,* edited by S. Sugarman and R. Rabin. New York: Oxford University Press.

Gusfield, J. Forthcoming. Alcohol in America: The twisted frames of morality and health. In *Morality and health,* edited by A. Brandt, S. Katz and P. Rozen. New York: Routledge.

Gusfield, J., J. Kotarba, and P. Rasmussen. 1979. *The world of the drinking driver: An ethnographic study.* Washington, D.C.: National Science Foundation.

Gusfield, J., J. Kotarba, and P. Rasmussen. 1981. Managing competence: An ethnographic study of drinking-driving and barroom behavior. In *Social drinking contexts,* edited by T. Harford. Washington, D.C.: Health and Human Services.

Gutman, H. G. 1977. *Work, culture and society in industrializing America: Essays in American working class and social history.* New York: Vintage.

Haddon, W., Jr. 1970. The problem drinker and driving: Questions of strategy in countermeasure choice and development. In *Community response to alcoholism and highway crashes,* edited by L. Filkins and N. Geller. Ann Arbor: University of Michigan, Highway Safety Research Institute.

Haddon, W., Jr. 1972. A logical framework for categorizing highway safety phenomena and activity. *Journal of Trauma* 12:193–207.

Haddon, W., Jr., and J. L. Goddard. 1962. An introduction to the discussion of the vehicle in relation to highway safety. In *Passenger car design and highway safety.* Mt. Vernon, N.Y.: Association for the Aid of Crippled Children, and Consumer's Union of U.S.

Haddon, W., Jr., E. Suchman, and D. Klein. 1964. *Accident research: Methods and approaches.* New York: Harper and Row.

Haight, F. 1985. Current problems in drinking-driving: Research and intervention. *Journal of Studies on Alcohol* supp. no. 10:13–18.

Hamilton, C., and J. Collins, Jr., 1981. The role of alcohol in wife beating and child abuse: A review of the literature. In *Drinking and crime,* edited by J. J. Collins, Jr. New York: Tavistock.

Handler, 1979. *Social movements and the legal system: A theory of law reform and social change.* New York: Academic Press.

Handlin, O. 1941. *Boston's Immigrants.* Cambridge, Mass.: Harvard University Press.

Hansen, M. 1940. *The Immigrant in American History.* Cambridge, Mass.: Harvard University Press.

Harford, T., B. Grant, and D. Hasin. 1991. The effect of average daily consumption and frequency of intoxication on the occurrence of dependence symptoms and alcohol-related problems. In *Alcohol in America: Drinking practices and problems,* edited by W. B. Clark and M. E. Hilton. Albany: State University of New York Press.

Harring, S. 1983. *Policing a class society: The experience of American cities, 1865 to 1915.* New Brunswick, N.J.: Rutgers University Press.

Harrison, B. 1971. *Drink and the Victorians: The temperance question in England, 1815–1872.* Pittsburgh: University of Pittsburgh Press.

Harrison, B. 1982. *Peaceable kingdom: Stability and change in modern Britain.* Oxford: Clarendon Press.

Harrison, S. S. 1960. *India: The most dangerous decades.* Princeton, N.J.: Princeton University Press.

Hart, H. L. A. 1968. *Punishment and responsibility: Essays in the philosophy of law.* Oxford: Clarendon Press.

Hayes, M. T. 1981. *Lobbyists and legislators: A theory of political markets.* New Brunswick, N.J.: Rutgers University Press.

Heath, D. 1975. A critical review of ethnographic studies of alcohol use. In *Research advances in alcohol and drug problems,* vol. 2, edited by R. Gibbins. New York: John Wiley.

Hedlund, J. H. 1994. If they didn't drink, would they crash anyway?—The role of alcohol in traffic crashes. *Alcohol, Drugs and Driving* 10:115–26.

Hedlund, J. and J. Fell. 1993. United States impaired driving policies and practices. In *Alcohol, drugs and traffic safety.* Cologne: Verlag TUV Rheinland.

Heilbroner, R. 1989. Reflections on capitalism. *New Yorker,* 23 Jan., 98–109.

Heise, H. E. 1934. Alcohol and auto accidents. *Journal of the American Medical Association* 103:739–41.

Helfgot, J. 1977. Professional reform organizations and the symbolic representation of the poor. *American Sociological Review* 39:475–91.

Hilton, M. 1984. The impact of recent changes in California drinking-driving laws on fatal accident levels during the first post-intervention year. *Law and Society Review* 18:605–28.

Hirschman, A. O. 1970. *Exit, voice and loyalty: Responses to decline in firms, organizations, and states.* Cambridge, Mass.: Harvard University Press.

Hobsbawm, E. J. 1963. *Primitive rebels.* New York: Praeger.

Holcomb, R. L. 1938. Alcohol in relation to traffic accidents. *Journal of the American Medical Association* 111:1076–85.

Hughes, E. 1958. *Men and their work.* Glencoe, Ill.: Free Press.

Hughes, E. N.d. Pullman, Illinois. Unpublished ms.

Husak, D. 1994. Is drunk driving a serious offense? *Philosophy and Public Affairs* 23:24–51.

Hutchison, R. 1991. Capitalism, religion and reform: The social history of temperance in Harvey, Illinois. In *Drinking: Behavior and belief in modern history,* edited by S. Barrows and R. Room. Berkeley and Los Angeles: University of California Press.

Ignatieff, M. 1983. State, civil society and total institutions: A critique of recent social histories of punishment. In *Social control and the state: Historical and comparative essays,* edited by S. Cohen and A. Scull. Oxford: Martin Robertson.

Illich, I. 1974. *Energy and equity.* New York: Harper and Row.

Inciardi, J. A. 1986. *The war on drugs: Heroin, cocaine, crime, and public policy.* Mountain View, Calif.: Mayfield.

Insurance Institute for Highway Safety. 1986. Highway death rate cut more than half since safety acts. *Status Report* 21, no. 11:1–3, 5.

Insurance Institute for Highway Safety. 1993. New facts about highway deaths show the lowest toll in 31 years. *Status Report* 28 (July 24).

Insurance Institute for Highway Safety. 1994. Then and now: Trends in deaths and death rates, 1975–93. *Status Report* 29 (August 20).

Jaakola, R., and H. Takala. 1971. *The problem of drunken driving in Finland.* Helsinki: Institute of Criminology.

Janowitz, M. 1978. *The last half-century: Societal change and politics in America.* Chicago: University of Chicago Press.

Jellinek, E. M. 1960. *The disease concept of alcoholism.* Highland Park, N.J.: Hillhouse.

Jellinek, E. M. 1977. The symbolism of drinking. *Journal of Studies on Alcohol* 38:852–66.

Jenness, V. 1993. *Making it work: The prostitutes' rights movement in perspective.* New York: Aldine.

Jensen, R. 1971. *The winning of the Midwest: Social and political conflict, 1888–1896.* Chicago: University of Chicago Press.

Jessup, J. 1979. The liquor issue in American history: A bibliography. In *Alcohol reform and society: The liquor issue in social context,* edited by J. S. Blocker, Jr. Westport, Conn.: Greenwood.

Jobson's Liquor Handbook. 1986. New York: Jobson's Publishing Corporation.

Johnson, P. E. 1978. *A shopkeeper's millenium: Society and revivals in Rochester, New York, 1815–1837.* New York: Hill and Wang.

Jones, R., and K. Joscelyn. 1978. *Alcohol and highway safety: A review of the state of knowledge.* Technical report no. DOT-HS-501207. Washington, D.C.: NHTSA.

Jones, G. S. 1983. Class expression versus social control: A critique of recent trends in the social history of "leisure." In *Social control and the state: Comparative and historical essays,* edited by S. Cohen and A. Scull. Oxford: Martin Robertson.

Judicial Council of California. 1985. Annual Report of the Administrative Office of the California Courts. Sacramento, Judicial Council of California.

Junker, B. H. 1960. *Field work: An introduction to the social sciences.* Chicago: University of Chicago Press.

Kaplow, J. 1980. Saint Monday and the artisanal tradition in nineteenth century France. Unpublished paper. Department of History, University of California, San Diego.

Kaplow, J. 1981. La fin de la Saint-Lundi. *Temps Libre* 2:107–18

Karp, I. 1980. Beer drinking and social experience in an African society. *Explorations in African Systems of Thought,* edited by I. Karp and C. S. Bird. Bloomington: Indiana University Press.

Katz, E., and P. Lazarsfeld. 1955. *Personal influence: The part played by people in the flow of mass communications.* Glencoe, Ill.: Free Press.

Keller, M. 1976. Problems with alcohol: An historical perspective. In *Alcohol and alcohol problems: New thinking and new directions,* edited by W. Filstead, J. J. Rossi, and M. Keller. Cambridge, Mass.: Ballinger.

Keller, M., and V. Efron. 1959. Selected statistics on alcoholic beverage. In *Drinking and intoxication: Selected readings in social attitudes and controls,* edited by R. McCarthy. Glencoe, Ill.: Free Press.

Kett, J. F. 1977. *Rites of passage: Adolescence in America, 1790 to the present.* New York: Basic Books.

Kitsuse, J. 1962. Societal reaction to deviant behavior. *Social Problems* 9:247–56.

Kitsuse, J., and A. Cicourel. 1963. A note on the use of official statistics. *Social Problems* 11:131–39.

Klein, D. 1985. *The impact and consequences of the 1982 law on drunk driving adjudication.* Oakland: Office of Court Services, Alameda County, Calif.

Kleppner, P. 1970. *The cross of culture: A social analysis of midwestern politics.* New York: Free Press.

Klerman, G. 1980. *ADAMHA prevention policy and review.* Washington, D.C.: Alcohol, Drug and Mental Health Administration.

Knowles, J. H., ed. 1977. *Doing better and feeling worse: Health in the United States.* New York: Norton.

Knupfer, G. 1984. The risks of drunkenness (or, ebrietas resurrecta). *British Journal of Addiction* 79:185–96.

Kotarba, J. 1977. The serious side of tavern sociability. Paper presented to the Society for the Study of Social Problems, August.

Kreitman, N. 1986. Alcohol consumption and the preventive paradox. *British Journal of Addiction* 81:153–63.

Krout, J. A. 1925. *The origins of prohibition.* New York: Knopf.

Kuusi, P. 1957. *Alcohol sales experiment in rural Finland.* Helsinki: Finnish Foundation for Alcohol Studies.

Lambert, R. 1963. *Workers, factories and social change in India.* Princeton, N.J.: Princeton University Press.

Landers, M. E. and J. K. Martin. 1982. *Drinking in America: A history.* New York: Free Press.

Landes, D. S. 1983. *Revolution in time: Clocks and the making of the modern world.* Cambridge, Mass.: Harvard University Press.

Latour, B., and S. Woolgar. 1979. *Laboratory life: The construction of scientific facts.* Beverly Hills, Calif.: Sage.

Lau, H. 1975. Cost of alcoholic beverages as a determinant of alcohol consumption. In *Recent advances in alcohol and drug problems,* vol. 2, edited by R. Gibbins, et al. New York: John Wiley.

Laurence, M. D., J. Snortum, and F. Zimring, eds. 1988. *Social control of the drinking driver.* Chicago: University of Chicago Press.

Leach, B. 1973. Does Alcoholics Anonymous really work. In *Alcoholism: Progress in research and treatment,* edited by P. G. Bourne and R. Fox. New York: Academic Press.

Lears, T. J. J. 1981. *No place of grace: Antimodernism and the transformation of American culture, 1880–1920.* New York: Pantheon.

Ledermann, S. 1956. *Alcool, alcoolisme, alcoolisation; donnés scientifiques de caractère physiologique, économique et social.* Institut National d'Etudes Démographiques, Travaux et Documents, Cahier no. 29. Paris: Presses Universitaires.

Le Goff, J. 1980. *Time, work and culture in the Middle Ages.* Chicago: University of Chicago Press.

LeMasters, E. E. 1975. *Blue-collar aristocrats: Life styles in a working-class tavern.* Madison: University of Wisconsin Press.

Lemert, E. 1962. Alcohol, values and social control. In *Society, Culture and Drinking Patterns,* edited by D. J. Pittman and C. R. Snyder. New York: John Wiley.

Lemert, E. 1967. *Human deviance, social problems and social control.* Englewood Cliffs, N.J.: Prentice-Hall.

Lender, M.E., and J. K. Martin. 1982. *Drinking in America: A history.* New York: Free Press.

Levine, H. G. 1978a. Demon of the middle class: Self-control, liquor, and the ideology of temperance in nineteenth-century America. Ph.D. dissertation. Department of Sociology, University of California, Berkeley.

Levine, H. G. 1978b. The discovery of addiction. *Journal of Studies on Alcohol* 39:143–74.

Levine, H. G. 1983. The committee of fifty and the origins of alcohol control. *Journal of Drug Issues* 13 (Winter):95–116.

Levine, H. G., and C. Reinarman. Forthcoming. The end of the epoch of prohibition? Social justice, public health and the future of drug policy. In *Crack in conservative America: "Demon drugs" and social justice,* edited by H. Levine and C. Reinerman. Berkeley and Los Angeles: University of California Press.

Lévi-Strauss, C. 1969. *The raw and the cooked: An introduction to a science of mythology.* New York: Harper and Row.

Lewis, D. C. 1992. Medical and health perspectives on a failing U.S. drug policy. *Daedalus* 121:165–94.

Lindesmith, A. 1965. *The Addict and the Law.* Bloomington: Indiana University Press.

Lofland, J. 1989. Consensus movements: City twinning and derailed dissent in the

American eighties. In *Research in social movements, conflicts, and change,* edited by L. Kreisberg. New York: JAI.

Los Angeles Times. 1989. Mental patients allowed to refuse drugs. 24 June.

Lundman, R. J. 1980. Police patrol work: A comparative perspective. In *Police behavior: A sociological perspective,* edited by R. J. Lundman. New York: Oxford University Press.

MacAndrew, C. 1969. On the notion that certain persons who are given to frequent drunkenness suffer from a disease called alcoholism. In *Changing perspectives in mental illness,* edited by S. C. Plog and R. B. Edgerton. New York: Holt, Rinehart and Winston.

MacAndrew, C., and R. B. Edgerton. 1969. *Drunken comportment: A social explanation.* Chicago: Aldine.

Maccoby, N., et al. 1977. Reducing the risk of cardiovascular disease: Effects of a community-based campaign on knowledge and behavior. *Journal of Community Health* 3:100–114.

Maddox, G. L., and B. C. McCall. 1964. *Drinking among teen-agers: A sociological interpretation of alcohol use by high-school students.* New Brunswick, N.J.: Rutgers Center of Alcohol Studies.

Maier, P. 1978. Popular uprisings and civil authority in eighteenth century America. In *Riot, rout, and tumult: Readings in American social and political violence,* edited by R. Lane and J. J. Turner. Westport, Conn.: Greenwood Press.

Mäkelä, K. 1974. The effects of an alcohol strike. *Drinking and Drug Practices Surveyor* 9:11–12.

Mäkelä, K. 1975. Consumption level and cultural drinking patterns as determinants of alcohol problems. *Journal of Drug Issues* 5:348–57.

Mäkelä, K., et al. 1981. *Alcohol, society and the state,* vol. 1. Toronto: Addiction Research Foundation.

Mäkelä, K., and R. Room. 1985. Alcohol policy and the rights of the drunkard. *Alcoholism: Clinical and Experimental Research* 9, no. 1:2–5.

Mannheim, K. 1949. *Ideology and Utopia: An introduction to the sociology of knowledge.* New York: Harcourt, Brace.

Manning, P. 1977. *Police work.* Cambridge, Mass.: MIT Press.

Markle, G., and Troyer, R. 1979. Smoke gets in your eyes: Cigarette smoking as deviant behavior. *Social Problems* 26:611–25.

Marrus, M. R. ed. 1974. *The emergence of leisure.* New York: Harper Torchbooks.

Marshall, T. H. 1965. *Class, citizenship and social development.* New York: Anchor.

Mather, L. M. 1979. *Plea bargaining or trial? The process of criminal case disposition.* Lexington, Mass.: Lexington Books.

Matza, D. 1966. The disreputable poor. In *Social structure and mobility in economic development,* edited by S. M. Lipset and N. Smelser, Chicago: Aldine.

Maxwell, M. 1950. The Washingtonian movement. *Quarterly Journal of Studies on Alcohol* 1:410–51.

Maxwell, M. 1962. Alcoholics anonymous: an interpretation. In *Society, culture and drinking patterns,* edited by D. J. Pittman and C. R. Snyder. New York: John Wiley.

McCarthy, J., and M. Zald. 1974. *The trend in social movements in America: Professionalization and resource mobilization.* Morristown, N.J.: General Learning Press.

McCarthy, J. D., et al. 1988. The founding of social movement organizations: Local citizen's groups opposing drunken driving. In *Ecological models of organizations,* edited by G. Carroll. Cambridge, Mass.: Ballinger.

McCarthy, R. 1958. Alcoholism: Attitudes and attacks, 1775–1935. *Annals of the American Academy of Political and Social Science* 315:12–21.

Mead, G. H. 1934. *Mind, Self, and Society: From the standpoint of a social behaviorist.* Chicago: University of Chicago Press.

Medicine in the Public Interest. 1976. *A study in the actual effects of alcohol beverage control laws,* vol. 1. Washington, D.C.: Medicine in the Public Interest.

Mehan, H. 1980. *Learning lessons: Social organization in the classroom.* Cambridge, Mass.: Harvard University Press.

Melbin, M. 1978. Night as frontier. *American Sociological Review* 43:3–22.

Merton, R. 1976. The sociology of social problems. In *Contemporary social problems,* edited by R. K. Merton and R. Nisbet. New York: Harcourt, Brace, Jovanovich.

Michelson, L. 1979. The effectiveness of an alcohol safety school in reducing recidivism of drinking drivers. *Journal of Studies on Alcohol* 40:1060–64.

Mills, C. W. 1943. The professional ideology of social pathologists. *American Journal of Sociology* 49, no. 2:165–80.

Monkkonen, E. H. 1975. *The dangerous class: Crime and poverty in Columbus, Ohio, 1860–1885.* Cambridge, Mass.: Harvard University Press.

Moore, M., and D. Gerstein, eds. 1981. *Alcohol and public policy: Beyond the shadow of Prohibition.* Washington, D.C.: National Academy Press.

Morgan, P. 1980. The state as mediator: Alcohol problem management in the postwar world. *Contemporary Drug Problems* 9:107–36.

Morgan, P. 1988. Industrialization, urbanization and the attack on the Italian drinking culture. *Contemporary Drug Problems* 15:607–26.

Morris, M. D. 1960. The recruitment of an industrial labor force in India with British and American comparisons. *Comparative Studies in Society and History* 2:305–28.

Mosher, J. 1978. Dram-shop liability and the prevention of alcohol related problems. Working paper No. F 80. Social Research Group, School of Public Health, University of California, Berkeley.

Mosher, J. 1980. The history of youthful drinking laws. In *Minimum drinking age laws,* edited by H. Wechsler. Lexington, Mass.: Lexington Books.

Mothers Against Drunk Driving (MADD). 1982. *National Newsletter* (Spring).

Moynihan, P. 1965. The professionalization of reform. *Public Interest* 1:6–10.

Mumford, L. 1938. *The culture of cities.* New York: Harcourt, Brace.

Muraskin, W. 1976. The social control theory in American history: A critique. *Journal of Social History* 2:559–68.

Nadelman, E. et al. 1994. The harm reduction approach to drug control: International progress. *Science* 33.

Nelson, B. J. 1984. *Making an issue of child abuse: Political agenda setting for social problems.* Chicago: University of Chicago Press.

Nichols, J. and H. L. Ross. 1990. The effectiveness of legal sanctions in dealing with drinking drivers. *Alcohol, Drugs and Driving* 6:33–60.

Nichols, J. L., et al. 1978. The specific deterrent effect of ASAP education and rehabilitation programs. *Journal of Safety Research* 10:177–87.

Nissenbaum, S. 1980. *Sex, diet and debility in Jacksonian America: Sylvester Graham and health reform.* Westport, Conn.: Greenwood.

Norris, J. L. 1976. Alcoholics anonymous and other self-help groups. In *Alcoholism: Interdisciplinary approaches to an enduring problem*, edited by R. E. Tarter and A. A. Sugerman. Reading, Mass.: Addison-Wesley.

O'Connor, J. 1973. *The fiscal crisis of the state.* New York: St. Martin's Press.

Odegaard, P. H. 1928. *Pressure politics: The story of the Anti-Saloon League.* New York: Columbia University Press.

Office of the Surgeon General. 1989. Surgeon general's workshop on drunk driving: Proceedings. Rockville, Md.: U.S. Department of Health and Human Services.

Oldenburg, R. 1989. *The great good place: Cafes, coffee shops, community centers, beauty parlors, general stores, bars, hangouts, and how they help you get through the day.* New York: Paragon.

Packer, H. 1968. *The limits of the criminal sanction.* Stanford: Stanford University Press.

Paredes, A. 1976. The history of the concept of alcoholism. In *Alcoholism: Interdisciplinary approaches to an enduring problem*, edited by R. E. Tarter and A. A. Sugerman. Reading, Mass.: Addison-Wesley.

Parker, D. A., and M. S. Harman. 1978. The distribution of consumption theory of prevention of alcohol problems: A critical assessment. *Journal of Studies on Alcohol* 39:377–99.

Parsons, T. 1951. *The social system.* Glencoe, Ill.: Free Press.

Parsons, T. 1957. The distribution of power in American society. *World Politics* 10:123–43.

Parsons, T., and R. Fox. 1952. Illness, therapy and the modern urban American family. *Journal of Social Issues* 8:31–44.

Pearson, G. 1983. Goths and vandals: Crime in history. In *Hooligan: A history of respectable fears*, edited by G. Pearson. London: Macmillan.

Pelz, D., and S. Schuman. 1974. Drinking, hostility and alienation in driving of young men. In *Proceedings of the third annual alcoholism conference of the National Institute on Alcohol Abuse and Alcoholism.* Rockville, Md.: National Institute on Alcohol Abuse and Alcoholism.

Perelman, C., and L. Olbrechts-Tytecka. 1969. *The new rhetoric: A treatise on argumentation.* Notre Dame: University of Notre Dame Press.

Pfohl, S. 1977. The discovery of child abuse. *Social Problems* 24:310–23.

Piliavin, I., and S. Blair. 1964. Police encounters with juveniles. *American Journal of Sociology* 70:206–14.

Pittman, D. J. 1967. Public intoxication and the alcoholic offender in American society. In *U.S. President's Commission on Law Enforcement and Administration of Justice.* Task force report; drunkenness. Washington, D.C.: U.S.G.P.O.

Pittman, D. J. 1991. Social policy and habitual drunkenness offenders. In *Alcohol: The development of sociological perspectives on use and abuse,* edited by P. M. Roman. New Brunswick, N.J.: Rutgers Center of Alcohol Studies.

Piven, F. F., and R. A. Cloward. 1971. *Regulating the poor: The functions of public relief.* New York: Vintage.

Plath, D. W. 1964. *The after hours: Modern Japan and the search for enjoyment.* Berkeley and Los Angeles: University of California Press.

Platt, A. M. 1969. *The child savers: The invention of delinquency.* Chicago: University of Chicago Press.

Plaut, T. F. A. 1967. *Alcohol problems: A report to the nation by the Cooperative Commission on the Study of Alcoholism.* New York: Oxford University Press.

Polich, J. M., and B. R. Orvis. 1979. *Alcohol problems: Patterns and prevalence in the U.S. Air Force.* Report no. R-2308-AF. Santa Monica, Calif.: Rand.

Popham, R. E., W. Schmidt, and J. DeLint. 1976. The effects of legal restraint on drinking. In *Social aspects of alcoholism,* edited by B. Kissin and H. Begleiter. New York: Plenum.

Popper, K. 1976. The logic of the social sciences. In *The positivist dispute in German sociology,* edited by T. Adorno, et al. New York: Harper and Row.

Powell v. Texas. 1968. 392 US 514.

Reid, D. 1976. The decline of Saint Monday, 1766–1876. *Past and Present* 71:76–101.

Regier, M. 1979. *Social policy: The study of a detoxification center.* Lexington, Mass.: Lexington Books.

Reinarman, C. 1987. *American states of mind: Political beliefs and behavior among private and public workers.* New Haven: Yale University Press.

Reinarman, C. 1988. The social construction of an alcohol problem: The case of Mothers Against Drunk Drivers and social control in the 1980s. *Theory and Society* 17:91–120.

Riesman, D., et al. 1950. *The lonely crowd: A study of the changing American character.* New Haven: Yale University Press.

Rieff, P. 1966. *The triumph of the therapeutic: Uses of faith after Freud.* New York: Harper Torchbooks.

Roberts, J. 1982. Drink and industrial work discipline in nineteenth century Germany. *Journal of Social History* 15:25–38.

Robertson, L., and A. B. Kelly. 1972. A controlled study of the effect of television messages on safety belt use. *Insurance Institute for Highway Safety* (June).

Robertson, L. S., R. F. Rich, and H. Ross. 1973. Jail sentences for driving while intoxicated in Chicago; a judicial action that failed. *Law and Society Review* 8:55–67.

Robinson, D. 1976. *From drinking to alcoholism: A sociological commentary.* London: John Wiley.

Rodgers, D. T. 1978. *The work ethic in industrial America, 1850–1920.* Chicago: University of Chicago Press.

Rodman, H. 1966. Illegitimacy in the Caribbean social structure. *American Sociological Review* 31:673–83.

Roebuck, J. and W. Frese. 1976. *The rendezvous: A case study of an after-hours club.* New York: Free Press.

Roizen, R. 1987. The great controlled-drinking controversy. In *Recent developments in alcoholism,* vol. 5, edited by M. Galanter. New York: Plenum.

Roizen, R. 1991. The American discovery of alcoholism, 1933–1939. Ph.D. dissertation. Department of Sociology, University of California, Berkeley.

Room, R. 1971. The effect of drinking laws on drinking behavior. Paper presented at annual meeting of the Society for the Study of Social Problems, Denver, Colorado, August.

Room, R. 1973. Notes on the implications of the lognormal curve. *Drinking and Drug Practices Surveyor* 7:18–20.

Room, R. 1974. Governing images and the prevention of alcohol problems. *Preventive Medicine* 3:11–23.

Room, R. 1977. A note on observational studies of drinking and community response. *Drinking and Drug Practices Surveyor* 13:17–22.

Room, R. 1984, Alcohol and ethnography: A case of problem deflation. *Current Anthropology* 25, no. 2: 169–91.

Room, R. 1985. Alcohol as a cause: Empirical links and social definitions. In *Currents in alcohol research and the prevention of alcohol problems,* edited by J. P. von Warburg, R. Muller and S. Wyse. Bern, Stuttgart, and Toronto: Hans Huber.

Room, R. 1991. Cultural changes in drinking and trends in alcohol problems indicators: Recent U.S. experience. In *Alcohol in America: Drinking practices and problems,* edited by W. B. Clark and M. E. Hilton. Albany: State University of New York Press.

Room, R. et al. 1979. Profile of policies and programmes for the prevention of alcohol-related problems. Berkeley: Social Research Group report.

Room, R., and S. Sheffield. 1974. *The prevention of drinking problems: Report of a conference.* Sacramento: State of California Office of Alcoholism.

Rorabaugh, W. J. 1979. *The alcoholic republic: An American tradition.* New York: Oxford University Press.

Rosen, G. 1968. *Madness in society: Chapters in the historical sociology of mental illness.* New York: Harper and Row.

Rosenzweig, R. 1983. *Eight hours for what we will: Workers and leisure in an American city, 1870–1920.* Cambridge: Cambridge University Press.

Ross, H. L. 1960. Traffic law violation: A folk crime. *Social Problems* 8:231–41.

Ross, H. L. 1977. Deterrence regained: The Cheshire constabulary's Breathalyzer blitz. *Journal of Legal Studies* 6: 241–79.

Ross, H. L. 1973. Law, science and accidents: The British Road Safety Act of 1967. *Journal of Legal Studies* 2:1–73.

Ross, H. L. 1982. *Deterring the drinking driver: Legal policy and social control.* Lexington, Mass.: Lexington Books.

Ross, H. L. 1984. Social control through deterrence: Drinking-and-driving laws. In *Annual Review of Sociology,* edited by R. Turner and J. Short. Palo Alto, Calif.: Annual Reviews.

Ross, H. L. 1992. *Confronting drunk driving.* New Haven: Yale University Press.

Rothman, D. J. 1970. *The discovery of the asylum: Social order and disorder in the new republic.* New York: Little, Brown.

Rothman, D. J. 1983. Social control: The uses and abuses of the concept in the history of incarceration. In *Social control and the state,* edited by S. Cohen and A. Scull. Oxford: Martin Robertson.

Rowntree, J., and A. Sherwell. 1900. *State prohibition and local option.* London: Hodder and Stoughton.

Rubinstein, J. 1973. *City police.* New York: Ballantine.

Rudé, G. F. 1959. *The crowd in the French Revolution.* Oxford: Clarendon Press.

Rudé, G. F. 1964. *The crowd in history.* Oxford: Clarendon Press.

Rudolph, F. 1962. *The American college and university: A history.* New York: Knopf.

Sacks, H. 1972. An initial investigation of the usability of conversational data for doing sociology. In *Studies in social interaction,* edited by D. Sudnow. New York: Free Press.

Sahlins, M. 1976. *Culture and practical reason.* Chicago: University of Chicago Press.

Said, E. W. 1978. *Orientalism.* New York: Vintage.

Saltz, R. 1989. Server intervention and responsible beverage service programs. In *Surgeon-general's workshop on drunk driving background papers.* Rockville, Md.: U.S. Department of Health and Human Services.

Scanlon, W. F. 1986. *Alcoholism and drug abuse in the workplace: Employee assistance programs.* New York: Praeger.

Schattschneider, E. E., 1960. *The Semisovereign people: A realist's view of democracy in America.* New York: Holt, Rinehart and Winston.

Schatzman, L., and A. L. Strauss. 1973. *Field research: Strategies for a natural sociology.* Englewood Cliffs, N.J.: Prentice-Hall.

Scheff, T. 1966. *Being mentally ill: A sociological theory.* Chicago: Aldine.

Schluchter, W. 1979. Value neutrality and the ethic of responsibility. In *Max Weber's Vision of History: Ethics and methods,* edited by G. Roth and W. Schluchter. Berkeley and Los Angeles: University of California Press.

Schmidt, W., and J. DeLint. 1970. Estimating the prevalence of alcoholism from alcohol consumption and mortality data. *Quarterly Journal of Studies on Alcohol* 31:957–64.

Schmidt, W., and R. E. Popham. 1978. The single distribution theory of alcohol consumption: A rejoinder to the critique of Parker and Harman. *Journal of Studies in Alcohol* 39:400–409.

Schneider, J. 1978. Deviant drinking as disease: Alcoholism as a social accomplishment. *Social Problems* 25:361–72.

Schur, E. 1980. *The politics of deviance: Stigma contests and the uses of power.* Englewood Cliffs, N.J.: Prentice-Hall.

Schutz, A. 1967. *The phenomenology of the social world.* Evanston, Ill.: Northwestern University Press.

Scott, R. A. 1969. *The making of blind men: A study of adult socialization.* New York: Russell Sage Foundation.

Scull, A. 1979. *Museums of madness: The social organization of insanity in nineteenth century England.* London: St. Martin's Press.

Seeley, J. 1962. Alcoholism is a disease: Implications for social policy. In *Society, culture and drinking patterns,* edited by D. J. Pittman and C. R. Snyder. New York: John Wiley.

Sennett, R. 1974. *Families against the city: Middle class homes of industrial Chicago, 1872–1890.* New York: Vintage.

Shakespeare, W. 1938. *Twelfth night.* In *The works of Shakespeare,* edited by T. Parrot. New York: Charles Scribner's Sons.

Siegler, M., and H. Osmond. 1974. *Models of madness, models of medicine.* New York: Macmillan.

Silver, A. 1967. The demand for order in civil society. In *The police: Six sociological essays,* edited by D. J. Bordua. New York: John Wiley.

Simpson, H. M., D. R. Mayhew, and R. A. Warren. 1982. Epidemiology of road accidents involving young adults. *Drug and Alcohol Dependence* 10:35–63.

Sinclair, A. 1964. *The era of excess: A social history of the prohibition movement.* New York: Harper and Row.

Singelmann, J. 1978. *From agriculture to services: The transformation of industrial employment.* Beverly Hills: Sage.

Skog, O. 1973. Less alcohol—fewer alcoholics? *Drinking and Drug Practice Surveyor* 7:7–14.

Snyder, C. R. 1958. *Alcohol and the Jews.* New Brunswick, N.J.: Rutgers Center of Alcohol Studies.

Sonnenstuhl, W., and H. Trice. 1991. The workplace as locale for risks and interventions in alcohol abuse. In *Alcohol: The development of sociological perspectives on use and abuse,* edited by P. Roman. New Brunswick, N.J.: Rutgers Center of Alcohol Studies.

Sontag, S. 1978. *Illness as metaphor.* New York: Farrar, Straus and Giroux.

Spector, M., and J. Kitsuse. 1977. *Constructing social problems.* Menlo Park, Calif.: Cummings.

Speiglman, R. 1985. Issues in the rise of compulsion in and/or treatment for driving under the influence of alcohol and California's drinking driver treatment system. In *Punishment and /or treatment for driving under the influence of alcohol and other drugs: Current concepts, experiences, and perspectives,* edited by M. Valverius. Stockholm: International Committee on Alcohol, Drugs and Traffic Safety.

Speiglman, R., and J. Gusfield. Forthcoming. Expediency and ideology in the courts: Twenty years of sentencing drinking drivers in El Cajon, California.

Spitzer, S. 1983. The rationalization of crime control in capitalist society. In *Social control and the state: Comparative and historical essays,* edited by S. Cohen and A. Scull. Oxford: Martin Robertson.

Spitzer, S., and A. Scull. 1977. Social control in historical perspective: From private to public responses to crime. In *Corrections and punishment,* edited by D. Greenberg. Beverly Hills: Sage.

Standard Encyclopedia of Alcohol Problems. 1930. Westerville, Oh.: American Issue Publishing.

Starr, P. 1978. Medicine and the waning of professional sovereignty. *Daedalus* 107:175–93.

Staudenmeier, W. 1987. Context and variation in employer policies on alcohol. *Journal of Drug Issues* 17:255–71.

Stewart, E. D. 1889. *Memories of the crusade: An account of the great uprising of the women of Ohio in 1873, against the liquor crime.* Columbus, Oh.: W. G. Hibbard.

Stinchcombe, A. 1963. Institutions of privacy in the determination of police administrative practices. *American Journal of Sociology* 69:150–160.

Stivers, R. 1976a. Culture and alcoholism. In *Alcoholism: Interdisciplinary approaches to an enduring problem,* edited by R. E. Tarter and A. A. Sugerman. Reading, Mass.: Addison-Wesley.

Stivers, R. 1976b. *A hair of the dog: Irish drinking and American stereotype.* University Park: Pennsylvania State University Press.

Straus, R. and S. Bacon. 1953. *Drinking in college.* New Haven: Yale University Press.

Summers, L., and D. Harris. 1978. The general deterrence of driving while intoxicated, vol. 1. DOT HS 803–582. Washington, D.C.: National Highway Traffic Safety Administration.

Sutton, F. X. 1959. Representation and the nature of political systems. *Comparative Studies in Society and History* 2:1–10.

Sykes, G., and D. Matza. 1957. Techniques of neutralization: A theory of delinquency. *American Sociological Review* 22:664–70.

Szasz, T. S. 1970. *Ideology and insanity: Essays on the psychiatric dehumanization of man.* Garden City, N.Y.: Doubleday.

Tabachnick, N. 1973. *Accident or suicide? Destruction by automobile.* Springfield, Ill: Charles C. Thomas.

Taylor, C. 1979. Interpretation and the sciences of man. In *Interpretive social science: A reader,* edited by P. Rabinow and W. M. Sullivan. Berkeley and Los Angeles: University of California Press.

Temperance Manual. 1836. Publisher unknown.

Thomas, C. W., and J. R. Hepburn. 1983. *Crime, criminal law and criminology.* Dubuque, Ia.: William C. Brown.

Thompson, E. P. 1967. Time, work-discipline and industrial captialism. *Past and Present* 38:56–97.

Thompson, E. P. 1978. Eighteenth-century English society: Class struggle without class? *Social History* 3:133–65.

Thompson, R. R., J. A. Tennant, and B. S. Repa. 1975. Vehicle borne drunk driver countermeasures. In *Alcohol, Drugs and Traffic Safety,* edited by J. Israelstam and S. Lambert. Toronto: Addiction Research Foundation of Ontario.

Tilly, C. 1981. The web of contention in eighteenth century cities. In *Class conflict and collective action,* edited by C. Tilly and L. A. Tilly. Beverly Hills: Sage.

Timberlake, J. H. 1963. *Prohibition and the Progressive Movement, 1900–1920.* Cambridge, Mass.: Harvard University Press.

Tongue, A. 1962. What the state does about alcohol and alcoholism. In *Society, culture and drinking patterns,* edited by D. J. Pittman and C. R. Snyder. New York: John Wiley.

Toulmin, S. 1950. *The uses of argument.* Cambridge: Cambridge University Press.

Treno, A. J., R. N. Parker, and H. D. Holder. 1993. Understanding U.S. alcohol consumption with social and economic factors: A multivariate time series analysis, 1950–1986. *Journal of Studies on Alcohol* 54 2:146–56.

Turner, R. 1972. Deviance avowal as neutralization of commitment. *Social Problems* 19:308–21.

Turner, V. W. 1969. *The ritual process: Structure and anti-structure.* Chicago: Aldine.

Turner, V. W. 1977. Variations on a theme of liminality. In *Secular ritual: A working definition of ritual,* edited by S. F. Moore and B. G. Meyerhoff. Amsterdam: Van Gorcum.

Tyler, S. A. ed. 1969. *Cognitive anthropology: Readings.* New York: Holt, Rinehart and Winston.

Tyrell, I. 1979. Temperance and economic change in the ante-bellum north. In *Alcohol, reform and society: The liquor issue in social context,* edited by J. S. Blocker. Westport, Conn.: Greenwood.

Ullman, A. 1953. The first drinking experiences of normal and addictive drinkers. *Quarterly Journal of Studies on Alcohol* 14:181–91.

Ungerleider, S., and S. Bloch. 1987. Assessing the various components of a drunk driving program from prevention to criminal justice intervention. *Oregon Psychology* 33:17–21.

Upjohn Institute for Employment Research. 1973. *Work in America: Report of a special task force to the secretary of health, education, and welfare.* Cambridge, Mass: MIT Press.

U.S. Congress. 1968. Committee on Public Works. *Alcohol and highway safety.* Washington, D.C.: USGPO.

U.S. Department of Commerce Bureau of the Census 1972. San Diego County 1970 Census of Population and Housing. Washington, D.C.: USGPO.

U.S. Department of Health, Education and Welfare. 1971. National Institute on Alcohol Abuse and Alcoholism. First special report to the U.S. Congress on Alcohol and Health. DHEW Publ. No. HSM-72–0900. Washington, D.C.: USGPO.

U.S. Department of Health, Education and Welfare. 1978. Third Special Report to Congress on Alcohol and Health. Rockville, Md.: National Institute on Alcohol Abuse and Alcoholism.

U.S. Department of Health, Education and Welfare. 1979. Public Health Service. *Healthy people. The surgeon general's report on health promotion and disease prevention.* Washington, D.C.: USGPO.

U.S. Department of Transportation. 1968. Alcohol and highway safety report. Washington, D.C.: USGPO.

U.S. Department of Transportation. 1974. National Highway Traffic Safety Administration. Office of Driver and Pedestrian Programs. *Alcohol safety action projects, evaluation of operations,* vol. 2. Evaluation of the Enforcement Coontermeasure Activities. DOT HS801 77. Washington, D.C.: USGPO.

U.S. Department of Transportation. 1991. Fatal Accident Reporting System. Washington, D.C.: National Center for Statistics and Analysis.

U.S. National Center for Health Statistics. 1973. Health resources statistics, 1972–73. Washington. D.C.: USGPO.

U.S. President's Commission on Law Enforcement and Administration of Justice. 1967. Task force report; drunkenness. Washington, D.C.: USGPO.

Van Gennep, A. 1960. *The rites of passage.* Chicago: University of Chicago Press.

Veblen, T. 1934. *The theory of the leisure class.* New York: Modern Library.

Vingilis, E. 1991. Problems detecting DWIs. *Alcohol, Drugs and Driving* 7:197–203.

Vingilis, E., and K. De Genova. 1984. Youth and the forbidden fruit: Experiences with changes in legal drinking age in North America. *Journal of Criminal Justice* 12:161–72.

Voas, R. 1975. Roadside surveys, demographics and BACs of drivers. In *Alcohol, Drugs and Traffic,* edited by S. Israelstam and S. Lambert. Toronto: Alcohol Research Foundation.

Voas, R. 1984. Estimating alcohol involvement in fatal crashes: A note on the reporting of BAC in the FARS. *Abstracts and Reviews in Alcohol and Driving* 5, no. 1: 20.

Wade, R. 1978. Violence in cities. In *Riot, rout and tumult: Readings in American social and political violence,* edited by R. Lane and J. J. Turner. Westport, Conn.: Greenwood Press.

Wagenaar, A. C. 1981. Effects of the raised legal drinking age on motor vehicle accidents in Michigan. *HSRI Research Review* 11:1–8.

Walleck, L., and D. Barrows. 1981. Preventing alcohol problems in California: Evaluation of the three year "winners" program. Report of the Social Research Group, School of Public Health, University of California, Berkeley.

Waller, J. 1967. Identification of problem drinkers among drunken drivers. *Journal of the American Medical Association* 200:124–30.

Waller, J. and H. W. Turkel. 1966. Alcoholism and traffic deaths. *New England Journal of Medicine* 275:532–36.

Walzer, M. 1969. *The revolution of the saints: A study in the origins of radical politics.* New York: Atheneum.

Weber, M. 1946. *Max Weber: Essays in sociology,* edited by H. Gerth and C. W. Mills. New York: Oxford University Press.

Weber, M. 1949. *The methodology of the social sciences.* Glencoe, Ill.: Free Press.

Wechsler, H. ed. 1980. *Minimum-age drinking laws: An evaluation.* Lexington, Mass.: Lexington Books.

Weed, F. 1985. Grassroots activism and the drunk-driving issue: A survey of MADD chapters. Paper presented at meeting of the Society for the Study of Social Problems, Washington, D.C., August.

Weinberg, I. 1974. Social problems that are no more. In *Handbook of social problems,* edited by E. Smigel. Chicago: Rand McNally.

Weiner, C. 1977. *The politics of alcoholism: Building an arena around a social problem.* New Brunswick, N.J.: Transaction.

Weitzer, Ronald. 1991. Prostitutes' rights in the United States: The failure of a movement. *Sociological Quarterly* 32:23–41.

Wendling, A., and B. Kolodji. 1977. *An evaluation of the El Cajon drinking driver.* Department of Sociology, San Diego State University, report to Department of Highways, California.

Westley, W. 1953. Violence and the police. *American Journal of Sociology* 59:34–42.

Wheelwright, P. 1964. *The burning fountain: A study in the language of symbolism.* Bloomington: Indiana University Press.

White, H. 1978. The fictions of factual representation. In *Tropics of discourse: Essays in cultural criticism.* Baltimore: Johns Hopkins University Press.

Whitehead, P. 1977. Alcohol and young drivers: Impact and implications of lowering the drinking age. Toronto: Department of National Health and Welfare.

Whyte, W. F. 1955. *Street-corner society: the social structure of an Italian slum,* 2nd ed. Chicago: University of Chicago Press.

Wilensky, H. L. 1975. *The Welfare state and equality: Structural and ideological roots of public expenditures.* Berkeley and Los Angeles: University of California Press.

Wilensky, H. L. and C. N. LeBeaux. 1958. *Industrial society and social welfare.* Glencoe, Ill.: Free Press.

Wiley, N. 1967. The ethnic mobility trap. *Social problems* 13:147–59.

Wilkerson, A. Jr. 1966. A history of the concept of alcoholism as a disease. Ph.D. dissertation, University of Pennsylvania, School of Social Work.

Wilkinson, R. 1970. *The prevention of drinking problems: Alcohol control and cultural influences.* New York: Oxford University Press.

Williams, A. 1986. Raising the legal purchasing age in the United States: Its effect on fatal motor vehicle crashes. *Alcohol, Drugs and Driving: Abstracts and Reviews* 2, no. 2:1–12.

Williams, A. 1992. The 1980s decline in alcohol-impaired driving and crashes and why it ocurred. *Alcohol, Drugs and Driving* 8:71–76.

Williams, A. et al. 1975. The legal minimum drinking age and fatal motor vehicle crashes. *Journal of Legal Studies* 4:219–39.

Williams, G., D. Clem, and M. Dufour. 1993. Surveillance report no. 27: Apparent per capita alcohol consumption: National, state and regional trends, 1977–91. Washington, D.C.: NIAAA, U.S. Dept of Health and Human Services.

Williams, R. M. 1960. *American society: A sociological interpretation.* New York: Knopf.

Williams, R. 1977. *Marxism and literature.* Oxford: Oxford University Press.

Wirth, L. 1949. Introduction to K. Mannheim, *Ideology and Utopia: An introduction to the sociology of knowledge.* New York: Harcourt, Brace.

Wolfe, A. C. 1975. Characteristics of late-night, week-end drivers: Results of the U.S. national roadside breath-testing survey and several local surveys. In *Alcohol, Drugs and Traffic Safety,* edited by S. Israelstam, and S. Lambert. Toronto, Canada: Addiction Research Foundation of Ontario.

Wrightson, K. 1981. Alehouses, order and reformation in rural England, 1590–1660. In *Popular culture and class conflict, 1590–1914: Explorations in the history of labour and leisure,* edited by E. Yeo and S. Yeo. Sussex: Harvester Press.

Wyllie, I. G. 1954. *The self-made man in America: The myth of rags to riches.* New Brunswick, N.J.: Rutgers University Press.

Zador, P. 1976. Statistical evaluation of the effectiveness of alcohol safety action projects. *Accident Analysis and Prevention* 8:51–66.

Zerubavel, E. 1981. *Hidden rhythms: Schedules and calendars in social life.* Chicago: University of Chicago Press.

Zerubavel, E. 1985. *The seven day circle: The history and meaning of the week.* New York: Free Press.

Zimring, F. E., and G. J. Hawkins. 1973. *Deterrence: The legal threat of crime control.* Chicago: University of Chicago Press.

Zola, I. K. 1972. Medicine as institution of social control. *Sociological Review* 20:487–504.

Zylman, R. 1968a. Accidents, alcohol and single-cause explanations. *Quarterly Journal of Studies on Alcohol,* supp. no. 4:212–33.

Zylman, R. 1968b. Police records and accidents involving alcohol. *Quarterly Journal of Studies on Alcohol,* supp. no. 4:178–211.

Zylman, R. 1970. Are drinking-driving laws enforced? *Police Chief* 37:48–52.

Zylman, R. 1973. Youth, alcohol and collision involvement. *Journal of Safety Research* 5:58–72.

Zylman, R. 1975. Mass arrests for impaired driving may not prevent traffic deaths. In *Alcohol, Drugs and Traffic Safety,* edited by S. Israelstam and S. Lambert. Toronto: Addiction Research Foundation of Ontario.

Index

Abortion, 10, 24–25, 172, 184

Absenteeism, 37, 58, 84, 268

Abstinence, 69–72, 95–96, 119; and the Temperance movement, 69–70, 173–74, 277; and the public designation of deviance, 173–74, 178, 181

Accident Analysis and Prevention, 300

Accident Research (Haddon), 269–70

Accidents, 13–14, 260–61, 285, 308–9, 318–20; statistics on, 209, 315, 319, 323–25; as a subject in DUI classes, 211–12; "second collisions in," 265, 269–70; and enforcement of DUI laws, 315–17; Fatal Accident Reporting Service data on, 315, 319, 323–25

Adam and Eve, 296

Addiction Research Foundation of Ontario, 286

Adolescents, 19, 20, 258. *See also* Juvenile delinquency; Minimum-age drinking laws; Minors

Advertising, 251, 258, 261–62, 285

African-Americans, 201, 247

Age, 18, 49, 51, 215. *See also* Minimum-age drinking laws

Aggression, 31, 75

Agriculture, 81–82, 84, 93

Air Force, 39, 52, 281

Air pollution, 23

Alcohol Beverage Control Boards, 36

Alcohol Control Policies in Public Health Perspective, 282, 286

Alcohol control policy, 54; frame and imagery in, 35–40; and benevolent repression, 75–97; and moral reform, 76–77; and social structure, 77–80

Alcoholics: and the welfare state, 13, 185–204; and the public designation of deviance, 171, 174, 179, 182–83; the construction of the DUI as, 220–28. *See also* Alcoholics Anonymous (AA); Alcoholism; Alcoholism movement

Alcoholics Anonymous (AA), 36, 182–83, 190–96, 304–5, 309; and DUI classes, 210, 213–14, 219, 223; and interviews of defendants by probation officers, 228, 229, 233–36; and the prevention of drinking problems, 274, 277; the Washingtonians and, 333n2

Alcohol in America (Clark and Hilton), 46, 50–52

Alcohol industry, 22, 84, 278, 283

Alcoholism: disease concept of, 21, 36, 192–96, 203, 205–7, 238, 277; as the obverse of "workaholism," 74; industry, overview of, 194–96; nine signs of, 212–13; four stages of, described by Jellinek, 213–14; imagery, implications of, 279–81. *See also* Alcoholics; Alcoholism movement

Alcoholism movement, 22, 36–37, 197–202; and the expansion of "troubled persons" industries, 198–99; and the fall of prevention, 276–79; "new," sources of, 290–93

"Alcohology," field of, 193

Alcohol Programs Office, 207–8

Alcohol Research Group, 51

Alcohol Safety Action Project, 262–63, 291

363

Index